FRANK LLOYD WRIGHT

FRANK LLOYD WRIGHT

ROBERT McCARTER

Phaidon Press Limited
Regent's Wharf
All Saints Street
London N1 9PA

Phaidon Press Inc.
180 Varick Street
New York, NY 10014

www.phaidon.com

First published 1997
Reprinted in paperback 1999,
2001, 2004, 2005
© 1997 Phaidon Press Limited

ISBN 0 7148 3854 3

A CIP catalogue record for this book is
available from the British Library.

8472

Printed in Hong Kong

Frontispiece: John Storer House,
Los Angeles, California, 1923,
view of entry terrace.

INTRODUCTION

Remember the impression one gets from good
architecture, that it expresses a thought.
It makes one want to respond with a gesture.

Ludwig Wittgenstein[1]

The Criticism of Persuasion

Architectural criticism should arise out of a debt of love. In a manner evident and yet mysterious, space seizes upon our imagination. We are not the same when we leave a building as we were when we entered it. Constructive criticism is the result of a powerful, transformative experience, the quality of which we seek to communicate to others, hoping they will also feel compelled to undergo the same experience. Great works of architecture take hold of and shake us, 'like storm-winds, flinging open the doors of perception, pressing upon the architecture of our beliefs with their transforming powers. We seek to record their impact, to put our shaken house in its new order. Through some primary instinct of communion, we seek to convey to others the quality and force of our experience. We would persuade them to lay themselves open to it. In this attempt at persuasion originate the truest insights criticism can afford.'[2]

This criticism of persuasion, as George Steiner so passionately and convincingly defined it above, is today ever more necessary because of the present dominance of 'information' over personal perception in the understanding of architecture. Today our 'knowledge' of the spaces and forms of architecture most often comes from media representations and verbal explanations – we need to be told what to remember about the space in which we are standing and how to 'interpret' the forms that shape our experience. It is rarely suggested in contemporary writings that our own actual experience of space has any value or should be the primary focus of study. This has led, inevitably, to our general lack of capacity for visual and spatial memory, noted by Josef Albers; while most people can recall a musical tune, the visual memory is so poorly trained in standard education that few can accurately remember a 'shape or form, the size of things, the extension of space and volume'.[3]

In our age of computer animation and information, virtual reality, and the disembodying influence of film and television, all sense of place – and even the need for places to house human life – is increasingly at risk of disappearing. In our age of biography, where emphasis is placed on the process and practically no notice taken of the product, any understanding of the architect's intentions as they are constructed in the actual built work seems increasingly irrelevant. By substituting information apprehended by viewing and reading for the direct physical experience, these two aspects of our contemporary world-view impede our access to Wright's spaces, which were designed to be understood through occupation, not through being read as bits of disembodied information.

Art historical scholarship – with its emphasis on the oxymoronic concept of 'original research' – has dominated recent studies on Frank Lloyd Wright, resulting in writings that have less and less to do with our experience of his spaces. Space and its inhabitation are not only being taken for granted in these studies, but are being avoided – after all, what is right there for all to experience cannot possibly generate 'original research' for the academic scholar. As a result, recent studies of Wright have been largely silent about spatial experience, particularly that of the interior.

Yet, something fundamental to our nature will not let us forget that the experience of space is of paramount importance to our understanding of architecture. The architecture that allows us to dwell and inhabit the earth, that gives space and form to our daily rituals, that houses the events out of which our lives are constructed is not the architecture revealed by historical 'research', but rather is the architecture of experience. In writing monographic studies on architects, authors usually attempt to add to our knowledge of the designers and their work. With Wright the situation is almost the opposite – one feels compelled to start afresh, to present Wright's architecture as if for the first time, to look past all the accumulated 'knowledge' so that we can experience the spaces themselves. To paraphrase Paul Valéry, seeing is forgetting the fame of the thing one sees.

This book is intended to encourage the desire to inhabit and experience the spaces left to us by Frank Lloyd Wright. In the context of the ever-widening split between our minds and bodies, fostered by the various electronic media and instruments of art historical research, the illustrated monograph on Frank Lloyd Wright seems an appealing anomaly, only slightly less anachronistic than the urge to actually experience space 'in the flesh'. It follows that readers should not feel satisfied that they 'know' these astonishing and phenomenal works of architecture, or the mind that made them, based solely on what may be found in this book. If, when they have finished, they feel compelled to visit Wright's buildings – to inhabit and measure them with their feet, their hands and their eyes; to experience directly the rich overlapping geometries of light, material and form; to sense how Wright shaped space to both allow and encourage our dwelling – I will have succeeded.

In the Cause of Architecture

In undertaking a study such as this, readers should first be reminded that Wright's total opus consisted of well over six hundred built works and a thousand unbuilt projects.[4] It was therefore necessary to select key works that epitomize the hundreds of buildings and projects, which it is not possible to cover in this monograph. In order that readers may understand the development of Wright's architecture through his career, it has been necessary to adhere to an approximately chronological sequence. At the same time, it is essential to make evident the underlying themes and principles that led Wright himself, at the end of his life, to see all his works as a unified series. In order to accomplish this, the opening chapter is devoted to an extended study of Wright's early years and the various sources of what I will call his design philosophy, while the following chapters relate Wright's works to each other in a manner that reveals shared themes and principles.

To achieve these two intentions – to make evident both the sequence and continuity of design principles – this study is organized in chapters presenting the major spatial, functional and constructional types developed by Wright in an approximate chronological order. However, in order to study certain building types (the skyscraper, for example), it has sometimes been necessary to reach across Wright's career and pull together designs that are temporally distant. For the most part, readers will find that the text moves progressively through Wright's life as an architect, collecting the selected works under provisional titles of my making.

By studying Wright's buildings, the spaces they define, and the fundamental ordering principles developed and presented here, we may better understand his system of design. The text and photographs are intended to present the consistent and systematic qualities underlying all of Wright's designs. Though cataloguing by biographical period or stylistic phase is the method most typically utilized by historians, Wright – the architect – described his life's work as being one singular effort, emphasizing not stylistic differences but the fundamental and unchanging ordering principles that determined his work throughout the seventy-year span of his career – a career devoted, as he said, to 'the cause of architecture'.[5] Therefore, the following chronological presentation, emphasizing key designs and those related to them thematically, is paralleled by an examination of the development of three primary principles, simultaneously active in Wright's design work, and singled out by him as fundamental to his understanding of architecture.

The first of these, and by far the most important, is his development of concepts and methods for making architectural *space*: how these ideas derived from his designs for interior spaces and their experience; how in Wright's architecture the occupant's movement (position) was critical to the experience of the spatial order (composition); and how he came to see all architecture as coming from what he called 'the space within'.

The second is his development of concepts and methods for ordering space through the manner of its *construction*: how this order determined his search for 'the nature of materials' and structures; how Wright employed different types of structure and construction materials, seeking those that would reinforce and make present his spatial system; and how he achieved a coherent tectonic order that encompassed both composition and construction.

The third is his development of concepts and methods for establishing the relationship between his architecture and the *landscape*: how Wright designed buildings wherein landscape, interior space, and construction materials are woven together to become the setting for the repeated rituals of daily life; and how Wright throughout his career endeavoured to give order to the developing American suburb, proposing collective and individual designs of spatial and social richness that remain unmatched to this day.

The Architecture of Experience

Returning to George Steiner's seminal insight into the nature of constructive criticism, the following will be an attempt to describe Wright's discoveries as to the nature of space and its inhabitation, which, rather than being subjected to the traditional methods of historical research, should suggest very different ways of construing experience.[6] Wright's hero-author Victor Hugo recalled the time when the building *was* the book for humankind, and Wright clearly intended his buildings to stand for themselves, not needing verbal explanations to be understood. To understand them, we must simply stand under them – stand where they are based, stand within their rich and powerful spaces. These spaces are made to move us, and we need no special training to appreciate them. If we are ever to understand Frank Lloyd Wright and his architecture, we must let his spaces teach us that which we may have forgotten: what it is to know the depth and beauty of the purely spatial experience; what it is to be in buildings that speak of the nature of the materials with which they are made; what it is to live in harmony with the natural landscape; what it is to truly inhabit architecture, and how it changes us forever.

TOWARDS AN AMERICAN ARCHITECTURE

The mind of this country has never been seriously applied to the subject of building. Intently engaged in matters of more pressing importance, we have been content to receive our notions of architecture as we have received the fashion of our garments and the form of our entertainments, from Europe.

Horatio Greenough[1]

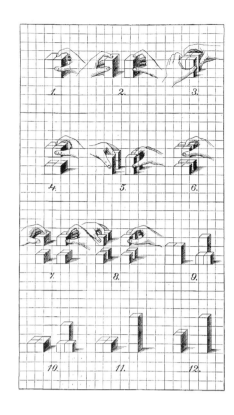

Left: 'Romeo and Juliet' Windmill, Taliesin, Spring Green, Wisconsin, 1896.
Above: Page from Friedrich Froebel's Kindergarten handbook. The Froebel training method introduced Wright to the formative geometries that would later become the basis of his architecture.

Frank Lloyd Wright was born in Richland Center, Wisconsin, on 8 June 1867, to William Carey Wright and Anna (Hannah) Lloyd Jones Wright. William Wright, the son of a preacher, was himself a preacher, musician, public speaker, school superintendent and jack of all trades, who had studied medicine and law; he was skilled at many things except continuous employment, and the family moved several times during Wright's youth in his father's search for a permanent profession. Anna Lloyd Jones was a teacher and part of the extraordinary Lloyd Jones family, a Celtic clan of religious revolutionaries who had settled near Madison, Wisconsin, in 1864. Wright's parents were married in 1866; Anna was twenty-seven at the time, and William, fourteen years her senior, was a widower with three children.

The influence of his father is most evident in Wright's love of music and ability to play the piano, his natural skill at a variety of tasks, his self-assurance and his confidence in public presentation. Frank also inherited from his father his tendencies to spend money on luxuries rather than necessities, to make occasional exaggerated claims and distortions of the truth, and to sometimes seek escape rather than confront difficult situations. While his mother gave extraordinary encouragement to her son, she may also have reinforced some of his habits through the excessive expectations and demands she made of him. It was through her family, the Lloyd Jones,

that she had the most positive influence and effect on Wright – he was later to take up a permanent and sheltered refuge in the valley owned by the Lloyd Jones family, building his home Taliesin among the family farmlands. It is indicative of the esteem in which Wright held his mother's family that at the age of eighteen he changed his name from Frank Lincoln Wright to Frank Lloyd Wright.

The Lloyd Jones family was very much involved in the developing American individualist and transcendentalist culture, which originated at least in part in the arrival of freedom-seeking refugees and rebels from Europe in the New World. In the nineteenth century, America still offered the possibility for a new beginning, and it was this that compelled Wright's maternal grandparents, Richard and Mallie Lloyd Jones, to emigrate here in 1844. They had been part of a Celtic clan in Wales that split away from the established Protestant church during the Methodist revival. They proudly considered themselves Dissenters and Nonconformists in their religious practices, and Frank Lloyd Wright's great-great-grandfather, Jenkin Jones, had founded the Unitarian – then called the Arminian – sect in 1726.[2] Upon arriving and settling in Wisconsin, the close-knit family adopted the motto, 'Truth against the world', and had soon assembled a sizable block of farmland in what came to be known, according to Wright, as 'The Valley of the God-Almighty Jones'.

After moving to McGregor in Iowa (on the Mississippi River), Pawtucket on Rhode Island, Essex in Connecticut and Weymouth in Massachusetts, the Wright family came back to settle in the Valley of the Lloyd Jones. The Wright family's stay in Madison proved to be the most permanent, but did not stop the disintegration of William and Anna's marriage; in 1883, Anna drove William from the house, and they were divorced in 1884. William's break from his family was complete, and Frank never saw his father again, nor did he attend his funeral in 1904.

Froebel Training and the Study of Nature

During the summers of his childhood, Wright had returned to work on the farm of his uncle James Lloyd Jones, in the valley near Madison, so the area was already familiar to him at the age of ten when his family moved there in 1877. The experience of working on his uncle's farm was to have a profound and lasting effect on Wright, being one of the primary sources of his great love of and respect for nature; it was reinforced and transformed into method by the Froebel training given to him by his mother, starting when he was nine years old. In his autobiography, Wright said that his mother had determined even before his birth that he would be an architect.[3] Her desire for the young Wright to succeed, in part to compensate for her failing marriage, combined with the high esteem in which her brother Thomas, the eldest of her siblings and a self-made architect and builder, was held by the Lloyd Jones, may very well have made architecture seem a suitably noble profession towards which to direct her eldest child and only son. It also seems likely, as Wright claims, that Anna attended the Philadelphia Centennial Exposition of 1876 with her sisters Nell and Jane, also teachers, and that there they discovered, and brought back for use in the Valley, the toys and instructions of the Froebel kindergarten educational system.[4]

Of the three fundamental formal experiences of Wright's youth that should be considered (literally) formative for his later architecture (the study of nature, the Froebel training, and the study of geometric ornament undertaken as part of his apprenticeship to Sullivan), the kindergarten training system developed by Frederich Froebel is of utmost importance, for it served as the method through which all three experiences could be correlated; it gave them a geometric spatial order. Froebel had himself first studied natural science (rock crystals), then studied architecture for two years, and finally became a teacher, working from 1807–9 with Johann Pestalozzi, whose school emphasized the principle of teaching and learning through voluntary activity on the part of the child. Froebel's own training methods, as described in the instructional handbooks that accompanied his training 'gifts', consisted of both philosophical and formal principles imparted to the child through a series of gifts or toys given in a predetermined sequence, increasing in complexity and subtlety as the child

grew up. As Grant Manson indicated in his seminal article of 1953, and as Richard MacCormac has shown in his more comprehensive article of 1974, the parallels – formal and to philosophical – between the Froebel illustrations and instructions and Wright's designs and thoughts are too numerous to be coincidental; despite recent questioning of its importance by historians, the Froebel training must be given a prominent place in the development of Wright's system of design.[5]

The Froebel training emphasized learning from nature, which reinforced and gave order to Wright's early experiences on his uncle's farm, and it introduced him to the formative geometries that would later become the basis for his architecture. At a fundamental level, this training was directed towards the development of analytical thinking. It taught the child to see that geometric forms and patterns structured every object in nature, and to see each object as 'a whole both in its organic unity and its component parts', as Froebel himself explained in the instruction manual.[6] The desire to create shape and form was considered a natural result for the child who was encouraged to observe, take to pieces, and reassemble things. The training intended that the child come to understand, through his own investigations in playing, that there was an inner coherence in all things and that the material and spiritual worlds were one. The training methods, according to Froebel, were to 'begin by establishing spatial relationships' and to operate through 'inference from the general to the particular, from the whole to the part'. This last is almost the exact wording Wright was later to use himself in describing his process of architectural design.

Froebel's educational system was nonverbal, non-representational and relied absolutely on the child's own analytically produced knowledge: 'It is not a question of communicating knowledge already acquired but of calling forth new knowledge.' Again and again as we examine the work of Wright, we will see evidence of his incisive analyses of natural forms, historical architectural forms, and even the forms of his own making; in this the Froebel training may be seen 'at work' in Wright's architectural designs. While there were clearly other important reasons for Wright's early development of such extraordinary capacities for design, his relationship with the Froebel training must at the very least be understood as the fortuitous meeting of an unusually comprehensive and effective method and an astonishing and perhaps unparalleled natural talent. In summary we may here say that Wright, as a result of this training, was far more interested in *designing* the world than in *representing* it; designing understood as discerning the underlying structure of nature and building with it. The principles resulting from this study became the foundation for Wright's mature design process; as he would later say, 'The form is a consequence of the principle at work.'[7]

Emerson and Transcendentalism

Frank Lloyd Wright was born in 1867 and, in order to begin to understand the man and his architecture, it is important to remind ourselves that, though he lived until 1959 and to the age of ninety-one, he was essentially a nineteenth-century man, already aged thirty-three at the turn of the century. Wright's fundamental beliefs were formed by the American transcendentalist thinkers; while he was growing up, Herman Melville (1819–91), Walt Whitman (1819–92) and his beloved Ralph Waldo Emerson (1803–82) were still alive; Henry David Thoreau (1817–62) and Horatio Greenough (1805–52) had only recently died and were still very much present in American culture. While Wright remained always at the forefront of modern architecture, continuing to amaze and surpass with his inventiveness and innovations even at the most advanced age, we should remember that at a fundamental level, his principles and beliefs had been formed at an early age by the comprehensive and powerful philosophy for living proposed by Emerson and the others – the only true American culture to appear since the founding of the nation less than a hundred years before Wright's birth. To be fully understood, Wright's work must be seen as a product not of our often doubtful and ideal-less twentieth-century society, but of the energetic and rigorous American transcendentalist culture of the nineteenth century.[8]

The philosophy underlying the Froebel system of kindergarten training found many parallels in the thinking of the American transcendentalists, especially in the work of Wright's lifelong inspiration, Emerson, who said, 'The intellect pierces the form, overleaps the wall, detects intrinsic likeness between remote things and reduces all things to a few principles.'[9] Wright was an inheritor of and a party to the vigorous transcendental tradition of nineteenth-century America exemplified and explicated by Emerson, Thoreau, Whitman, Melville and Greenough. Eventually Wright came to believe that he had given this transcendental thought built form and thereby connected it to Oriental philosophies in which he found many parallels.

This evolving American culture had a strongly critical aspect, opposed as it was to the attitude of dominating nature that characterized the emerging industrial age, seeking to achieve instead a harmony with nature.[10] Wright displayed a boundless confidence, also typical of the transcendental thinkers, that democracy in America could achieve the liberation of the individual man, the creation of an indigenous collective culture, and a dynamic integration of the evolutionary forces of nature, all this to be played out across the enormous spaces of the continent. As Charles Olson said in his study of Melville, 'I take SPACE to be the central fact to man born in America, from Folsom cave to now. I spell it large because it comes large here. Large and without mercy. It is geography at bottom, a hell of a wide land from the beginning. The fulcrum of America is the Plains, half sea half land, a high sun as metal and obdurate as the iron horizon, and a man's job is to square the circle.'[11]

Because man himself was a product of nature, Emerson believed that man was thereby eminently suited to intuit the principles of nature. Related to this was Wright's belief that the true function of architecture was to tell man about his own nature; as Emerson said, 'truth was in us before it was reflected to us from natural objects'. Nature was seen by Emerson as the result of an endless combination and repetition of a few fundamental laws and forms. We shall see that Wright, in seeking to clarify his design methods beginning at the turn of the century, analysed nature and its underlying geometric structures, using their purity of form and clarity of purpose to critique his own architecture. Emerson said that 'we are always reasoning from the seen to the unseen'; this is a perfect parallel to Froebel's training, which found expression in Wright's habit of 'seeing into' or 'seeing from within', as he called it. The following chapters will reveal how Wright was always profoundly affected by materials and construction methods, reflecting his constant search for a comprehensive constructional and compositional order similar to that which he found in his analyses of nature's forms.

Following Coleridge's 'such as the life is, such is the form', the transcendentalists held that each physical thing was the consequence of, and had consequences for, spiritual thought. 'All form is an effect of character,' as Emerson said; Wright put it more pointedly, stating that 'the sins of architects are permanent sins.'[12] Wright also felt that character was an effect of form, and that an inhabitant's character could therefore be positively affected by architectural form and space. In his work, Wright endeavoured to make present the ancient understanding of building as a sacred act and buildings as sacred places. All form had moral meaning, and nature was the model; 'esteem nature a perpetual counselor, and her perfections the exact measure of our deviations,' as Emerson stated.

It is most important for us to see that, for Wright, the philosophical ideals of integrity and natural order were not merely 'means' of designing – they were visions of the world as it should be. His design principles should thus be understood as having both formal and moral implications. In a way quite similar to the Froebel training, this transcendental philosophy also instilled confidence in one's own abilities to access the formative and moral power of nature's 'perfections'. Thus while Charles Baudelaire asserted that 'doubt or the absence of faith is the particular vice of this century; simplicity, that is an immediate access to things, has become a divine privilege which only the truly great possess,' Wright, on the contrary, exhibited a pure belief in the ideal of a perfect 'simplicity', and in the possibility of its realization in architecture.[13]

Wright was profoundly affected by Emerson's belief that only the individual, through the discipline of principles learned from experience, could effect the integration of culture and nature needed in America. Emerson held that the individual's powers of perception and analysis were vastly superior to those of any society, and that one should concentrate on one's own particular strengths and abilities: 'Insist on yourself; never imitate. Your own gift you can present every moment with the cumulative force of a whole life's cultivation.' Wright's combative stance in his dealings with the press and public can be traced to Emerson: 'Whoever would be a man, must be a nonconformist'; 'Nothing is at last sacred but the integrity of your own mind'; 'To be great is to be misunderstood'. Yet, as developed in Emerson's writings, this emphasis on the validity of the individual experience was essentially optimistic; it encouraged the reader to search history for the fundamental principles of human existence, to look beyond the particular failings of contemporary society to find the essential and unchanging nature of man. It was Thoreau who observed, 'The improvements of the ages have but little influence on the essential laws of man's existence.'[14]

Emerson and the transcendentalists had themselves been affected by the writings of Horatio Greenough, an American sculptor and writer, who lived much of his life in Rome. He wrote extensively on modern man's relationship to historical form, and architecture was of particular interest to him, as it seemed to be less dependent upon direct copying of precedents than the visual arts. Greenough's method for learning from history was succinctly stated: 'Let us learn principles, not copy shapes.'[15] He first enunciated the principle 'form follows function' (in 1852) and held that 'the edifices in whose construction the principles of architecture are developed may be classed as organic'. Paralleling his contemporary Froebel, Greenough called for the close study of nature and the development of forms from an inner conception: 'Instead of forcing the functions of every sort of building into one general form, adapting an outward shape for the sake of the eye or of association, without reference to the inner distribution, let us begin from the heart as the nucleus, and work outwards.'

Sullivan and Chicago
This concept of developing from a nucleus or seed-germ was critical to the architectural philosophy later proposed by Louis Sullivan (1856–1924), who inherited this transcendental and functionalist tradition. Sullivan, the architect Wright was later to call his *Lieber Meister* – the only architect whose influence Wright ever publicly acknowledged – clearly felt compelled to remedy Greenough's charge that 'the mind of this country has never been seriously applied to the subject of building'. Sullivan keenly felt the absence of a particularly American architecture, yet warned against efforts to speed its arrival

by 'transplanting or grafting' historical styles onto the American continent.[16] He felt that any truly organic American architecture would only develop on a regional basis, with variations dependent upon local climate, landscape and building methods and materials, rather than on arbitrary formal or theoretical preconceptions – a statement as valid today as when he made it.

Having left the École des Beaux-Arts in Paris before finishing his studies, Sullivan was sceptical as to whether contemporary architectural education in America, based as it was on the French classical school, would encourage the development of forms that followed functions. In another statement that seems remarkably applicable even today, Sullivan observed that architectural education in his day did not cultivate what he called the 'common sense' of analytical thinking and was instead:

> dependent upon the verbal explanation and comment of its exponents. A knowledge of their vocabulary is often of assistance in disclosing softness and refinement in many primitive expedients, and revealing beauty in barren places. Familiarity with the current phraseology of the applied arts is also useful in assisting the student to a comprehension of many things apparently incomprehensible. Metaphor and simile are rampant in this connection, a well-chosen word often serving to justify an architectural absurdity.[17]

Sullivan believed a more comprehensive training, starting well before college, was the only way to instil the analytical understanding of nature needed for organic design. Written to remedy the condition of the typical architecture school graduate, Sullivan's only book on architectural education is titled, significantly enough, *Kindergarten Chats*.

In his own work Sullivan built from his belief that nature could give form to architecture through a dialogue between structure and ornament. He began by concentrating on clarifying the tectonic elements, believing that the structural frame, then being developed in steel for the commercial buildings of Chicago, was fundamental to all architecture: 'When the lintel is placed upon two piers, architecture springs into being.' In order to create a truly organic architecture, on the other hand, he believed that ornament must be '*of* the surface and substance, rather than *on* it'. Remarkably similar to Froebel's training methods, and developed from the study of the same natural geometries, Sullivan's theory of ornament was in effect both a philosophy and a method of formal composition; it introduced Wright to the world of ancient forms and geometries that served as the beginning for all his subsequent designs.

Sullivan's studies of *The Grammar of Ornament* by Owen Jones, of 1856, undertaken together with Wright after he joined the office, were to be essential in the final crystallization of both their geometric design methods.[18] Sullivan's debt to Jones is evident in the close parallels between the texts of *The Grammar of Ornament* and his own

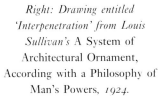

Right: Drawing entitled 'Interpenetration' from Louis Sullivan's A System of Architectural Ornament, According with a Philosophy of Man's Powers, *1924.*

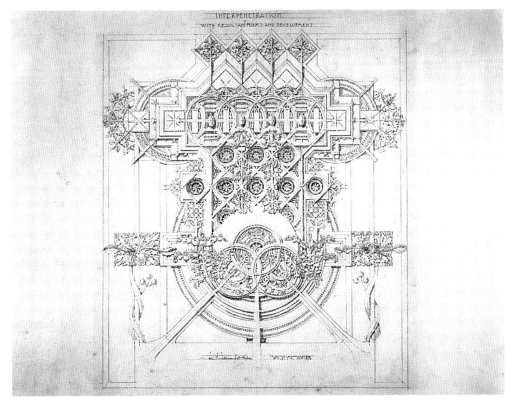

A System of Architectural Ornament According with a Philosophy of Man's Powers, published in 1924, the year of his death. In his relationship with Wright, correctly characterized by Otto Graf as being similar to a medieval guild apprenticeship, Sullivan was the final, catalytic event in Wright's formation as an architect, bringing into focus the formal and philosophical principles learned in his youth, and by example directing Wright towards the development of a new American architecture.[19]

The place of Wright's youth and early practice is also important for our understanding of his later direction as a thinker and architect: in the last quarter of the nineteenth century, many of those living in Chicago and the Midwest considered their region to be the most likely location for the development of a truly American culture. To the Midwestern way of thinking, the East, epitomized by New York and Boston, was dominated by a European-trained élite, who quite naturally utilized European models in projecting an idealized culture for the New World. The South was still recovering from the devastation of the Civil War, which ended only two years before Wright's birth, and the West remained a frontier, largely unsettled and uncivilized. Only in the Midwest, with Chicago at its centre, was there the combination of industry, growth and independent thinking many believed necessary for the projection of a truly American vision of life in the New World.

The fire of 1871 had destroyed 1,700 buildings in Chicago, leaving over 100,000 homeless. In the reconstruction that followed, Chicago rose as the most progressive and advanced city in America, with some of its greatest achievements occurring in architecture, where a combination of energetic commercial growth, the demand for fireproof construction, and high land costs led to the invention and rapid development of what came to be known as the 'skyscraper'. In Chicago, John Wellborn Root (c1850–91) and Daniel Burnham had built several multistorey, masonry-clad, wrought iron-structured buildings by 1884; architect-engineer William Le Baron Jenney (1832–1907) developed and built the first masonry-clad, completely steel-framed structure in 1885; and Henry Hobson Richardson (1838–86), considered the father of American architecture by his contemporaries, built his last great work in Chicago, the Marshall Field Warehouse, completed in 1887, one year after his death.

Apprentice to Architecture

In the same year, after completing two semesters of study in engineering at the University of Wisconsin – undertaken while working in the office of his professor Allan Conover – Wright left Madison at the age of twenty, to go to Chicago, where he first worked in the office of J Lyman Silsbee, architect to Wright's uncle, Jenkin Lloyd Jones. Later Wright attempted to portray himself as an outsider

DOUZIÈME ENTRETIEN   (fig. 18)

SALLE VOÛTÉE

with no connections, making his entry into the Chicago architectural community by merit alone, while in fact his uncle held a powerful position in the city, and had hired Silsbee to design both the All Souls' Unitarian Church and the family chapel in the Valley. The Rev Jenkin Lloyd Jones brought to his parsonage Jane Addams, Susan B Anthony, Booker T Washington and William Jennings Bryan, among others, and the young Wright would be associated with various members of this progressive liberal group in Chicago, giving his first major public lecture, entitled 'The Art and Craft of the Machine', at Jane Addams's Hull House in 1901.

Wright only worked in Silsbee's office for a year, but Joseph Connors has made a convincing case that Wright developed one of his fundamental precepts of design in reaction to Silsbee's methods.[20] In the design of the largely domestic work in his office, Silsbee was influenced by the houses of H H Richardson, practising what Vincent Scully would later call the 'Shingle Style', defined by its picturesque massing, made possible by the formal flexibility of wood shingles, the dominant material. As Wright wrote in his autobiography, 'Silsbee got a ground-plan and made his pretty sketch, getting some charming picturesque effect he had in mind. Then the sketch would come out into the drawing room to be fixed up into a building, keeping the floor plan near the sketch if possible. The picture interests

him. The rest bores him.'[21] Wright was later to reject this use of 'the sketch' as a generative element in design, saying that his own designs were 'conceived in three dimensions as organic entities, let the picturesque perspective fall how it will. No man ever built a building worthy of the name architecture who fashioned it in perspective sketch to his taste and then fudged the plan to suit. Such methods produce mere scene-painting. A perspective may be proof but it is no nurture.'[22] This idea of the perspective as 'proof', which Connors traces also to the French medievalist and architect Eugène Emmanuel Viollet-le-Duc (1814–79), whose *Discourses on Architecture* Wright had studied, represents in Wright's work 'a rare marriage between an abstract system of design and the requirements of the eye'.[23]

In 1888, as construction was underway on the Hillside Home School Wright had designed for his school-teacher aunts in the Valley, Wright secured a position at the Chicago firm of Dankmar Adler and Louis Sullivan, where he began work with the other young draftsmen in the office on the drawings for the monumental Auditorium Building which, when completed in 1890, would be the largest building in Chicago. It was doubtlessly this commission, for which the office received much publicity following its award in 1886, that attracted Wright to Adler and Sullivan; only later would he be introduced, by Sullivan himself, to the

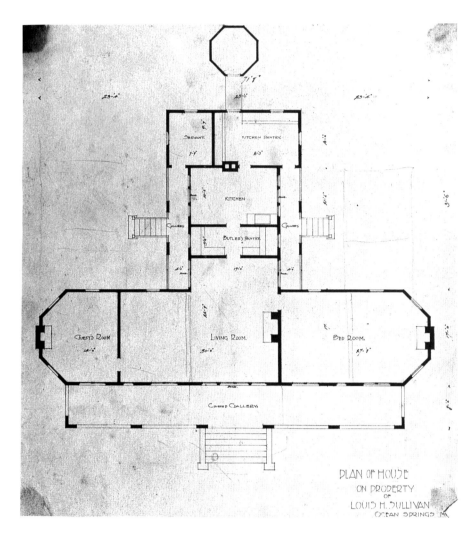

PLAN OF HOUSE
ON PROPERTY
OF
LOUIS H. SULLIVAN
OCEAN SPRINGS MS

process of design, and to the philosophy and system of ornament that were to have such a lasting impact on him.

At the same time, it is also clear that the twenty-one year old Wright's abilities were at once appreciated by thirty-two year old Sullivan who, after working briefly for the Philadelphia architects Frank Furness and William Le Baron Jenney, had himself been hired by Adler at the age of only twenty-four, going into partnership with him three years later. Wright soon became Sullivan's chief designer, entrusted not only with the translation of his sketches into construction drawings, but with commissions for houses that, while inappropriate for an office now exclusively concerned with large public and commercial structures, were nevertheless required to be undertaken; as Wright said, 'Adler and Sullivan refused to build residences. The few imperative, owing to social obligations to important clients, fell to my lot out of office hours.'[24]

In June 1889, a year after joining Adler and Sullivan, Wright married Catherine Tobin, who he had met at his uncle Jenkin Lloyd Jones's All Souls' Church. In the fall he built his house in Oak Park, paying for the construction with a loan from the office. Wright acknowledged in his autobiography that this loan was given under the condition that he not undertake any 'moonlighting' or independent commissions while employed at Adler and Sullivan.[25] Wright's interest and ability to keep to this promise were

soon tested, having to provide for not only his wife, but his mother and two sisters, who had come to live in the neighbouring house in Oak Park; and in the spring of 1890, Frank Lloyd Wright, Junior, the first of the couple's six children, was born. In the same year Wright took the commission for the A W Harlan House in Hyde Park, the first of what he would call his 'moonlight' houses, done at home at night after a day in the office of Adler and Sullivan. Predictably, the cycle continued with more house commissions coming his way in the rapidly growing suburbs of Chicago, and Wright's own habits of exquisite dress and extensive socializing, necessary both to achieve the appearance of the gentleman he had learned from his father and to develop the clientele for his emerging practice, added to the financial pressures to pursue his own 'moonlight' practice.

In the office, Wright soon gained in importance until he was almost indispensable to Sullivan; here was the perfect disciple, the qualities that Wright had developed from childhood – an astonishing ability to visualize and manipulate complex forms, a quick study of design methods, an innate understanding of geometry, a voracious capacity to learn, a wide-ranging interest in ideas, and a sharp and ready wit – made it possible for Sullivan to develop his theoretical insights in talks with Wright, and to turn over to Wright the parts of buildings which did not particularly interest him. As Wright said, 'A good pencil I became in the Master's hand, at a time when he sorely needed one. Because I could be this to him he had more freedom now than he had ever enjoyed before.'[26] It was during this period that Sullivan was focusing on the development of his own highly personal design philosophy, writing to Walt Whitman for encouragement, but otherwise tending to isolate himself from most of his Chicago contemporaries. Adler was the primary source of the office's steady flow of clients and commissions, which from 1887 to 1895 numbered over ninety. In 1890, when the firm of Adler and Sullivan moved to the top floor of their Auditorium Building's tower, the office plan showed that, other than the two partners, only Wright had a private office, located next to Sullivan's, which he shared with his friend George Elmslie, who he had brought over from Silsbee's office.

Indicative of the degree of faith and confidence Sullivan developed in Wright is the fact that he entrusted the twenty-three year old Wright with the design of houses not only for Adler and his own mother, but even for himself. Wright's plan for Sullivan's own vacation house at Ocean Springs, Mississippi, in 1890, already shows the cruciform plan and organization of services in a back wing that would later be fully developed by Wright in such designs as the Cheney House of 1903 and the Hardy House of 1905. But such early hints of what is to come do not prepare us for the James Charnley House, designed by Wright for Adler

and Sullivan and built in 1891 on Astor Place in Chicago; one of the greatest works of architecture of its period, surpassing the similar urban houses of Wright's mature contemporaries such as McKim, Mead and White, this is an absolutely astonishing work for an architect not yet twenty-four. Here we not only see Wright suddenly leap to a new level of both abstraction and synthesis in architectural form, but we can also see the importance of the Froebel training and analytical thinking he had learned at an earlier age.

In the exterior form of the Charnley House, Wright achieves a distillation of the purest forms: eliminating all but the essential, he produces a massing that is at once tight, flat and yet highly dynamic, composed of parts that, as Werner Seligmann said, 'are interdependent and interlock like Japanese joinery,' its details all the more powerful for their severity.[27] The brick body of the house rests on a base of smoothly finished ashlar stone, which lifts in the centre to frame the entry; the brick mass is recessed at the centre above the door to receive an ornamented loggia. The window openings in the brick wall have no frames and, with the exception of a cornice and the loggia, there are no projecting mouldings or details on the facade, and the stone and brick together produce a flush and smooth wall. Wright said: 'In this Charnley city-house on Astor Place I first sensed the definitely decorative value of the plain surface, that is to say, of the flat plane as such.'[28]

Left: Plan of Louis Sullivan's Cottage, designed by Frank Lloyd Wright, Ocean Springs, Mississippi, 1890.
Right: View of Michigan Avenue elevation, Auditorium Building, Chicago, Illinois, 1887, Adler and Sullivan. The office of Adler and Sullivan, which Wright joined in 1888, was located in the tower at the rear left.

Above: James Charnley House, Chicago, Illinois, 1891, view from the street; the house was designed by Frank Lloyd Wright for Adler and Sullivan.

The sophisticated composition of the Charnley House facade, at once powerful and restrained, is an extraordinary achievement, one that sets a standard of excellence rarely matched even today.

Yet it would be in the development of interior space that Wright was to make his greatest contribution, and in the Charnley House we can barely discern its first indications. Entering the low, small door, we discover that the plan is simple and tripartite, corresponding to the facade, with a skylit central stair hall opening upwards to the full height of the house, surrounded by a screen composed of square vertical wood strips, which extends the tight, flat detailing of the facade to the interior.

While Wright's own accounts of his time in the office of Adler and Sullivan focus on these residential designs, he was involved during the days with all the projects active during his five years in Sullivan's employ, including the Auditorium, the Dooley Block of 1890, the Getty Tomb of 1890, the Anshe Ma'ariv Synagogue of 1890, the Transportation Building (for the Columbian Exposition) of 1890, the Wainwright Building of 1890, the Wainwright Tomb of 1892 and the Schiller Building of 1891. While he frequently describes himself as carrying out the designs of Sullivan, one may suspect that Wright's hand was more active in at least some of them; most notably, the Schiller Building, which included a theatre at its base and exhibits

the balance and tension between the horizontal and vertical that is more evident in the work of Wright than that of Sullivan during this period. Wright wrote in his autobiography, 'the Schiller building, Chicago – a building, owing to Sullivan's love for his new home in the South [designed by Wright], more largely left to me than any other so far.'[29] It is also interesting to note that Wright was to open his own office in the Schiller Building after his departure from Adler and Sullivan.

The break with Sullivan occurred in 1893, and the exact circumstances are known only to the two principals. Wright said that Sullivan discovered his 'moonlighting' projects and fired him. That Sullivan would in fact have been aware of these outside commissions by Wright before this time is suggested by Sullivan's having walked past the Harlan House on the way to work every day for ten months; also, Sullivan's brother lived directly across from two other Wright 'moonlight' commissions, the George Blossom and Warren MacArthur houses.[30] Given Sullivan's probable foreknowledge of these houses, it seems likely that there were other factors involved in the timing of this falling out between the two headstrong designers. In any event, after five years at Adler and Sullivan, Wright opened his own office in 1893, sharing the top floor of the Schiller Building – a space remarkably similar to Sullivan's office at the top of the Auditorium Tower – with his old friend from

Silsbee's office, Cecil Corwin, who had been the architect on record for Wright's 'moonlighting' projects.

Fall and Rise of the Chicago School

Though Wright was later often to imply that Sullivan was the only American architect of this period attempting to both build in an innovative manner and develop an indigenous architectural style, Chicago of the late 1800s in fact had numerous architects working in a vein similar to Sullivan, and his buildings during this period did not always surpass the work of his Chicago contemporaries to the degree that has often been implied.[31] Most importantly, Richardson's Marshall Field Wholesale Store, finished in 1887, was essential to Sullivan's understanding of the formal potential of the wall as a massive and flush expression of the building's structure. The degree of his debt to Richardson during this period is reflected both in the Auditorium Building and in the Walker Warehouse of 1888. In its proportion and suppression of the horizontal (spandrel or transom) in elevation, Root's Mills Building in San Francisco of 1890 resembles Sullivan's Wainwright Building in St Louis of the same year, yet there is no question that in the Wainwright Building Sullivan was the first to achieve a pure expression of the ornament-clad, vertically oriented structure as a frame; he went on to perfect it in his Guaranty Building in Buffalo of 1895 and Bayard Building in New York of 1897.

On the other hand, it was Root's Reliance Building, largely designed before his tragic death in 1891, and completed in Chicago by 1895, that fully developed the ideas on the fundamental relation between a building's non-load-bearing wall or cladding and its underlying structure first proposed by the German architect Gottfried Semper (1803–79), whose writings Root had translated and published.[32] The completed Reliance Building presented to Sullivan and the other Chicago architects a stunning reinterpretation of the skyscraper, emphasizing the horizontal cladding rather than the vertical structure; Sullivan's last skyscraper, the Carson Pirie Scott (formerly Schlesinger and Mayer) Store of 1899, is directly indebted to Root's precedent-setting design.

This loosely defined school of architectural thinking that had developed in Chicago by 1890 was splintered by the World Columbian Exposition, opened in Chicago in 1893. But rather than being a uniquely critical moment in the development of modern architecture, the Exposition is better understood as one of a series of 'crises' in the ongoing development of an American architecture. Well before the Exposition, architects had turned to the classical forms of ancient Greece and Rome: Thomas Jefferson and Benjamin Latrobe, to name only the most prominent, used classical forms in building the public monuments of the young American nation, as Wright was well aware. However, while classical architecture was nothing new in

Right: The Schiller Building with the German Opera House and Garrick Theatre, Chicago, Illinois, 1891, designed by Louis Sullivan and Frank Lloyd Wright. After leaving Adler and Sullivan, Wright opened his office on the top floor of the tower.

America, the particular academic interpretation being put forward by the École des Beaux-Arts and its associated schools first emerged in Wright's time. Americans such as Jefferson and Richardson had endeavoured to adapt and redefine the classical and other historical precedents to embody qualities they understood to be particularly American. The followers of the Beaux-Arts school, on the other hand, were setting forth a much more uniform interpretation, academically 'correct', and explicitly non-contextual – intended to be the same around the world.

That this academic tradition, as it came to be called, was so appealing to an America eager to establish and display its recently attained position as a global power, reveals a basic aspect of the American character still true today: the belief that form alone is sufficient. This belief is precisely what motivated the architects who planned Chicago's Columbian Exposition: if America could produce the world's largest and most extravagant collection of buildings in the 'approved' classical style, its culture would surpass that of its rivals. American architects felt compelled to address the archaic mysteries of their New World, yet were simultaneously fascinated by the 'answers' of academic styles; as a result, the development of an American architecture has often been a seemingly unreconcilable struggle between archaic, contextual forms (derived from the functional and structural precision of

nature) and sophisticated, universal styles (defined by academic models).

The delicate balance of this struggle between the indigenous (best represented in 1890 by the Chicago skyscraper) and the universal (the classical models of the École) is evident in the early preparations for the Exposition itself. The Chicago firm of Burnham and Root had been selected in early 1891 to coordinate the design for the Exposition – a great success for the architectural community of Chicago, which had always been second to that of (strictly classical) New York. Yet in April the brilliant John Wellborn Root died suddenly of pneumonia, and Daniel Burnham selected Charles Atwood to replace Root as his designer. One can only imagine how different the Exposition would have been if Root, one of the most influential and inventive designers of his time, had lived to direct its design. As it actually happened, however, Atwood's classical training, together with Burnham's own decision to require strictly classical precedents for the Exposition designs – a decision much easier to make in the absence of the innovative Root – established the direction of its architecture. With the exception of Sullivan's formally reserved yet ornamentally exotic Transportation Building, the Exposition consisted almost entirely of academically defined classical architecture, such as the Fine Arts Building designed by Atwood.

While this event has been bemoaned in modernist architectural histories as a turning away from the indigenous American architecture just beginning to emerge in Chicago – resulting in its loss, or at the very least in a substantial setback, from which it took fifty years (in Wright's estimation) to recover – it is perhaps more likely that Burnham's dictation of the classical language at the Exposition was exactly the challenge needed to crystallize what was later to be called the Chicago School of architecture. In this regard, it is interesting to note that, though founded by a group of draughtsmen in 1885, two years prior to Wright's arrival in Chicago, the Chicago Architectural Club became active and influential in its support and promotion of both the Arts and Crafts movement and the emerging American school of design only after the so-called 'disaster' of the 1893 Exposition.

This Will Kill That: Style and Monumentality

It is certain that Wright, a true Lloyd Jones rebel, operated best when he was in the minority, battling for that which he thought right: 'Truth against the world.' Yet the extent of the indecision felt in this moment by American architects can be seen even in Wright, who was evidently not then as absolutely opposed to academically defined classicism as he later suggested; his entry for the Milwaukee Library Competition of 1893 is an extraordinarily powerful essay in classical architecture, one that Patrick Pinnell has shown

looked beyond the work of the Beaux-Arts architects to learn directly from the monuments of classical antiquity.[33] Only in hindsight, after over forty years of engaging the struggle between the archaic and the academic in his own work, could Wright say of the Exposition's opening in 1893, 'Fateful year in the culture of these United States. They are about to go Pseudo-Classic in Architecture.'[34] The attentive reader will note that even here, in this seemingly dismissive statement, Wright's use of 'pseudo' implies that one may still access the 'true'; the original monuments of classical antiquity.

Kenneth Frampton has noted the problematic aspect that monumentality presented to both Sullivan and Wright during these years.[35] A primary reason for Wright's return to the precedents of classical antiquity was undoubtedly their capacity to embody the monumental, to be the 'great book of stone', according to the heroic interpretation of architecture Wright had found in his early reading of Victor Hugo's *Notre Dame de Paris*.[36] In the chapter that was to have such a profound effect on Wright, entitled 'This Will Kill That', Hugo, speaking directly to the readers, says that up until the fifteenth century 'the material and intellectual forces of society all converged on that one point: architecture,' and that 'whoever was then born a poet became an architect,' because

architecture was the principal register of mankind, that during that period all ideas of any complexity which arose in

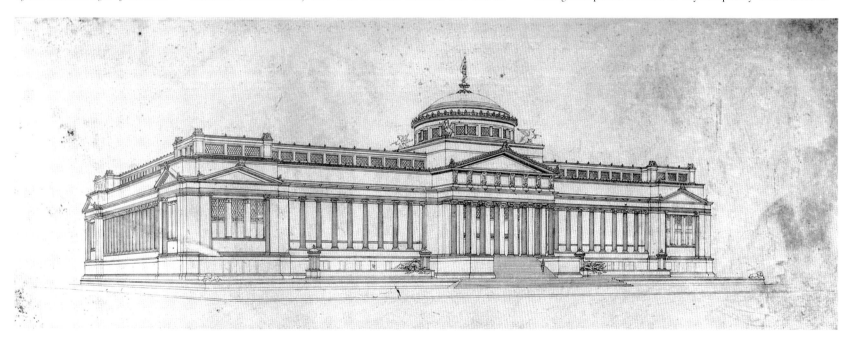

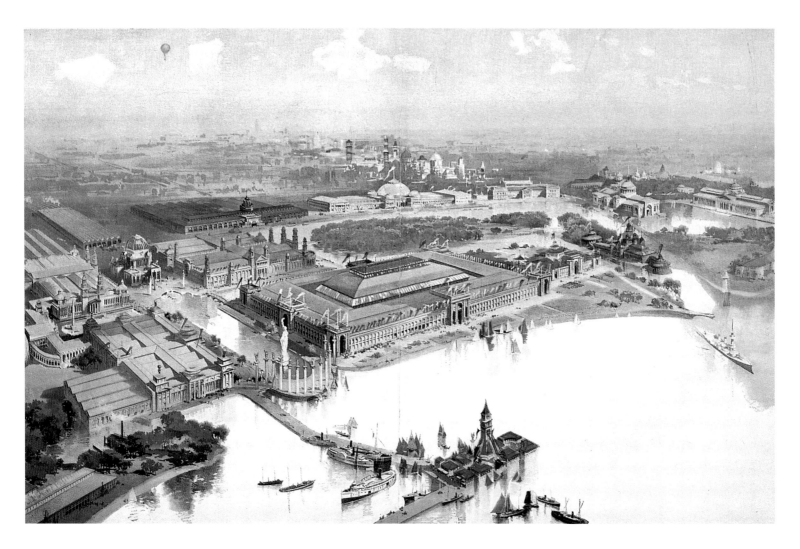

the world became a building. And why? Because every idea, be it religious or philosophical, is concerned to perpetuate itself, because the idea that has moved one generation wants to move others, and to leave some trace.

In the fifteenth century, Hugo states that everything changed: with the invention of the printing press 'the human mind discovered a means of perpetuating itself which was not only more lasting and resistant than architecture, but also simpler and easier ... The book was to kill the building.' Yet this new means of perpetuating ideas did not possess the place-making qualities of the monument after which Hugo's story is named: 'In the days of architecture, thought had turned into a mountain and

taken powerful hold of a century and of a place. Now it turned into a flock of birds and was scattered on the four winds, occupying every point of air and space simultaneously.' Hugo goes on to tell what was to happen to architecture after this event:

And so you see how, starting with the discovery of printing, architecture gradually dried up, it atrophied, and was denuded ... from the sixteenth century on, architecture's malady became apparent; it was no longer the essential expression of society; it turned miserably into a classical art; once it had been Gallic, European, indigenous, now it became Greek and Roman; once it had been true and modern, now it became pseudo-antique. This was the decadence we call the Renaissance ... It was the setting sun which we all take to be the dawn.

At this point in the narrative all seems lost: 'Let there be no mistake, architecture is dead, dead beyond recall, killed by the printed book.' Yet in the very next paragraph, Hugo holds out a last hope with this strange prophesy: 'The great accident of an architect of genius might occur in the twentieth century just like that of Dante in the thirteenth.' In his paraphrasing of this chapter in his 1901 lecture 'The Art and Craft of the Machine', Wright makes a revealing modification to Hugo's timetable: 'if architecture rise again, reconstruct, as Hugo prophesies she may do *in the latter days of the nineteenth century* ...' (my emphasis).[37] Wright's unique combination of the missionary and the messianic, nurtured from infancy by his mother's insistence that he would be an architect – as a Lloyd Jones, he could be nothing other than a revolutionary architect – can also be traced to the deep effect on Wright of Hugo's story of the death, and possible rebirth, of the beloved mother-art architecture. Did Wright, as is suggested by his change in Hugo's prophesy, to make it better fit his own biography, see himself as the 'architect of genius' who was to revive architecture?

An answer of sorts may be found in the revealing story Wright tells in his autobiography: the same year as the opening of the Exposition, Wright was invited to a meeting with Daniel Burnham, arranged and held in the house of Wright's good friend – and future repeat client – Edward C Waller. Related with overtones suggesting parallels to Christ's temptation by the devil, Wright tells how after dinner he was locked in the 'cozy' library with Burnham, who made him an almost unbelievable offer: Burnham, at that time perhaps the most powerful architect in America, would pay full expenses for Wright, accompanied by his family, study first for four years at the École des Beaux-Arts in Paris, then for two years in Rome, with a job in Burnham's office upon his return. Wright thought this offer was 'splendid, frightening'.

After what must have been agonizing moments, for what was being offered was also the promise of guaranteed wealth and influence, Wright declined the offer, saying that Sullivan had spoiled him for the Beaux-Arts. To Burnham's objection that all the great architects of the day favoured the classical, Wright recalls saying, 'if John Root were alive I don't believe he would feel that way about it. Richardson I am sure never would.' While we may perhaps doubt that Wright was quite so bold in referring to Burnham's deceased partner, it seems clear that the offer was in fact made and declined; "'I'm spoiled, first by birth, then by training, and" – this had now come clear under pressure – "by conviction, for anything like that.'"[38]

FIRST RECORDED in his autobiography written almost forty years after the event, Wright's rejection of Burnham's offer was by no means also a rejection of the classical architectural heritage Burnham represented. In fact, while Wright felt certain that he must continue Sullivan's search for an 'indigenous' form of modern American architecture, he had never been less certain of the part to be played in that search by the great monuments of classical antiquity. Victor Hugo's 'architect of genius', as Wright eventually came to see himself, would first go through a difficult period of trying and often failing before achieving a modern American architecture. Discovering the appropriate means to engage architectural history in the making of this new architecture – the relation between tradition and innovation – was the task to which Wright now turned.

TRADITION AND INNOVATION IN THE EARLY WORK

The intellect is a whole and demands integrity in every work. This is resisted equally by a man's devotion to a single thought and by his ambition to combine too many.

Ralph Waldo Emerson[1]

Left: Frank Lloyd Wright House, Oak Park, Illinois, 1899, detailed view of the front elevation and porch. Arguably Wright's first fully independent built work. Its unique presence in the rapidly growing, wealthy and progressive suburb of Oak Park would prove essential to the success of Wright's young practice.

In his sympathetic and important study of Wright's early career up to 1910, subtitled *The First Golden Age*, Grant Manson begins with the following assertion: 'Students of the career of Frank Lloyd Wright inevitably discover that any attempt to account for his accomplishment in customary terms of example and influence does not work. Sooner or later they are faced with the fact that *it is essentially spontaneous*' (my emphasis).[2] Manson here alludes to the presumption, typical in the writings of architectural historians, that Wright's forms and spaces resulted from the direct formal 'influence' of the works of his predecessors, achieved through the process of copying their forms; all the historian need do is to track down the 'source' for each of Wright's works. This concept of influence through the direct copying of forms was a method developed by architectural historians for comparisons to be made after the fact, and does not address the complex process of formal design and spatial development which actually takes place in the mind of the architect at work.[3]

While Manson was correct to point out that the traditional assignment of 'influence' was entirely insufficient in addressing the extraordinary work of Wright, Wright's own assertion that no previous architecture had any impact on his thinking and his work was also not the whole story. While later generations of modern architects might have been able to truthfully claim an ignorance of history,

Wright could not. Based as it is on this claim of historical 'innocence' by Wright, Manson's explication of Wright's design method – that it was 'essentially spontaneous' – is equally insufficient.

Even though he remembered being bold and decisive in declining Daniel Burnham's extraordinary offer, which would have required him to embrace academic classicism, in 1893 Wright had not yet resolved what form his architecture should take. After telling the Burnham story in his autobiography, Wright on the very next page offers an observation, in describing his own early independent work: 'I couldn't invent terms of my own overnight.'[4] Indeed, Wright's earliest period, from the opening of his own practice in 1893 until his arrival at the definitive design for the Prairie House in 1903, consisted of ten long years of serious struggles in design – far more difficult and convoluted than what we might have expected to follow the early success of the Charnley House – which resulted in a number of works to which Wright himself later makes little reference. Wright did in later years claim that designs for the Prairie Period buildings were 'shaken out of his sleeve', perhaps leading to Manson's impression that the design process was somehow 'spontaneous', but closer studies have revealed the far more complicated path taken by the young architect in achieving the systematic approach to design that finally allowed him to produce the great works of his Prairie Period.[5]

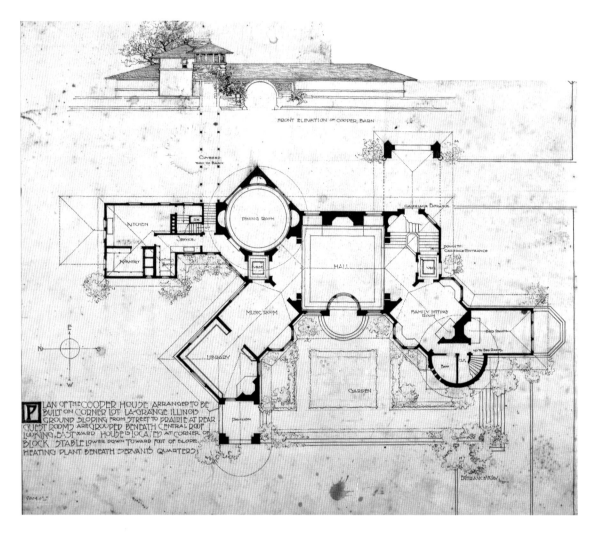

FRONT ELEVATION OF COOPER BARN

PLAN OF THE COOPER HOUSE ARRANGED TO BE BUILT ON CORNER LOT LA GRANGE ILLINOIS GROUND SLOPING FROM STREET TO PRAIRIE AT REAR GUEST ROOMS ARE GROUPED BENEATH CENTRAL ROOF LOOKING EASTWARD HOUSE IS LOCATED AT CORNER OF BLOCK STABLE LOWER DOWN TOWARD FOOT OF SLOPE HEATING PLANT BENEATH SERVANTS QUARTERS

Above: Henry Cooper House project, La Grange, Illinois, 1890, plan of house and elevation of stables. The plan was probably based on McKim, Mead and White's Wave Crest House of 1885.

Wright's classical design for the Milwaukee Library competition was not his only effort in this vein during this period; indeed, almost all his earliest houses, done while still at Adler and Sullivan and during the first years of his independent practice, may be characterized as either 'classical' or 'shingle', and were based upon domestic designs by architects such as Richardson, Bruce Price, Silsbee and, most notably, McKim, Mead and White – whom Wright called Richardson's 'elite running competition'. The question as to what degree Wright was indebted to these architects in his earliest work has been debated at some length, but in examining the works themselves, two things immediately become evident: first, that Wright did indeed utilize these houses by other architects as the starting points for his earliest designs and, second, that each of Wright's designs far surpassed its respective 'model' in quality and resolution.

As he had done in the Charnley House, Wright, despite having no 'terms' of his own, would at least excel at the use of someone else's. While Wright is usually presented as an inventor of 'new' forms, the fountainhead of innovative ideas for twentieth-century architecture – which, indeed, he often was – we should also note that at certain pivotal moments throughout his career he did not operate as a creator of 'original' architectural forms but as the designer who brought the forms used by others to their highest

possible level; he did them far better than anyone else, as if to show all the others 'how it should be done'. It is this that led Henry Russell Hitchcock, in answering his own question as to why Burnham would have made his extraordinary offer to Wright, to state that 'Wright was then [in 1893] almost certainly the ablest academic designer in Chicago.'[6]

Evidence for this somewhat startling assertion can be seen not only in the Milwaukee Library and Charnley House designs, but also in the houses Wright did by 'moonlight' while still at the office of Adler and Sullivan. The first of these houses was Wright's own in Oak Park of 1889 (which we will examine at length shortly); when compared to the elevation of the Chandler House, designed by Bruce Price in 1885 – which Vincent Scully claimed was the 'model' for Wright's design – Wright's house is far more forceful and exacting in its articulation of masses and elements, bringing the 'Shingle Style' to an entirely new level of formal precision. The second of these houses was most likely the Henry Cooper House project, designed around 1890; Wright later claimed that it was a drawing of this house that he showed to Sullivan in applying for work in 1887, leading some to mistakenly date it to that time.[7] Werner Seligmann has compared the Cooper House plan to that of its probable model, the Wave Crest House of 1885 by McKim, Mead and White; noting the precise geometries and rigorous axial

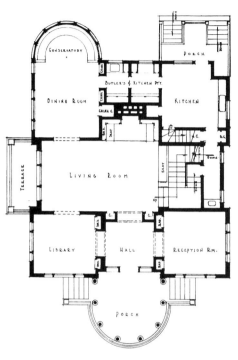

planning of the twenty-three year old Wright, he observes how McKim, Mead and White's 'pales by comparison'.[8]

The George Blossom House, Chicago, Illinois, 1892

The George Blossom House, with its base, pilasters and entablature as well as its Serliano windows, is Wright's most explicitly classical domestic design, and is most likely related to the H A C Taylor House of 1886, again by McKim, Mead and White. Almost exactly as he had done in the Charnley House, Wright creates a tight and restrained severity in the elevations of the Blossom House by using the materials – in this case wood siding and trim – with absolute precision; the wood siding, like the thin tight-set brick of the Charnley House, gives the primary texture and horizontal character to the elevations, while the trim elements crisply define the edges and corners. Also as in the similarly two-storeyed Charnley House, Wright places the lower windows of the Blossom House directly on the base of the house block, attaches the upper windows to the entablature as if they were hung from it, and recesses the central portion of the tripartite facade slightly so that the corner bays read as towers. The low, hipped, pyramidal roof, with overhangs on all four sides, emphasizes the simple square massing of the house.

The plan of the Blossom House is also quite remarkable: a nine-square grid with the central bays recessed slightly, it contains a cruciform plan – a device of the greatest importance in Wright's later work – set within four square corner blocks. Despite the static, symmetrical qualities of this geometry, Wright achieves a rotating, folding movement sequence by filling two arms of the cruciform with the stair and the fireplace; placing the dining room – the 'goal' of the movement sequence that starts at the front door – in one of the corner blocks; and positioning the living room asymmetrically along that path. In plan and elevation, this shift in the movement path is quite clearly marked at its beginning and end by the one-storey semicircular protrusions at the front door and dining room. Despite the seeming precision of the floor plan's geometry, the rear of the house – where two bay windows protrude from the cubic mass and no trim elements are used – exhibits the intentional dissolution of the perfect form on the 'service' side of the house, which was to become typical in Wright's designs. The corner cut off the kitchen, along with the pilasters, mark the limit of the perfect square in plan, and free up this back elevation for the expression of specific service functions.

The interior of the Blossom House, like many of Wright's houses, is rarely discussed in the existing literature; yet even at this early date it is clear that Wright was developing many of his formal innovations first in the interior spaces of his buildings. Many of his design

Above: The Frank Lloyd Wright House, Oak Park, Illinois, 1889, plan of ground level.
Above right: The George Blossom House, view of living room looking towards stair, fireplace and inglenook at left centre.

conceptions dealt primarily with what he would later call 'the space within' – the enclosure and definition of inhabited space. While the exteriors of many of these early works are tightly bound, severely detailed cubic volumes, the interior spaces are frequently much more open, and it is here that the interpenetrating spaces, which would characterize Wright's mature architecture, first appeared to be experienced by the occupants. In an effort to overcome the silence in the existing literature concerning the experiential qualities of the spaces within Wright's buildings, and because of their importance to Wright's design development, this study, whenever appropriate, will give primary emphasis to the aspect of interior experience.

After entering the Blossom House through the square hall, flanked on axis to either side by the square library and reception room, we move into the living room through an arched opening. Even though we have moved on axis from the entrance door directly to the centre of the square house plan, it is clearly one end and not the centre of the rectangular living room into which we have been deposited. The way directly ahead is blocked by the fireplace, and the stair to the right weaves up and out of sight behind three layers of screens made of thin vertical wooden rails. Between the inglenook fireplace and the seat set into the stair is one of the first re-entrant corners in Wright's work

– a simple yet highly plastic formal device of major importance to the development of the Prairie House.[9] Turning left to face the only window in sight, which opens on to a terrace at the other end of the living room, we can now see that the three primary rooms of the house – the living room with dining room and library that flank it on either side – together form a T-shaped volume, and that we are standing at its base. The occupant of the Blossom House is in this way reoriented upon reaching the centre of the house, and the rooms related to entry (hall and reception) now appropriately fade from view with this new reading of the interior.

We should note 'in passing' – a phrase wonderfully suggestive of movement through space – the precision and beauty of the flush-wood detailing of the inglenook, its seats to either side, and the stair, all of which are folded out of the continuous horizontal wood panelling that splits the elevation of the living room into two equal zones; the darker lower half, defined by the horizontal panelling, folds to define spaces by closing on itself; the lighter upper half, defined by the vertical wood rails of the stairs and windows, is open to the spaces beyond. The height of the wood panelling, over five feet, gives it the feeling of being an independent, freestanding wall that does not reach the ceiling – another idea that Wright develops to great effect in the Prairie Houses.

The re-entrant corner, developed as an interior spatial transition in the Blossom House stair hall, is first expressed on the exterior in the Allison Harlan House, which was built in Chicago in 1892; with its tripartite plan, its tight cubic massing, and its second-storey loggia – complete with ornament similar to Sullivan's – the Harlan House is closely related to the Charnley House of the previous year. Yet the roof overhang which projects all around the Harlan House, the loggia which appears to hang from it, and the terrace wall at the ground together compose a series of horizontal layers, giving this house a strong sense of spatial depth, registered in the shadowed facade. The window pattern, details and even the massing of the Harlan House are, upon closer inspection, highly complex, and suggest that the building has been disassembled in the mind of the designer into its constituent elements, which were then refined and reassembled – exhibiting Wright's rapidly developing ability to integrate diverse architectural forms and spaces.

The Frank Lloyd Wright House, Oak Park, Illinois, 1889

It can be convincingly demonstrated that the other, non-classical model for Wright's houses of this period was in fact his own house in Oak Park, built in 1889, one year after he started work at Adler and Sullivan. This house should be considered Wright's first fully independent built work; though he had prepared the drawings for his two aunts' Hillside Home School, built in the Valley the year before, he did not have the freedom in design there that he had in his own house. When we consider this modest little house, we find that it is full of suggestive details and spatial implications; we should assume that it was intended to exemplify Wright's architectural ideas. The quality of its subtle yet unique presence in the rapidly growing, wealthy and progressive suburb of Oak Park would prove essential to the success of Wright's young practice.

The massing of the house is deceptively simple and yet memorable: an enormous pyramidal gable floating over the recessed ground floor. The gable is sheathed entirely in wood shingles, but despite their pronounced texture, Wright achieves an astonishing and unexpected quality of tautness and smoothness in the facade, already exhibiting the control and precision in the use of materials that would mark the later Charnley House. In the gable a row of windows are set behind thinly edged frames, topped by a projecting cornice and half-round clerestory, lighting the room that at first would be Wright's studio, and later his children's bedroom. Only the front surfaces of the two bay windows on the ground floor are aligned flush with the surface of the gable, while the rest of the facade is recessed into the shadows of the gable, behind the terrace wall rising from the ground.

While the front elevation of the house, dominated by the gable, is symmetrical, the entrance is not central but through the bay on the right. Entered thus off-centre, the ground-floor plan has been developed to allow movement to rotate to the left, 'pinwheeling' around the conceptual and ceremonial centre of the house, the fireplace, together with its inglenook and built-in seats. It should be noted that the fireplace is not at the geometric centre of the plan, having been moved back to allow space for the larger living room. Our experience in occupying the interior of the house is nevertheless centred on the fireplace; upon entry the stair disappears around to its right, the living room opens directly off it, the dining room opens to its left and the kitchen hides behind it.

The off-centre (geometrical) position of this ritual (experiential) centre of the house allowed Wright to develop diagonal views and off-centre movement patterns in both the living and dining rooms. In the living room, the crossing of the diagonal connecting the fireplace and bay window with the diagonal (of movement) connecting the openings to the stair hall and dining room, will be seen again in numerous other designs, including that for Fallingwater. As in the Blossom House, after entering we turn twice – once in each direction – passing through the living room to reach the 'goal' of the dining room; indicative of its importance in Wright's definition of the rituals of domestic life, in both houses the dining room is the only primary space he allows to protrude from the basic massing of the house.

The plan for this small house Wright designed for his family was based on the then-standard builder's prototype, named the 'four-square' because of its four basic spaces on the ground floor: entry/stair, living room, dining room and kitchen.[10] The variations and developments that Wright was to bring forth from this simple plan in the next few years are positively staggering. Wright's experimentation in this little house with nontraditional means of defining and connecting space was not 'hesitant', as Manson asserts; in occupying this house, we are aware of the subtle but effective presence of formal and spatial devices that would later see wider and more explicit use.[11]

Upon entry, we literally confront the stair, which, emerging from the right corner, protrudes well past the middle of the entrance hall, and around which we must move to reach the living room. This stair, typical of many in Wright's work of this period, is an astonishing exercise of abstract geometric rigour, with its sharply defined rectilinear woodwork that folds around corners and goes easily from horizontal to vertical, moving smoothly from stair tread to seat, seat arm, railing cap or wall trim. In this stair, the first thing we experience upon entry, Wright shows that as early as 1889 he was already capable of highly articulated formal transformations, having one element evolve into another, each distinct and precisely defined. This was possible because each element shared the same material and straight-line geometries, as in the Froebel wood blocks.

Above: Frank Lloyd Wright House, living room as seen from the entrance foyer.
Far right: Frank Lloyd Wright House, dining room.

Moving into the living room, we find something similar happening to the entire space. The plaster walls are divided almost exactly at eyelevel (as in the Blossom House) by a wooden-trim strip the same height as the stair rail, fireplace mantel and built-in cabinets; the walls are left white above this trim line and tinted darker below it. One foot below the plaster ceiling, a continuous horizontal wood-trim board circles the room, tying it together and defining its boundaries; below this are aligned the window tops and the unframed openings between rooms; above this a one-foot section of wall bonds with the ceiling, as if the ceiling were folded down. The result is nothing short of astonishing: the lower parts of the wall seem to be free to move, to slide along under the smooth wooden band, so that the numerous openings in the living room – which respond to the dynamics of movement in this small house – do not overcome the calmness elicited by the smooth, simple ceiling, folding down to enclose us. In this way, the living room is a direct reflection of the facade: the serenely stable and massive gable hovering over the open and active (projecting and receding) ground floor.

The elements of interior space in this house are manipulated in a manner remarkably similar to those found in traditional Japanese domestic architecture, yet Wright's first trip to Japan does not occur for another sixteen years, and his first recorded visit to a Japanese building – the Ho-o-den reconstruction at the Exposition – does not occur for another four years. At the time he designed his own house, however, it is evident that Wright was already familiar, through publications, with Japanese culture that he came to deeply admire, and it seems that he treated this 'model' as he had the others: he analysed and distilled it in a personal reinterpretation, using it as the starting point for his own design. His house indicates that Wright had analysed the manner in which the traditional Japanese screen walls do not touch the ceiling, and are free, literally, to move below the beam that circles the room above door height. He had also learned how the all-enclosing roof of the Japanese temples could dominate the elevation, allowing the walls to 'fill in' the shadowed space between roof and ground. Yet with its massive pyramidal gable, Wright's house and those he developed from it tended towards a more compact cubic form and massing, rather than the distended floating lightness typical of the Japanese buildings. The question of monumentality still concerned the young Wright, and he was not yet ready to give up mass, as it remained his most reliable means of achieving monumentality.

THE WARREN MacArthur House, built in Chicago in 1892, is similar to Wright's own house in the relationship between the heavy, massive gable and the projecting and recessing entrance floor. The plan, never analysed in studies on

Wright, holds a surprise: the fireplace stands between the entrance hall and the dining room with open passages on either side, exactly as would occur sixteen years later in the Robie House.[12] The plans of the Robert Emmond House, the Robert Parker House and the Thomas Gale House, all of 1892, are divided down their centres by a bearing wall; on one side are the kitchen and other services, and on the other the three primary rooms of the house – parlour, library and dining room – are lined up side by side. The octagonal parlour and dining room are symmetrically disposed on either side of the square library, which has the fireplace, with large openings connecting all three. This 'tripartite' plan, here already clearly formed, would be later developed by Wright as one of the two primary plan types for the Prairie House. Overemphasis on the exterior form, and a lack of analysis of the interior spaces of these early works, has led to the general assumption that Wright 'invented' the spatial forms of the Prairie Houses only after a certain date (1900 is usually cited). Yet, as these examples indicate, Wright was in fact only perfecting and articulating concepts that had been present even in his earliest works.

The William Winslow House and Stables, River Forest, Illinois, 1893

The William Winslow House and Stables are an essential step in the development of the Prairie House; this is because it was in this house – and even more so in the stables – that Wright first developed the exterior forms and elevational concepts that would allow him to begin to give shape on the outside to the dynamic qualities of interior space and plan he had already built inside his earlier houses. It should come as no surprise, then, when we are struck by the similarity between the brick base that rises over halfway up the front elevation of the Winslow House and the wooden panelling that rises halfway up the living-room walls of the Blossom House: the top of each is crisply defined by a cornice moulding, and the dramatic change in materials in both cases allows the surfaces above and below to be developed in different ways. Just as he was doing on the interiors of his houses, Wright was trying to do on the exteriors, separating and articulating the components that defined the house – the foundation slab, the terrace, the wall, the entrance, the window, the chimney and the roof. As he had discovered in designing the interior spaces, when the elements are thus separated, they gain in both independence and identity; when the elements are also derived from similar geometries, they gain in their ability to be related and reintegrated.

The one and one-half storey brick volume, framed with white stone trimwork, is carefully proportioned to emphasize its heavy contact with the ground; the centre portion, with the entrance door carved out of the layered white stone panel set into the brick, projects forward and is matched by the similarly detailed horizontal plane of the

TRUTH IS LIFE.

GOOD FRIEND, AROVND THESE.
HEARTH STONES SPEAK NO EVIL
WORD OF ANY CREATVRE · · ·

terrace. The half-storey space between the cornice topping the brick mass and the widely overhanging roof is filled with heavily textured terracotta panels; the windows take up the entire space of this terracotta panelling, extending from the cornice to the moulding under the roof. The result is that the roof seems to float above the brick mass, almost as if it were physically or structurally separated. In this initial effort, the effect is purely visual, as the wall is structurally continuous from ground to roof, but the Winslow House is Wright's first attempt to separate and articulate the elevation as a series of, potentially, independent horizontal layers; layers that would later allow the similar spatial layers of the interior to give form to the exterior.

The plan and interior of the Winslow House are notable for the degree of emphasis and independence accorded the fireplace. Located in this instance at the geometric centre of the rectangular volume of the house, the fireplace and its inglenook directly face not the living room but the entrance door. Three steps up on its own podium – a hierarchically more important floor level shared with the stairs and dining room – the hearth is here a fully independent room, commanding a volume at its front equalling the living room, the extent of which Wright is careful to indicate in plan by drawing the carpet pattern encompassing the upper and lower levels; this reading is further reinforced by the stencilled frieze that runs around the top of the entire volume. The dining room, once again the only room

allowed to escape the basic volume of the house, is projected directly backwards from the fireplace mass.

After confronting the hearth upon entry, we again move in a rotational manner around the fireplace, first to the right into the living room, a rectangular space which we enter and exit – to the dining room – at the corners. In moving through these three primary rooms of the Winslow House, the entrance hall, the living room and the dining room, we enter and move along the edges – not the centres – of the rooms, and in each case the centre of the room is blocked to physical passage. This organization of the ground floor as an L-shaped configuration of entry-living-dining wrapped around the fireplace and kitchen block became the typical plan Wright utilized to implant an unexpectedly dynamic movement pattern within houses characterized by cubic or compact rectangular exterior massing.

While the Winslow House, as has often been suggested, may appear to strain somewhat with the contradictory readings of its severely flattened front and the divergent volumes of its back, the stables Wright built behind the house are, by comparison, more relaxed, unified and integrated in their overall design. With the Winslow Stables, Wright, in one seemingly effortless leap, brings forth the primary formal characteristics of the Prairie House: the interpenetration of the two principal volumes, resulting in a cruciform plan at the second level, and the elevations composed of continuous horizontal layers –

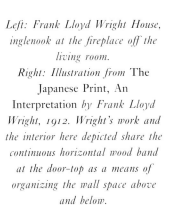

Left: Frank Lloyd Wright House, inglenook at the fireplace off the living room.
Right: Illustration from The Japanese Print, An Interpretation *by Frank Lloyd Wright, 1912. Wright's work and the interior here depicted share the continuous horizontal wood band at the door-top as a means of organizing the wall space above and below.*

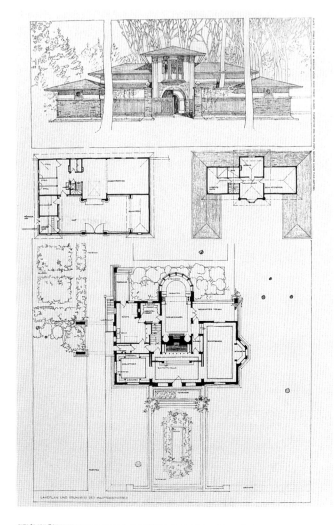

elevations composed of continuous horizontal layers – foundation slab, low brick wall, stucco band (incorporating the windows) and overhanging hipped roof; each layer being free to assume different dimensions and shapes to that above and below it.

These primary elevational elements of Wright's Prairie Period designs – shared by the Winslow House and Stables – have often been thought of only as a 'style', and discussed largely as exterior forms. That these layered elevations were created by Wright to allow for increased freedom in plan, making possible the multiple overlapping spaces that characterize his early designs, has been overlooked. It is interesting to note that even Wright's apprentices did not always understand the spatial intentions of these formal developments. Charles White, after having been an apprentice in the Oak Park Studio for only six months, was able to grasp Wright's division of massing in elevation; in a letter of 1904 he included a sketch of a typical Wright house design, with its base, wall, window band, and overhanging roof as continuous horizontal spatial layers. He went on to say, 'All features of the design have some recognition in the plan.'[13] This is far indeed from Wright's principle that the plan is the *solution* and the elevation is the *expression* of the design idea.[14]

IN THE A C McAfee House project of 1894, Wright began to develop the possibilities implied, in plan, elevation and

Above: William Winslow House, River Forest, Illinois, 1893, ground-floor plan of the house (below), plans and elevation of the stables (above).
Right: William Winslow House, view of the street front. The horizontally layered elevation allows for increased freedom in plan.

massing, by the use of horizontal layers. The house is asymmetrical, the living room and library aligning to form a primary linear volume, with the stair and kitchen-dining block projecting to each side.[15] The openness implied in plan (as presented in the Wasmuth portfolios), where the living room appears almost to be a loggia, is denied in the elevation, where only a row of small windows are punched out of the large blank wall. On the other hand, the elevation does reflect the asymmetry of the plan, through each of its elements being allowed to develop independently, exemplified by the change in height of the low wall at the dining-room windows.

The Isidore Heller House was built on a long narrow lot in Chicago in 1896. As seen in the plan, the entrance is between the living room, which faces the street, and the dining room, which faces the sideyard. We enter off-centre in the hall, and the stair lands diagonally across the narrow space. The living and dining rooms are both cruciform in plan, each being formed of a higher rectangular volume interpenetrated by a lower one, which opens niches to either side. The living room is on an axis with the entrance hall, while the dining room, entered at its end, opens to the left at the end of the hall. While these two rooms are formally resolved in themselves, their composition in the overall plan is less so.

In the Joseph Husser House, built in Chicago in 1899, Wright returns in plan to the complex axial composition of

independent geometries of the early Cooper House (1890), using Richardson's Winn Memorial Library of 1877 as its 'model', and making a confident reinterpretation. But the strongly individual geometries of the rooms are not well integrated in plan, and the massing and elevations are an even less successful attempt to develop the loosely jointed composition of the McAfee House project. In fact, a number of Wright's house designs of this period – such as those for J Baldwin, N Moore, O Goan, G Furbeck and R Furbeck – appear somewhat uncertain and unresolved in plan; their massing and elevations, with the return of the arched windows Wright had earlier eliminated from his work, are at times almost chaotic.

The cause for the slow but certain unravelling of Wright's design method during this period was his belief that he should provide a totally unique form for each of his clients, even as their numbers rapidly increased; this belief of Wright's was an interpretation of individuality in architecture which he now found increasingly difficult to accomplish in his actual designs.

Wright's Second Froebel Training

There is little doubt that Wright's training as a child in the Froebel kindergarten method was instrumental in the development of his enormous capacity for formal and spatial invention and composition. Yet a more important aspect of the Froebel system's effect on Wright's

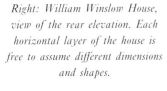

Right: William Winslow House, view of the rear elevation. Each horizontal layer of the house is free to assume different dimensions and shapes.

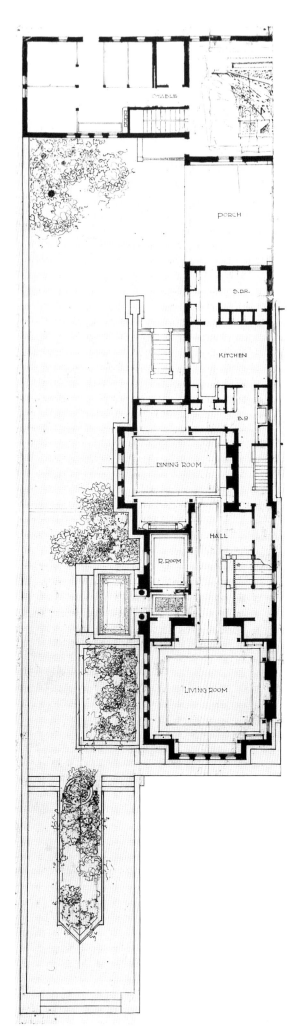

Right: Isidore Heller House, Chicago, Illinois, 1896, ground-floor plan.

and renewed immersion in the Froebel training system while utilizing it to teach his own children from 1895–1900. Meryle Secrest has noted: 'He saw the method's possibilities anew when his own children began playing with them, and, of course, his wife was also teaching Froebel's method.'[16] During that critical period, while Wright was struggling to achieve a clarity of function and simplicity of composition in his own architectural designs, he was every afternoon instructing his children in the Froebel system, reading for himself the instructional manuals provided for the parent, which included detailed diagrams of optimal solutions and texts describing the intended results in the child's creative capacities, thinking and philosophy; all this taking place in the playroom Wright had built on to the second storey of his Oak Park house in 1894, expressly for the purpose of providing a place for his wife to give Froebel training to his own and the neighbourhood children.

We should remember that the Froebel system is, among other things, directed towards the development of a limited group of generative geometric and spatial forms, which are both discerned in nature and to be utilized as repetitive, typological elements of composition. This view of natural order is totally opposed to the primary idea upon which Wright had become fixated in his earliest domestic design work – that each individual client requires a unique design: 'There should be as many kinds of houses as there are kinds of people and as many differentiations as there are different individuals.'[17] This self-imposed demand for endless formal invention in Wright's work had clearly reached a crisis point by 1897, and the perceived need to make something totally new and unique for each client was straining even Wright's prodigious formal capacities.

In his hours away from the Oak Park studio – and the struggle to invent the multitude of forms seemingly called for by his own design dictum – returning to the Froebel training, with its blocks, its square grid table-top work mats, its paper strips for weaving and its suggestively worded manuals, must have been a refreshing diversion for Wright. At some point it clearly became more than a mere diversion, for here in this kindergarten system he was using to train his children as his mother had trained him, there was another way of making that did not rely on formal invention but rather on repetitive use of a limited group of elements and their configuration into a few spatial types. Sometime in the late 1890s, Wright realized that the Froebel training, with which he was now doubly familiar, held the key to resolving the design dilemma he had created for himself in his architectural work, saying, 'the individuality of those concerned may receive more adequate treatment within legitimate limitation.'[18]

As we have seen, the development of the Prairie House was by no means instantaneous or spontaneous, and the sequence of house designs Wright produced from 1885 to 1900 reveals the emergence step by step. While at times Wright seems to have despaired of succeeding in his search for a systematic design process, in looking at his designs from this period in sequence, we are today able to see the influence and critical aid

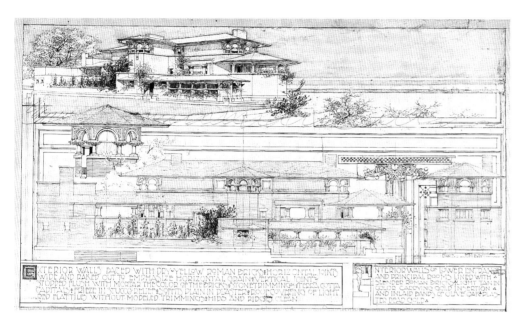

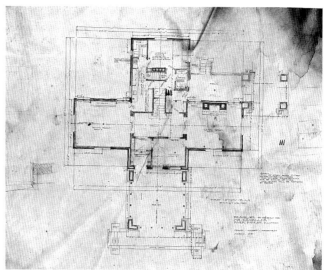

Above: Joseph Husser House, Chicago, Illinois, 1899, analytique drawing, with perspective and elevation details.
Above right: Edward Waller House project, River Forest, Illinois, 1898, plan. In this project, Wright first proposed the fully articulated cruciform plan.

provided by the design and analysis logic implied in the Froebel training: by the architectural conceptions of type, variation on a theme and the use of a limited number of forms that were imbedded in it.[19] While Wright probably did not read the Froebel instruction manuals when his mother utilized them in instructing him as a child, the words no doubt sounded familiar to him as he read them at the age of thirty; so much of his own design philosophy had been shaped by it. Richard MacCormac has noted the close parallels – far too close to be coincidental – between quotations from the Froebel instruction manuals and Wright's own philosophical statements from throughout his career.[20] Yet this hardly seems surprising when one recognizes that the renewed exposure to the highly geometric Froebel training, its instruction manual, and its strongly integrated philosophy was clearly instrumental in Wright's breakthrough in the design of the Prairie House.

THE RESULTS of this re-exposure to the Froebel training can be seen in the geometric precision and simplicity of the Edward Waller House project of 1898, where Wright first proposed the fully articulated cruciform plan, with the entrance hall in the very centre of four single-room 'wings': entrance porch, living room, dining room and kitchen-stair. This plan was later built out almost exactly in the Barton House of 1903, but here already the living and dining

rooms are rotated ninety degrees to the entrance hall by the placement of the fireplace and buffet, respectively, which face across the axis linking the three rooms. These rooms are separated not by doors, but by beams dropped across the ends of the entrance hall to mark the thresholds of each space. This project was not built, and around 1899 there seems to have been a brief hiatus in Wright's busy design practice; as after all such slow periods in his career, Wright would emerge having reconsidered and refined his design concepts, appearing to leap to a new level of resolution in his work. This resolution first took form in Wright's greatest innovation of this period, the Prairie House.

THE DEVELOPMENT OF
THE PRAIRIE HOUSE

We must make the shapes, and can only effect

this by mastering the principles.

Horatio Greenough[1]

Left: Susan Lawrence Dana
House, Springfield, Illinois, 1900.
A beautifully interwoven
composition of brick, stone coping,
terracotta panels, stained-glass
windows and copper-edged roofs.
Above: 'A House in a Prairie
Town' project, Ladies Home
Journal, *1900. By publishing his*
designs in this popular American
magazine, Wright presented his
houses to a wide audience.

The Prairie House was the name Wright gave his new designs for the American suburban home, a type of house characterized by a degree of both spatial freedom and formal order previously unknown in either the Old or New World. In the two houses designed in 1900 for publication in the *Ladies Home Journal* in 1901, Wright arrived at the two cruciform plan 'types' that were to serve as the starting point for virtually every Prairie House. Patrick Pinnell has convincingly shown how these two plans were directly derived from the simple little 'four-square' plan of Wright's own house of 1889.[2] It is therefore of the greatest importance to note that Wright moved from using the works of other architects as his 'models' or starting points to using his own work as the theme for variation. As Colin Rowe has noted, the Prairie Houses exhibited from the very start an:

> astonishing finality … These houses are the monuments of an
> unerringly consistent development; and to informed observers
> of the time it was apparent that here a plastic statement of
> the very highest relevance was in the process of delivery, that
> here a definite answer had already been given to those
> questions which many of the most advanced buildings of the
> day seemed to exist merely to propose.[3]

The publication of these two seminal designs by Wright in the *Ladies Home Journal*, a popular magazine with broad national readership and great influence among homemakers,

rather than a professional architectural journal, was hardly accidental. Throughout his career, Wright went to great efforts to present his designs for domestic living to the widest possible audiences – directing his accompanying texts to those considering building their own homes, rather than to those who might be employed to design them. From the start of his practice in Oak Park, Wright wanted to present his ideas directly to potential clients and avoid the necessity of being represented as part of the larger and more anonymous architectural profession, and he published in *Ladies Home Journal* and other popular magazines numerous times during his career. In the United States, architects would not consider advertising for another seventy-five years, but in 1900 Wright already understood the need for direct communication with the American family.

The first *Ladies Home Journal* design, called 'A Home in a Prairie Town', develops the 'tripartite' plan previously discussed; the living room is flanked by – and completely open to – the library and dining room on either side, and the fireplace and a bay window projecting onto a covered terrace form the cross axis, with the kitchen and stair behind the fireplace occupying the fourth arm of the cruciform. The second, called 'A Small House with "Lots of Room in It"', develops the 'pinwheel' aspects of the Wright House plan; centred on the fireplace, the four wings of the cruciform contain the entrance and stair, living room, dining room and kitchen, encountered in that order upon entry, and one moves from room to room only at the corners – each room centres on the fireplace, which has separate hearths for each room. Due to Wright's use of the cruciform for both plans, light and views are provided on three sides to all the major rooms on the ground floors – even to this day an exceptional condition in house design, but one that would become the norm for Wright. In both plans, the bedrooms are on the smaller second floor.

These two plan prototypes were first built in 1900 as the Warren Hickox House and the Harley Bradley House, respectively, both in Kankakee, Illinois. The enormous spaciousness produced by the tripartite plan is evident in the Hickox House, where the dining-living-library rooms (here interestingly labelled 'alcove room-room-alcove room') together form an unbroken volume of almost sixty by twenty feet in size, subdivided only by beam drops and short stub walls. How entry is to be accomplished is not a simple problem in this plan; Wright here brings the entrance in from behind and to one side of the fireplace, providing for internal circulation and stairs – as in 'A Home in a Prairie Town' – parallel to the three-room configuration, along the back side of the fireplace.

The independence attained by each room in the pinwheel plan is evident in the Bradley House; Wright emphasizes this by giving the living room and the dining room different proportions and ceiling beam patterns that are rotated ninety degrees to one another, reinforcing the focus of each room back towards the central fireplace. The scale of the two *Ladies Home Journal* designs was quite modest, and in the side alcoves off the living room, and the extensive service area and outbuildings of the Bradley House, we can see the difficulty Wright had adapting these compact, minimalist designs to the requirements of clients with more grandiose intentions. As Wright himself often said, an architect's limitations are his best friends.[4]

The Board and Batten Cottages

The projects for the Henry Wallis Cottage of 1900 were the first of a series of designs for summer cottages or second homes where Wright's careful orchestration of the economies necessitated in simple wood construction achieved an exceptional coherence of form. Yet this in no way hindered – and perhaps even helped – Wright's continued development of his spatial concepts; in the Wallis Cottage projects, we see Wright experimenting with the position of the fireplace, testing its effect on the relations between the various rooms in the plan. In the first project, Wright places the fireplace at the geometric centre of the square house plan; freestanding, fronting the living room, the fireplace has space open to either side, defining the edges of all three major rooms. In the second project, Wright pulls the fireplace back across the entrance hall, so that, while it still faces the living room, it occupies all three

Below left: 'A Home in a Prairie Town' plans.
Below right: 'A Small House with "Lots of Room in It"', perspective.
Bottom: Harley Bradley House, view of the living room.

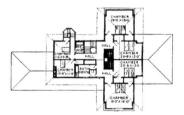

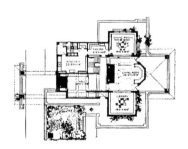

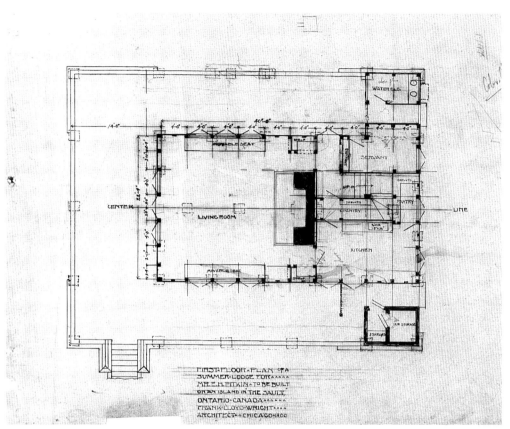

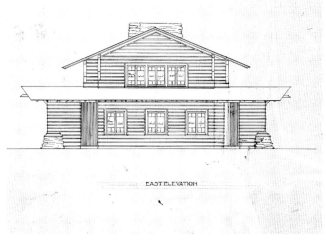

EAST ELEVATION

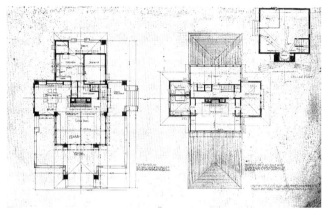

Top left and right: Summer Cottage for E H Pitkin, Sapper Island, Ontario, Canada, 1900, plan and elevation.
Above right: Charles Ross House, Lake Delavan, Wisconsin, 1902, plans.
Above: Henry Wallis Summer Cottage second project, Lake Delavan, Wisconsin, 1900, plan.

rooms – or perhaps none of them – producing a rich ambiguity of spatial definition in this modest little design.

In the E H Pitkin Summer Cottage, built in Ontario in 1900, Wright achieves an early synthesis of geometry, space and construction method. The house is designed on a rigorous four-foot grid, with a continuous wood platform floor and terrace; the walls are made of four-inch by four-inch wood posts, placed four feet on centre, with horizontal board and batten siding, the whole is topped by a wood-framed roof, exposed inside. The plan consists of one large rectangle, surrounded on three sides by a deep terrace, made by running the wooden floor directly from inside to outside, and flanked on the other side by two small service blocks. The fireplace, placed off-centre in the plan, divides the living room from the kitchen and stair. A large pitched roof covers the main rectangular two-storey volume, and a smaller pitched roof runs along the back, tying the one-storey service blocks to the kitchen. The whole has a distinctly Japanese feel, in the profiles of the roofs and the strong presence of the grid and wood in its construction, and is an altogether remarkable design – simple, tight, efficient and yet elegant.

In massing, the Charles Ross House, built in 1902 on Lake Delavan, Wisconsin, is a two-storey cruciform; on the ground floor the wider volume holding the living room and kitchen is intersected by the narrower volume containing the entrance and dining room, with the fireplace at the centre. If we complete in plan the rectangular shapes of the entrance hall, living room and dining room, we can see that the missing corners of these three rooms overlap, with the fireplace standing in this interlocking joint. With this house, Wright moved from simply opening previously discrete rooms one to another, by removing the walls between them, to having the rooms overlap and interpenetrate each other, by removing the corners and pushing the spaces towards one another. One is made more aware of this overlapping condition by Wright's use of simple rectangular geometries for the rooms, and he employs these again in defining a somewhat different reading for the main floor; the wooden veranda forms a square with the narrow volume containing the entrance and dining room, and the main spaces of the house may be seen as a T-shaped volume standing on the veranda, with the kitchen and services projected out to the rear – typical of Wright's handling of these elements.

The cottages built for George and Walter Gerts in 1902 are one-storey wooden constructions that display the simplicity and beauty of this method of building, as developed by Wright. Both cottages extend horizontally to cover exterior terraces; in the George Gerts Cottage, Wright projected its entrance across a bridge, and in the Walter Gerts Cottage, he extended its roof to either side of the living room, which is centred on the fireplace,

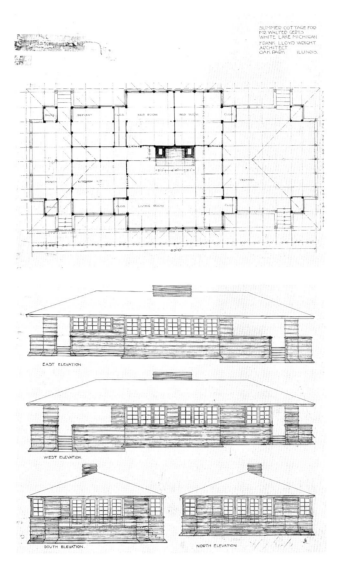

SUMMER COTTAGE FOR
MR WALTER GERTS
WHITE LAKE MICHIGAN
FRANK LLOYD WRIGHT
ARCHITECT
OAK PARK   ILLINOIS.

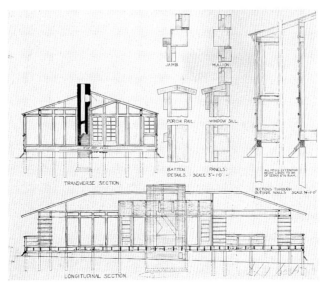

Above: Walter Gerts Summer Cottage, Whitehall, Michigan, 1902, plan and elevations.
Right: Walter Gerts Cottage, sections and details. The roof in this building is extended, supported by two pairs of freestanding piers, to either side of the living room. The construction method of this house is related to that of the 'Romeo and Juliet' Windmill of 1896.

supporting this extended roof on two pairs of freestanding piers – exactly as he would do in the Evans House of 1908. The working drawings for these cottages, with the 3-foot by 3-foot planning grid explicitly shown in red ink, reveal the degree to which the form of the building was a direct revelation of the method of construction. In occupying these houses in the woods, we are made subtly aware of the formal and structural tension between the wood frame of vertical four-inch by four-inch posts spaced at three-foot intervals – exposed on the interior between plastered panels and on the exterior between the windows that run in a continuous band under the roof – and the cladding of horizontal wood boards one foot in width, with two-inch battens nailed over their joints.

It should be noted that the construction method common to all these houses, which relies on the vertical wood frame being braced and stabilized laterally by the horizontal board and batten siding, was given its first test by Wright in the 'Romeo and Juliet' Windmill built for his aunts in the Valley in 1896; as Wright noted in a lengthy section of his autobiography, despite the doubts of the various relations about the structural stability of this slender tower, it never fell victim to the winds it harnessed.[5] Today, almost one hundred years later, it has been renovated, the siding replaced, and appears as good as new – an altogether remarkable design indicative of Wright's application of the lessons learned from his acute studies of the structural implications of natural forms.

The Susan Lawrence Dana House, Springfield, Illinois, 1900

The Dana House is often left out of the canonical studies of Wright, usually because it was a renovation and addition, not a totally new house. We must look carefully to discern the original house in the final plan, however, as it was completely folded into Wright's new construction – this was so skilfully accomplished that several scholars have even assumed that the original house was largely demolished.[6] Almost as if the original house were one of Wright's friendly limitations, rather than the impediment we might imagine it to be, Wright developed the final plan as a pinwheel around the fireplace, showing that this plan type was applicable even to much larger and more complicated houses. More importantly for our purposes, we are completely unaware of the configuration of the original rooms in the completed Dana House, which contains perhaps Wright's greatest interior spaces of this period.

In examining the plans of this house, we are struck by the openness of the rooms to one another. The tendency over the previous two hundred years had been for architecture to rely more and more on corridors and one-door rooms, increasingly emphasizing functional separation and individual privacy, often resulting in the elimination of the incidental or unplanned meeting. Yet, in the Dana House we can see Wright opposing this tendency with another, one described by Robin Evans as 'an architecture arising out of the deep fascination that draws people towards others; an architecture that recognizes passion, carnality, and sociality. The matrix of connected rooms might well be an integral feature of such buildings.'[7] The Dana House plan contains no corridors and all the rooms – including the master bedroom – have more than one way in and out; the rooms are connected *enfilade*, in a series, necessitating movement through rooms to reach other rooms. This type of planning, which predominates the common rooms of Wright's Prairie House, encourages chance meetings and the shared experience of the spaces of the house. The result is what might best be described as a familial relation among the various rooms of the house, a direct reflection of Wright's idealized vision of family life taking place around the table and fire.

We enter the Dana House through an arched doorway on to a tiled landing three feet below the main floor level; looking up into the double-height hall, with its arched fireplace repeating the form of the doorway we just entered, we are immediately aware of the full vertical volume of the house. At the second level, directly over the fireplace, a piano is set into the brick wall under a screen of wooden slats, and there is a continuous walkway around the edge of the room. Our way directly ahead is blocked, so we must take the stair to the left, which places us under the low ceiling of the loggia overlooking the garden to the left; to the right, beyond the brighter volume of the hall, are a pair of glass doors leading into the living room.

From this position assumed immediately upon entering, we are drawn directly ahead across the loggia into the dining room, also double-height and brightly lit, with a barrel-vaulted plaster ceiling and an apsidal seating area projected at the rear. This dining room is one of the most beautiful spaces of its kind in Wright's work; framed by projecting beams resting on square columns in each corner and further enclosed by the high backs of the wood-slatted chairs, it is as if we were in a room inside a room inside a room. Wright's leaded glass, coloured in rich earth tones in the windows and encasing the hanging lamps and sconces, along with the dark woodwork and golden coloured plaster, gives the room the sense of being buried deep inside the forest; reinforcing this are the ornamental patterns Wright developed from various plant forms. The hanging lamps are certainly among the most beautiful objects Wright ever designed, and the quality of repose in the dining room has rarely been equalled.

In our circulation we rotate around the pair of fireplaces that form the core of this house; we can move through the sitting room or back through the entrance hall to access the living room. The living room is a T-shaped space, the ceiling lower to the sides and higher in front of the fireplace, standing free with its pairs of glass doors to either

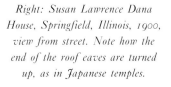

Right: Susan Lawrence Dana House, Springfield, Illinois, 1900, view from street. Note how the end of the roof eaves are turned up, as in Japanese temples.

side; this living room prefigures quite closely that of the Robie House eight years later. The plan of the living room is repeated in the bedroom above where the fireplace stands between the two beds, which are joined back together by their own shared set of canopy beams. Also off the loggia is a glazed corridor that leads to the gallery-library, which together with the dining room, living room and entrance hall constitute the four wings defining the pinwheel plan.

Upon entering the gallery-library from the corridor, we can see over a balcony the full height of the space, giving a similar view overlooking the entrance hall and dining room as to that from the second floor of the main house. The gallery-library is a three-storey, freestanding structure, lit by a long band of windows on both sides, with a barrel-vaulted ceiling similar to that of the dining room; the gallery-reading room is above and the studio-library below, with another fireplace anchoring the far end. Like the dining room, the gallery-reading room is one of Wright's greatest spaces, capturing the open yet enclosed quality he was seeking for the Prairie House. The ribs of the curved ceiling bear on a pair of arched beams to either side, structurally integrating the space in both directions; the windows slid up behind and to the outside of these beams, so that the ceiling appears to fit down between the walls, creating another layering of space even more explicit that that of the dining room. On the floor below, this slot of space between the two layers of the wall and the vault above

is occupied by the bookcases, which project from the wall and do not touch the ceiling, creating small rooms in the larger room in a way very similar to the dining table and chairs. Indeed, throughout this house the furniture, built-in or freestanding, is fully integrated into the design and contributes to the definition and characterization of the spaces to a degree rarely matched in this century.

The exterior of the Dana House, a beautifully interwoven composition of brick, stone coping, stained-glass windows and doors, pressed metal friezes and copper-edged roofs, is notable for Wright's earliest employment of paired sets of piers in terminal elevations and the continuous bands of casement windows in the space above the brick wall, under the roof overhang. The fact that the paired piers do not reach the roof gives the roof a sense of floating over the windows below, which, coupled with the way Wright has turned up the end of the roof eaves, relates the roofs to those of Japanese temples. The large massing of the Dana House is effectively controlled and given scale by Wright's design of long thin volumes that intersect and interpenetrate at right angles, resulting in a dynamic and yet balanced composition.

The Ward Willits House, Highland Park, Illinois, 1901
Often called the first true Prairie House, the Willits House also marks the full development of Wright's wood frame and stucco system of construction. Capable of appearing

Right: Dana House, plans. The plan contains no corridors; rather the rooms are arranged enfilade, *necessitating movement through rooms to reach other rooms, encouraging a shared experience of the spaces of the house.*

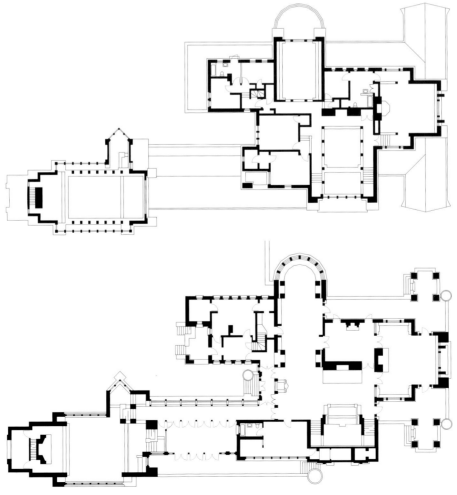

Below: Dana House, view from rear garden towards main house, with gallery and library to right.
Right: View from balcony into studio or gallery.
Far right: View from doors of living room towards entry hall and loggia.

either as a massive wall, in the living-room corners, or as a light screen, in the floating entrance soffit, this composite construction system allowed Wright to give form to his emerging conceptions of interior space. While the repetitive rhythm of the wood frame is revealed in the posts between the windows, running along under the roof in continuous bands, this 'revelation' is not complete; that is, the posts between the windows reveal only a portion of the framing, the major part of which remains concealed beneath the sheathing and plaster needed for horizontal stability. When it is also noted that the floor line between the two storeys is suppressed, the vertical wood members running uninterrupted from foundation to roof, past the floor joists which frame into them, we may consider that this house reveals the order of (rather than literally revealing) the balloon-frame system used in its construction. On the front of the Willits House, Wright applied vertical wood-trim boards on the exterior, over the plaster, aligned with and nailed through to the matching vertical framing members underneath, reinforcing the ambiguity of the resulting form – appearing both monolithic and articulated.

The plan of the Willits House is a direct development of the plan for 'A Small House with "Lots of Room in It"', a cruciform, pinwheel plan with the entrance-stair hall, living room, dining room and kitchen rotating about the fireplace. The living room and kitchen are in the main two-storey

block that is set ninety degrees to the street, while the entrance and dining room are in a thinner volume that intersects the first to form the cruciform. The ground-floor roof, covering the entrance and dining room, is extended along the axis of these rooms, parallel to the street, covering the porte-cochere to the right and a terrace off the end of the dining room to the left. These roof extensions are supported by four piers set well outside the main volume of the plan, marking out the long horizontal sweep of the roofs that complement the vertical mass of the living room and master bedroom above.

From the street we are confronted by this latter symmetrical form which not only has no discernable entrance, but is further blocked by the terrace wall projected towards us. Typical of Wright's later buildings, we are first presented with the major mass or volume – clearly housing the main space (living room) of the house – and yet we must move around this mass, in a way very similar to the circulation around the fireplace mass inside, and enter from the side. Here we should notice that Wright has taken advantage of the broad space covered by the roof extensions to either side by having the entrance hall move slightly forward towards the street while the dining room, the 'goal' of our entry sequence, moves slightly backwards away from the street, towards the woods behind the house. Entry is incremental, by moving along the walkway, under

Left: Dana House, dining room.
Right: Dana House, the upper
central portion of leaded glass
window, in the master bedroom.

the roof overhang, turning to the left we go up three stairs, now enclosed by a low wall and a set of windows into the reception room, through the front door, turn right, then turn left and up five more stairs, turn left again and we are finally in the living room – the room occupying the mass we confronted from the street.

The entrance and stair hall is open the full height of the house, and the ceiling light at the top is turned forty-five degrees and set off-centre to the stair opening, suggesting the rotating movement pattern to come. The stair is enclosed and shaped by a series of wood screens, beams and plaster panels; both binding and juxtaposing horizontal to vertical as it weaves its way up through the house, this is one of the most dynamic spaces of its kind in Wright's work. The living room and dining room are centred on two openings of the fireplace, which projects into each a seat and screen wall only on one side; neither room has a wall of any sort at the inner edge of the room, and the fireplace forms the fourth 'wall' for each. From the entrance one looks through the wood slat screen into the living room, but one must go around the screen to actually enter it, while from the living room one can see through to the dining room, but again one must go around the screen to get there; in doing so we enter the living and dining rooms along their edges, and see into them diagonally rather than frontally, both important developments in Wright's efforts to achieve interconnected interior spaces.

The living room, with closed corners and cubic volume, is symmetrical and dominated by the planar surfaces of the plaster ceiling and wood floor; the vertically oriented fireplace faces a similarly ordered set of glass doors out on to the terrace, balanced by the horizontal composition of matching built-in cabinets under three square windows at the sides of the room. The only articulations of the ceiling in the living room are two beams running across the axis of the fireplace, which mark the location in the ceiling above of steel beams necessitated by the width of the room; as is typical of his designs, Wright creates composite systems of construction and structure, and then carefully articulates these in a way that enhances the spatial experience. The dining room could hardly be more different, and is at once more open and more complex in its form, appearing to have no walls in plan, only small posts separated by glass. As it was built originally, with its columned cabinets on the side opposite the bank of doors along which we enter, its skylit beamed ceiling, and its vertical, wood slat, high-backed chairs, the dining room appears almost woven from lines in space, with what little surface is left broken into small pieces by the enveloping wood trim.

Interlocked House and Landscape

In the William Fricke House of 1901 and the W E Martin House of 1902, both built in Oak Park, Wright attempts to

Above: Ward Willits House, Highland Park, Illinois, 1901, view from the street.

combine the aspects of both the pinwheel and tripartite plans, while continuing to develop the ability of plaster and wood trim to frame more and more complicated and interlocked spaces – in both houses, the free-spanning beams of the dining room and the folded surfaces of the stair are particularly powerful examples. In positioning symmetrical volumes or elements within an asymmetrical matrix, both plans are quite dynamic in their disposition of volumes and in the resulting internal movement patterns; in the Fricke House the fireplace again stands free at the end of the living room, with passages open to either side – by now evidently a typical solution during Wright's early Prairie Period.

In both the Fricke House and the W E Martin House, we enter along a narrow hall that splits the living and dining rooms, and which is anchored at one end by the stair while the other end reaches out to the garden to end in a pavilion or terrace. Entering the W E Martin House down this hall with its stained-glass toplight, we first encounter the end of the foyer, which moves off to the right, then we see through a wall opening into the living room beyond, which moves off to the left; here we experience how the act of entry ties together the spaces of these houses. Both the Fricke and W E Martin Houses are pushed up against one edge of their lots, allowing their gardens to occupy the centre of the sites; the rooms of both houses are interlocked and meshed with the spaces of their gardens, creating a remarkable interdependence between house and landscape, neither appearing complete without the other.

Wright's intention to overlap house and landscape is even more explicit in the unbuilt project for the Edward Schroeder House of 1911, where the L-shaped plan of the house is turned and pivoted to interlock with the garden in a most extraordinary manner. The site is divided into two distinct zones, a formal axial garden and entrance court running east–west across the north end of the large lot and an open grass field to the south, both ending at the lakeshore to the east. In the Schroeder House project, Wright designed two bar-like building masses, a one-storey garage set in the centre of the symmetrical entrance garden and the three-storey house projected into the grass field, the two bars set at ninety degrees to one another. The first floor of the house bridges the driveway reaching from the field to rest on the corner of the garage, creating the L-shaped plan of the whole. The fact that the formal rooms of the house are placed in the open field and the service elements of the house are placed on the axis of the entrance garden creates an unmatched interaction with nature in the suburban setting; here Wright pivoted and projected the house out of the 'urban' entrance court and into the 'rural' field. This focus on the garden, and the removal of the compositional centre of the design from house to garden, would characterize Wright's Usonian Houses of 1937–59.

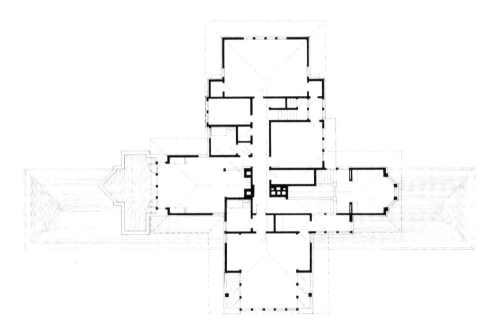

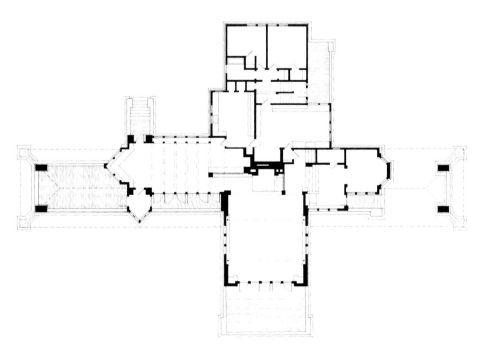

A complementary direction, where the house focuses in on itself and is set very much as an object in the landscape, can be seen in the Arthur Heurtley House of 1902. Wright holds the house within a compact rectangular volume, lifting the main rooms to the first floor and allowing them to rotate and interlock within the strict confines of the heavy brick walls; the living and dining rooms, oriented at ninety degrees to one another, have hipped, wood-trimmed plaster ceilings hung like tents under the single enveloping roof. While Wright was to occasionally experiment with this containment of dynamic interior spaces within a tightly defined exterior volume – the character of his own seminal house in Oak Park – he was to move more and more towards the extension of the 'arms' or wings of cruciform plans out into the site, letting the geometry of the houses redefine their suburban landscapes.

The Francis Little House, built in Peoria, Illinois, in 1902, is related to the Fricke House in plan, particularly in the way the entrance, living room and dining room are composed, but its massing is much more compact; a two-storey rectangular block interpenetrated by a one-storey block, which is extended to produce the entrance porch. The larger mass is oriented perpendicular to the road along one side of the site, and to enter we move around the main block to the middle of the lot; again the garden and covered terrace are given the centre of the site. The manner in which the stair and entrance hall separate yet join the living room and dining room in the Little House, along with its massing, are clarified and strengthened by Wright in his designs for the J J Walser House, built of wood frame and plaster, and the George Barton House, built of brick, both of 1903; it is with these houses that Wright achieves the perfection of his small tripartite plan type.

The George Barton House, Buffalo, New York, 1903

The Barton House, later built into the complex of domestic structures designed for Wright's brother-in-law Darwin Martin, is on the exterior a simple cruciform intersection of two rectangular volumes of one and two storeys, with brick walls and overhanging hipped roofs. In plan, the taller volume contains the living and dining rooms at either end on the ground floor, with the bedrooms above, while the lower volume holds the entrance porch and kitchen at either end; the stair hall is defined by the intersection of the two volumes. We enter by moving first towards the porch, meeting a wall we turn right up a half-flight of stairs under the roof overhang, turning left we open the door and move into the entrance hall, turning right again we move into the space between the living and dining rooms, the stairs straight ahead. The space we are in is framed by four freestanding piers, set four feet in towards the centre of the square formed by the intersecting rectangles of the plan; these piers do not reach the ceiling but support free-spanning beams at door-top height that run parallel to our direction of entry.

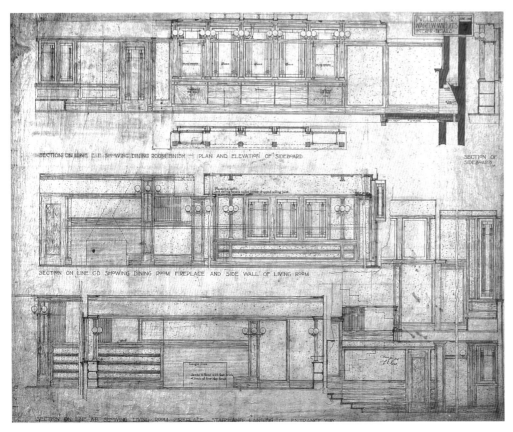

Section on line e.e. showing dining room finish.   plan and elevation of sideboard.   Section of sideboard.

Section on line CD showing dining room fireplace and side wall of living room.

Section on line AB showing living room fireplace stair hall and landing of entrance way.

*Above: Willits House, construction
drawings, interior elevations of
dining room and living room.
Below: Willits House, view
from entrance and stair hall
to living room.
Far right: Willits House,
dining room.*

Counteracting this direction of space towards the stair are the piers themselves, which are not square but rectangles oriented laterally, and the fact that the living room and dining room, and the stair hall between them, are all covered and drawn together by the same ceiling, which runs unobstructed right across the top of the free-spanning beams and piers. Not only did Wright eliminate the walls between these spaces, but he fused them together by having the ceiling and floor running continuously through all three, without frames, thresholds or other divisions. Upon closer study, we realize that, by moving in towards the centre of the plan, the four piers have effectively relocated the inner edges of the dining room and living room inside the lower intersecting volume, achieving in both directions the 'tartan' grid – a larger central space flanked on each side by smaller spaces (often called an *a–b–a* rhythm) – that was to be essential to Wright's plans and elevations. The overall effect is that the built-in furniture, stair, fireplace and plastered wall panels are all freestanding within the matrix implied by the piers, beams and wrapping wood trim.

On the exterior, the two-storey volume is clad solidly in brick up to the stone sill on the underside of the second-storey windows, and the lower floor has closed corners and windows carved out of the centre of the elevations. The windows on the first floor run as a continuous series around the corners, between the protective brick parapet and the roof, which is cantilevered all around, casting these windows into deep shadow. Thus, contrary to what we might expect, the 'public' rooms of the house – the living and dining rooms – have closed corners and small windows in the centre of the elevations, while the 'private' rooms of the house – the bedrooms – have open corners and continuous windows giving broad views all around. This is a result of their position in section relative to the street and the possibility of being seen from the outside; in the lower rooms we need protection from views almost at the same level, and thus have only small windows set deep into the masonry, while in the upper rooms, we are protected from being seen by the high parapets and overhanging roof, and are free to overlook the site at the height of the treetops through the continuous row of windows.

The Darwin Martin House, Buffalo, New York, 1904
The Darwin Martin House, built when Wright was only thirty-seven years old, is without doubt one of his greatest achievements, a solution to his efforts to define appropriately open yet monumental forms for American architecture, rooted in the suburban landscape. Starting with the exquisitely crafted site plan, Wright organized the enormous house – conservatory, Barton House, garage, greenhouses and pergola – as a series of cruciform pavilions of varying scales, their axes skilfully crossed and recrossed to produce a pattern of centres woven into the landscape. Elements properly considered part of the landscape here

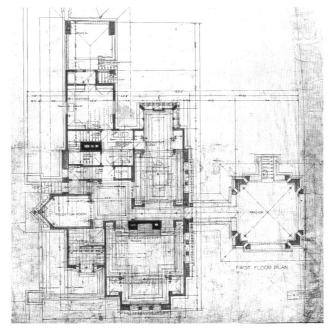

Above: George Barton House, Buffalo, New York, 1903, view from the street. The house is a simple cruciform intersection of two rectangular volumes of one and two storeys, with brick walls and an overhanging roof.
Above right: William Fricke House, Oak Park, Illinois, 1901, dining room.
Right: Fricke House, ground-floor plan.

have a presence in the plan almost equal to the spaces of the house. These include: the existing trees; a carefully organized 'floricyle' (a large semicircle of blooming plants, which Wright carefully specified as to height, colour and season) centred on the living room terrace; plantings held in rectangular areas defined by low walls extending from the house into the site; and the formally organized flower gardens to either side of the pergola.[8]

The degree to which the house is open to the landscape on all sides, through terraces, pergolas, walkways, balconies and the windows, which make the plan seem more open than closed, leads us to conclude that, for Wright, the space of the house by definition included its site. The landscape was framed and formed by the same low, outriding brick walls that defined the interiors of the house; like roots of the house, these simultaneously gave order to the landform and anchored the house to the site. Very few American suburban houses from any period can compare to the Darwin Martin House in its weaving together of house and landscape, both as plastic form and as inhabited space.

The exterior of the Martin House is a series of compositional variations on the theme of a taller vertical volume interpenetrated by a lower horizontal volume, all covered with overlapping low hip roofs. The box-like lower floor of the Barton House has here been sliced open, the surfaces separated into their constituent parts – piers, low earthbound walls, spanning beams and windows, now simply filling the spaces between masonry masses – and reorganized into a tightly ordered and powerful composition of horizontals and verticals. While, like all of Wright's houses, the Martin House is dominated by the horizontal of the roof, paralleling the horizon line of the earth, the more subtle vertical patterning of the leaded glass, the posts and proportions of the casement windows,

Above: Edward Schroeder House project, Milwaukee, Wisconsin, 1911, perspective.

Right: Site plan of Francis Little House, Peoria, Illinois, 1902, site plan. The garden and covered terrace are given the centre of the site.

Below: Edward Schroeder House, site plan. The L-shaped plan is turned and pivoted to interlock with the garden.

Far right: George Barton House, perspective and plans.

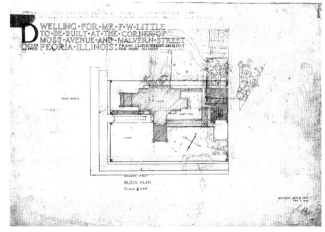

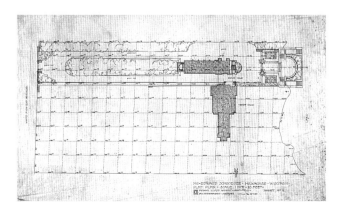

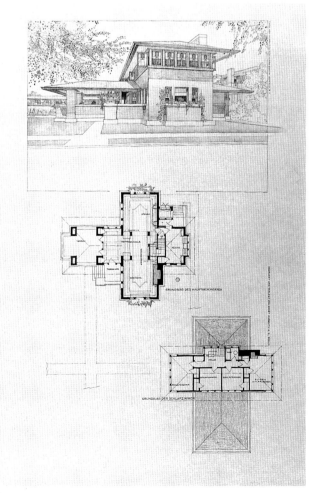

and the paired piers allude to the presence and scale of the standing human figure.

The plan of the Darwin Martin House is a development, to an astonishing degree of resolution, of the 'A Home in a Prairie Town' prototype for the tripartite plan, first presented only three years before. The main rooms form a cruciform, with the primary symmetrical tripartite grouping of the living room flanked on either side by the dining room and library interpenetrated by a secondary volume that runs from the entrance-stair hall, around the fireplace, through the living room, and out on to the main covered terrace. As a whole, the plan is a beautiful composition of piers of various sizes and orientations, hierarchically proportioned to their height in elevation; the larger piers in plan are taller, the smaller piers in plan are shorter. The fireplace, the largest and highest of these pier groupings, generates an axis which was crossed by that formed by the next largest piers, those at the extreme ends of the three rooms; this axis is in turn recrossed again, by an axis parallel to that of the fireplace generated by the piers at the end of the terrace, and so on.

A second, related rhythm is set up by the eight square clusters (each composed of four small, square piers) which frame the living room at the intersection of the cruciform, the entrance hall and the kitchen-reception room block; each pier cluster housing the service elements of the plan. Amazing designs in and of themselves, the pier clusters support the major steel beams framing the second floor as well as the free-spanning beams at door-top level. They house the radiators in their central space; they are fitted with bookshelves of about five feet in height between each pair of piers (four total to each cluster); they are pierced with casement windows in the open spaces between the piers above the bookcases to let the heat out into the rooms and to allow views through the house; and they have the lighting fixtures attached to their tops.

As a whole, the plan presents a highly complex, rich and powerfully articulated series of interlocked symmetrical spaces, and the individual sets of elements in the plan have a purity, precision and balance rarely achieved in architecture. It is no wonder that for the next fifty years, Wright would have the plan of the Darwin Martin House prominently positioned on the wall of his office draughting rooms; we may safely assume that this plan represented for Wright a kind of perfection to be sought in all his designs.

From the street we enter the house by first walking towards the porte-cochere at the far left end, then turning right and walking along the edge of the house and up a half-flight of stairs, then turning to the left under the roof overhang we find the front door, standing between two of the pier clusters. In the entrance hall, we are in a space which would seem to be at the centre of the house – due to the presence of the fireplace – and which is open in all directions: to the left the reception room and stair, to the right the living room and terrace, straight ahead to the

Below left: Darwin Martin
House, Buffalo, New York, 1904,
view from the street. A solution to
Wright's efforts to define
appropriately open yet monumental
forms for American architecture,
rooted in the suburban landscape.
Below: Darwin Martin House,
site plan. The house is organized
as a series of cruciform pavilions
of varying scales, their axes
crossed and recrossed to produce a
pattern of centres woven into the
landscape.

astonishing perspective made by the pergola structure, which leads to the conservatory, and up through the double-height space to the second floor.

Moving past the fireplace into the living room we enter a space not so much contained as woven: the library and dining room, each a small cruciform with corner piers, interlock and overlap with the living room through their shared ceiling, which appears to float over the enormous length of the three rooms. The thresholds between these rooms are suggested by the pairs of free-spanning beams seven feet off the floor that leap from each pier cluster to the next in all four directions, paralleled originally by curtains running on poles under the beams. The floor and the ceiling, the only continuous planes, define the space in its ultimate vertical dimension, but the horizontal definition is much more complex, requiring the experience of inhabitation and movement to be fully understood. We seem to be in a forest of pier-trunks and beam-limbs, the light flickering through numerous apertures in the distance. The fireplace, which is itself opened at the hearth to let space pass through, and the opening above the terrace doors, which allows us to see the terrace roof continuing right into the living room from outside to inside, reinforce the perception that space is here being defined by multiple rather than singular layers, making possible several interpretations of the same space. Closure and thresholds are here only implied, and cannot be drawn or photographed; our perception of these spatial definitions and edges is determined by our position in the space itself.

Unlike the Barton House of just the year before, in the Darwin Martin House Wright abandons the traditional floor-to-ceiling wall altogether, composing in plan and elevation with freestanding independent elements, so that the feeling of moving within a matrix implied by piers, beams, low walls, screens, built-in furniture and wrapping wood trim, which Wright had achieved in certain of his interior spaces, is here experienced throughout. Plans drawn of the floor, the soffit plane and the ceiling give three completely different definitions of the volumes; due to this canopy of layers, the resulting rooms are much more complex and rich than their relatively low height would lead one to expect. The plan published by Wright in the Wasmuth portfolio is cut at eyelevel, around five feet off the floor, and shows an extraordinary open quality – there appear to be only piers, with no walls at all. Yet by simply sitting down we find ourselves within a protective enclosure of low masonry walls and heavy built-in cabinets, with views suddenly limited to the interior realm. The difference between sitting and standing in the Martin House is astonishing; for Wright the drawn plan was only one of many horizontal layers of space carefully modulated to the occupant's activity and the resulting position of the eye.

The piers that articulate the exterior and interior are ambiguous elements, both structurally and spatially. As something between a wall and a column, the pier not only stands as an isolated element but also gives direction to

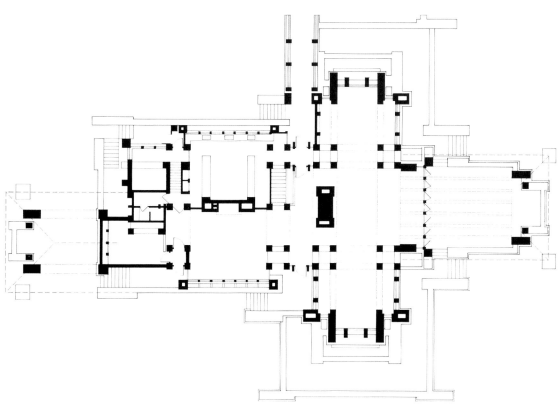

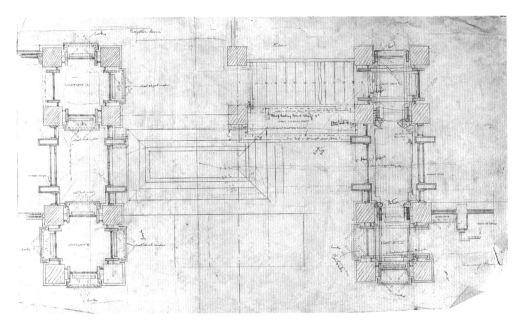

Above: Darwin Martin House, construction drawings illustrating plan of heating and light brick pier-cluster 'units' at the entrance. Right: Period photograph showing view from the entrance to the loggia and conservatory, with living room and open fireplace to the right, and the stair to the left. Below: Period photograph of a brick pier-cluster heating, lighting and book storage 'unit'.

space. When constructed of brick, as they are here, the vertical piers rise straight to the roof and simultaneously fuse with the neighbouring horizontal walls. Wright wrote:

> Brick lends itself to articulation in plan and is an easy material to use architecturally. Bricks naturally make corners and the corners are easily used in the play of light and shade. The Martin House is an organized brick-pier building. It is when assembling groups of piers in rhythmical relation to the whole that brick comes out best according to its nature.[9]

In the library elevation, which dominates the entrance side of the house, the intermediate pair of piers goes all the way up to support the roof, while the outermost pair of piers, turned ninety degrees from the first, reach only to the parapet under the second-storey windows, and the smallest innermost pair of piers reach only to support the first floor; three pairs of piers and lintels are 'nested' one inside the other, giving an indication of the layering of space within. The piers are carefully spaced away from each other by small slots of stained glass, so that when inside the house it is a slice of light that separates and articulates the piers. In looking at the exterior of this house, we are at first aware only of the massive masonry piers and low walls; the glass stands back, almost unseen in the protective shadows of the piers and overhanging roof.

In the Martin House, Wright attempted to develop a universal building system, applicable to both large-scale public projects and small-scale residential projects, continuing aspects of the Larkin Building of the previous year, which had been commissioned from Wright by Martin, the chief operating officer of the company.[10] The vertical structure, as indicated above, is a series of brick piers hierarchically scaled relative to their height and structural loads, which stand on the concrete foundations and ground-floor slab. These piers in turn support primary steel beams, running under the concrete slab first floor, and concrete lintels, running under the double layer (inside and out) brick spandrel 'beam' walls, which go from the top of the ground-floor window to the sill of the first-floor windows. The roof is framed in wood, with wood posts between the continuous window band carrying the load down to the concrete lintels below.

The wood trim strips applied to the respective ceilings clearly articulate the difference in the structures between the floors; in the living-room ceiling the steel and flat concrete slab structure of the first floor above is indicated by the smooth centre of the ceiling, with the trim running parallel to the steel beams at the edges of the volume; in the bedroom ceilings the regular rhythm of the sloped wood frame structure of the roof above is indicated by evenly spaced trim strips applied to the sloped plaster ceilings. The application of interior plaster also serves to articulate and clarify the structural hierarchy; the brick of the supporting piers is exposed inside and out, while the brick interior faces of the non-supporting low walls at the ground

Right: Period photograph looking from the living room to the terrace; the furniture was custom-designed for the Darwin Martin House by Wright himself.
Below: Period photograph of the dining room.

floor and the supported spandrel 'beam' walls at the first floor are plastered. The result is that the interior of the Martin House, while spatially highly complex, is clearly legible as to the hierarchy of its structural elements: primary (brick piers), secondary (steel beams) and tertiary (concrete floor slabs and lintels).

What I have been describing at the Darwin Martin House, built in 1904 – where Wright achieved perhaps his most complete synthesis through the integration of structure, construction, utilities, built-in furnishings, glasswork, landscape and the extraordinary interpenetration and layering of spaces, all tied together through our movements in occupying the house – no longer exists, except in black-and-white period photographs. Today the Martin House stands stripped of its built-in cabinets, most of its stained glass and light fixtures, and all its carpets and furniture; on the exterior, the pergola, conservatory, plantings and garage are gone, replaced by new apartment buildings. The incomprehensible gutting of this house and its site, destroying forever both the definition of the interior spaces and the relationship of the house to the landscape, is surely one of the saddest mistakes of our often short-sighted generation. This is an irreparable loss, denying for all present and future generations the experience of one of the greatest spaces ever built, calling into question our ability to control our speculative attitude towards what we choose to call 'real estate', and casting doubt

on our commitment to understanding and preserving our common place-making heritage.

WRIGHT'S PRAIRIE Houses exemplify his intention to create intimate interior spaces for family life situated in the prairie suburb, in a landscape given order through the positioning and anchorage of the house to its site. The 'breaking of the box', Wright's description of his opening of corners to join previously discrete rooms within the house, resulted in a new reinterpretation of family life taking place in the single 'great room', an important idea of this period. Yet in Wright's Prairie Houses there remain layers of definition given by low walls, screens, varying ceiling heights and built-in furniture, producing spaces that are both great and intimate in scale, open and obscured to view, buried deep within the masonry cave of the house and projected out into the landscape with only the tent-like roof for cover. In Wright's Prairie Houses, compartmentalized, sequestered volumes fed by corridors were replaced by a more open plan of interlocking rooms, allowing a variety of possible paths and interpretations of spatial boundaries. In this way individuals were not required to give up their privacy to gain the sense of belonging to the larger family. With this new type of house, intimate and protected within yet opening to survey the landscape without, Wright in 1900 created a place that would prove most appropriate to the American family life of the new century.

THE INTROVERTED PUBLIC SPACE

Radical though it be, the work here illustrated is dedicated to a cause conservative in the best sense of the word. At no point does it involve denial of the elemental law and order inherent in all great architecture; rather, it is a declaration of love for the spirit of that law and order, and a reverential recognition of the elements that made its ancient letter in its time vital and beautiful.

Frank Lloyd Wright[1]

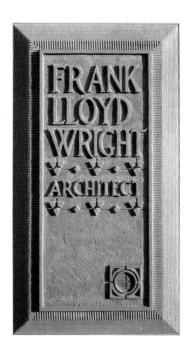

Left: Frank Lloyd Wright Studio, Oak Park, Illinois, 1895, entrance loggia. The studio was built as an addition to Wright's house of 1889.
Above: Wright's plaque at the entrance doors of his studio.

Frank Lloyd Wright's first nationally publicized series of essays, written in 1908 at the age of forty-one and entitled *In the Cause of Architecture*, opens with the statement which heads this chapter: a direct challenge to the exclusive control over the interpretation of architectural history claimed by the followers of the Beaux-Arts school. This rather amazing and somewhat startling statement would appear to contradict many long-held presumptions about Wright's process of design and its relation to history. Wright has been consistently interpreted through his own rhetoric of the 1950s, late in his life, when he maintained that architectural history and the earlier buildings of other architects were irrelevant to his work. Yet in 1908, at the peak of the Prairie Period, when he had already completed many of the buildings for which he is today most famous, we hear him saying something altogether different about his relation to history.[2]

Wright was later to state the same intention towards history by saying that in order to remain true to what he termed 'Tradition' (the great monuments of man's past) he had to deny the 'traditions' that dominated his own day (the formally derivative designs of the Beaux-Arts-trained academic classicists).[3] John Dewey, the American philosopher who was Wright's contemporary, also defined this difference in approaches to tradition:

The trouble with the academic imitator is not that he depends upon traditions, but that the latter have not entered into his mind; into the structure of his own ways of seeing and making. They remain upon the surface as tricks of technique or as extraneous suggestions and conventions as to the proper thing to do.[4]

With his statements, and more importantly with his own design works of this period, Wright sought to reclaim ancient architecture for those who would examine it analytically, searching for the underlying principles that shaped it; to accomplish this he could not allow ancient architecture to be claimed and defined by those merely seeking models for copying.

The Frank Lloyd Wright Studio, Oak Park, Illinois, 1895

One of the clearest indications of this occurs in the entrance of Wright's own architectural office and studio, built as an addition to his Oak Park House of 1889. On the four piers that define the entrance loggia, Wright placed bas-reliefs that depict most prominently a floor plan which is apparently that of a portion of the Baths of Caracalla, built in AD 217 in ancient Rome.[5] We find this even more interesting when we realize that Wright's own plan for his studio complex is quite close to what has been depicted on the piers. While this is perhaps the only time that Wright so overtly suggested that his architecture had a specific historical source, it could not have been a more 'public' declaration, there for every client to see as they entered his office. It was as if Wright was establishing at the outset his knowledge and command of the great architecture of the past; despite the 'radical' appearance of his forms, the client should be assured that they sprang from the most ancient and fundamental sources. It is not incidental that Wright displays a plan, not an elevation or formal element such as a column, in this emblematic entry reference; Wright developed his residential plans from the plan of his own house, and as Jonathan Lipman has shown, Wright was to base the plans for his public buildings on the plan of this studio.[6]

On the exterior of the studio complex, we are faced with a series of pure volumes packed along one side of the small corner site; the square studio and the smaller octagon of the library stand on either side of the entrance and office block. At first glance, these three seem to have been rendered as independent elements, their frontal surfaces not aligned and their heights varying. Yet Wright has fabricated these out of a common set of materials, and the brick and dark wood shingles and trim wrapping across their surfaces tie them together. We should take note of the way in which Wright was able to achieve a sense of depth in this shallow site by pulling the entrance loggia forward, interlocking it with the continuous brick wall that runs the length of the site, and pushing the studio and library back behind the wall, so that they seem to rise up out of the garden.

Wright also emphasizes the verticality of the studio and library by transforming their geometric definitions from bottom to top. The lower portion of the studio is square in plan, with a brick base and shingle top interlocked around a long horizontal window, above which emerges an octagonal top with windows all around. The library begins at the ground as an octagon of brick which transforms to a series of eight corner piers with shingles and high windows between, topped by a square cornice projection, aligned with the street and studio, with a shingle-clad octagon emerging at the roof. The result of the whole, including the pyramidal mass of the original house, is the impression of powerful independent spaces bound together by some mutual purpose, an introverted labyrinthine compound of the type Wright was to propose again and again for complex programmes in urban settings.

Entering through the loggia, we find that there are two equal doors at either end of the narrow space; we must choose to go right or left, as the centre is closed. Pushing open the small door at the end of the loggia we must immediately turn to enter along the edge of the reception hall, under a low plaster ceiling. The centre of the room is dominated by the three parallel leaded-glass skylights running across our direction of entry, with chairs facing a long worktable for drawings that is integrated with windows set between the piers and bas-reliefs of the loggia. A large door opens to the studio, a smaller door to the corridor leading to the library, and two secondary doors across from

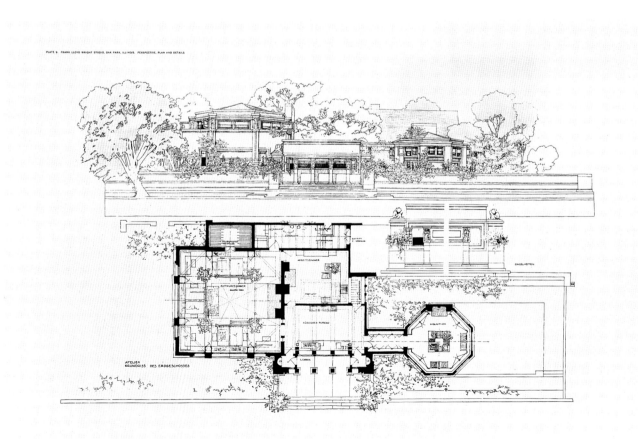

PLATE 9. FRANK LLOYD WRIGHT STUDIO, OAK PARK, ILLINOIS. PERSPECTIVE, PLAN AND DETAILS

the entrance doors lead to Wright's private office and a stair, respectively.

If we use the light and size of doorway as cues, we first turn left into the studio itself, the largest and most well-lit space in the building. The studio is a wonderfully complex space, layered in both plan and section; a square plan subdivided into a nine-square by the wooden pier-cabinets with their interlocked set of free-spanning beams that crisscross the room just above door height. A square opening in the centre lets us see to the octagonal mezzanine, which is supported by a series of chains hung from the radial beamed ceiling above. The furniture Wright designed for the studio carefully articulates the space; under the corners of the mezzanine opening and the intersections of the free-spanning beams four square cabinets stand on the floor, dividing the space into the nine smaller volumes – seven draughting spaces and the fireplace arranged around the central two-storey volume. Natural light is introduced high up, between the beams, on the lower floor, and through a series of continuous clerestory lights on the octagonal upper floor; the result is that while there is ample light for working, there are no direct eyelevel views out to the street and surrounding neighbourhood – the views are directed up, into the tree tops.

When the studio complex was in use, we would have first been led by Wright not into the studio but into the library,

through the tunnel-like hallway. As we have noted, this is the route we are least likely to take upon entering, if left to our own devices, for its seems remote and private. Even though it is the most exposed volume in the studio complex, standing free as an object in the garden, once inside it we feel completely enclosed, introverted, unable to see out of the small high clerestory windows, folded into this small world entirely of Wright's making. Wright created this library not so much for books as for his own collection of beautiful objects – such as Japanese wood-block prints, medieval decorative art, fabrics, dried flowers and ceramics – and drawings, models and stained-glass windows from his own work. As a result there are few bookshelves and numerous cabinets and pivoted display panels taking full advantage of the eight faces of the octagonal plan.

Taking note of the single table in the centre of the room, with the four low chairs set around it, the whole illuminated by the high clerestory windows and the skylight at the centre of the ceiling, it becomes clear that this was a room for presentation and edification. Wright used this room to educate and indoctrinate his clients in his comprehensive spatial and formal system of design, so that the library – with its fireplace – may be understood as an exemplar of the dynamic, integrated and yet protective and secluded spaces typical of his houses. David van Zanten has indicated that Wright also used the library as 'a museum-

laboratory', where he could educate his draughtsmen in the appreciation and manipulation of abstract form.[7]

Wright himself practised and experimented with whatever material lay closest at hand. He would stop work each day in the studio, sending his draughtsmen out into the nearby fields to collect wild flowers, which he would then arrange according to his studies of the ancient Japanese art of *Ikebana*, the result displayed in the corner of the studio and criticized by the collected office staff. He would bring home gas-filled balloons, spending hours in the vaulted playroom helping his children arrange the brightly coloured spheres in different patterns by tying them to furniture and playing out their strings to varying lengths. He insisted on arranging ever-new and ever-more dynamic compositions using the dining table, chairs, tablecloth, napkins, glasses and silver – all of which he had designed, as a result delaying many a meal in the Wright household. Many of Wright's clients relate the story of his unexpected visits to their completed houses while they were gone; upon their return they would find their furniture completely rearranged in a new dynamic order, a gift from their architect.

Wright would regularly rearrange the furniture in his own living room, photographing the result to document it, and then rearrange it again. These furniture arrangements tended to take the form of dynamic compositions playing off against the regular geometries of the rooms themselves. It is interesting to note that, despite the stable, symmetrical forms of his studio and library, Wright's own private office – almost never photographed – displays a strong rotational imperative, reflected in the asymmetrical arrangement of the skylight, desk and window, which are pushed to the edges and corner of the space. This process of experimentation extended to the physical fabric of Wright's home and studio; during the time he lived in Oak Park, from 1889 to 1909, Wright made numerous renovations, additions, extensions and alterations to his house and studio, always attempting to achieve a more dynamic interaction of space and occupation. So extensive and continuous was this work that it seemed as soon as one construction project was completed Wright would start another; neither the house nor the studio were off limits in this constant experimentation. Because of this continuous renovation of his own inhabitation, recent efforts to restore the house and studio have had to confront the fact that there was no 'typical' condition during the twenty years of use by Wright – what we see today is a necessary arbitrary 'freezing' of what in reality was a highly dynamic, constantly changing set of spaces and forms.

An American Monumentality

A substantial contract from the Luxfer Prism Company, for whom Wright was to produce high-rise designs utilizing their patented window glass, allowed Wright to undertake the extensive and expensive additions of the studio and library to his small Oak Park house in 1895. While Wright's conception of the high-rise was to differ dramatically from that of Sullivan and the other early Chicago architects (as we shall see later in Chapter 9), we should note here the fact that the primary legacy Wright received from the Chicago School – the Chicago frame or steel-framed office tower – was incapable of dealing with the need for the monumental in forming the public realm. As a manifestation of the economic determination of scale, the universal planning grid, and the production of uniform interiors to be styled later by what Wright called the 'inferior desecrators' (interior decorators), the Chicago frame skyscraper was a projection of private commercial interests at a scale previously given only to public buildings, yet totally lacking any sense of the monumental.

That Wright was aware of this is reflected in his work as early as 1894, in his project for the Monolithic Concrete Bank, an all-concrete structure published, oddly enough, in *Brickbuilder Magazine*. The plan is a simple rectangle, the space divided into five bays by engaged piers carrying ceiling beams. The elevation of this building is severe, yet with a highly articulated ground plane projected for the front of the building; the walls are bevelled or sloped slightly outwards as they go from top to bottom, and as a result the piers emerge from the walls 'in eminently plastic fashion', as Wright put

it.[8] The whole, though small, could not be more monumental, and is in fact directly related to Egyptian temple fronts. The singularity of the space, and the manner in which it is born from a fusion of its form, structure and material, is exactly the opposite of the Chicago frame building.

Wright clearly understood that the systematic production of universal space could not give form to monumental public buildings, and in his Waller Amusement Park project of 1895 he developed his own alternative: the systematic composition of unique places. In what may also be seen as Wright's answer to the 'White City' of the 1893 Chicago Exposition, this project for Wolf Lake proposed a series of pavilions arranged around a semicircular canal and on the circular island at the centre. Close examination of these pavilions, as Wright designed them in plan and perspective, reveals plan fragments matching Unity Temple, the Martin House, the Ullman House and even a small Imperial Hotel. Here in 1895, almost the entire set of plan types that Wright would utilize in the Prairie Period were projected in the pavilions of this unbuilt design, as numerous geometrically rigorous and systematically developed variations on the theme of the cruciform interlocking of spaces and the rhythmic disposition of pier groups. This astonishing project may be considered as Wright's equivalent of Piranesi's 'Campo Marzio' etching; the repository and record for all manner of speculative forms to be utilized and realized in later designs.

Right: Frank Lloyd Wright Studio, library. Wright created this room not so much for books as for his own collection of objects. Overleaf: Frank Lloyd Wright Studio, entrance foyer; the entrance loggia is to the left, the draughting room lies ahead, and Wright's private office is to the right.

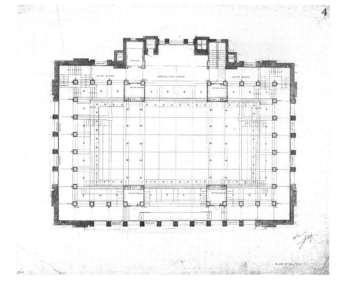

Above: Monolithic Concrete Bank project, 1894, perspective.
Right: Wright's final project for the Abraham Lincoln Center, Chicago, Illinois, 1900, plan of balcony level.
Below: Amusement Park project for Edward Waller, Wolf Lake, Illinois, 1895, site plan.

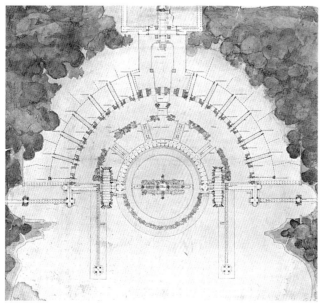

Wright's further development of the search for public monumental form can be seen in his project for the All Souls' Building begun in 1897, later called the Abraham Lincoln Center, and finally built in 1901 – in a considerably different form – by Wright's associate Dwight Perkins, after Wright felt he could no longer carry on without straining his relationship with the client, his uncle, Jenkin Lloyd Jones. The Abraham Lincoln Center project of 1900 accomplishes a breakthrough in public design similar to that which Wright achieved the same year in house design with the *Ladies Home Journal* houses. Many of the elements that would not be built until the Larkin Building of 1903 and the Unity Temple of 1906 are here already fully developed. The plan of the main sanctuary floor has four freestanding piers carrying the structural and mechanical loads, stairs in the building's corners, seating on the floor and in balconies, light introduced from clerestories set high on the back walls, and an entrance along the edge to either side of the pulpit – all as it would be in Unity Temple. The elevation and section have a brick pier-and-lintel window-wall with solid corners and a skylit open volume running the full height of the office floors, respectively – all as it would be in the Larkin Building.

In the elevation, Wright's subtlety in distinguishing between the entrance foyer, sanctuary volume and the office floors, while still maintaining the unity of the building, is masterful. The stepping in of the masonry piers in elevation – at the base the corner is composed of three sections of brick while at the top the corner is composed of only one – allows the reading of a building (entrance foyer at ground floor) within a building (sanctuary on second and third floors) within a building (three office floors above), each with its own corner pier that reaches the ground. This design clearly establishes that Wright possessed a rich and comprehensive design vision for urban public spaces, and was actively engaged in attempting to adapt certain aspects of Sullivan's achievements in high-rise design in the making of an urban monument.

Wright turned to the problem of the public institution sited in the open landscape with the design of the Hillside Home School, built for his aunts Ellen and Jane in 1902, in Spring Green, and which he incorporated as part of his own draughting-room complex for Taliesin in 1933. This building is related to the Martin House of two years later, being composed of primary cruciform assembly volumes linked by long linear rows of classroom spaces and loggias. The stone piers and walls rise directly from the ground, looking as if they could have grown there; the smallest pair of piers is set forward to support a terrace, the next larger pair frame the projected glass walls of the cruciform volume, and the corners – the largest pier set – reach up to support the roof. The pyramidal roof meets the vertical wood posts between the windows at its edge, so that the lighter wooden volume defined by roof and window posts

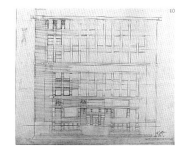

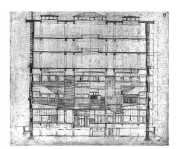

interlocks in section and plan with the heavier stone volume defined by the piers and walls; few buildings have ever achieved a stronger anchorage to both the earth and the sky.

The assembly room has four stone piers set into the room, an enormous fireplace in one arm of the cruciform, and a square opening set on the diagonal connecting the upper and lower floors. One corner of this unexpected diagonal opening is carried by the giant lintel over the fireplace, and the various parallel and diagonal beams focus the space of this room in towards this central space. This is one of the only ostensively public spaces by Wright with extensive glazing at eyelevel; as a private school, this building was at best only semi-public in nature, and Wright presents this through a synthesis of private and public attributes drawn from his other works.

The Yahara Boathouse project of 1905 is breathtaking in the degree of its abstraction and precision of form. Intended for use by the University of Wisconsin rowing crew, the building is a simple bar stretched out along the edge of the lake, the wider lower floor fitted with racks for the long thin boats, with entry at the narrow ends, and the thinner upper floor holding lockers and showers, with a terrace above the ground-floor volume on either side. The exterior presents two sets of four piers; the taller two-storey piers, which rise up to carry the long flat roof (cantilevered well beyond each end), bisect the space defined by the lower one-storey piers.

The stairs are set between the taller piers at either end, and at the ground the doors open between the tall and shorter piers. The front of the building, facing the water, is solid, presenting no openings for entry. The boat landings, each fully the length of the building itself and projected several feet out into the water, are laid out to either side along the edge of the lake, stopping after interlocking with the lower pier nearest the water.

The solid wall of the boathouse nearest the water has no foundation, spanning from landing to landing, and we can see the wood-pole columns holding the boats inside coming down to the ground behind; it would appear that the building floats above a rocky shore. Given the lack of any board or shingle indications on the elevations, the material Wright intended for this building is most likely stucco on a wood frame structure. The intriguing revelation of lightness just described would be possible to achieve using wood frame, but the severely rectangular form also suggests cast concrete, and it is not surprising that Wright himself later referred to the Yahara Boathouse project as seminal in his development of Unity Temple.

The Larkin Company Administration Building, Buffalo, New York, 1903

In 1902, at the age of thirty-five, Wright received the commission for the Larkin Building through Darwin

Martin, chief operating officer for the company, for whose brother Wright was designing a house at that time in Oak Park – the W E Martin House discussed earlier. The design was completed early in 1904 and the building constructed by 1906; it is one of the greatest works of architecture of the modern era.[9] Wright's new building for the Larkin Company served as administrative headquarters for the prosperous soap manufacturer – their factories facing the site – and housed their expanding mail-order business. Wright's apprenticeship with Adler and Sullivan had well prepared him to design the type of office building the Larkin Company had in mind, advanced in its functionalism, construction and servicing, and progressive in its moral import.

This last intention was directly reflected in the Larkin family and company officers' friendship with Elbert Hubbard, the creator of the Roycrofter movement in America, who had worked for the Larkin Company until 1893 (and whose personal wardrobe of wide-brimmed hat, cane, cape and scarf tied at the neck Wright had already taken as his own), and in their study of Emerson, whose works were read to the Larkin Company employees during work breaks. Wright's design was not only to be functionally a model place to work but, as Jack Quinan has indicated, was to direct 'the employees away from the common notion of work as mindless drudgery and toward the belief that work well done is inherently edifying. The

Larkin executives and their architect, Frank Lloyd Wright, sincerely believed in the virtue of work.'[10]

The plan of the Larkin Building was developed from the atrium or light-court building type, where the offices are wrapped around an enclosed, top-lit space that runs the height of the building. Wright's designs of early 1903 showed the symmetrical main office block, centred on the open court – the stairs defining the court's narrow ends – and the services located in a smaller annex block attached to one side of the building, with the entrance made through this annex; the same bi-nuclear planning Wright would apply to almost all public buildings, a feature which originated in his own Oak Park Studio. In this early plan, the vertical ventilation shafts are attached to the side of the building near the corners, and it was not until late 1903 that Wright moved the stairs to the corners to create freestanding independent service and stair shafts, leaving the rectangular mass of the office building free of vertical obstructions.[11]

As Wright wrote:

not until the contract had been let to Paul Mueller [Wright's contractor and structural engineer from Sullivan's office] and the plaster-model of the building stood completed on the big detail board at the centre of the Oak Park draughting room did I get the articulation I finally wanted. The solution that had hung fire came in a flash. I took the next train to Buffalo to try to get the Larkin Company to see that it was worth

Below left: Larkin Company Administration Building, Buffalo, New York, 1908, period photograph, view from the manufacturing buildings across the street.
Below right: Larkin Building, side elevation.
Bottom right: Larkin Building, plan of top floor, with dining room and kitchen.

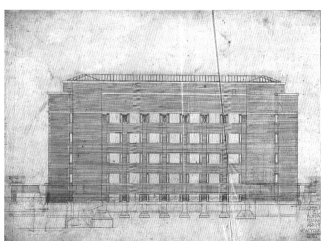

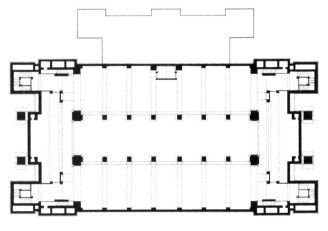

Below: Larkin Building, period photograph of entrance.
Bottom: Axonometric of typical office bay of Larkin Building.
Below right: Larkin Building, President's Office, note its location on the main floor; view to left into toplit central workroom, furniture custom-designed for Larkin Company by Wright.

thirty thousand dollars more to build the stair towers free of the central block, not only as independent stair towers for communication and escape but also as air intakes for the ventilating system. It would require this sum to individualize and properly articulate these features as I saw them … Mr. Larkin, a kind and generous man, granted the appropriation and the building as architecture, I felt, was saved.[12]

At this same time the annex stair is similarly pulled away from the main block in plan so that entry is accomplished by moving between the major and minor volumes, just as in Wright's own Oak Park Studio.

The result of this projection of the stairs away from the building's corners, perfected in early 1904 by Wright's insertion of a narrow strip of glass between the exhaust ducts, on the side of the main block and the stair and intake ducts, was a power and plasticity in the facade and massing that were to have an enormous impact on both Wright's own later work and the work of generations of European and American architects. On the exterior the stairs became one of a series of pylons or towers interlocked with the woven assemblage of vertical piers and recessed horizontal spandrels that composed the window wall, all rendered in brick with concrete-edge trim top and bottom. The stair and exhaust towers, which together formed the corners of the structure, ran unobstructed from ground to roof, with only a thin band of concrete marking the location of the toplights inside.

Wright called the building that resulted 'a simple cliff of brick'.[13] Indeed it had a severity unlike anything else of its time, seeming to relate more to the stark rectilinearity of ancient monuments: 'It wears no badge of servitude to foreign "styles" yet it avails itself gratefully of the treasures and the wisdom bequeathed to it by its ancestors.'[14] Wright labelled a sharply angled perspective of the Larkin Building with the words 'grammar of the protestant', saying that the building was a protest against the use of historical styles. 'Here, again, most of the "critic's architecture" has been left out. Therefore the work may have the same claim to consideration as a "work of art" as an ocean liner, a locomotive or a battleship', Wright said in 1910, claiming an aesthetic merit for such pure expression of space years before the more famous similar comparison by Le Corbusier.[15] However, the exterior is more than a rejection of the use of historical styles: it is the first fully developed application of Wright's abstracted formal system, locking together interior space, structure, services and material – the system that would almost immediately be applied to other programme types, as in the Darwin Martin House – and represents the emergence of Wright's mature architecture.

As is true of all Wright's buildings, though it is rarely remarked upon, the Larkin Building is carefully designed to be seen up close from the street, resulting in a rather exaggerated vertical perspective; the glass is recessed to

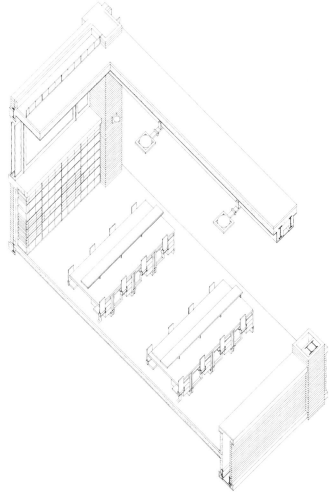

produce shadows between the brick pylons and piers, making them legible in their hierarchic order from standing eyelevel. It is interesting to note that following the Larkin Building's publication in 1908, Wright was as upset with the magazine's use of photographs taken well above eyelevel as he was with the unsympathetic criticism; he stated that it is imperative to 'know the building *on the ground*' (Wright's emphasis).[16] From that viewpoint, the monumentality of the whole is indeed extraordinary. On the side elevation the office floors are read through their windows between piers and spandrels; also indicated are the dimensions of the light court within, the blank facade at the top houses the dining room and conservatory, and the exhaust towers and stairs frame the building on either side. On the fronts (the building faces both streets), the two central piers, which carry spherical sculptures, indicate the dimension of the light court within, and the stairs bracket the mass to either side; there is no entry in the centre of this main building block.

On one side is the annex stair tower with a fountain at its base next to what must be the entrance; a sheet of horizontal water falls into a basin, seemingly sliced off by the flat slab of stone mysteriously suspended, set flush in the brick stair wall, with the words 'Honest labor needs no master; Simple justice needs no slaves' inscribed on it. Passing this fountain and climbing the stairs into the deep shadow of the brick walls, we move through two layers of all-glass doors (the first such doors in the world) and enter the reception area, relatively dark and low in height – sixteen feet, the standard height for all the office floors in the Larkin Building. On the outside edge of the entrance space are the correspondence areas for visitors, and straight ahead the semicircular reception desk projects out towards us from the other side, with the elevators behind.

To either side of the reception desk the ceiling and floor continue smoothly, without a beam drop, carrying us into the centre of the main building. We step out into the light court, having entered it at the middle across its narrower dimension; suddenly and unexpectedly the ceiling drops away and we look up seventy-five feet to the square-gridded skylight at the top of the space, the piers shooting up uninterrupted from floor to ceiling. The lower, darker, horizontal, rotating entry sequence, compressing and then releasing us into the taller, lighter, hidden, vertical central space, is typical of Wright's public and private designs, and indicates the degree of his mastery in orchestrating the perceptions of those inhabiting his buildings through movement, space and light; the human eye adjusts to the dark so that by the time we enter the central court, it appears to be brighter than out-of-doors, which we recently left behind.

The building is organized in a way that surprises most who assume that the company officers, as is typical, occupied the top floor: in the Larkin Building they occupied the entrance floor, at the bottom of the light court, where they could be seen by all the workers above; the top floor is instead occupied by the employee restaurant, with a conservatory a half-level above, and a brick-paved roof terrace for the use of the employees another half-level above. The building's functional layout directly reflects the progressive ideals of the architect and management, and Wright developed the typical working floors to focus on the central space, wherein inspirational aphorisms were inscribed in the topmost spandrels of the light court, illuminated by the skylight.

The office floors were thirty-two feet wide by sixteen feet high – a double-square in section – with the windows on the outside wall set seven feet six inches off the floor, so that the views were directed upwards to the sky; under the windows were built-in metal filing cabinets. On the inner court side of the floors, a low wall of only three feet in height (also with built-in filing cabinets) allowed the workers to easily overlook the space below, and introduced generous light from the skylight above into the work spaces. The result was that at eyelevel, even for a seated worker, the office floors are open to the inner court and closed to the exterior. This introverted, toplit building, with views only of the sky and its own central space, gave form to Wright's vision of the public realm in America.

The company's collective ideals are exhibited in the concentration of ornament in the central court so as to demarcate those spaces used by all the employees – the piers, unadorned shafts of brick running past the office floor levels, are at their tops clad with terracotta patterned blocks, square clusters of spherical lights, and panels inscribed in gold leaf with inspirational words, marking the restaurant and conservatory floor, just under the flat skylight. The sacred aspect both Wright and the company executives wished to impart to the public workplace is indicated by the organ that was later placed at the end of the light court on the restaurant level, the various religious and transcendentalist speakers invited to address the employees in the central space, and most notably by the introduction of diffused light – 'Wright's medium of transcendence' – into the very centre of the company and its building.[17]

The building housed 1,800 office workers who would daily process more than five-thousand customer letters in well-lit, fireproof surroundings that kept out the soot of the industrial neighbourhood. This latter consideration involved the filtering, cooling and heating of air, or what we today call air conditioning; the first such application to an office building, following directly upon Carrier's first such installation (in a factory) of 1902. Indeed, in the Larkin Building Wright developed numerous innovative and seminal building and service technologies. Among them were: the folded and punched sheet-metal desks with integral cantilevered chairs that could be pivoted out of the way; the first wall-hung toilets and toilet partitions;

Far left: Larkin Building, period photograph, view from the dining room at the top floor into the central space, with the skylight above and workfloors across.
Above: Period photograph showing a detail of the terracotta castings and the lamps at the top of the interior piers.
Right: Period photograph of a typical floor showing the high windows to the outside above, built-in filing cabinets to the left and lower openings to the toplit central space at right.

magnesite floors, copings and desk tops for sound-absorption; double-paned window glazing for thermal and acoustical benefit; and air conditioning, with intake at the top of the building, introduced through integral ducts built into the piers and beams with the steel structure, with the exhaust drawn out of the rooms at the ceiling in summer and at the floor in winter. All of these made for easy cleaning and an excellent working environment.

In addition, the annex contained a classroom, a branch of the Buffalo Public Library, a lounge and lockers for the employees. The top-floor restaurant, which could serve up to six hundred people at a time, had windowless outer walls, focusing in on the light court. The eight-person dining tables specially designed by Wright had raised posts at their narrow ends, so that it was not possible to sit at the 'head' of the table – a clear indication of the democratic attitude of the company officers, whom with their spouses took their lunches here with the employees. Of particular note is the quality and quantity of natural light on the office floors; Wright had promised that the building would be 'as light as all outdoors', and he had designed it to provide a far higher level of natural light than any other office building of its time.[18] Indeed, the relatively narrow office floors, lit from both sides, had more natural light than may be found in many present-day American office buildings.

After the solid 'cliff of brick' of the front elevation, we are surprised to see that the plan, cut eight feet up at window height, is not unlike that of the Darwin Martin House; a pattern of hierarchically ordered piers of various sizes, with no continuous wall surfaces. The structure of the Larkin Building is an internal steel frame clad in brick with the outer walls composed of load-bearing brickwork. The interior steel columns are cast in concrete inside the piers, the steel joist beams are doubled so as to allow the placement of the air ducts between, and the spandrels are supported by steel truss girders; in all cases the structure and the air-conditioning ducting are fully integrated and carefully revealed.

The proportioning of the plan and section are precise: the main block is a double square, as are the office floors in section, the light court is three squares in height in its narrow dimension and a golden section in the larger dimension, and the piers are set sixteen feet on centre so as to create a perfect square in section with the sixteen-foot high floors. As Otto Graf has indicated, the entire spatial and ornamental programme for the Larkin Building is 'a fugue on the theme of the cube'; Wright developed the sculpture, light fixtures, furniture, ornament, elevations, plans, sections and spaces from various ways of unfolding the square and cube.[19] The building focuses on the light court, which most clearly embodies Wright's design

intentions; as Quinan, who has done so much to help us recall this great building, put it:

> The Larkin light court thus can be seen to exemplify Emerson's belief in the unity of all things in nature and the aspiration of all matter to a spiritual ideal ... The hierarchy – from plain, solid piers to elaborate capitals to living plants (from dead to living matter), and then, with light accenting gilded inscriptions, to the realm of ideas – is wholly Emersonian.[20]

Due to the decline of the mail-order industry in America, Wright's administration building was modified in both programme and form by the owner starting in the 1920s. The most drastic of these changes came in 1939, when the administrative and mail-order functions on the lower three floors were removed and replaced by the Larkin Company department store. This direct sales effort ultimately failed, as did the Larkin Company, and in 1943 the Larkin Building was sold to a contractor who subsequently abandoned the building, forcing the City of Buffalo to purchase it in 1945. The city was unable to sell or use the building, and in 1949 sold it for demolition with the promise of a new taxable construction on the site.

It is difficult for us to understand why this great building, which has had such an enormous influence on architecture around the world, was demolished in 1950. As Quinan points out, if the building's site had been valuable for rebuilding, this would give us a reason, albeit insufficient for such a loss.[21] Today, more than forty years later, the site where the building once stood is covered in weeds, and is not even used as a parking lot.

Unity Temple, Oak Park, Illinois, 1905

In the summer of 1905, the wood-frame sanctuary of the Oak Park Universalist congregation was completely destroyed in a fire, and Dr Johonnot, the pastor, offered the commission for building a new church to Wright, a member of the congregation. Wright began designing what he would call Unity Temple that summer, and construction was finished in 1908. This was a particularly busy time for Wright, with the works in Buffalo underway and many new projects coming into his growing office. It was also the period directly following his first trip to Japan to study first hand the culture he had so long admired from a distance (he returned in May 1905).

Unity Temple is arguably Wright's greatest public work, and it is the only building where he left us an extensive and detailed description of the design process. Wright rarely wrote or spoke about his process of design, preferring to refer to the larger struggle to introduce new architectural ideas against prevailing trends. Therefore the chapter in Wright's autobiography entitled 'Designing Unity Temple' is an almost unique revelation on his part, indicating the esteem in which he himself held this work. Wright's trepidation about being misunderstood in even this one description of his design process may be heard in his conclusion, but we should also note the following aspects that I have emphasized: the visual/spatial reading to complement the verbal story, and the presence of underlying principles and analytical methods of study. As he wrote:

> Now, even though you are interested in architecture this story is more or less tedious. Without *close study of the plans and photographs as it is read* it must bore you. I have undertaken here, for once, to indicate *the process of building on principle* to insure character and achieve style, as near as I can indicate it *by taking Unity Temple to pieces*. Perhaps I am not the one to try it. It really would be a literary feat and feast were it well done. (My emphasis.)[22]

In designing Unity Temple, Wright first considered 'the philosophy of the building', which for him involved a questioning of all preconceived forms; whereas the pastor had assumed Wright would give the congregation a 'little white New England church, lean spire pointing to heaven', Wright began by saying, 'let us abolish, in the art and craft of architecture, literature in any symbolic form whatsoever ... why the steeple of the little church? Why *point* to heaven?' So simply posed, yet with this question Wright establishes a fundamental principle in his definition of architecture: forms that 'point' to, or refer to something absent are *representations*, not architecture – architecture makes things present, it is a *presentation* of man in his most noble aspects.

To the church building committee, Wright proposed a temple where God would be present in the gathering of people, a concept close to the essence of the Unitarian faith, which his mother's family had so much to do with shaping. When asked by the building committee, 'What would such a building look like?' Wright could not cite a precedent for the exterior image; the design must be developed from within – from this idea of a space for gathering: 'The first idea was to keep the noble room for worship in mind, and let that sense of the great room shape the whole edifice. Let the room inside be the architecture outside.'

Wright's next step in explaining his design is somewhat unexpected: 'What shape? Well, the answer lay in the material. There was only one material to choose – as the church funds were $45,000 – to "church" four hundred people in 1906. Concrete was cheap.' While at first we might presume that Wright is simply being responsible by keeping construction costs down, we should remember that at this time reinforced concrete was a relatively new material in America, one used mostly for industrial buildings, covered with an exterior cladding of 'finer'

Below: Sanctuary interior.
Below right: Entry level plan; north is at the top.

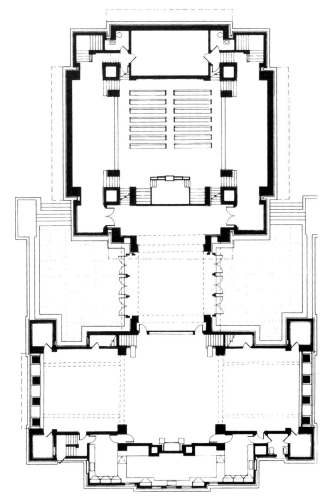

Left: Unity Temple, view from sanctuary balcony looking towards pulpit and organ screen.
Above: Unity Temple, view up to leaded glass skylights and hanging lamps.

materials. What Wright was proposing would be the first public building of any type in America to be built entirely of exposed concrete:

Why not make the wooden boxes or forms so the concrete could be cast in them as separate blocks and masses, these grouped about an interior space in some such way as to preserve this sense of the interior space, the great room, in the appearance of the whole building? And the block-masses might be left as themselves with no facing at all? That would be cheap and permanent and not ugly either.

Something far more than simple economic determinism is at work here; Wright's principle of integrity called for the building to be 'thoroughbred, meaning built in character out of the same material', and therefore reinforced concrete was the only material possible. Wright's particular sense of economy, reflected in his praise of the bare wall surface, in his call for simplicity and getting the most from the least effort, and in his statement that limits are the architect's best friend, led him to believe that the economic, monolithic material of his proposal was not simply a means, but an end:

Too monumental, all this? It would be simply noble. The wooden forms or molds in which concrete buildings must at that time be cast were always the chief item of expense, so to repeat the use of a single form as often as possible was necessary. Therefore a building, all four sides alike, looked like the thing. This, reduced to simplest forms, meant a

building square in plan. That would make their temple a cube – a noble form in masonry.

The modular grid present in Wright's work – the repetition of a single form mentioned above – was used as a method of formal and economic control, and Wright believed pure geometries were inherently virtuous. In his praise of the 'noble' cube, we can hear his poetic mentor, Walt Whitman:

Chanting the square deific, out of the One advancing, out of the sides,

Out of the old and the new, out of the square entirely divine,

Solid, four-sided, all sides needed.[23]

Wright's plan for Unity Temple is closely related to the centralized churches of the Renaissance, being similarly based on pure geometries of the square and cube, which Wright turned to for the same reasons as the architects of the Renaissance: they were geometrically perfect, 'divine' as Whitman said, and they made perfection present in space when built – an appropriate space in which to worship God. The continuity of ordering principles between Wright's Unity Temple and the centralized churches of the Renaissance can be seen in an axonometric drawing by Leonardo da Vinci, located in the lower margin of folio 310V of the Codex Atlanticus. The drawing depicts a volumetric analysis of Bramante's design for Saint Peter's in Rome: a cube, divided in plan in both directions into three zones – a larger central space flanked by two smaller spaces – with the square corners anchored to the base while the central cruciform is lifted up. Exactly the same analytical diagram can be made of Unity Temple.

Also similar to Renaissance centralized churches, Unity Temple is ordered on a rigorous system of proportion: the primary central space of the sanctuary a square in plan (1:1 proportion) and a cube in volume (measured from the floor to the glass of the skylights); the secondary arms of the cruciform – entrance cloisters and balconies surrounding the main space – are half-size double-cubes (1:2 proportion). In plan and section, the four double squares of the secondary spaces are gathered around and open into the central space, geometrically dependent upon it as their centre in the overall cruciform volume, while the four square corners, containing the stairs, anchor and bound the composition.[24] Wright said, 'Geometry is the grammar, so to speak, of the form. It is its architectural principle.'[25] Wright was closer to the Renaissance architects than any of his Beaux-Arts-trained contemporaries, not in the use of classical styles or forms, but in his belief in the timeless validity of fundamental ordering principles: 'Principles are not invented, they are not evolved by one man or one age.'[26]

Unity Temple is first seen as a grey cubic mass standing solidly on its corner site, the clerestory windows are set on the top of high blank walls, under the shadow of the overhanging roof; though this clearly houses the primary volume of the church, there are no openings for entry at ground level on any of the three sides visible from the street. We follow the sidewalk around either side, where we become aware of the lower volume of Unity House behind, going up a set of stairs behind a low wall and turning to find a bank of doors between the primary and secondary masses; as Wright said, 'the entrance to both [is] to be the connecting link between them'. This connecting entrance foyer is the lowest space in the building; the skylit main room of the Unity House, into which the four school rooms open, can be seen through a glass partition to one side, while a solid wall faces us across the depth of a corridor to the other side.

Turning twice more as we walk into this dimly lit 'cloister', we move around the outer edge of the building, skirting the main sanctuary, the floor of which is four feet above the level of the cloisters. Through the opening between the sanctuary floor and the cloister ceiling, we can see from the darkness of the cloister up into the sanctuary space, illuminated from above by skylights and clerestory windows. In this way Wright notes that 'those entering would be imperceptible to the audience. This would preserve the quiet and dignity of the room itself.' Wright allows us, before entering, to see into the main space without ourselves being seen, making it possible for us to make a comfortable, discreet entrance: 'Those entering the room in this way could see into the big room but not be

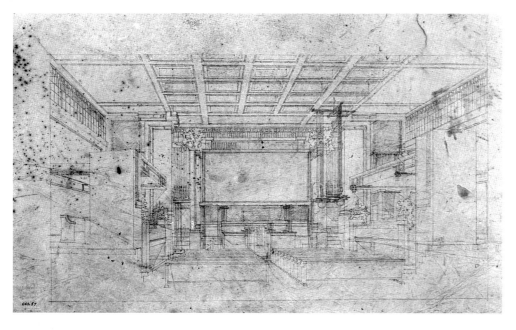

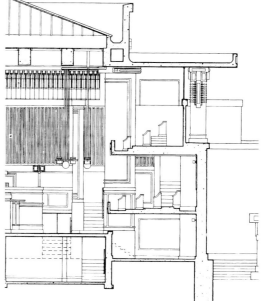

seen by those already seated in it.'

We turn and move up the stairs in the back corner, or along the edges of the four square piers that support the main space, and enter the main space of the sanctuary. A total of seven turns and a walk the equivalent of almost twice the length of the entire building were required to get from the street to sanctuary. Again, as in the Larkin Building, Wright's careful control of the light during our prolonged, rotating and dimly lit entry sequence makes the central space seem brighter than out-of-doors.

And what an astonishing space we are in! The ceiling is opened above the central cube into a grid of beams, into which are set twenty-five stained-glass skylights in a complex pinwheeling pattern. Clerestories run full width across the tops of each balcony just under the roof; the ornamented piers that support the roof's four large overhangs are set outside these windows, and can be seen through the patterned glass. With the exception of the thin slits of stained glass that separate the stair masses from the outside walls, light only enters the sanctuary from above – there are no views out at eye level – and the light is filtered, coloured amber and made geometric by the patterns of the leaded windows and skylights; as Wright said, the space is flooded 'with light from above to get a sense of a happy cloudless day into the room ... the light would, rain or shine, have the warmth of sunlight'.

While on the exterior Wright presented us with a concrete structure rendered as a solid cubic mass standing on the ground, inside Wright constructed a space defined by concrete rendered as floating coloured planes, centred by the golden light falling from above. Concrete as mass and concrete as an free-spanning structure are played off against each other in our readings of exterior and interior. Yet at this point in his narrative Wright says, 'For observe, so far, what has actually taken place is only reasoned *arrangement*,' indicating that for him this complex spatial and formal dialogue between inside and out is but a matter of 'the concrete expression of concrete'; the architect was discovering the nature of the material and giving form to its spatial and structural possibilities. Wright indicated how he eagerly learned from the contractor, Paul Mueller, who also built the Larkin Building, and from the construction process itself, something that was true throughout his career, though it is rarely acknowledged, 'together we overcame difficulty after difficulty in the field where an architect's education is never finished'.

There are no walls defining the inner cubic volume, only the horizontal front surfaces of the balconies and the vertical corners of the four square concrete piers, which are both structure and service ducts, carrying the double layer of balconies on all four sides of the room as well as the ceiling. All the surfaces are rendered as homogeneous planes by Wright's monolithic use of concrete; these planes appear to have been 'folded' to create enclosure. Wood strips or trim boards are utilized to define, explain, indicate, divide and relate the surfaces, and to articulate the continuity of surface around corners and between ceilings and walls. The continuity of planar surfaces indicates a similar continuity and plastic manipulation (folding) of the space defined by the planes. There is a constant play between the monolithic massive planes and the thin eloquent articulation of wood stripping that outlines openings, joins planes and gives an interpretation of the space: the underlying structure-pattern of the space made visible and articulated as a rhythm of the form. Wright 'called it *continuity*. It is easy to see it in the folded plane [which] enters here emphasized by *lines* merging wall and ceiling into one. Let walls, ceilings, floors now become not only party to each other but *part of each other*, reacting upon and within one another; continuity in all.'[27]

In the sanctuary of Unity Temple the congregation is faced more towards each other than towards the pulpit; this is appropriate to the question and discussion format of the Unitarian worship services, and is a direct result of the square floor plan. Wright placed hidden doors to either side behind the pulpit and organ, which are thrown open after the service, allowing the congregation to exit directly from the sanctuary in to the entrance foyer, without going back through the cloisters: 'it seemed more respectful to let [the congregation] go out thus toward the pulpit than turn their backs upon their minister as is usual in most churches.'

Far right: Unity Temple, detail view of pulpit and organ screen

Across the entrance foyer, and at the same floor level, is Unity House, the Sunday school building; Wright distinguishes it as more domestic than the sanctuary not only with this name but with the fireplace that dominates its double-height skylit central room, off which the four classrooms open, two to either side, at the same floor level and in balconies above. While the central room is square in plan, the overall volume of Unity House is rectangular, stretched across the site behind Unity Temple. The stained-glass skylight in Unity House does not centre on the main space, as does the skylight in the sanctuary, but overlaps into the classrooms to either side, integrating the three spaces.

On the exterior, the independent volumes Wright created in plan through 'taking Unity Temple to pieces' are separated and articulated. The corner stair towers of Unity Temple stand free, sliced away from the mass of the building by thin windows running their full height, recessed to produce a sharp shadow line. The four cruciform roof cantilevers align with the blank wall masses below and project from a central cubic volume rising from the central cube of the sanctuary, its outside corners interlocking with the inside corners of the stair towers. The volumes of the lower mass of the Unity House are similarly articulated, and the whole complex is then carefully integrated. The moulding at the top of the low wall at the entrance is pulled

through Unity House so as to form the base for the ornamented columns in front of the windows. The moulding at the top of the Unity House is pulled across, forming the top of the entrance element and the base for the ornamented columns in front of the clerestory windows at the top of the Unity Temple. Finally, the moulding at the top of the stair towers on Unity Temple is pulled through behind these columns to become the window sills. This interweaving of lines and planes produces a bonding of independent forms that recalls in a most subtle manner the dynamic folded planes and woven trim lines of the interior.

The complexity of the geometries and interlocking spaces in Unity Temple and Unity House are simply staggering; we wonder how Wright could have conceived such as space. In Wright's narrative of the design process, he said:

> Holding all this diversity together in a preconceived direction is really no light matter but is the condition of creation. The ideal of an organic architecture is often terribly severe discipline for the imagination. I came to know this full well. And, always, some minor concordance takes more time, taxes concentration more than all besides. Any minor element may become a major problem to vex the architect. How many schemes I have thrown away because some one minor feature would not come true to form! Thirty-four studies were necessary to arrive at this concordance as it is now seen. Unity House looks easy enough now, for it is right enough. But it was not. Many studies in detail as a matter of course yet remain to be made, in order to determine what further may be left out to protect the design. These studies never seem to end and in this sense no organic building may ever be 'finished'. The complete goal of the ideal of organic architecture is never reached. Nor need be. What worthwhile ideal is ever reached?

WITH THE design and construction of Unity Temple, Wright achieved his goal of realizing a monumental architecture appropriate for America. The characteristics of this architecture differed considerably from previous definitions of monumentality – this is perhaps best exemplified by Wright's emphasis on interior space rather than exterior form: on the introverted experience of transcendence through the medium of top-light rather than the extroverted expressions of historical styles. It is interesting to note that it was on Unity Temple's interior – the design of which was only completed during construction – that Wright first felt he had achieved 'the concrete expression of concrete', the highly plastic capacity of this material that allowed space, function, form, structure and construction to be fully unified. Today, nearly one hundred years after they were realized, Wright's early public buildings appear to have been built only yesterday. At once new and old, ancient and modern, these structures owe no obvious debt to any historical style, yet recall the great monuments of the ancient world in a manner we still find deeply moving.

THE EXTROVERTED HOUSE

A space is something that has been made room for, something that is cleared and free, namely, within a boundary, Greek *peras*. A boundary is not that at which something stops but, as the Greeks recognized, the boundary is that from which something begins its essential unfolding – comes into presence. That is why the concept is that of *horismos*, that is, horizon, the boundary. Space is in essence that for which room has been made, that which is let into its bounds.

Martin Heidegger[1]

Left: Frederick Robie House, Chicago, Illinois, 1907. Above: 'A Fireproof House for $5000', another of Wright's Ladies Home Journal *projects, 1906. The house was proposed to be built on a small suburban site, tight against neighbouring buildings.*

As we have seen, Wright's public buildings invariably focus on introspective, top-lit central spaces, protected by solid walls that deny eyelevel views outwards. Introverted at ground level with their closed exteriors and open centres, these buildings are vertically oriented, opening up and out in section and massing, directed towards the sky. These public buildings are cubic in form, composed of pure geometries with clear, distinct edges and boundaries. On the other hand, Wright's private Prairie Houses tended to be extroverted, opening outwards with views in all directions and anchored by the heavy solid hearths at their centres. With their exteriors open under overhanging eaves, their closed solid centres, and their horizontal orientations, they open down and out in section and massing, directed towards the horizon, the earth line. The Prairie Houses are pyramidal in form, often composed of incomplete or interrupted geometries with multiple edges and ambiguous, overlapping boundaries. Both the extroverted private houses and the introverted public buildings were developed by Wright as sacred spaces, with their concealed, spiralling, revelational entrance sequences reinforcing the importance of the centre in the daily rituals of each building; the public building's central space as nave and the private house's hearth as altar.

Wright spoke of the spaces within his Prairie Houses as being both caves and tents. The resolution of this dichotomy – heavy and light, earth and sky, horizontal and vertical – is experienced in the interiors of these houses, where the light plaster ceilings with their floating folded planes, free-spanning beams and woven glass skylights hover over and gather around the heavy dark brick fireplaces, terraces and low walls anchored to the earth. In defining the Prairie House, Wright said, 'the way the walls rose from the plan and the spaces were roofed over was the chief interest of the house.'[2] The spaces of these houses fused two conceptions of dwelling: the dark, earth-bound, anchored and protected centre of domestic ritual – the sense of belonging to the family and to a place – and the centrifugal expansion of space and view to the distant horizon in all directions – the sense of freedom and individual independence.

This paradoxical pair was combined in Wright's vision of the house in the flat prairie of the American Midwest landscape: 'I saw the house, primarily, as livable interior space under simple shelter. I liked the *sense of shelter* in the look of the building.'[3] This came from the manner in which the roof and other 'horizontal planes in the building, those planes parallel to the earth, identify themselves with the ground – make the building belong to the ground'.[4] Yet Wright always returned to the idea that the character and identity of a house comes from the space within: 'What I have just described was on the *outside* of the house. But it

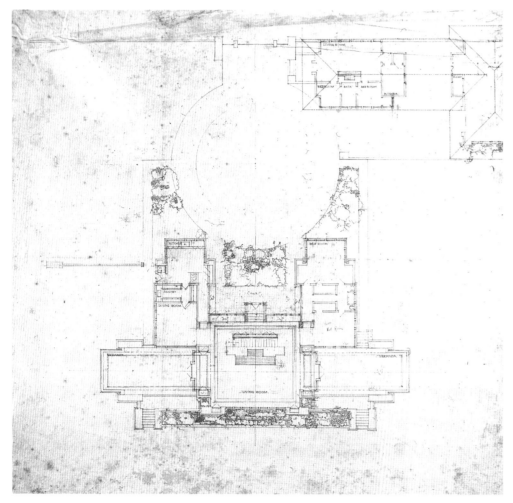

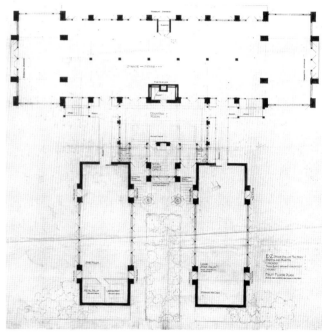

was all there, chiefly because of what had happened *inside*.'⁵ In this pursuit of ever-more precisely formed and subtly nuanced interior spaces, Wright developed variations which explored the expansive volumes of the 'tripartite' plan type to produce imbedded, impacted, truncated, extended and pinwheeled cruciform plans; these were complemented by his development of a third major plan type, based on the cube.

Imbedded Cruciform Plans

In these designs, the cruciform-shaped public rooms of the house are imbedded, either in plan or section, in the private and service spaces, presented and framed almost like a diamond in its setting. The unbuilt project for a summer house for Edward Waller in Charlevoix, Michigan, of 1902 is developed from the tripartite plan type, but in this case Wright flanked the central living room with two exterior, covered verandas, defined by four enormous freestanding piers, rather than creating three interior spaces in *enfilade*, as he had in the Darwin Martin House. The house is also symmetrical, an ordering device Wright normally reserved for public buildings; indeed, this plan will later reappear in the design for a public building – the E-Z Polish Factory of 1905 for the Martin brothers in Chicago. Two wings, containing the services and bedrooms, are attached to the edges of the living room and oriented ninety degrees to the axis joining the living room and verandas; these are

projected forward to form an entrance court. We would have thus entered this house from behind the fireplace, which stands free in the living room, and the primary facade of the house is oriented away from the street. The direction of movement set up by the entrance is blocked and redirected along the cross-axis to either side by the fireplace, the piers defining the corner of the living room, and the verandas and their piers.

Edwin Cheney House, Oak Park, Illinois, 1903

The plan of the Edwin Cheney House, built in 1903, is a variation on this same theme, and it is symmetrically organized in plan, with only slight deviations at the entrance and kitchen. The main rooms of this tripartite plan are developed as a single cruciform space, with the larger living room, anchored on the interior edge by the fireplace, flanked and open to the dining room and study to either side. The hipped plaster ceiling with dark wood-trim boards runs unbroken through all three rooms, with free-spanning beams carried by pairs of piers defining the thresholds at either edge of the living room. The space in front of the fireplace, where we enter the house, and the projected square bay window opposite, which opens to a terrace, are covered by flat ceilings at the level of the beams. The kitchen is opposite the entrance, on the other side of the house, and the bedrooms are at the rear of the house, lined

up in a row along the corridor behind the fireplace.

The main floor of the house is set up on a podium made by the basement, the whole brick volume covered by one low pyramidal roof, with four piers set out at the corners of the front yard, which is enclosed by a low brick wall. The bedrooms project out into the rear yard, beyond this bounding wall; the main 'public' rooms of the house (living room, dining room, study and kitchen) are thus contained within the bounded yard defined by the corner piers, while the 'private' rooms (bedrooms and bathrooms) are left outside. The low wall thus divides the house just behind the fireplace, which falls into the bounded yard, so that while in the living room we feel we are standing at the protected centre of several layers of walls, starting in the yard. This is an example of the unique and effective manner in which Wright defined and integrated the interior and exteriors of these suburban houses: 'My sense of "wall" was no longer the side of a box. It was enclosure of space affording protection … But it is also to bring the outside world into the house and let the inside of the house go outside.'[6]

Impacted Cruciform Plans
In these designs, the cruciform plan has been impacted or folded in on itself, producing an experiential density and tension between the space-defining elements. The three projects for the Harvey Sutton House of 1905 propose several astonishing variations of the tripartite plan type. The first scheme has the central living room inserted between the dining room and library and projecting out into the landscape. The second scheme locates the fireplace at the centre of the cruciform, with the space of all four rooms flowing freely around it. In the third scheme the three rooms in the tripartite plan are all of equal width, so that the movement forward of the fireplace from the rear wall results in a projection of the living room the same distance at the front of the house.

In the Barton Westcott House, built in 1907, Wright aligns the dining room, living room and reception room along the inside wall, with a shallow square bay projected across from the fireplace. The boundaries between the three rooms are wonderfully subtle in this house, with the inside wall and the outside wall giving overlapping, contradictory readings. While two wood slat screens, housing seats and terminating in freestanding piers, are projected from the ends of the fireplace, reaching a little over halfway across the width of the room, the space defined by these arms sits inside the space defined by the edges of the projecting window bay on the opposite wall.

Thomas Hardy House, Racine, Wisconsin, 1905
The Thomas Hardy House, built in 1905, was developed from Wright's unbuilt project for a summer lodge for J A

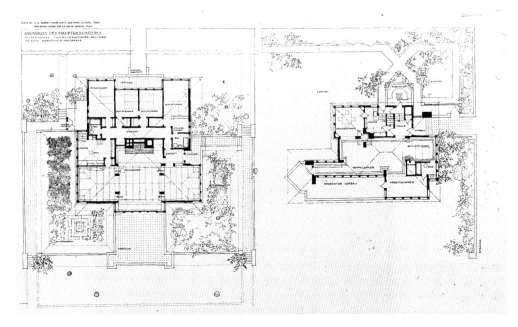

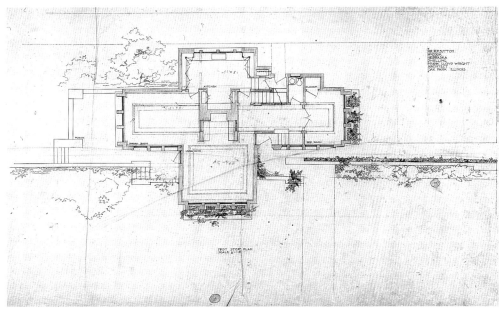

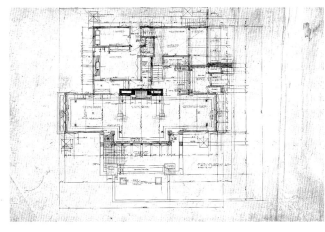

Above: Edwin Cheney House (left) and project titled 'House for an Artist' (right), ground-floor plans; the latter is probably intended as a pied-à-terre for Wright himself, published on the same page and next to the house he had designed for his lover, Mamah Cheney.
Centre: Second project for Harvey Sutton House, McCook, Nebraska, 1905, ground-floor plan.
Right: Barton Westcott House, Springfield, Ohio, Illinois, 1907, ground floor-plan.

Scudder in Ontario of the previous year. Both houses were proposed for the edge of steep embankments dropping to the water below, and the Hardy House is stretched out along the breakline of the ridge overlooking Lake Michigan. The plan takes the tripartite arrangement, typically used only for the main rooms of Prairie Houses, and stacks all the volumes of the house within it to produce a compact three-storey design, anchored into the site in section. The plan of the Hardy House is composed of a larger central square interlocked with two smaller squares to either side; into the spaces defined by the overlaps of these squares Wright places closets and stairs, thereby creating a service zone at the edge of all primary rooms. Wright 'restates' the plan form, as he was so often to do, in the ornament of the house; in this case in the pattern of the leaded-glass windows of the entrance hall.

On the relatively flat and closed street facade, Wright suggests the split-level nature of the house's section by suppressing the floor line beneath the stucco finish, letting the wood-trim boards run without a horizontal break from the windows at the entrance level to the windows at the top, tucked under the roof. As in Wright's own studio, there are two equal 'front' doors, one at each end of the building; in the Hardy House we enter near the middle of the three-storey section. The entrance hall is a narrow space behind the fireplace, which we move around and up into the living room, a double-height volume facing the lake. Flanking the living room to either side are bedrooms, which in turn open to square walled gardens; while the living-room windows face along the direction of our entrance to the lake, the bedrooms windows are oriented along the slope, parallel to the lakeshore. The second floor has two bedrooms and a balcony at the top of the stairs overlooking the living room below. On the bottom floor the dining room is in the centre, under the living room, with the kitchen and servant's bedroom to either side. The dining room opens on to a large terrace which projects towards the lake; from the lake side, in the famous perspective drawing by Marion Mahony, the house is anchored to the hillside by the interlocking of the garden walls stretched along the ridge top and the dining-room terrace projecting out into space.

Truncated Cruciform Plans

In these designs, the cruciform plan has been truncated, one of its wings or arms being removed or compressed back into the central volume; the truncated extension is marked by the slight projection at the centre of the plan, which interlocks with the exterior space of the garden. The project for the Thaxter Shaw House of 1906 develops its T-shaped plan as a series of formal, symmetrical, independent pier clusters, which when combined with its large scale, give the house the feeling of a public building, very similar to the E-Z Polish Factory. The Pettit Mortuary Chapel of 1906 is also T shape in plan, consisting of an enclosed volume which interlocks

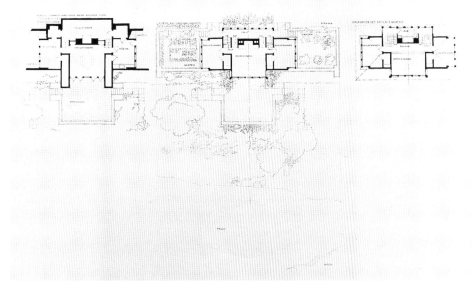

*Above: Thomas Hardy House,
Racine, Wisconsin, 1905, view of
street side.*
*Right: Thomas Hardy House,
plans: lower level with dining
room (left), middle level with
living room (centre), and upper
level with bedrooms (right).
Entrance occurs halfway between
the lower and middle levels.*

with an open, covered volume at the fireplace. Double doors are set on either side of the fireplace at the end of the enclosed volume to allow movement all around the fireplace, which becomes a freestanding element when the doors are opened.

The unbuilt 1906 project for a Studio-Residence for Richard Bock, Wright's favourite sculptor, has a one-storey T-shaped plan with the tripartite library-living-dining room intersected by the double-height studio volume at the rear. The fireplace sits at the juncture of the two spaces and circulation between them occurs to either side of it. Across from the fireplace, mirroring the studio volume in plan, Wright planned an entrance terrace framed by two pairs of piers, one set inside the other, facing a reflecting pool. The whole is rendered in rigorously abstract flat wall and roof planes, with the windows set in a square grid; the double-height volume of the studio is ringed with clerestory windows where it rises above the roof of the rest of the house.

The Walter Davidson House and the Isabel Roberts House, both built in 1908, along with the Oscar Steffens House of 1909, all have cruciform plans with the central volume as a double-height living room with a gallery overlooking it on the first floor; the wing to the right is the dining room; the wing to the left is an open covered porch; and the kitchen and service spaces, with the bedrooms above, are loosely assembled at the rear. These are the only examples of

Wright's carrying out the two-storey vertical central space called for in his seminal 'Home in a Prairie Town' project of 1901; in these houses he resolves the front elevation by expressing the double-height volume with a single set of windows and posts that rise uninterrupted to the roof.

Extended Cruciform Plans

In these designs, the cruciform plan is extended to either side so as to emphasize one of the plan's axes over the other, resulting in a longer primary volume interpenetrated by a shorter secondary volume. The A P Johnson House, built on Lake Delavan, Wisconsin, in 1905 incorporates the square overall plan of the Cheney House, while extending two covered verandas, supported on two pairs of piers, which flank and extend the axis of the tripartite main room. The two-storey square mass of the house, anchored at its centre by the massive chimney and covered by a pyramidal roof, is sliced through at its midsection by the one-storey roof that reaches to cover the two verandas to either side, marking the cantilevered extension of the tripartite plan that was to culminate, after many attempts at perfecting the scheme, in both the Robie House and the Evans House. The River Forest Tennis Club of 1905, while not a private house, develops this spatial concept with its long thin volume in which two fireplaces stand freely, with a zone for movement left open along each edge. The E A Cummings

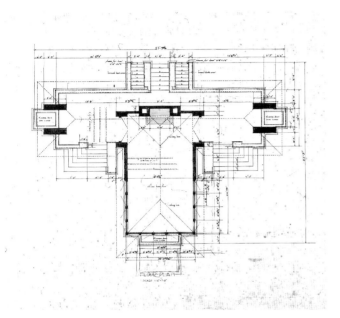

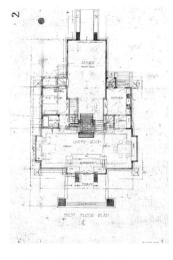

Real Estate Office project of 1905 presents a similar single volume running the length of the building, with other spaces collected in the base of the T-shaped plan, the whole also related to the truncated cruciform plan above.

In the F F Tomek House of 1907, built in Riverside, Illinois, Wright placed the living room and dining room at opposite ends of a continuous primary volume, separated by the freestanding fireplace and entrance stair rising up in the centre, with the service spaces and bedrooms in a cubic block set back and to one side. The dining room does not match the living room in width, and the two rooms are connected along the edge only on one side of the fireplace; the stair up to the bedrooms taking up the same zone next to the dining room on the other side. Wright had but one more step to take to arrive at the design for the Robie House. As Joseph Connors said:

> What is interesting about ... the jump from the Tomek to the Robie House, is that it allows us to see Wright standing in front of his own work and criticizing it. Very few modern visitors are tempted to be as critical as Wright himself apparently was with his own work. For most people the Tomek House would be progressive enough. It is a superb design in the abstract, but also a very appealing place to live. Only Wright would have been capable of the imaginative dissatisfaction that led to the Robie House. He pushed every idea to the limit ...[7]

Frederick Robie House, Chicago, Illinois, 1907

Late in 1906 Frederick Robie, a thirty-year-old inventor, maker of bicycles, and proud owner of experimental automobiles, approached Wright and commissioned him to begin designing a house for his young family. He was typical of Wright's clients of this period in Oak Park: many of whom were engineers and technicians who had become managers of growing manufacturing companies and who often were – as Robie – younger than their architect.[8] Robie had made some preliminary diagrams of the layout he wanted and had been told by contractors and architects to whom he had shown them, 'I know what you want, one of those damn Wright houses.' For Robie the next step was obvious: 'I contacted him, and from the first we had a definite community of thought. When I talked in mechanical terms, he talked in architectural terms. I thought, well, he was in my world.'[9]

Robie found a corner site in the Hyde Park section of Chicago, near the University, which he bought in early 1908.[10] Woodlawn Street, on to which the narrow face of the site opened, was lined with blocky three-storey houses all aligning with the required thirty-five-foot setback from the street and lot line. In designing the Robie House, Wright stopped the interior space of the living room at this setback line, as required, but made the house appear to go almost to the street line by extending the brick terrace walls and

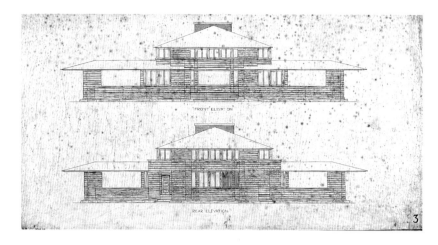

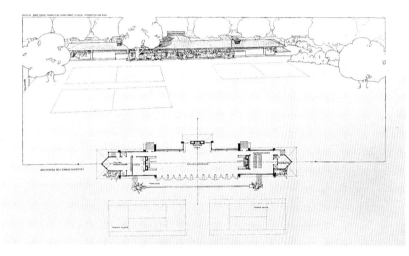

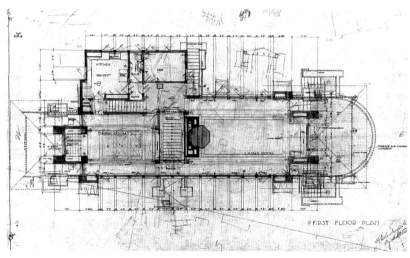

the roof cantilevers, projecting them far beyond the neighbouring facades. The block to the south had not been built out as yet, giving a view to the Midway Park on the long side of the site. Wright lifted the main floor a full storey off the ground, so that the occupants could look out through the continuous expanse of glass doors in the living and dining rooms which face south, protected from the sun by the roof overhang. The heights and pyramidal massing of the brick piers and walls in section are carefully calculated to allow views out from the main-floor rooms but block views into the rooms from the sidewalk.

As in most of Wright's best work, the overall massing of the Robie House is surprisingly simple; in the ground-floor plan two rectangles – the primary rooms and the service spaces – seem to be sliding past each other, and where they overlap rises the square plan of the upper bedroom floor. On the exterior, we are most aware of the long horizontal volume containing the primary rooms which is placed on the corner, nearest both streets; the cubic first-floor floats over the lower floor towards one end. In viewing the house from the street, we are confronted with a series of brick piers and connecting walls which step back as they rise up, above which we find a continuous row of leaded-glass openings set between brick posts recessed deep under the shadow of the long, low hipped roof, with its knife-edged copper gutters and extraordinary cantilevers at either end covering open-air terraces. The chimney rises through this roof at its centre, with the low walls and roof of the bedroom floor locked into it on one side. The whole seems to be composed of masses that are interlocked, delicately balanced, yet ready to move.

We immediately wonder, how do these walls and roofs stay up? Architects may guess – correctly – that there are steel beams hidden in these horizontal roofs and walls that leap unsupported across such enormous distances, but while the house expresses its vigorous structuring of space, it does not reveal the actual structure. Wright's concept of coherence between spatial composition and structural construction did not require the literal exposure of structure: 'Why should you always expose structure? I call it *indecent exposure*.'[11]

Wright valued the cantilever – which he considered his greatest structural discovery and contribution – for the space it at once liberated and defined, not for any revelation of structure it allowed. The heroic extension of the front roof cantilever over the terrace is structured by two beams buried within the depth of the roof and bearing on brick piers hidden in its shadows. Though unexposed, these steel beams are subtly revealed in the folded and dropped ceiling along the edges of the main rooms inside. On both exterior and interior the steel beams transform space and experience, they are revealed through the spatial freedom they allow, and they are made present in the spaces they create; Joseph Connors has noted that 'Wright's reputation as a great innovator in the realm of structure has obscured the fact that he is also a brilliant visual psychologist.'[12]

Wright often said that he worked 'in the nature of materials', but this nature was profoundly inflected by the spatial and experiential intention of the design. In the Robie House, there is a wonderful play between the vertical, load-bearing brick piers and the long brick balcony, which appears to be a type of beam leaping across the distance between the piers. This long span is clearly an 'unnatural', indeed impossible structural use of brick, which has no inherent spanning capacity when laid in a horizontal running bond; the steel beam that is doing the real work of structural spanning is buried behind the brick.[13] In this way Wright contradicts expectations he himself sets up: the

vertical brick piers demonstrate the 'normative', load-bearing use of brick, and thereby serve as the perfect foil for the mysteriously floating brick balcony wall that spans between them. Rather than the literal expression of the brick's constructive nature, Wright employed the brick's capacity to give character to space. In the Robie House, Wright used extremely long thin bricks, finishing the vertical joints with brick-coloured mortar flush to the face of the brick while deeply raking the horizontal white mortar joints, resulting in the all-pervasive horizontal shadow patterns that weave together the many surfaces of the elevation.

The spatial openness of the plan is already evident to those making a close examination of the exterior. The plan of the living and dining rooms achieves a level of perfection and precision rarely matched even in Wright's own work. The fireplace, open to both sides, anchors the centre of the space, with continuous open movement zones down both sides of the entire volume. These narrow movement zones are lined by leaded glass doors on the south side, which open to the balcony behind the 'floating' brick wall and end in doors leading to the covered terrace. The centre zone, defined by the width of the fireplace, terminates at either end in projecting diagonal bay windows, framed by the pairs of piers that carry the steel beams in the ceiling.

The volume containing the kitchen and other services is dominated by walls, while the volume containing the living and dining rooms is composed of piers of various sizes and repetitive lines of posts between windows and doors. Sets of four piers are nested one inside another: defining first the inner volume scaled by the width of the fireplace; enclosing this are the four piers set at the outer edges of the rooms; set in front are the two piers turned towards the street to frame the long balcony at the edge of the living and dining rooms; enclosing this entire volume are the four large piers that define the height of the terrace wall and the now-destroyed garage court wall; and set in front are the two piers and wall framing the sunken garden opening off the ground-floor rooms. The whole is composed of a series of spaces nested one inside another, layers of brick walls and piers of varying heights defining a complex and dense sequence of boundaries.

Entering the Robie House is no simple matter, as we have come to expect with Wright. While we are drawn to the long south facade, due to its dynamic play of layered walls, roofs and deeply shadowed spaces, no entry is to be found there; in fact, from this perspective the house appears rather defensive in character. The entrance is found on the other side of the house, off the narrow street front, half-way in at the middle of the site, hard against the inner lot line. Walking all the way around the projecting terrace, we move in along the edge of the forward mass, towards a dark space ahead. We are enclosed in the cool shadows of the entrance

court on the north side, with the mass of the house on our right and a low garden wall on our left; we move under the overhanging brick spandrel-beam and in the darkness find the door.

When it was originally built we came into the centre of the entrance hall, a blank plaster wall directly ahead and the brick side of the fireplace, with a stair going up at its edge, to our right. The family playroom and billiard room open to either side through leaded-glass doors, but we are drawn to the stairs, above which the ceiling has been carved away, allowing us to see the space rising up to the main floor. Mounting the stairs, we turn twice more and arrive in the upper foyer facing away from the long south facade; in plan this foyer overlaps between the primary volume, housing the living and dining rooms, and the secondary 'service' volume behind. Opening off its inner corners are a balcony overlooking the entrance court and the stair up to the bedrooms. The outer corners open into one of the movement zones connecting the living and dining rooms. The foyer's outer edge is defined at the centre by the side of the fireplace, on the dining room side by the woodwork and low walls around the stairs, and on the living room side by the freestanding pier, vertical wood slay wall and inglenook seat. These latter have since been removed, so that the foyer is now open directly to the living room in a way that Wright never intended. Moving along the narrow edge zone, we enter 'the great vessel'.[14]

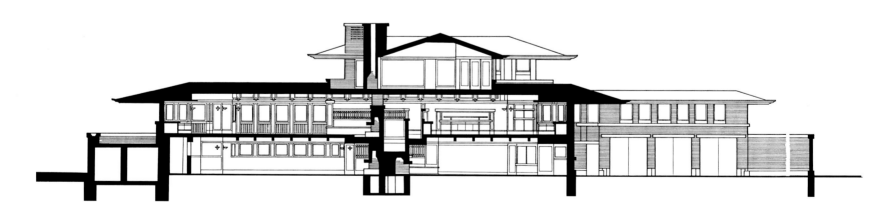

Left: Robie House, detail of south elevation showing planters at the terminals of the horizontal brick walls and the east roof cantilever.
Below left: East–west section looking north.
Below: Plans.
Below right: View of the terrace at the west end of the living room, under the roof cantilever. Wright valued the cantilever for the space it defined and liberated.

Entering the living room along the edge of the fireplace, we see ahead to the prow-like bay window at the far end. We must turn first to face the long line of leaded-glass doors opening to the south and then turn again to finally face the fireplace. There are no real walls in the living room, only plaster-faced posts between the windows and doors; by folding down over the door and window tops, the plaster ceiling acts to enclose the space, 'giving generous overhead', as Wright said.[15] The ceiling over the edge or movement zone is seven-feet and six-inches in height, while the ceiling over the centre space is nine feet high, the two held together by the continuous wood-trim boards, which bend to follow the ceiling line as they cross the room, are spaced to align with the door posts.

The leaded-glass windows and doors are continuous around the entire living room; these prismatic designs capture and retain light, holding it within their sparkling geometries, so that enclosure is perceived as lines woven in space. Rudolph Schindler was later to say that these leaded glass apertures are 'a dissolution of the building material into a grid – leaded glass – as the ground dissolves and becomes lost in the tree branches'.[16] The pattern Wright uses in the Robie House glasswork utilizes flattened diamond shapes and diagonal geometries that subtly echo the bay windows at either end of the great double room; the proportions of the diamond shapes can be fitted exactly into the main floor plan.[17]

As is typical for Wright, the beauty of his geometric patterns and folded coloured planes is matched by the subtlety with which the structural and mechanical elements are integrated into the fabric of the building. The radiators for heating are set into the wall under the windows along the north side of the living room and were placed in the floor under a brass grille set in front of each of the doors along the south side of the room. Two types of lights are integrated into the construction of the house: the spherical fixtures projected into the centre of the room along the edge of the folded ceiling and the hidden lights recessed into the ceiling above the edge movement zones, each behind a wooden grille, casting what Reyner Banham called 'a modulated dappled light through it onto the floor in front of the windows'.[18]

At the point where the ceiling folds, going from its lower edges to the higher centre, are the two steel beams that support the roof cantilevers; the ceiling reflects the flat planar space of the steel structure rather than the diagonal slope of the roof above. Along the edge of the roof eaves are openings that allow air into the space between the flat ceiling and the sloped roof – as do the wooden ceiling grilles hiding the recessed lights – and the chimney has a separate flue for venting the hot air that collects under the roof. The roof overhangs to the east, south and west are each of different length, exactly calculated to shade the glass doors and bay windows in summer and let the sun in to warm the

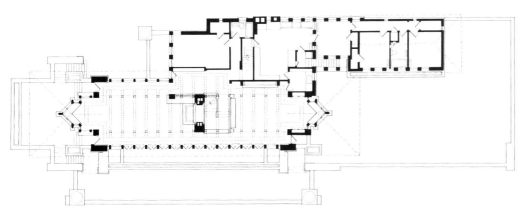

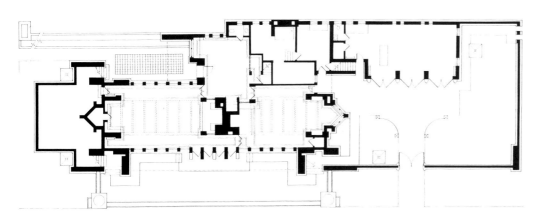

Left: Robie House, view from the west terrace to the entrance court. The front door is within a shaded recess below the balcony.
Above: View from the dining room past the fireplace to the living room. There are no real walls in the living room, only plaster-faced posts between the windows and doors.
Above right: View from the living room towards the dining room, with the fireplace on the left.

rooms in winter; as Banham noted, 'at mid-day on Midsummer day, the shadow of the eaves just kisses the woodwork at the bottom of the glass in the doors to the terrace … Nothing else that anybody else did for decades was to match [the Prairie Houses'] easy mastery of environmental control.'[19]

In the living room of the Robie House, the centre of the room is blocked from physical passage by the fireplace, yet open at the top to partial view, making us aware of the differences between the experiences and the paths of the eye and the body, the visual and the haptic. Facing the fireplace as it originally stood, with the seat and wood pier standing forward on the left, we would have seen that though the space along both edges was open to the dining room beyond, only on the right did the glass doors run continuous into the next space; the pier and seat moving forward on the left combined with the doors sliding away on the right imply a rotation that we follow under the lower movement zone along the right edge and into the dining room.

This dining room, perhaps more than any other by Wright, indicates the importance of the furniture, built-in and freestanding, which Wright designed specifically for each space. As this furniture is now lost, we must study the period photographs to understand the power of this place of domestic ritual. The stair was originally separated from the room by a five-foot-high wall of vertical wood slats, so that

upon entering and arriving at the top of the stairs, the dining room would have been screened from view. These wood slats are matched by those forming the tall backs of the dining chairs, which when gathered around the dining table formed a space, the chair backs higher than the seated person's head. This 'room' within the dining room formed by the chairs is reinforced by Wright's placement of four piers at the corners of the dining table – where the space within this inner 'room' would otherwise leak out; these piers are topped by cubic stained-glass lamps that echo the diagonal patterns of the leaded-glass windows. The wooden sideboard against the far wall presents a reduced scale version of the main elevation of the house, and the rug patterns in the entrance hall, dining room and living room present three 'interpretations' of its floor plan. When the family sat down at this table, they were enclosed within multiple layers of space and self-referential form; the family meal was clearly the most important ritual in Wright's vision of the house. At the end of his life, Robie himself said of this house, 'I think it's the most ideal place in the world.'[20]

Pinwheeled Cruciform Plans
In the earlier of these designs, one axis of the cruciform plan is emphasized and its volume enlarged, while the two wings on the other axis are sheared away and positioned diagonally across from each other. In the later versions, the plans are

101

developed from that of the first floor of the Robie House; but here instead of the the public and private masses shearing, it is the two primary volumes of living room and dining room that slide past one another, often oriented ninety degrees to each other, touching only at their edges and interlocking only at their corners. Both types of the pinwheeled cruciform plan impart a rotating movement sequence to the design.

In the project of 1904 for the Robert Clark House, Wright begins with a cruciform plan, with the living room, dining room, entrance and kitchen each in a separate wing, centred on the square hall; the bedrooms are on the second level. Wright transforms this cruciform by moving the dining room in plan back behind the fireplace to where it can be connected to both the kitchen and the hall; he also moves the dining room in section, lowering it (along with the kitchen) a half-level down and placing a covered veranda above it, so that both dining room and veranda are open to the central hall. Also notable in plan are the four piers Wright has set in the corners of the living room; these not only define the threshold between the living room and hall, but create a narrow movement zone along each edge of the room, leaving the centre of the room free for furnishing.

In the H J Ullman House project, also of 1904, Wright further develops the plan and section proposed for the Clark House, but abandons its solid exterior walls for the interlocked pier system of construction he had perfected in the Darwin Martin House of the year before. In the Ullman House project, the four piers are set into the central square hall, fused with the fireplace, the spatial zone they create at the edge of the hall being used to house the open stairs that go down to the entrance and dining room and up to the veranda and bedrooms. Wright expands the hearth to take up the remainder of the central hall, its inglenook-seating walls forming the edge of the stairs to either side. As he did in the Darwin Martin House, Wright develops each room in the project for the Ullman House as if it were an independent pavilion set in the landscape, the house closely bound to its site through its network of projecting walls, walkways, pools, planters and gardens.

E E Boynton House, Rochester, New York, 1908

In the plan of the Boynton House, built in 1908, Wright does not attempt the geometric precision of the Robie House; indeed, the living room and dining room, each symmetrical volumes with a large bay-window projection, are oriented in different directions and loosely joined by the entrance hall. The fireplace again stands free, with movement possible around both its sides. It is the deeply inset beams and soffits at the tops of the doors and windows that marks this house as unique; rarely until the Usonian Houses forty years later would Wright manipulate the ceilings of rooms this dynamically. The dining room has no less than three primary ceiling heights, layered across the

Above: Robie House, leaded glass windows in 'prow' at the west end of the living room.
Right: Period photograph of the dining room, showing the leaded glass lamps.
Right: Living room details.
Far right: View of the living room and fireplace. The built-in seating and freestanding wooded screen walls around the fireplace have been removed, and the furniture is not the custom-designed originals Wright had built for the house.

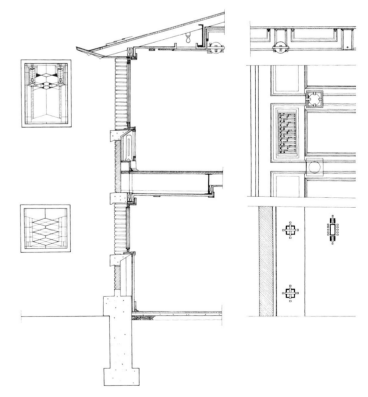

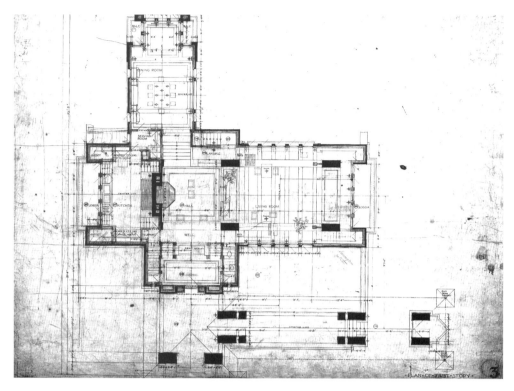

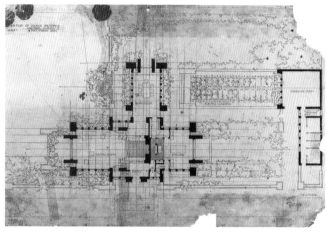

room from the windowed 'breakfast bay' (lowest), up to the clerestory zone (highest) and folding back down to the stained-glass recessed-lighting panels (middle). The plaster ceiling and soffits are crossed and recrossed by dark wood-trim boards, first in one direction, then in the other. In the living room, the centre of the room has a high ceiling, while the beam banding the room at door height cuts across the face of the fireplace and projects deep lower soffits at the windows to either side and over the veranda which opens across from the fireplace. The overall experience is of a highly dynamic weaving of interdependent spaces, creating many planar layers of plaster and leaded glass, which affords a sense of depth and protection to the space despite the large number of windows.

Meyer May House, Grand Rapids, Michigan, 1908

The plan of the Meyer May House, built in 1908, is quite different from Wright's typical house plans, similar only to the W R Heath House of 1903. The living room and dining room are pushed to the front and back (respectively) of the house, so that they are open to each other only at a single corner, and the entrance hall runs between them, separating and joining them. The reason to study the May House is not primarily for this planning experiment on Wright's part – though it does result in a particularly dynamic movement pattern – but because of its recent renovation back to near

perfect original condition.[21] As it stands today, the May House is perhaps the only Prairie House where we can experience the full depth and richness of Wright's original construction.

The exterior vestibule has the door on the right; entering a double-height space, within less that ten feet, Wright turns us three times, offering us glimpses of the entrance hall and dining room through the six-foot-high wooden slat screens, finally letting us enter the hall along its back edge, facing the living room. Moving along the edge in entering the living room, to our left is what seems almost an all-glass bay facing the terrace, with windows along the front and sides as well as stained-glass skylights overhead. The entire room is ringed by a wood band at door-top height, and this wood board bisects the centre of the upper window in this bay. Ahead and around to the right is the fireplace, screened from the entrance by a bookshelf-lined wall that does not reach the ceiling. The walls and ceilings of all the spaces are plaster with wood trim, the floor is wood, and the fireplace is brick – its horizontal joints painted gold, so that light sparkles from the masonry with or without a fire; 'It comforted me to see the fire burning deep in the solid masonry of the house itself', Wright said.[22] Moving back across the entrance hall, at the end of which we glimpse the veranda, we enter the edge of the dining room, a serene and simple space with the four-posted dining table in place;

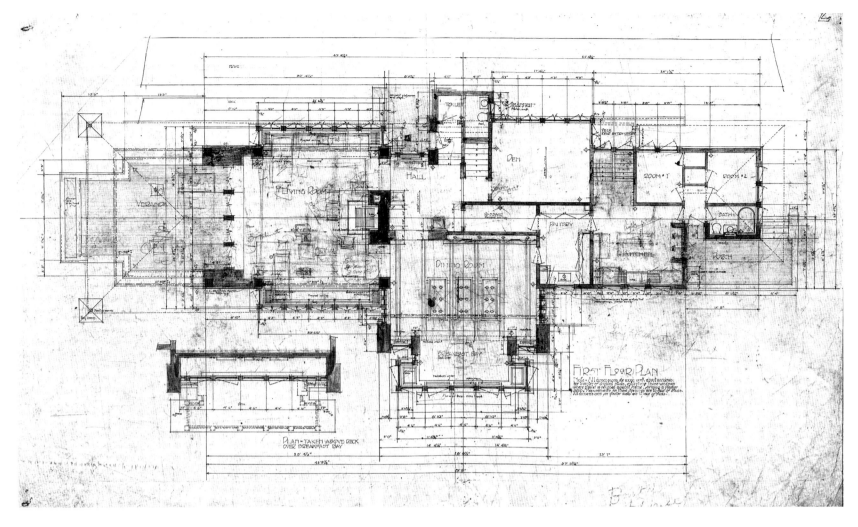

when the stained-glass lights are on at its corners, the play between the natural light coming through the leaded-glass windows and these lamps is magical.

Rotated Cubic Plans

In these designs, the plan is concentrated in a square or cubic volume, with the rooms inside pivoting around the central fireplace, resulting in a dynamic rotational movement sequence within a deceptively static exterior mass. The project for *Ladies Home Journal* called 'A Fireproof House for $5000', designed in 1906, crystalizes the development of this third major house-plan type in Wright's Prairie Period, following the dominant tripartite and secondary pinwheel plans. Unlike these two earlier prototypes, both of which are cruciform in volume, this project for an all-concrete house is a return to the cubic massing of Wright's own Oak Park House of 1889 and the Blossom House of 1892. Wright here presents a different relationship between living and dining rooms, in that the two rooms are opened to each other by being wrapped around the fireplace. The development of this deceptively simple plan can be seen in the P D Hoyt House, the Frederick Nicholas House and the Grace Fuller House, all of 1906; it is presented in its purest form in the 'Fireproof House' of the same year.

The square plan is divided first in half, with the fireplace standing at the exact centre of the house, facing into the living room that occupies the front half of the square; the dining room occupies the right rear quarter, and the kitchen is set in the left rear quarter so that the living and dining rooms are wrapped around three sides of the square. The whole is cubic in massing, with closed corners, symmetrical facades, and a flat roof cantilevered all around. The entrance is developed as a separate mass inserted into the cube, so that we move across the face of the fireplace as we enter, and a free-spanning wood beam is the only thing separating the dining room from the living room. The cubic exterior of this small house remains static and centred while the interior space is highly dynamic and rotating in nature. This compact cubic plan was built almost exactly a number of times, starting the very next year with the Stephen Hunt House in LaGrange, Illinois.

Emil Bach House, Chicago, Illinois, 1915

This cubic plan type was further developed in Wright's project for a 'Suburban House' of 1911, and built out in its definitive form in the Emil Bach House of 1915. The Bach House is on a tight, semi-urban site; its heavy, dense, brick lower floor with its closed corners protects the major rooms of the house from views in, while the plaster-clad first floor, less threatened with being seen from the street, projects bedrooms with corner windows in all four directions. The

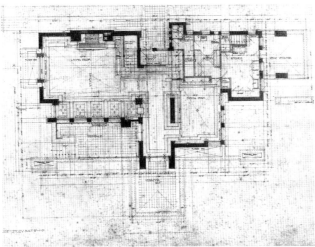

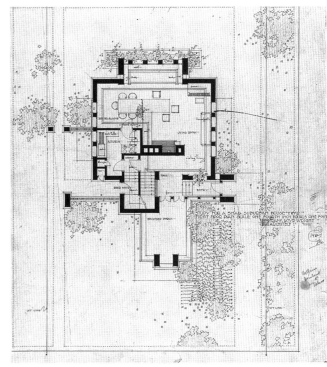

Left: Meyer May House, Grand Rapids, Michigan, 1908, view of the dining room, with original furnishings. Integral leaded glass lights are incorporated on the corner posts of the dining table. (Recent restoration by Steelcase Corporation.)
Above: View of exterior from the street.
Above centre: Ground-floor plan. The living and dining rooms are pushed to the front and back of the house, with the entrance hall both separating and joining them.
Above centre, top: Emil Bach House, Chicago, Illinois, 1915, exterior view.
Above right: Suburban House project, 1911, plan. The cubic plan type was developed in this design and built out in the Emil Bach House four years later.

lower floor is directly developed from the cubic 'Fireproof House' plan of 1906, while the upper floor unfolds into a small cruciform plan, with each bedroom projected out in its own short 'wing'. As a result of this vertical development from cubic, heavy and closed to cruciform, light and open, the Bach House is a compact form with extraordinarily dynamic qualities, and was a unique attempt by Wright to join the most successful aspects of the brick and plaster Prairie Houses. As was true of all houses utilizing the cubic plan type, the static, symmetrical and axial reading of the exterior form is contradicted by the dynamic, asymmetrical and rotational character of the interior space and its movement patterns.

We enter by moving all the way around the cubic mass to its right, where a covered entrance porch is projected out from the back of the square plan. We go up four steps to the entrance hall, which opens towards the back to a covered porch (since destroyed by an addition) and towards the front to the living room. Moving into the living room, we are now facing the street, and directly ahead our way is blocked by a set of shelves and cabinets projecting from the fireplace; we must move around these, entering the room along its outer edge. The living room wraps around the fireplace into the dining room, as was typical in these plans, so that together the two primary rooms occupied three of four quarters and corners of the

square plan – the kitchen and stair in the other. But here the fireplace faces to the right, to the south where the main windows of the living room open, rather than the street, as we might have expected from the formal pier-framed bay that projects from the house's front facade. Instead of finding a symmetrical room behind this bay, we discover that it opens off the considerably more ambiguous space joining the living and dining room. In the Bach House, there is not even the free-spanning beam to delineate the boundary between the two primary rooms – they are completely and smoothly fused into a single space.

The outer walls on the two major elevations of this double room are symmetrically divided by windows and closed corners, but the inner elevations of the rooms, defined by the fireplace and built-in dining table, are developed to express most energetically the asymmetrical character of this rotating, L-shaped space. The fireplace is the first by Wright to have an asymmetrical plan, its lintel extended to the left and butting into a brick mass set forward to the right. Shelves and a seat are projected forward from the right side of the fireplace, while the dining table and cabinets are projected backward, around the corner into the dining room to the left. In plan the fireplace is a Z shape, clearly expressing the rotational dynamic of the movement pattern in this space.

Below left: Project for
'A Fireproof House for $5000',
published in Ladies Home Journal,
1906, exterior perspective and
perspective view
of living room (below).
Below centre: 'A Fireproof House
for $5000', exterior perspective
and plans, alternate site and
ground-floor configurations (left),
and upper level.
Below right: Emil Bach House,
construction drawings showing
details of chimney and
built-in furniture.

Robert Evans House, Chicago, Illinois, 1908

The importance of the site in Wright's work is evident in the design for the Robert Evans House. While the compact 'Fireproof House' – and the later Bach House – were proposed to be built on small suburban sites, tight against neighbouring buildings, the Evans House is set on a spacious open hilltop, and here Wright unfolds the cubic plan type, combining it with the extended cruciform plan in a development and perfection of the scheme for the A P Johnson House of 1905. Wright's most extraordinary development in the Evans House is his setting of four large one-storey freestanding piers into the landscape, two on either side of the central, cubic, two-storey portion of the house; the inside edges of these piers align with the outside edges of the cubic volume. A single-storey hipped roof spans across between these pairs of piers, supported by beams running between them, intersecting the two-storey cubic mass of the house, which is topped by a pyramidal roof that projects out on all sides.

The cubic central volume of the Evans House is rotated with the orientation typical of the other house plans of this type, so that the living room, which occupies one half of the square-floor plan, is oriented to the left rather than directly facing the street and public entrance; Wright projects a raised porch surrounded by low walls out under the cover of the lower roof. The dining room is placed directly behind the fireplace so that it is centred on the living room's axis

of symmetry, and projects out the right side of the cubic volume; also covered by the lower roof on this right side are the porte-cochere and entrance stairs. The entrance occupies the near right corner of the square inner portion of the plan, with the kitchen and stair taking over the right rear corner. Between the closed corners, the central open portion of all four elevations of the cubic mass are projected out, framed by pairs of piers at the main floor, with window bays on the second floor.

The result of this setting of bounds through the placement of the terminal piers outside the enclosed volume of the house is a powerful combination of the cubic, vertical, closed centre and the spreading, horizontal, open roof and walls at the ground; the Evans House is at once anchored at its centre and reaching out at its edges. The horizontal roof extension captures outside space and draws it into the house; it also allows the interior spaces of the house, such as the dining room, to move out of the central cubic volume. Engaging the tension between the precisely defined space of the cubic central volume and the equally precisely defined space of the four piers and their horizontal roof and layered low walls, Wright develops his typical entrance sequence.

We cannot directly enter what is clearly the primary volume, and must instead move around it to the right, stepping within the bounded space defined by the four piers, under the low roof, turning left behind the low wall,

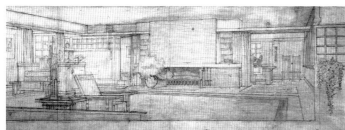

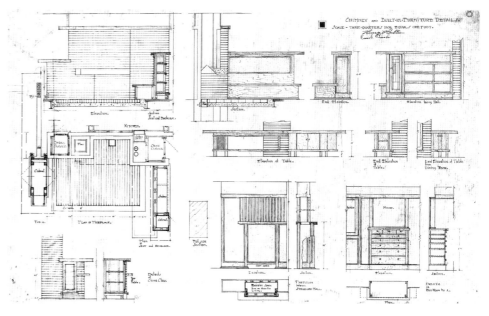

Above: Robert Evans House, Chicago, Illinois, 1908, view of dining room and plans. Above right: Robert Evans House, exterior view from the street.

up several stairs to the door. The lower ceiling, at beam or door-top height, follows us into the entrance hall, projecting into the living room to wrap the fireplace, retreating into the stairs and kitchen, reappearing again over the porch. The rest of the living room has a higher ceiling, as does the dining room, where the ceiling is folded up to recessed stained-glass light panels at the centre of the room. On the ground floor Wright uses white plaster walls, dark wood-trim, door-top beams and soffits, and vertical wood-slat screens both outside and inside in order to allow the inside to come outside and the outside to come inside, contradicting our initial hermetic reading of the central cubic mass.

In Wright's private houses, the service spaces are usually ordered by a different compositional logic than the rest of the building. In the Evans House, the kitchen is ruled out of the symmetrical order that organizes the primary rooms within pure geometrical forms; instead it creates a nongeometric, disordered back side of the house, away from the public view and entrance. Wright placed the kitchen and service spaces outside the spatial bounds set up by the four terminal piers that order the rest of the house. In addition, the service zone interrupts the pure cubic form of the central volume of the house, engulfing one corner as it attaches itself to the house. At the first floor the bedrooms

are held inside the cubic volume of the house, but their more informal planning suggests their secondary importance relative to the rigorously ordered and axially aligned public rooms of the ground floor.

IN HIS house designs Wright constructed a hierarchy of public, private and service spaces, expressing this order in plan, interior volume and exterior form. Rather than being a mistake, or the result of careless disinterest on Wright's part, or even the first full flowering of free-plan functionalism, all of which have been asserted, this distinction between the geometrically and axially ordered primary volumes and the more casually or loosely organized service spaces is clearly intentional. Wright, with his astonishing formal capacity and relentless pursuit of integrated perfection, was surely capable of placing the kitchen and other service elements in the same geometric envelope that held the other volumes of the house, if he had wished. But had he done so, the expression of the relationship between the secondary service spaces and the primary spaces they served would have been lost. Such perfect integration of all spaces within a pure geometric volume was almost always reserved by Wright for public structures, producing a precise distinction in his work between public and private buildings.

THE COURTYARD DWELLING

Left: Aline Barnsdall, 'Hollyhock'
House, Los Angeles, California,
1919, view of the courtyard. The
client, heiress to an oil fortune,
approached Wright in 1915
with the idea of constructing a
complex of buildings, including her
own house, centred around an
experimental theatre.
Above: Avery Coonley House,
Riverside, Illinois, 1907,
exterior view. The house bounds
the crest of a low hill on its large
wooded site.

Beginning with the Darwin Martin House of 1903, Wright developed for his larger house commissions a more open, less compact spatial order, involving the interlocking and interweaving on larger sites of a series of cruciform spatial focal points or pavilions, rather than the singular pyramidal form more typical of the smaller Prairie Houses. In the Harold McCormick House of 1908 and the Avery Coonley House this was distilled into Wright's own particular variant on the courtyard type, wherein the large, U-shaped house wraps and defines a courtyard, but in a loose and open-ended manner that allows for the creation of symmetrical, geometrically defined rooms within the overall asymmetrical fabric of the house and its outbuildings. In studying the beautiful site plan Wright prepared for the Coonleys, we should note that of the various buildings constructed on the site, only the garage and stables are given anything even approaching a symmetrical, cruciform shape. Indeed, at first glance the main house itself appears to be the most informally organized building in the complex; it is the landscape – in particular the enclosed gardens and large pool – that centres and focuses the entire composition.

In the large wooded site, Wright defines the courtyard space not by the construction of a wall that runs all around it, but by drawing the volumes of the house around the top of the low hill on which the house is set and by framing the courtyard partly with landscape elements such as the trellis,

pool and low walls. The courtyard is implied rather than literal; as we experience it, we find that it is sufficiently defined, even if formally incomplete. The space of this courtyard, only loosely confined, is allowed to 'leak out' by openings between the buildings and even by driveway openings cut through the first floor of the house and bridged by the rooms of the second floor.

The entrance drive enters the site from the west, passes under the kitchen and along the southern edge of the entrance court, exiting under the guest wing. It is flanked by a walkway that cuts straight through the site and across one edge of the courtyard. Another linear spatial element defining the edge of the court space is the walled garden projecting off the guest bedroom and flanked at its end by a pair of freestanding piers. The courtyard itself is divided into a paved entrance and service court nearest the main house and the flower and vegetable garden defined by the trellis and stables further out. The service drive enters the site from the north, passing right through the garage (similar to the way the main drive passes through the wings of the main house), discreetly sliding in along the east edge of the entrance court, gaining access to the service area, in the corner near the kitchen, walled off from the rest of the paved court.

In plan, the lower floor, split into three separate buildings by the entrance drive, is dominated by the playroom, its fireplace flanked by inglenook seats and wood-slat screens, terminating in a pair of piers. This central and most intimate space faces out, and is in turn enveloped by the U-shaped outer edge of the playroom which opens in towards the fireplace. The playroom is defined by these symmetrical sets of nesting volumes, and is in turn framed by a pair of piers behind which are positioned the two stairs, on either side of the fireplace. These are all finally surrounded by another U-shaped wall, opening out to the main terrace and pool, anchored at its ends by two enormous piers.

Though symmetrical, this playroom plan, with its open corners, interlocked, independent volumes and implied enclosure, shares its compositional logic with the courtyard. The working drawing for this lower floor contains some intriguing erasures: faint outlines show earlier positions of the playroom's outer wall, one being all the way back at the outer edge of the inglenook fireplace. This would have resulted in the living room, which sits above the playroom, hovering over an open, covered and deeply shadowed terrace. As it was finally built, only the two narrow corridors to either side of the stairs allow exterior space to deeply penetrate the volume of the house, and the living room sits on the solid, closed volume of the playroom.

Another characteristic of the Coonley House not typical of the traditional courtyard house is the fact that the primary rooms of the house, all lifted to the second floor, look outwards to the surrounding landscape rather than inwards to the courtyard. The upper floor is composed of two sets of rooms, each clustered at a corner; the more public rooms such as the living room, dining room and entrance hall, as well as the kitchen, servant and service spaces are at the west corner while the bedrooms are gathered around the east corner. Wright clearly articulates the transition between these two areas by inserting in the plan a shift in the middle of the main linear volume that defines the south side of the court, exactly where private and public zones of the house come together; the study is placed at this juncture, acting as the space of transition.

The living room and dining room, oriented ninety degrees to one another and facing out from the two sides of the corner they share in plan, are each centred on a fireplace, covered with a hipped plaster ceiling, and surrounded on three sides by continuous bands of clerestory windows. The living room overlooks the pool and terrace to the south, and when we refer again to the complete site plan, we see that the living room is located at the exact centre of the site. This again is unlike a traditional courtyard house, where the court itself occupies the geometric centre; here, as in many of Wright's houses, the relationship between the building and the landscape is one of interdependence and interpenetration, point and counterpoint.

As it was originally built, we would have approached the house from the west, moving past the edge of the dining room above and passing under the kitchen, which spans the

Right: Coonley House, site plan, the main house is below and the stables on upper right. The landscape centres and focuses the whole composition.

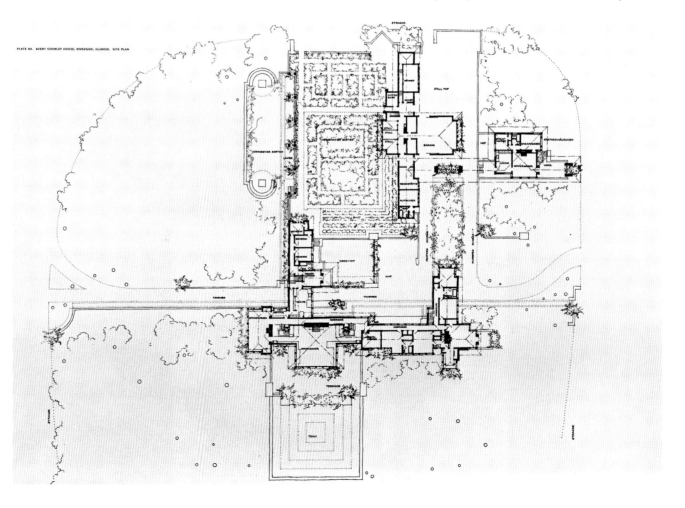

Above: Coonley House, view of the entrance courtyard.
Right: Perspective view of the living room.

driveway. The wood-frame house is clad in white stucco plaster, with large sections coloured, scored and set with tiles in bold square patterns, banded top and bottom by wooden-trim boards.[2] These patterned planes are transformed by this texturing of their surfaces so they appear to be lightweight screens, floating across the driveway openings and between the larger symmetrical masses of the projecting rooms above. Ahead of us is the entrance court, and immediately to the right, under the cover of the bridge, the front door is tucked back behind a pier; to enter, we must turn all the way around and go back parallel to the way we came.

From the entrance hall three steps to the left take us up to a landing where we can see into the playroom and where the stair descends from the main floor. Turning as we mount the stair towards the light above, we arrive facing a wall and turn left to enter the dining room, past one side of the freestanding fireplace, drawn in by the abundance of light coming from the windows on three sides. We again turn twice, reversing directions to move past the other side of the fireplace, down the sky-lit gallery to the living room.

This gallery, its symmetrical twin opening on the other side of the living room, is one of Wright's most dynamic and beautiful interior spaces. In the period photograph taken from the living room, Wright carefully composed and arranged the furniture and carpets so as to capture the sense of interpenetrating spaces: the forest mural above the bookcases to either side of the fireplace runs along the wall behind the stair, which is surrounded by a low wood-panel wall; the peaked ceiling – with its wood and stained-glass skylight – runs down one side of the space, interlocking with and carving into the larger living-room ceiling (floating above the free-spanning beam at its edge), and terminating in the brick back wall of the dining-room fireplace; the hallway itself occupies the other side of the space, with the opening into the dining room at its end; the long carpet runs through the doorway into the dining room, while the carpet at the living room end is turned ninety degrees to the longer carpet, running under the table next to the bookshelves; this table itself stands on both this carpet and the main carpet of the living room, occupying both rooms, and is in turn crossed by the cloth Wright has draped across it. With its numerous crossed trajectories of space and form, there is nothing casual about this photograph – Wright's hand is everywhere evident, and by his use of furniture and carpets to reinforce the dynamism of the built-in elements, the result is richly suggestive of the traces left by our movement and occupation.

The living room of the Coonley House is one of Wright's greatest achievements, a space of repose, as he defined it; the large, heavy and massive fireplace balanced by the

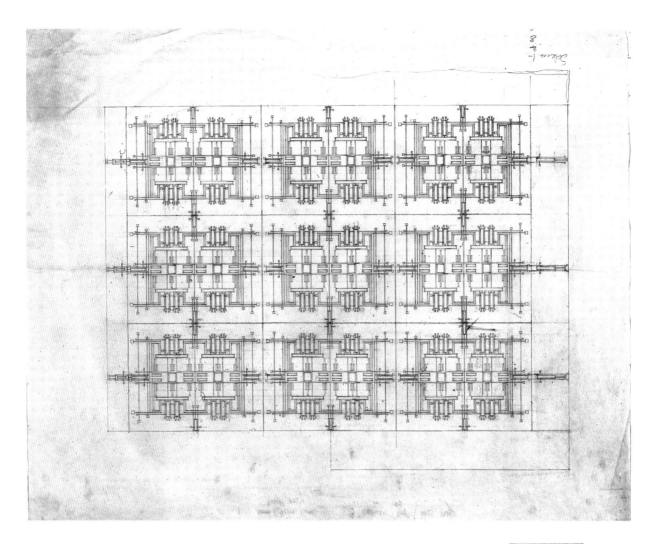

floating, folded and rhythmically modulated planes of the ceiling – cave and tent. The long horizontal forest mural running under the edge of the ceiling behind the fireplace joins with the series of casement windows running unbroken around the other three sides of the room to lift the ceiling free of any sense of support – light emanates from the electrical fixtures recessed into its edges and from the skylights in the galleries to either side, and the forest is visible (in mural or window) all around.

Wright's preference for the casement window (which swings open like a door) – as opposed to what he called the 'poetry-crushing' guillotine window (which slides vertically to open) – came from his emphasis on the experience of occupying the spaces inside; the casement window operates as the human arm swings, out from the centre, and the opening is full, not halfway like the guillotine window. Here in the Coonley House they are filled with a delicate pattern of leaded and coloured glass, and the overall effect makes us feel that we are deep in the forest, sheltered next to the fireplace, yet free to look out from our higher vantage point over the site below. Though the Coonley House does not possess the geometrical purity and rigorous order of many of the more famous Prairie Houses, it is important to note that Wright himself felt it was his best house of this period.

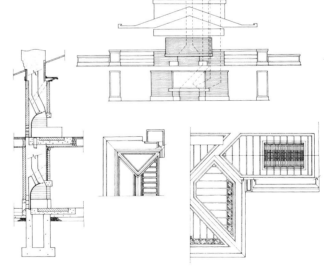

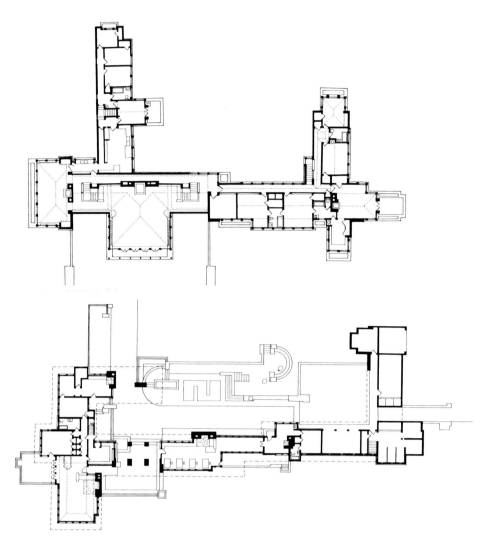

Above: Plans of Coonley House (above) and Taliesin (below) shown at the same scale. Opposite: Taliesin, Spring Green, Wisconsin, 1911–25.

The Oak Park Studio and the Prairie School

Shortly after the opening of his own practice in 1893, Wright began to operate from his studio in Oak Park, employing a number of talented young architects, including Barry Byrne, Charles White, Marion Mahony, Walter Burley Griffin and William Drummond, among others. These were not apprentices, as Wright would later have at Taliesin, but true associates; while it is clear that Wright was the designer for the office – none of these architects ever claimed otherwise – these young designers were nevertheless able to engage in critical discussions with Wright during the development of the designs. The extraordinary quality of design that marks Wright's Prairie Period is at least partially due to this constructive criticism from his associates, and the efforts on Wright's part to educate and instil in these associates his emerging principles for building form and space.

As a founder of the Chicago School, where, as David Van Zanten has noted, 'the foremost issue was always how one put things together', Wright developed a system of design that was intended to be harmonious, logical and inevitable, where 'geometric purity was a means to expedite assembly, achieving a kind of mechanical self-generation in architectural composition'.[3] To this end, Wright often presented his designs in general form to his employees; as a former apprentice stated: 'The development of all implied but not

delineated portions of the project then became the problem of the student draftsman, subject to the master's approval and correction.'[4] By the time of the Coonley House, Wright had become, with Sullivan's decline, the leader of the loosely defined Chicago School or 'New School of the Midwest', which included in addition to his own associates a number of former colleagues from Silsbee's and Sullivan's offices, including George Mahler and Grant Elmslie, among others.

While the spatial and formal concepts Wright developed in his Prairie Houses continued uninterrupted in his work, his private life during this period was another matter.[5] Wright had from the start spent more time and energy on his practice than on his marriage and family – even the renovations of his own house seemed to be a distraction from the family. As he himself wrote: 'Young husband more interested in the house than in his bride, so the young wife said to him again and again.'[6] Sometime after building the house for Edwin Cheney in 1903, Wright began an affair with his client's wife, Mamah Borthwick Cheney, that was to culminate in 1909 with Wright abandoning his wife and six children to go to Europe with Mrs Cheney.

Wright had been asked to produce a volume of drawings for the publisher Wasmuth of Berlin, and in 1909 he moved to Fiesole, Italy, near Florence, to undertake the drawings.[7] In doing so, Wright left his successful practice in the hands of a recently hired associate, foregoing the chance to build

very large and expensive houses recently commissioned from him by Henry Ford and Harold McCormick, two of America's most important industrialists. As a subtle reference to Wright's travel companion, we should note the only time the plans of two different houses appear on one plate in the first Wasmuth portfolio: Wright placed 'A House for an Artist', an astonishingly dynamic project clearly intended for himself, side by side with the plan of the Cheney House, the house he built for his lover.

Soon after Wright's sudden removal to Europe, the Oak Park Studio employees began to disband, opening practices of their own, sometimes with work from former clients of Wright. Wright later berated his former associates for using his forms, opening his second 'In the Cause of Architecture' article with the statement, 'Style, therefore, will be the man. It is his. Let his forms alone.' Yet he also wrote in the same article: 'Were no more to come of my work than is evident at present [1914], the architecture of the country would have received an impetus that will finally resolve itself into good.'[8] Indeed, just as the Columbian Exhibition had actually been the provocation that helped bring the Chicago School into existence in 1893, Wright's abandonment of his Oak Park practice resulted in the blossoming of the Prairie School. Wright's former associates and followers were now on their own, out from his considerable shadow, and his influence spread even as he criticized the results.[9]

Taliesin, Spring Green, Wisconsin, 1911, 1914 and 1925

In Europe, the first Wasmuth portfolio was to have enormous influence following its publication in 1910, and this only increased the following year when Wasmuth produced a second Wright portfolio, this one containing photographs of built works.[10] Wright returned from Europe in 1911 to find his practice dissolved, his clients gone, and his wife Catherine demanding that he renovate his studio into apartments in order to raise money to support his six children. Even as he opened an office in downtown Chicago, Wright began construction of a home and office in the Lloyd Jones family valley near Spring Green, Wisconsin.

Wright called this house Taliesin, the name of an ancient Welsh poet, also meaning 'shining brow'. This seemed an appropriate name to Wright, given his decision to attenuate the house and wrap it around the hill, leaving the top of the hill to be enclosed in the loosely defined entrance court. He wrote: 'I knew well that no house should ever be put *on* a hill or *on* anything. It should be *of* the hill. Belonging to it. Hill and house should live together each the happier for the other.'[11] In this design, similar to the Coonley House of 1908 and the A W Cutten and Sherman Booth Houses, both of 1911, Wright developed the large domestic complex as a series of semi-independent pavilions, linked by pergolas and woven in an informal manner into its site.[12] From its first inception, the domestic portion of Taliesin was

Left: Taliesin, view along the drive at the edge of the hilltop courtyard.
Above: View from the bottom of the hill towards the house's cantilevered lookout balcony, entered from the dining room.
Right: Ground-floor plan of the original 1911 construction.

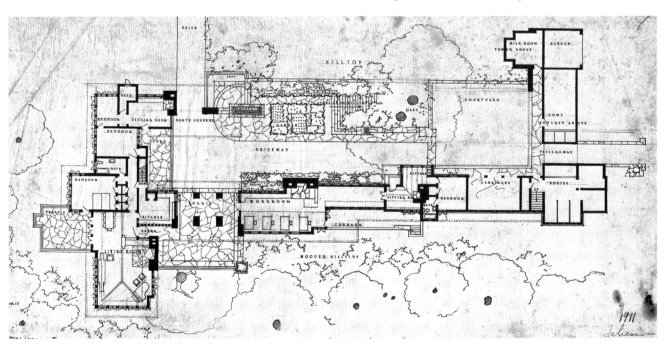

basically asymmetrical and L-shaped in plan, wrapped around a garden – the same basic scheme that would be used for the majority of the Usonian Houses, the first of which was built over twenty-five years later.[13] Again, as he had done with his home and studio in Oak Park in 1889–95, Wright developed first in his own house the spatial order which was used extensively in his later domestic commissions.

The first Taliesin had the living-dining room and bedroom projecting out from two sides of the east corner of the hill, sharing the southeast-facing terrace between them. The low one-storey design consisted of the private house which was separated from the draughting room and office by an open-air loggia, providing a spectacular view back across the valley upon entry. The courtyard opened to the southwest, anchored at the corner opposite the house by the garage, stables, servants' quarters and service buildings. The house was entered directly from the loggia, and one came in from behind and along the edge of the fireplace. Ahead was the dining table and beyond that the terrace, to the left opened the living room with views out in three directions.

The living-dining room was again photographed with the furniture and carpets carefully arranged by Wright: the folded plaster ceiling opens off to the right, while on the floor the rug moves left out the terrace door; the dining table and chair (an astonishingly abstract design for 1911) are moved slightly left of centre, while the Japanese screen behind is moved slightly to the right of centre – nothing is

allowed to occupy the exact geometric centre of the space, and everything seems to be in balance. The house's large piers and fireplace walls were built of flat stones from nearby hills and stream beds, laid roughly so that they protruded in small ledges as they had in their original condition. Stucco, made of the yellow sand from the Wisconsin River, covered the wood frame construction of the walls where continuous bands of casement windows wrapped around the main rooms, and the wood frame and cedar-shingle hipped roofs hovered over it all.

In 1914, as Wright worked in Chicago on the construction site of the Midway Gardens, at Taliesin a deranged servant killed seven people with a hatchet, including Mamah Cheney and her children, and burned Wright's house to the ground. This incomprehensible disaster seemed to make Wright's commitment to Taliesin all the stronger, and he soon began its reconstruction and enlargement.

The draughting room had not been destroyed in the fire, and the residence in this second Taliesin (1914) was built directly on the ruins of the first. New details, such as the roof ventilators over the kitchen, brought into the otherwise quiet entrance court the dynamic 'crossed trajectories' of the Robie House.[14] On the downhill side of the house, Wright developed and concentrated the habitable volume in the middle of the elevation or section such that the upper and lower edges of the house were allowed to merge with the sky and ground, respectively; the rock walls meet the

PRELIMINARY STUDY OF
TALIESIN SPRING GREEN
WISCONSIN

*Left: Taliesin II, period
photograph taken in 1914 of
the entrance loggia and the
hilltop courtyard.
Above: Taliesin II, aerial
perspective of the 1914
reconstruction, after the
devastating fire earlier that year.
Right: Taliesin I, period
photograph of 1911 (probably
taken by Wright), view from the
living room to the dining alcove,
with furniture arranged
by Wright.*

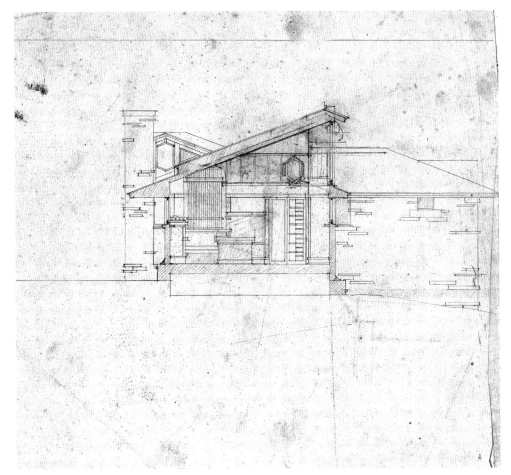

Left: Taliesin II, period photograph of 1914 (probably taken by Wright), showing a view of the loggia with furniture arranged by Wright.
Above left: Section through the architecture studio and office.
Above right: Period photograph of 1914 (probably taken by Wright), showing a view of the studio and office, with plaster models of the San Francisco Call Building and the Larkin Building.

earth, the vertical posts of the screened loggia turn the corner (without horizontal members – a vertical interpretation of the corner window) to merge with the sky, and the low, horizontal plaster wall spans the entire elevation, holding the main-floor level of the house. Once again, in a photograph taken by Wright, we see him arranging the furniture in a dynamic configuration in the corner of the loggia, as if to give further evidence that the basic underlying spatial order of this house depends on the space formed by corners and edges, rather than centres; while the courtyard occupies the centre of the site, we inhabit its edges.

Taliesin burned again in 1925, the fire apparently caused this time by a lightning strike, and Wright again rebuilt it that same year, larger and even more permanent. First seen from below, across the lakes created by a series of dams designed by Wright, we approach Taliesin by circling the hill and climbing up to enter the hilltop courtyard from behind the house, through its southward, open side. The driveway originally ran along the southeast edge, with the crown of the hill on our left and the private dwelling on our right; straight ahead was the loggia that separated the workspaces from the dwelling. At the other end of the house, where the service wing wraps around the other side of the hill, Wright built a tower, the only two-storey element to rise above the hilltop. Neil Levine has said:

The tower indicates the deepest penetration of the house into the hill and can thus be read as an eccentric vertical axis staking the building to the site as the house unwinds in a spiraling, counterclockwise direction around the hill to the entrance. Instead of revolving around an internal element, like the fireplace core of the typical Prairie house, Taliesin takes its direction from an external, natural feature of the landscape.[15]

Standing in this court, we are aware that the floor of the house is set well below the top of the hill, the crown of the hill rises above the low roof eaves, enclosed by the house and given an intimacy of place impossible for a typical exposed hilltop. Water, driven uphill using a waterfall-driven pump in the dam below – the dam which, as Wright said, 'raised the water [level] in the valley to within sight of Taliesin'[16] – runs through a series of fountains, channels and pools placed around the hilltop courtyard. We find large oak trees occupying the grassy court, with low rock walls making the transition at the edges. As Wright said, here 'it was not easy to tell where the pavements and walls left off and the ground began',[17] and the fountains and gardens draw us into the terraced entrance space at the loggia.

The interior spaces of Taliesin are ordered in a way quite different from the Prairie Houses; the wings and rooms are loosely organized, without the symmetry and formal order either in the parts or their groupings that was typical of

Wright's earlier work. Here the order is more subtle and less geometric, determined instead by the circumstances of the natural topography of the hilltop and the specific orientation and views to the surrounding landscape. Taliesin, as we visit it today, has the entrance to the dwelling through a line of square stone piers to the southeast; the original drive has been closed and the dwelling's garden room has been built across it. Upon passing through the piers, which open into a loggia at the centre of the plan, we turn left down a hall that terminates in the living room.

Ahead our way is blocked by the bookcase and inglenook-seat wall that extends halfway into the room, and the ceiling opens up overhead in a series of interlocking folded plaster planes angled at the gentle slope of the roofs outside, with clerestory windows opening in several directions. We must turn to the right, moving around the dining table and chairs; now directly ahead is the 'Birdwalk', an extraordinarily long and narrow balcony cantilevered out across the valley, giving a view of the Lloyd Jones family chapel. The room is banded above door height by a wood board-faced soffit, which hovers over the entrance from the hall, the fireplace, and opens its lower ceiling generously over the extension Wright added to the living room's southeast side. Turning as we pass the end of the freestanding wall, we now see the full length of the room,

and windows open on three sides, giving expansive views to the hills on the other side of the valley. Turning back, we see both the vertical lift of the ceiling centring over the dining table, giving it a sense of being a room within a room, and the horizontal mass of the fireplace's stonework, beautifully composed of smaller slabs holding up the single enormous stone that spans the opening. While, in our experience, this fireplace is the centre of gravity for the entire house, we should note that it is not at the geometric centre of the plan.

Wright's own bedroom-study was added to the other end of this wing, where before there had been an enclosed garden, the room and its large terrace facing southwest. Anchored back to the rest of the house out of which it protrudes by a fireplace we pass upon entering, this room is opened on three sides to the views of valley, hillside and hilltop with continuous windows and glass doors. The ceiling is low and flat, a square section ringed with six-inch tall clerestory windows rises in the centre of the room. The glass wall on to the terrace slides open so that the two spaces may be joined in good weather, and one may enter the courtyard gardens directly from here. Period photographs do not show the bed, and suggest that Wright spent most of his time in this room working on his designs, able to oversee the courtyard, and thus the rest of the complex, from this vantage point.[18]

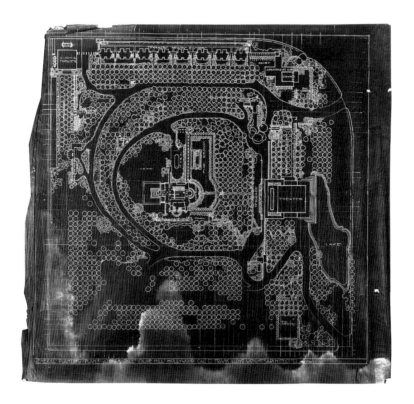

The architectural studio is entered from the original loggia, and today is a large space not unlike the living room, with a high, folded, hipped plaster ceiling with wood-slat ribbing running the direction of the joists beneath. The studio focuses on the stone fireplace, where the ceiling is folded back up to produce a higher space at the hearth. Built into the courtyard wall, the fireplace is located at the corner of the room between the wider studio and the narrower library beyond, and along with the cubic stone vault for Wright's drawings and Japanese prints, it serves to anchor the lighter plaster planes of ceiling and walls. The draughting room activities were removed to the Hillside School complex in 1932, so we must refer to period photographs to sense the density of occupation evident in this studio when it was still in use. There are very few views out of the studio, and the loosely dynamic arrangement of the furniture, dominated by the huge stones of the hearth, presents a comfortable, cave-like refuge, with large plaster models (of the Larkin Building, Abraham Lincoln Center and San Francisco Press Tower) set at various heights around the room. At Taliesin Wright built his own complete, self-sustaining world: the fruit trees, vegetable gardens and farm providing sustenance for the dining table, while in the studio he gathered his earlier works around him to sustain him as he worked at his drawing table.

Aline Barnsdall, 'Hollyhock', House, Los Angeles, California, 1919

Aline Barnsdall, heiress to an oil fortune, approached Wright as early as 1915 with the idea of constructing a complex of buildings, including her own house, centred around an experimental theatre. At first apparently she was uncertain in which city the theatre should be built, and she did not settle on a specific site until 1919, when she bought the 36-acre Olive Hill in Los Angeles.[19] Wright had begun a series of generic hilltop schemes prior to Barnsdall's purchase of the site, but even afterwards design work proceeded slowly due to his involvement with the design and construction of the Imperial Hotel, which would take him to Tokyo for extended periods during the construction of the Hollyhock House.

Wright insisted from the beginning that the existing olive orchard on the hill be retained, and required new trees first be planted to fill in the empty spaces within its grid. Wright's overall site plan for Olive Hill eventually grew to include: Barnsdall's residence sitting atop the hill, facing west, a long wing extended to the north where the garage was located; the theatre behind it to the east with an apartment building for actors to its north side; streetfront shops with terrace houses above along Hollywood Boulevard to the north, anchored at one end by a cinema; and two directors' residences (A and B) scattered on the

*Below: Corner of the courtyard,
with stair to the roof terrace.
Below right: Construction drawing
details of the living room.*

side of the hill. Only the Barnsdall's Hollyhock House and the two directors' residences were to be built, the drawings executed and construction were supervised by his son Lloyd Wright and Rudolph Schindler, arguably the most gifted designer ever to work with Wright.

The main house is closely related in plan to the Edward Waller House project of 1902, in its T-shaped composition of the three main spaces, and to the Midway Gardens and the Vogelsang Dinner Gardens project, both of 1913, in its enclosure of a square courtyard behind. Barnsdall's blend of public and private in the programme for her theatre-house, or house-theatre, seems to have led Wright to design the house as an integration of symmetrical front rooms and asymmetrical secondary rooms around the court behind. The living room occupies the central volume, a double-square in plan, which is in turn flanked to either side by the music room and library. Wright utilizes paired piers to frame severely cut openings in these rectangular volumes, and separates the closed primary volumes with open loggia-like spaces, aligned with the inside edges of the courtyard.

The three front rooms are separated from those behind by a series of connected spaces including the entrance foyer, the loggia between living room and courtyard, and the hallway to the private wing of the house. On the north side of the courtyard are the dining room, kitchen and servants' quarters; on the south side are the conservatory, gallery and nursery; and the bedrooms bridge the rear or

east side of the courtyard on the first floor. There is a carefully considered asymmetry in the courtyard, with the living-room facade opening in the shadow of the loggia to the west facing the opening to the pool at the eastern end, while the pier-lined arcade on the north side faces the glass-enclosed gallery to the south. Each volume has a measure of independence in plan, and the joints between them are often open, adding to this impression.

While we may have noted the closed corners and extensive wall surface in the plan of the Hollyhock House, nothing from Wright's earlier work prepares us for the series of heavy, massive forms that we find inhabiting the top of Olive Hill. The beautiful ink-wash perspective drawing, apparently executed by Wright's son Lloyd in 1921, showing an aerial view of the Hollyhock House, is virtually an exact match with the view of the so-called Nunnery, a Maya structure at Uxmal, seen from the Pyramid of the Magician: the walls flat near the ground and sloped back above, with a horizontal decorative frieze at their juncture; the proportions and dimensions of the thin, long, rectangular, flat-roofed massive volumes with roof terraces, set so that their ends do not align and their joints therefore remain open and of course the distinctive central courtyard. As this drawing is not taken from any existing vantage point on Olive Hill, while the Nunnery at Uxmal can *only* be seen from above at this angle, we are left to wonder if Wright provided this clue to confirm that, as has

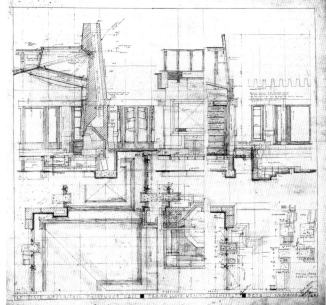

Top: Aerial perspective of the Hollyhock House, drawn by Lloyd Wright.

Above: Nunnery at Uxmal, Yucatan, Mexico, as seen from the 'Pyramid of the Magician'. This famous view, widely published in the early part of this century, was probably used by Wright and his son Lloyd in laying out the aerial perspective of the Barnsdall House. The drawing's massing details at the corners, and beveled upper portions, closely parallel this view, and it is possible that the Wright drawing was begun by tracing over a photograph of the Nunnery.

Overleaf: View from the semicircular amphitheatre in the garden, under the bridge, through the courtyard to the entrance loggia.

been suggested, he was at this time attempting to make a direct relation in his work towards the great monuments of the Maya in the Yucatan – powerful examples of indigenous place-making, which are not of European origin.[20] Wright had never given up his search for an appropriate American form of monumentality, and perhaps this task pressed upon him all the more forcefully as he took up residence in Japan to build the Imperial Hotel.

With its major apertures being clusters of windows recessed behind paired piers at the centre of each elevation (again similar to the solid brick lower floors of Prairie Houses such as the Barton House of 1903), this largely single-storey house presents an image of solidity hardly matched even by Wright's public commissions, with which it would at first glance appear to share its construction in reinforced concrete. But his search for monumentality had in this case taken Wright away from his sense of appropriate and expressive use of construction materials, for the Hollyhock House is in fact built of wood frame and hollow tile faced with stucco, and only the decorative details are made of cast stone – an early form of unreinforced precast concrete.

Despite this fact, Henry Russell Hitchcock, in his monograph on Wright of 1942, states that the Hollyhock House is a 'domestic use of exposed poured concrete'.[21] Hitchcock researched and wrote his book, titled

significantly enough *In the Nature of Materials*, under Wright's supervision at Taliesin, and with his approval. We can only assume that Wright agreed to this false assertion because poured-in-place reinforced concrete is what he wished the Hollyhock House had been built of, rather than the lightweight wood and thin stucco. Wright perpetuated this myth by labelling a photo of Hollyhock Residence A as 'Glass and Concrete' in a 1928 publication.[22] He was to address and remedy this matter of the tectonic 'ethic' in his work with the remarkable series of concrete block houses built in Los Angeles in the next few years.

In the entrance court to the north of the house, we confront a distinctly asymmetrical facade, its centre hidden behind the foliage of a flower garden. The entrance is indicated by a pergola which extends from the house along the south edge of the entrance court, and from which the inner columns are dropped in the last section to produce a cantilevered roof. Where the columns return to both sides there is a half flight of stairs up. Moving along this asymmetrical pergola, we find the door recessed deep into the mass of the house ahead; we must move into a small space, where the walls are stepping in as they rise, to find a solid pair of precast concrete entrance doors, each weighing 300 pounds – yet they open easily, and in this unexpected and astonishing way we enter the house. To our left the dining room opens immediately up four stairs, to

Above: View of the living room with the fireplace on the left, and the built-in couch and table at the centre.
Far right: Corner of the living room with the 'Hollyhock' motif in cast stone cladding on the column.

our right the music room is visible through a screen of vertical wooden slats, and directly ahead is the loggia, between the courtyard and living room. The low ceiling of the entrance pergola follows us in to the loggia, where it lifts to either side, and the light level suddenly rises as well. Across the sun-drenched court we can see the circular pool under the second-storey bedroom 'bridge', and the stepped semicircular 'seating' in the garden behind.

Turning, we enter the living room which is dominated by the fireplace at the centre of the south wall to our right. Placed asymmetrically in plan (as it was in certain Prairie houses such as the Barton House), this fireplace reorients the room about itself and simultaneously allows the axis generated by the courtyard to run uninterrupted through the house. As we have noted, the larger portion of the house – that surrounding the courtyard – is asymmetrical in plan, and the position of the fireplace now draws our attention to the subtler asymmetries within the front portion of the plan, such as the music room which is open to the living room while the library is closed off by a solid wall. Along with the fireplace, these asymmetrical aspects respond to the movement sequence, which does not primarily utilize the axis of symmetry, and the location of entry, which comes in from one side of that axis.

The fireplace itself is an amazing element, assembled from randomly sized and smoothly finished blocks of cast stone, it carries on its mantel an asymmetrical design, purportedly portraying Barnsdall as an Indian princess sitting on a throne surveying distant mesas, but only recognizable as an abstract design related to Wright's designs at the fireplaces of the Imperial Hotel. Unique in all of Wright's designs, this fireplace mass is topped by a skylight, covered by a wood-slat screen, and the fireplace's hearthstone seems to float in a pool of water. Carried in channels under the foundations, this water flows from the circular pool at the end of the courtyard, through the fireplace pool, and out to the square pool at the front of the house – originally connected to a small waterfall above the theatre, which would have completed the axis that binds the house to the court and the site.[23] In this fireplace (as he would again at Fallingwater), Wright brings together in one place the four elements: earth, fire, water and light (or air).

The living-room ceiling is made up of gently sloping coloured plaster planes elegantly trimmed in wood and edged by a wood-faced soffit that rings the room at door-top height and carries recessed uplights; it is similar to those in Wright's original Taliesin and the beautiful living room of the second Francis Little House, built in Wayzata, Minnesota in 1912.[24] The furniture in the living room, recently restored, responds to the fireplace, skylight and pool; two enormous couches, each set at a forty-five-degree angle to the fireplace and anchored at their outer edges with

133

large vertical uplights, dominate the centre of the room, and block movement on its central axis.

The dining chairs Wright designed for the Hollyhock House may be best understood literally as stage props for the dramatic public dinners the room was intended to house. It is certain that here Wright sacrificed comfort to the design coherence of the whole, for these chairs do not look inviting. On the other hand the leaded-glass windows,

with their delicate diagonal patterning, are among the most beautiful Wright ever designed, creating in the porch off the nursery a crystalline web-like network in space, casting thin lines and coloured splashes across the floor. At the back of the house, the sleeping alcove off Aline Barnsdall's second-storey bedroom, which is open to the nursery below (its full height enclosed at the exterior by a continuous vertical wall of leaded glass set between two piers) lets us feel as if we are occupying the treetops, and provides an unexpectedly private and intimate place amid this very public house.

ON THE whole, the Hollyhock House strikes those who enter it as distinctly theatrical in character, most appropriate for the home of Aline Barnsdall, who intended to play a pivotal role in the development of the American theatre, and who was responsible for the introduction of many modern innovations, both in acting and its setting. This theatrical character to be found in Wright's courtyard houses as a group was if anything even more prominent in his public buildings designed in the same period, which were likewise organized around and focused upon a central courtyard.

THE COURTYARD
PUBLIC SPACE

What *is* reality here in this so familiar object
we call a drinking glass? The answer is, reality is
the space within into which you can put something.
And so it is with everything you can
experience as reality.

Frank Lloyd Wright[1]

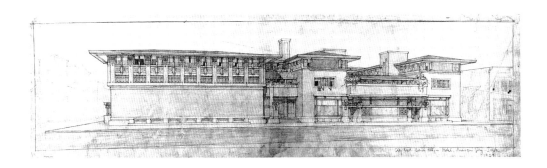

Left: Project for Cinema, San Diego, California, 1905, perspective of front elevation. The elevation is a closed at the top, with the opening for entry made between heavy masonry piers at the base.
Above: City National Bank and Hotel, Mason City, Iowa, 1909, perspective from the street.

In the later Prairie Period, from 1909 to 1920, Wright designed a series of public buildings that focused in upon interior courtyards; introverted, opening upwards, and not allowing eyelevel views out, as was typical of his earlier public buildings, these interior court spaces tended to be less vertical in orientation and more directly related to the horizontal terraces of their own interior landscapes. In contrast to the private courtyard houses we examined in the last chapter, which are asymmetrical in plan, these public courtyard spaces are rigorously symmetrical, continuing Wright's use of symmetry as a way of distinguishing and delineating the public and private realms. While symmetrical, these courtyard public buildings are rarely entered on centre, or on any axis of symmetry; rather they utilize the spiralling movement around the edges of the solid central mass typical of all of Wright's work.

In these designs the solid central elevation often is broadly extended into a horizontal mass, as first seen in the Yahara Boat Club project of 1905. Wright had earlier developed designs intended for urban 'infill' sites, where, due to shared party walls with the buildings on either side, the front elevation had to act simultaneously as the closed protective wall and the revelation of spaces within. The Cinema San Diego project of 1905, the various designs for a Bank for Frank Smith of 1904, and the unbuilt design for Wright's own office in Chicago's Goethe Street of 1911, all present a closed solid block at the top of the elevation, with the opening for entry made between heavy masonry piers at the base.

The City National Bank and Hotel, built in Mason City, Iowa, in 1909, is one of Wright's most interesting designs of the period, though it is rarely studied. On the irregular site, Wright placed the rectangular (double-square) banking hall at the corner, facing the main street; inside is a two-storey volume with two enormous piers carrying two beams that split the space down the centre over the front door. The broader side of the banking hall faces the smaller side street, and behind the bank is the hotel, a U-shaped mass opening towards the street, filled in at the lower floors by the lobby and terrace above. The banking hall has only high windows and is closed at eyelevel – with a single entrance at the centre, while the hotel is entered through two equal front doors at each edge – focusing inwards on to the glass-roofed café on the ground floor, and the rooms look into the light court on the two upper floors. The elevation along the side street is a masterpiece of integration, with the bank being closed at its lower level and open above while the hotel is open below and closed above; with this complementary massing and fenestration pattern, Wright brings the disparate functional elements into a highly resolved and beautifully proportioned composition.

Wright explored the theme of an enclosed volume that opens to a lower walled garden as early as 1898 in the

Right: Project for Frank Lloyd Wright Studio and Residence, Goethe Street, Chicago, Illinois, 1911, perspective of street front.

Mozart Gardens Restaurant project, where an enclosed volume is set along the street, entered only at its ends, with a larger terraced garden and bandstand behind. A similar design was proposed for the Larkin Company Pavilion, a temporary exhibition building constructed in Jamestown, Virginia, in 1907; while today all that remains of this building is a single perspective drawing, it indicates that a taller mass, with projecting central volumes in elevation and re-entrant corners, sat partly within a larger, lower mass, with receding central volumes in elevation and projecting piers anchoring the corners – the same relation as that of Unity Temple to Unity House.

The Avery Coonley Kindergarten project of 1911 is a cruciform in plan. It has a central wall of high windows and a pair of identical entrances at either end (as in Wright's Oak Park Studio and the Hardy House), a pair of freestanding fireplaces – each opening to both sides – at either edge of the central volume (as in the River Forest Tennis Club), and a double-height volume encompassing the central crossing space of the cruciform and its rear wing (as in the Bock House), which extends into the walled garden behind – anchored there by a large freestanding fireplace with a fountain and pool at its back. (The whole design is very similar to Wright's Banff National Park Pavilion of 1911.) The kindergarten project, with its layering of horizontal and vertical planes, its extended cantilevers at the entrance and stairs, its double-height central space opening to the garden behind, and its long closed wall along the front elevation, punctuated by an arcade of piers, is in turn the direct design precursor for Midway Gardens. Once again we see how Wright designed projects of a similar programme in sequence, as variations on a common spatial theme, so that each becomes a sketch design for the next. It was this that allowed Wright to say of the design for Midway Gardens: 'The thing had simply shaken itself out of my sleeve. In a remarkably short time there it was on paper.'[2]

Midway Gardens, Chicago, Illinois, 1913
In his autobiography, Wright begins his description of Midway Gardens by recalling how his client, Edward Waller, Jr (son of the Waller in whose house the Burnham offer was made), said, '*I want to put a garden in this wilderness* of smoky dens, car-tracks and saloons' (my emphasis).[3] Wright's Midway Gardens is a courtyard public building set in an urban rather than suburban context, where he carefully and effectively brings the landscape into the city by creating within the building an enclave of 'natural' forms, the courtyard designed as a walled garden. Here the vertical orientation towards the sky common to his public buildings is not simply 'a skylit transformation of the walled paradise, it is a garden in fact, open to the sky', as Jonathan Lipman has noted.[4]

Constructed on a square site, 300 feet on each side, the design placed the 'winter garden', the major enclosed space,

Right: City National Bank and Hotel, perspective of bank interior.
Centre left: Larkin Company Exhibition Pavilion, Jamestown, Virginia, 1907, perspective.
Centre right: Project for Avery Coonley Kindergarten, Riverside, Illinois, 1911, ground-floor plan.
Bottom: Avery Coonley Kindergarten, perspective from the street.

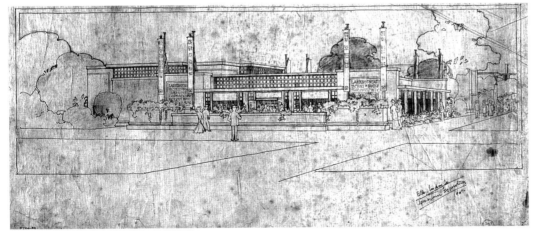

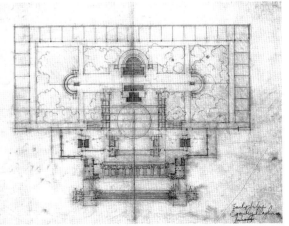

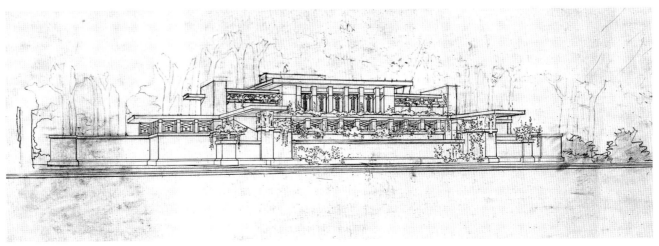

along the main street at the east edge of the site, with tall entrance pavilions set at the corners at either end of it.[5] As Wright said, 'two tall welcoming features: flat towers topped by trellises intended to be covered with vines and flowers and ablaze with light to advertise the entrances to both summer and winter gardens.'[6] The majority of the plan was occupied by the 'summer garden', a series of landscaped, paved garden terraces that stepped down towards the bandstand at the back of the site. These were flanked on the left and right by two-storey open-air arcades or galleries, similar to the mezzanines that overlook the central spaces in Unity Temple and the Larkin Building, which originate in the entrance towers and terminate in stairs leading to the lowest terrace, their patterned walls extending to wrap around the bandstand.

The symmetrical primary axis of the design originates in the winter garden, passes through the summer-garden terraces and terminates in the bandstand at the other end of the site. The major outdoor cross-circulation is the upper terrace, at the same level as the side arcades or galleries in which it originates, placed between the two primary volumes of the winter garden and the summer garden; it is in the same position as entrance occurs in Unity Temple.[7] The major interior cross-circulation runs parallel to the upper terrace, includes the wide hallways or promenades that originate in the entry towers and pierces the centre of the winter garden; on the street side of this interior circulation spine the bar and club room are placed. The huge kitchen is set in the basement under the winter garden and upper terrace, with stairs emerging at the lower terrace and dumb-waiter lifts set in two corners of the interior winter garden. Ramps emerge out in the summer-garden terraces next to low roofed drink stands and tunnels run under the arcades to dumb-waiter lifts at the edges of the lowest terrace near the bandstand.

Wright's beautiful aerial perspective drawing of Midway Gardens, with its carefully inked foliage and red dots of colour to indicate the tile patterns of the walls, gives the best overview of the design, and indicates to what degree Wright considered it a work of both landscape and architecture.[8] When he was unable to finish the construction to the level of detail that he had hoped to achieve, he wrote sadly that there was no money 'to plant the big trees at the corners of the Gardens' and to plant the flowering vines that were to climb up the tops of the entrance towers.[9] Seen from this elevated perspective, we are aware of the extensive roof terraces over the winter garden, and the balconies projecting from every tower.

Midway Gardens was built by the faithful Paul Mueller, contractor for Unity Temple and the Larkin Building; it was constructed of brick-clad steel columns and beams, steel trusses (over the winter garden), hollow brick piers carrying ventilation shafts, load-bearing brick walls and concrete floors; the walls inside and out being clad with brick, square

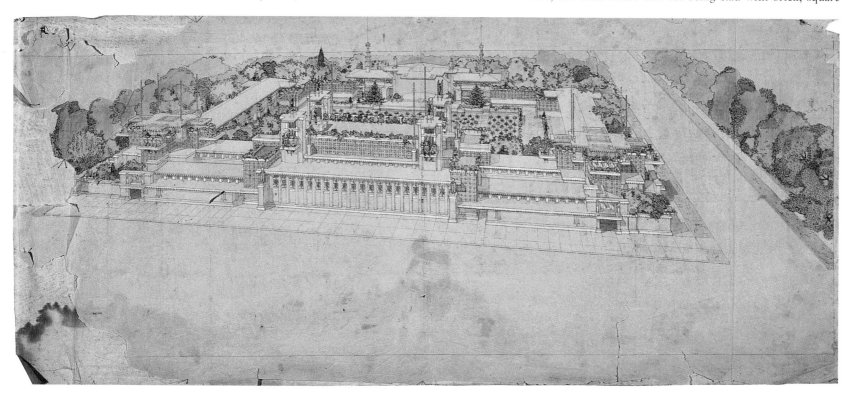

terracotta tiles, stucco plaster, coloured and patterned square site-cast concrete blocks, and site-cast coloured and patterned concrete trim; metal, stone and coloured glass decorative details abounded. From the street, we are confronted with a brick-walled enclave, piers marching across its closed main facade as the stair towers and belvederes rise above the heavy lower masses, their spires, trellises and cantilevered balconies inviting us to find our way to the space within. Entry is indicated by the canopies cantilevered from the corner towers or 'belvederes', as Wright named them in plan, which reach across the sidewalk near the street corners at the two ends of the building.

We enter by first moving under these canopies, the low ceiling suddenly giving way to the three-storey, top-lit, trellis-roofed entrance hall, an open-air square pavilion with four square columns set into its centre, defining the four circulation paths that cross here: the two entrances from the street, the axis to the winter garden (terminating in a glass-enclosed volume that projects into the belvedere) and the arcade along the sides of the summer garden. In winter, we move along the edge of the belvedere to access the door at the side of the glass foyer; only at this point do we enter an enclosed, heated space. We go down several steps and walk along the 'promenade', the cloakroom is to one side and a walled sunken garden to the other, the ceiling drops over our heads again as we move under the balcony and

emerge in the winter garden. It is a large, three-storey space lit by windows at the rear of the side balconies and by leaded-glass clerestories at the very top.

The plan of the winter garden is related to that of the Christian Catholic Church of 1911–15 (discussed in Chapter 14), while the section is related to that of the Larkin Building of 1903. The rectangular main volume is anchored at its corners by four-pier pairs that enclose the stairs and are flanked by the toilet rooms. The tiled main floor is composed of a series of small interior terraces which are stepped back as they rise from the centre to the edges, similar and parallel to the terraces of the summer garden, with one mezzanine balcony on each of the wider sides and two, one above the other, on each of the narrower ends. Each set at a half level above the next, these balconies appear to grow from and intertwine around the stair towers anchoring the corners, where clusters of spherical lights are hung from the ceiling on long cables carrying small decorative cubes, spheres and pyramids. The ceiling is a massive hovering plane with no indication of the deep steel-truss structure above, from which it hangs; unlike almost all Wright's other central public spaces, the winter garden is not top lit – a clear indication of the primary importance in this design of the exterior garden space. Stairs opening from the centre of the smaller balconies at either end climb from lower side roof terraces to the highest roof terrace

Above: Midway Gardens, period photograph of the entrance and stair tower.
Far right: Midway Gardens, period photograph of view along the street facade.

over the winter garden; this can be accessed as well by the four corner stairs, which culminate in small balconies projected out over the summer garden or the street.

In the summer, we move down the arcade from the entrance belvedere, entering the summer-garden terraces without ever having passed through a door; we have been outside, under cover the whole way in, and now we step out into the open air to take our seat. Period photos taken while the building was occupied, usually at night, show it filled with people, the towers lit by floodlights, the decorative spires – called 'electric needles' by Wright – carrying a profusion of lamps, the sculpture lit in profile by small bulbs, and the tables on the garden terraces illuminated by the poles holding diagonally stepped square lights. In the daytime, the sunlight made complex patterns as it struck the square block walls or passed through the trellises, terracotta panels and metal trimwork at the roof edges. From the summer-garden terraces, the winter garden appears at yet another set of surrounding walls, its patterned spandrels spanning from edge to edge so that it seems to have no mass and contain no volume, its closest edge the same height as the open arcades to either side. The gentle stepping down of the terraces towards the centre, the permeable boundaries of arcades and balconies, the layering of walls, floors and roofs, the profusion of patterned planes and forms and the vibration of their ornamented surfaces, all combine to create

enclosure without any sense of constraint: our eye is free to move, yet we cannot see anything that is not part of Wright's self-contained garden of delights.

Much of the sculpture, furniture, lighting fixtures, dishware, decorative patterns and details Wright designed for Midway Gardens were executed with the help of Richard Bock and Alfonso Ianelli. Wright designed the bandstand based upon his experience with the Auditorium Building and other opera houses and theatres designed at Adler and Sullivan, and it proved to be remarkably effective. For both eye and ear, the whole has a degree of cohesion and integration that is exceptional even in Wright's work. As he wrote:

> I meant to get back to first principles – pure form in everything, weave a masonry fabric, a beautiful pattern in genuine materials and good construction. Forms could be made into a festival for the eye no less than music made a festival for the ear ... the straight line, square, triangle and circle I had learned to play with in the Kindergarten were set to work in this developing sense of abstraction to characterize the architecture, painting and sculpture of the Midway Gardens.[10]

Midway Gardens was designed, built and opened in a remarkably short period of time, and though it did not have the plantings, coloured walls and coloured glass to be set into the concrete tiles, and 'gay coloured balloons of various sizes in great numbers [that] were to have flown high above

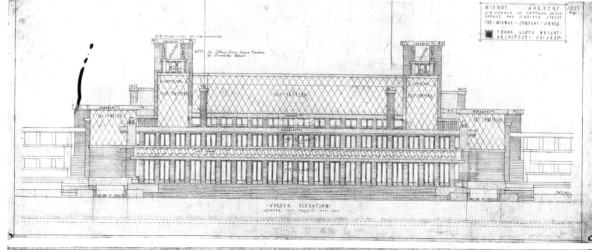

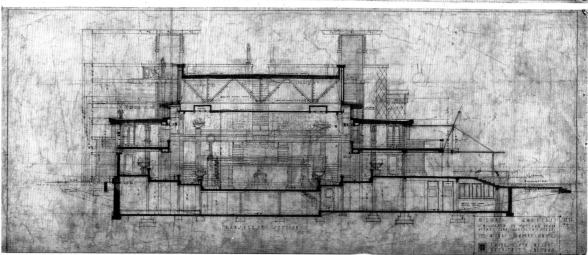

the scene, anchored to the electric needles and tower features'; and though the 'sky-frames on the four towers' were never completed as Wright designed them, it remains without question one of his greatest works. Though unfinished, its opening was a smashing success. As Wright said: 'as brilliant a social event as Chicago ever knew. In a scene unforgettable to all who attended, the architectural scheme and colour, form, light and sound had come alive. And this scene came upon the beholders as a magic spell.'[11]

The spell was broken when Prohibition put the Midway Gardens and all other places of entertainment out of business in 1920. This magical place, which Lipman rightly calls Wright's 'most essential rendering of the consecrated public space', passed through several owners, who painted the concrete and turned the summer garden into an ice rink.[12] It was finally, as Wright put it, 'mercifully destroyed' in 1929, and he ironically notes that the contractor who demolished the building found it so solidly constructed that he lost more than his bid.[13] While Prohibition was eventually repealed, we cannot bring back a demolished building – Midway Gardens is yet another of Wright's greatest works lost to us forever.

Imperial Hotel, Tokyo, Japan, 1914–22
Just following the opening of Midway Gardens, Wright received a delegation from Japan in search of an architect for the new Imperial Hotel, to be built in Tokyo on a site across from the Imperial Gardens and Palace. His visitors were moved by Taliesin, where, beyond the more obvious evidence, such as the profusion of Japanese wood-block prints Wright had collected and displayed, they no doubt sensed the effects of Wright's lifelong sympathy for Japanese building and culture. Wright had visited Japan briefly before, as early as 1905, but with this commission he would spend the next several years of his life there, now having the time to study directly what he had before only known from prints and books. He wrote: 'the Japanese house naturally fascinated me and *I would spend hours taking it all to pieces and putting it together again.* I saw nothing meaningless in the Japanese house.'[14] (My emphasis.)

Wright stated that the Japanese prints, about which he had written a book in 1912, had 'taught me much. The elimination of the insignificant, a process of simplification in art in which I was myself already engaged, beginning with my twenty-third year, found much collateral evidence in the print.' Wright had long found Japanese art and architecture to be 'nearer to the earth and a more indigenous product of native conditions of life and work, therefore more nearly *modern* as I saw it, than any European civilization alive or dead.'

We see here the difference between Wright's definition of what it was to be a 'modern' architect and the definition

Above right: Period photograph of the view from the bandstand to the 'winter garden', the service from the kitchen is through the covered stairs at left and right middleground.
Right: Period photograph of the view from the side terrace across the main garden dining space, with the 'winter garden' on the left.

that was just beginning to emerge from Europe, and which would be formalized in the 1932 Museum of Modern Art exhibition entitled 'The International Style'. Wright believed that to be 'modern', architecture must engage with the earth, its foundation, by employing the 'indigenous' materials and programmes of one's period and place, yet also following the timeless principles of 'simplification' and 'elimination of the insignificant'. Wright believed that the stylistic appearance of a building was perhaps its least 'modern' attribute, and he saw the Europeans as promulgating merely a new formal style they called 'modern architecture', which was *not* 'modern' precisely because it required its practitioners to reject the ordering principles underlying the great buildings of the past. On the other hand, Wright believed that his own work displayed the understanding that to be 'modern' one must first rediscover the demanding precision of the discipline of architecture, a tradition he found to be very much alive in the arts and architecture of Japan.

Wright's design for the Imperial Hotel, while unprecedented in scale in his earlier work, is related in plan to the larger cruciform house designs, such as that for Darwin Martin of 1903, C Thaxter Shaw of 1906, and Harold McCormick of 1907, as well as a series of public commissions, such as the Horseshoe Inn of 1908, the Midway Gardens of 1913, the Vogelsang Dinner Gardens project of 1914 and the United States Embassy project in Tokyo of 1914; these latter all are characterized by a bi-axial, symmetrical, central volume with lower wings projected to either side, framing the garden space in which the primary volume is set. Wright's initial design for the Imperial Hotel, developed at Taliesin in 1914, established the basic plan: a symmetrical volume containing a series of public rooms on several levels is set in the centre and flanked to either side by long, narrow, three-storey guestroom wings that run the entire length of the block. A pool of water is set in front of the main central entrance, in the entrance court made between the two guestroom wings, so that we cannot approach the entrance on axis from the street, yet beyond this pool we are brought back to the centre, making this one of the very few Wright buildings with a central, axial entrance.

In the central volume, the lobby, dining room and auditorium (with the ballroom above and cabaret below, the three rooms together a self-contained, cruciform building) are aligned from front to back, with the main circulation cross-axis – the 'promenade' – separating the dining room and auditorium, while a smaller circulation cross-axis – consisting of two 'bridges' – separates the lobby and dining room. The promenade is the centre of social life within the hotel, as early in the twentieth century it was customary for guests to meet visitors and each other here in the promenade rather than in their private guestrooms; this is reflected in the fact that the promenade was provided with

Above: Imperial Hotel, view of the theatre.
Right: First scheme for Imperial Hotel, aerial perspective.
Far right: Imperial Hotel, view of the fireplace in the parlour.

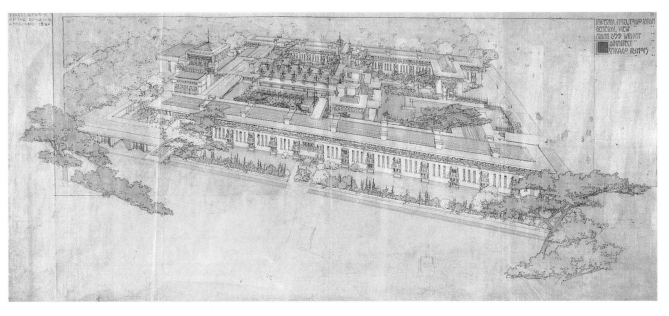

extensive groups of seating along its entire 300-foot length.[15] This wide promenade also connects the two guest wings to each other and to the central group of public spaces, as well as acting as the foyer to the auditorium and overlooking the dining room. Kenneth Frampton has noted that the Imperial Hotel:

> derived in both plan and section from Midway Gardens. The restaurant/winter garden of the Chicago complex reappeared as the auditorium and lobby of the hotel, while the flanking arcades of the gardens themselves became transformed into its residential wings. The internal murals and reliefs also extended Midway themes, while the galleried accessways of the hotel recalled the cafe terraces of the Midway layout.[16]

An aerial perspective of the preliminary design for the Imperial Hotel, quite similar to that drawn for the Midway Gardens, shows Wright's initial intention to utilize flat roofs and to provide, in addition to the dining terraces to either side of the dining room, a large central roof terrace overlooking the entrance. This was removed from the final design, which was completed by Wright in Japan with the assistance of a number of architecture students from the University of Tokyo and Antonin Raymond, a talented Czech-American architect who would remain in Japan for the rest of his life. Wright had a large plaster model of this final design built while he was in Japan, showing the hipped roofs that were used throughout.[17]

Wright's memories of the project indicate that both he and the client were obsessed with the dangers posed by earthquakes – as well they should have been, for Tokyo was a large city in a zone of high seismic activity, and earthquakes were nothing new to the Japanese; as Wright said, 'the fear of the temblor never left me [as] while I planned the building'.[18] The site had more than sixty feet of soft soil – Wright called it 'mud' – below the topsoil, rather than bedrock or any other typical bearing strata. Wright asked, 'Why not float the building upon it?' proposing the idea of a shallow foundation system, consisting of thousands of concrete 'pins', borings of nine inches diameter by eight feet deep made in the topsoil and filled with concrete, two feet on centre, the tops of which were then embedded in the wall footings, and the whole bound together with a thick mat slab of reinforced concrete at grade.[19]

Wright next addressed the problem of the size of the building, and the fact that if rigid and solid it was likely to break up in an earthquake; he proposed dividing the building into parts to produce a 'flexible structure', with joints running from roof through to foundation. Wright placed the plumbing, gas and electrical lines in trenches separated from the foundations and all major load-bearing elements, giving them flexible coiled or bent joints, so that they would remain intact and unruptured in an earthquake.

Above left: Frederick Bogk House, Milwaukee, Wisconsin, 1916, exterior view; heavy cubic masonry massing with highly articulated window surrounds.
Above right: Bogk House, view of the living room looking towards the dining room.
Far right: West elevation of the Bogk House.

Wright later claimed that he developed the entire structure as cantilevered from central supports, so as to avoid floors collapsing when exterior walls moved in earthquakes: 'Why not carry the floors as a waiter carries his tray on raised fingers at the centre – *balancing* the load.' While he would employ exactly this cantilever system of structure in his series of skyscraper designs (the first of which he undertook in 1923), it is evident that this was only a wishful description of the Imperial Hotel, as the exterior walls are clearly load-bearing in the final design, and indeed are battered to help brace against lateral movement. These walls were double shells of masonry, the exterior layer of thin bricks and the interior of hollow masonry tile, the whole 'poured solid with concrete to bind them together'. No steel beams or columns are indicated in any of the working drawings (though this does not rule out their possible use), and the basic structure of the Imperial Hotel would appear to have consisted of reinforced concrete piers, beams, walls and floors. The building was once again constructed under the direction of the remarkable Paul Mueller, who had by this time repeatedly brought Wright's designs into existence. The nonstructural materials used to clad the building were Oya stone, which Wright called 'a workable light lava weighing as much as green oak', brick screens, terracotta and metal; all were 'lightened by ornamental perforations enriching the light and shadow of the structure'.

The exterior of the Imperial Hotel is extraordinarily rich, the golden brick and white Oya stone are woven together, playing off against each other, the whole is 'a jointed monolith with a mosaic surface of lava and brick'. The building is heavy and massive, the end elevations consisting of symmetrical cubic volumes nested one within another. In stepping the massing of the whole and opening it on one side towards the Imperial Palace gardens across the street, resulting in perhaps the only partially extroverted public building of Wright's career, Wright was clearly responding to the important site and client. Yet the specific forms of the building should not necessarily be presumed to have been drawn from the actual context; while Jonathan Lipman makes a case for the influence of the Edo Castle nearby in the Palace gardens, the battered walls of the Hotel go back to Wright's own early Monolithic Concrete Bank of 1894;[20] the closed brick lower volume topped by continuous windows and hipped roof overhang are found in all of Wright's Prairie Houses such as the Barton House of 1902; the turned-up roof edges are found in the Dana House of 1900; and the nested cubic masonry volumes and other elements of the Hotel's elevation are found in the Edward Schroeder House project of 1911 (also the fireplace), the Jerome Mendelson House project of 1912, the Kehl Dance Academy project of 1912, the LaGrange Schoolhouse project of 1912 and the Carnegie Library project of 1913.

This last series of projects suggests that Wright was already moving towards heavier, complexly ornamented, monumental forms in his work even before receiving the commission for the Imperial Hotel. We should note that Wright continued to develop these forms as work on the Imperial Hotel proceeded, both in other projects in Japan, such as the Yamamura House of 1918 and the beautiful Jiyu Gakuen School of 1921 (currently threatened with destruction), and at home, in works such as the State Bank of Spring Green project of 1914, the Emil Bach House of 1915, the E D Brigham House of 1915 and the Frederick Bogk House of 1916. Yet Wright nevertheless felt that he had made an appropriate offering to his beloved Japanese culture: 'No foreigner yet invited to Japan had taken off his hat to Japanese traditions. When foreigners came, what they had back home came too, suitable or not.'[21] Wright's own forms and spatial concepts were so closely tied to his years of study of traditional Japanese building culture that he was in the unique position of being a foreigner able to bring forms from 'back home' which were nevertheless 'at home' in Japan. As Sullivan was to write: 'It was not an imposition upon the Japanese, but a free will contribution to the finest elements in their culture.'[22]

This is particularly true in the hotel's interior, where we enter under a low ceiling that follows us in from the porte-cochere, going up several sets of stairs, and then emerging into the triple-height lobby. The four cruciform-and-square piers that support the flat concrete ceiling are perforated from top to bottom, their corners a woven fabric of terracotta panels and carved Oya stone, within which are mounted integral lights. As in the Larkin Building, the brick spandrels of the mezzanine balconies that ring the lobby are banded top and bottom – in this case with ornamented Oya stone blocks. Wright emphasized the horizontal flow of space by suppressing the vertical brick joints, finishing them flush with the face of the brick and using mortar whose colour matched the brick, while emphasizing the horizontal brick joints, raking them deeply to cast strong shadows and colouring the mortar to contrast with the brick. This had an enormous impact on the character of these interior spaces, greater even than on the exteriors, due to the close proximity for the inhabitant of these articulated masses.

The elevation of the lobby that leads to the dining room beyond is one of Wright's most powerful spatial compositions: vertical and horizontal are dynamically balanced, and the thickness of the massive construction is matched by the many layers of space in both plan and section. The hotel's interior spaces are both protected, buried deep inside thick heavy masonry, and free flowing; the closed cubic masonry masses of the exterior are complemented by the spatial interpenetrations and freedom of movement experienced in the interior. The inhabitant is simultaneously provided with refuge from the world outside and vistas of a rich and complex space within. The

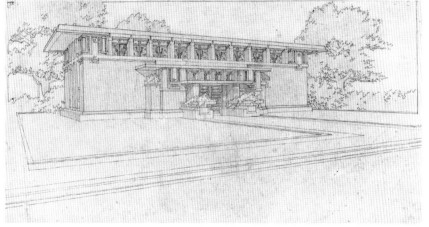

introduction of natural light, through high windows and narrow slots of glass, is used to separate and articulate piers, walls and ceilings, opening up the heavy massing to allow inhabitation to take place.

Overall, the light in the public spaces of the Imperial Hotel is rather dim compared to that found in American public buildings, but it is typical of Wright's work, where the overhanging eaves and leaded glass frequently result in softly lit interiors. In this we should remind ourselves that the light levels shown in photographs of Wright's buildings are most often considerably higher than that experienced in reality by the human eye. In the West, the modern movement in architecture, and indeed the entire era starting with the Enlightenment, called for 'more light', as Goethe was supposed to have said on his deathbed; ever more light – light seen as an inherent good, the more of it the better. In his work it is clear that Wright understood that there was no meaning to light without darkness, and that *shadow* was the realm of experience, not the shadowless light of the modern world. As Wright said: 'Shadow itself is of the light.'[23] As was often the case, we find that in his work Wright opposed the more instrumental aspects of modernism and the Enlightenment, particularly when they resulted in a truncation of experiential possibilities.

In Japan, Wright noted that 'light here is something soft to beguile the eyes', and that 'black, in itself a property, is

revelation here'.[24] This particular quality of shadow comes from the Japanese culture of 'half-light', fully articulated by the novelist Jun'ichiro Tanizaki in his book, *In Praise of Shadows*; it is interesting to note that in this book Tanizaki mentions only one building by name – Wright's Imperial Hotel – praising its 'indirect lighting'.[25] In describing the world defined by shadows, where light and dark are equally valued, Tanizaki is quite close to Wright's sensibility as evidenced in the Imperial Hotel: too much light makes things and spaces shallow, whereas shadows give depth; light falls on the object, whereas shadows occupy space; in shadowed spaces, gold seems to draw light to itself (as in Wright's inserting gold leaf into the horizontal brick joints of his interiors); the heavy, overhanging roofs create the shadows in which inhabitation occurs; and, finally, 'we find beauty not in the thing itself but in the patterns of shadows, the light and the darkness, that one thing against another creates. Were it not for shadows there would be no beauty.'[26]

The patterned, woven fabric of brick and lava (Oya stone) that defines the public spaces of the Imperial Hotel is composed of Wright's richest collection of modular units, square patterns and geometric ornament. The dining room is structured by a series of brick piers which stand forward from the low brick wall and are bonded to the ceiling beams by large carved lava brackets, with passages running along

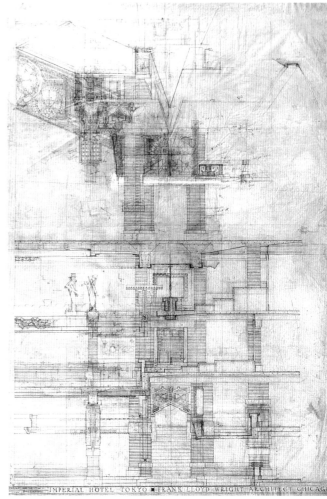

IMPERIAL HOTEL TOKYO ■ FRANK LLOYD WRIGHT ARCHITECT CHICAGO

both sides on both first and second levels. The promenade is framed by angled 'arches', trimmed with carved lava and springing from brick piers, with a gallery overlooking it from the upper level. The auditorium and ballroom, cruciform in plan, are structured by four enormous clusters of four piers each (a gigantic version of the pier-clusters in the Darwin Martin House), and the latter is topped by a ceiling composed of folded tetrahedral shapes.[27] Created out of carved Oya stone, brick screens, terracotta panels, wood, coloured plaster and specially designed rugs, the public spaces are so complexly and completely woven into a unified composition that one can never feel certain that all has been explored. Impossible to describe in any comprehensive manner, the Imperial Hotel was the source of endless variations for Wright's imagination, as evidenced by the 700 or so drawings that were produced, most of which document the design of interior details.[28]

The richly ornamented and patterned public spaces of the hotel are complemented by the simple and spare detailing of the guestrooms, which are furnished with either traditional Japanese *tatami* mats or Western bedroom furniture. In the latter, Wright took the opportunity to design cabinets and furnishings that nest and interlock in the most ingenious manner, drawing inspiration from the asymmetry of the traditional Japanese *tokonama*, the niche off the tea room where the spirits dwell, in the shadows.

The Imperial Hotel was completed and opened after Wright departed Japan in 1921, and had its greatest moment in 1923, when the most powerful earthquake in Japanese history hit Tokyo, levelling large portions of the city. Wright was to wait ten long days before receiving news of the Imperial Hotel in the form of a telegram from his client and defender, Baron Okura: 'Hotel stands undamaged as monument to your genius, hundreds of homeless provided by perfectly maintained service.'[29] Wright's 'jointed monolith' had held firm, one of the very few buildings to ride out the quake. The pools at the entrance and in the gardens – almost removed in final budget cuts – provided water to stop the fires spreading from neighbouring buildings. Hailed by Louis Sullivan in his article of 1924, written shortly before his death, the Imperial Hotel remains one of Wright's greatest accomplishments, structurally and spatially; his gift to the Japanese culture that had taught him so much.

While the hotel was able to survive one of the largest earthquakes in history, it was not to survive the domination of Japan by Western ideas. In 1967, real-estate development pressures in Tokyo dictated that Wright's 'low-rise' Imperial Hotel should give way to a 'high-rise' replacement, but what was really lost in the demolition of this great work of architecture will never be fully measured – certainly not by the careless instruments of land speculation.

Avery Coonley Playhouse, Riverside, Illinois, 1911

Wright's courtyard public buildings all defined spaces that were distinctly theatrical in conception, and he developed a series of actual theatres that utilized the corner entrance, perimeter circulation and stepped floor of perhaps his most theatrical design, Midway Gardens. The primary movement sequence of the Imperial Hotel terminated in a theatre, whose cruciform floor plan is shared with most of Wright's other theatres, beginning with the earliest, the Coonley Playhouse. The Coonleys, who in 1908 had approached Wright to build the house discussed in the last chapter, also commissioned from him several semi-public buildings for their extensive properties, including an unbuilt kindergarten of 1911 and the Playhouse, built in 1912.

This design of the Coonley Playhouse is based directly on the project for the Bock House, and brings Wright's cruciform plan type to its highest level of resolution. The plan consists of a square interpenetrated by a cruciform; the crossing of the arms of the cruciform is marked within the square by four brick piers set in from its corners. The two narrower wings to either side contain the kitchen and workshop, respectively, and the two equal entries are set in the forward corners of the square. The primary volume runs from front to back and contains the seating area at the front, the stage on the far side of the square, framed by the piers and backed by the brick fireplace, with the service-

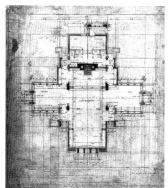

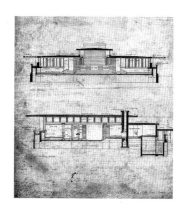

dressing rooms at the rear. This public volume, extending from the front elevation to the fireplace at the back edge of the square, is lifted up to be one and one-half storeys in height, with clerestories running along both of its sides. While not centred in the overall plan, due to the dressing rooms behind the fireplace, Wright 're-centres' this public space by framing it with inset piers and ceiling beams symmetrically spaced in from either end.

The front elevation consists of three vertical windows running up to the roof, sliding past the horizontal beams and soffits on both interior and exterior. The interior and exterior are both composed of abstract flat planes of walls, piers, roofs and trellises: verticals and horizontals balanced and woven together to produce a dense and powerful space and form. Wright plays off the precision and symmetry of the overall form in the leaded-glass windows, each of which presents a different asymmetrical composition of lines, circles and squares of various primary colours – extraordinarily abstract designs for this time, equal to anything then existing in painting and the other arts. In recent years this brilliant work has been tragically defaced, the windows and furniture removed to various museums and private collections. Like so many of Wright's works, the building is gravely reduced by the loss of any of its carefully integrated glasswork, furniture, lights and rugs; Wright's buildings require them all to be fully understood and experienced.

THE MODIFIED cruciform plan of the Coonley Playhouse was adapted for the Kehl Dance Academy project, proposed for Madison, Wisconsin, in 1912. This brilliant urban party-wall design has shops and a director's apartment on the street and, behind, two double-height dance halls, one above the other. A square light court flanked by two generously scaled stairs divides the private spaces fronting on to the street from the school behind. Each dance hall has a stage and balcony at opposite ends, so they may be used for both practice and performance. The larger lower hall, located at street level, takes the form of a cruciform, with four service spaces occupying the corners and, like the Coonley Playhouse, one of the arms of the cruciform is the elevated stage and the main axis is reinforced by being double height with clerestories running down both long sides.

The Barnsdall Theater project of 1918–20 was also cruciform in plan, here housed within a square volume, similar to Unity Temple in its relation between interior space and exterior form. This project, which was to be built on Olive Hill in Los Angeles as part of the Hollyhock House complex for Aline Barnsdall, involved a degree of integration and interpenetration of stage and audience that was almost unprecedented in its time.[30] The beautiful perspectives of the theatre's interior indicate, however, that Wright's first priority, as always, was the clarity of the

Below: Period photograph looking from the audience towards the stage and fireplace.
Below right: Avery Coonley Playhouse, period photograph looking from the stage area to the audience.

public space and its definition through rigorous and evident geometric enclosure; he had no intention of sacrificing this to the emerging requirement for a recessive audience and an increasingly flexible stage.

In 1921, Wright designed another theatre on Olive Hill for Barnsdall, the Community Playhouse project (called the 'Little Dipper'); again he proposed a cruciform plan, in this case four inset corner piers framed four arms which ended in triangular 'prows', a stage and fireplace set in the smallest arm and tiered seats built into the wings to either side. A combination of this design and that for the Coonley Playhouse was the basis for Wright's 'Kindersymphonies' Playhouses project for the Oak Park Playground Association of 1926. The 'Little Dipper' theatre was the only design for the Hollyhock complex which Wright proposed to be built with his textured concrete block, employed two years later in the California houses discussed in the next chapter.

The New Theater project designed in 1931 for Woodstock, New York, is a further development of Wright's ideas for this building type, involving a hexagonal plan with the audience on three large banked planes that reach around to embrace the stage. The (usual for Wright) double entries are set at either edge of the building, right and left, so that we approach the building from behind the stage and dressing area, ascend a ramp (one set to either side of the building), enter one of the lobbies, continue moving in the same direction we entered, now walking along the outside wall to the back of the room, where we finally turn and move back down towards the central stage; to enter we have to go all the way from one side of the building to the other. In the Cinema and Shops project for Michigan City, Indiana, of 1932, Wright proposed a very similar design, including the hexagonal geometry and elongated entrance sequence, only here the whole is internalized between urban party walls.

Wright's first design for the Hillside Playhouse at Taliesin of 1933, to be housed in an existing cruciform volume of the Hillside Home School of 1902, utilized the hexagonal seating of the New Theater at the lower level and suspended a balcony overhead from four corner supports. The opening for this balcony is a rectangle with triangles added to the two narrower ends, allowing a smaller version of the bevelled outside seating of the main floor to occur above. The design for this balcony floor would be deployed by Wright in the Chapel for Florida Southern College five years later, while the plan of the backstage service area of the New Theater would be employed by Wright without substantial change on the penthouse level of the Johnson Wax Building of 1936, including the circular stairs anchoring the corners of the half-hexagon plan. In the mezzanine level below, Wright built a theatre for the Johnson Wax employees, a semicircular volume with a ceiling of plaster semicircles stepping up towards the centre and a plywood floor – the only public space with a wood floor in the building.

*Below: Aline Barnsdall Theater,
perspective of interior, looking
from the audience towards
the stage*

Right: Project for Kehl Dance
Academy, Madison, Wisconsin,
1912, mezzanine floor plan. The
modified cruciform plan of the
Coonley Playhouse was adapted
for this project.
Far right above: Dallas Theater
Center (now known as the Kalita
Humphries Theater), 1955, plan.
Wright built a revolving circular
stage which he had discovered in
the kabuki theatres of Japan.
Far right below: Kehl Dance
Academy, perspective view
from the street.
Below: Second project for Aline
Barnsdall Theater, Olive Hill,
Los Angeles, California, 1918,
view of the plaster model with the
roof hinged open.

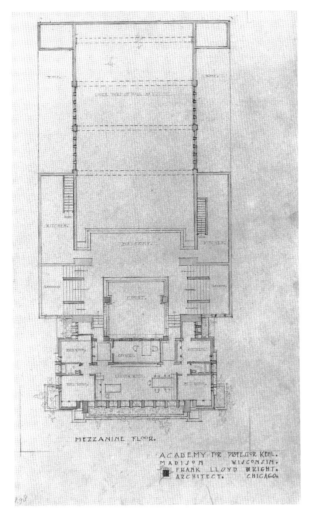

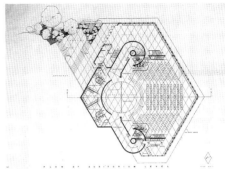

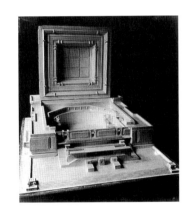

The design for the New Theater is again used by Wright for the Florida Southern College Theater project of 1938, without substantial change save for the elimination of the circumnavigating entrance sequence. In 1940, Wright employed the New Theater design again for the Community Church built in Kansas City, this time with circular corner stairs removed but the entrance sequence intact; Wright disavowed this design when its construction was removed from his control. The New Theater design, virtually unmodified except in scale, is again employed by Wright in the Music Building project proposed for Florida Southern College in 1946 and the 1949 project for a new theatre for the Theater Corporation of Hartford; it was finally built as the Dallas Theater Center (today called the Kalita Humphries Theater) in 1955. First conceived by Wright in 1915 in his designs for Aline Barnsdall's Chicago theatre project, the merging of audience and actors that characterized the development of the modern theatre is here amply evident; no longer do we have 'the audience sitting in one box looking at the performers in another box', as Wright said.[31] In the Dallas Theater Center, as he had done previously in the Imperial Hotel theatre, Wright built the revolving circular stage he had initially discovered in the traditional kabuki theatres of Japan.

THIS REDEPLOYMENT by Wright in new buildings of devices drawn from ancient Japanese kabuki theatre is again indicative of his unique vision of what it was to be a modern architect. During the period in which Wright made the designs discussed above, the vast majority of 'modern' architects were becoming ever-more fixated on the building articulated as a free-standing object, to be apprehended as a purely sculptural form. In direct opposition to this tendency, we find Wright focused on the courtyard as a prototype for both public and private buildings, embracing and developing the courtyard's propensity to produce theatrical effects most often associated with enclosed urban spaces. Wright, in later life so often labelled the anti-urbanist, was here not only well-anchored in the ancient tradition of urban courtyard design (going back before the Romans and Greeks), but actively engaged in adapting this traditional device to American contexts and modern programmes.

THE CONCRETE-BLOCK HOUSE

What we call space is relative to the existence
of whatever structures we may choose to conceive.
The architectural structure interprets space, and
leads to hypotheses on the nature of space.

Paul Valéry, 'Introduction to the
Method of Leonardo da Vinci', 1894.[1]

*Left: Alice Millard House, known
as 'La Miniatura', Pasadena,
California, 1923, exterior view
across the ravine and pond.
Above: Project for Harry Brown
House, Genesco, Illinois, 1906,
perspective. Labelled 'First block
house' by Wright.*

Throughout his life as an architect, Wright attempted to relate the spaces and forms of his designs to the structures and materials with which they were made. Wright believed this was essential if his buildings were to be edifying for those who inhabited them: *aedificare*, the ancient word for building, means both to edify (instruct) and to build (construct) with an ethical intention. Wright engaged in a constant search for a comprehensive order that would encompass both *composition* and *construction*, an order similar to the fusion of structure, material, form and space that he found in his studies of nature. In his architecture, Wright sought the integration of form and space in natural elements such as the crystalline geometries of rock formations, which he termed 'proof of nature's matchless architectural principles', and the dynamic structure of the sahuaro cactus, which he called 'a perfect example of reinforced building construction.'[2]

Wright attempted to develop forms from the rhythm inherent in each particular system of construction he used, so that the construction might in turn be integrated with and responsive to the spatial idea – achieving what he termed simplicity, 'There is only one way to get that simplicity. And that way is, on principle, by way of construction developed as architecture.'[3] Essential to Wright's architecture was his understanding that the way a space is made or constructed is directly related to the way

it is experienced. Construction was not simply a means to some end; it was an essential part of the final experience of life that took place within, and thus was to be fully integrated in the process of design.

In his designs Wright utilized what he called the 'unit system' of square-grid planning, a 'highly developed expression of structure', which provided the 'sympathetic frame for the life going on within'.[4] Wright directly relates this to the geometries found in nature: 'In the logic of the plan what we call standardization is seen to be fundamental groundwork in architecture. All things in nature exhibit this tendency to crystalize; to form mathematically and then to conform.'[5] This square grid or 'unit system' that underlay all of Wright's designs operated as both an essential compositional and scaling device and as a measure and organizational method for construction – both being required in his view to achieve integral order and organic rhythm. The uniform grid gave a basic stability that allowed variations within the matrix, such as the production of modulated order (the 'tartan' or *a-b-a* spacing), and acted to coordinate and integrate all elements and spaces (the parts) into the composition of the house (the whole).

In his working drawings, from the very start of Wright's career, the square grid appears as a way of eliminating the dimension lines and making the modular construction evident:

All the buildings I have ever built, large and small, are fabricated upon a unit system – as the pile of a rug is stitched into the warp. Thus each structure is an ordered fabric. Rhythm, consistent scale of parts, and an economy of construction are greatly facilitated by this simple expedient – a mechanical one absorbed in the final result to which it has given more consistent texture, a more tenuous quality as a whole.[6]

It is typical to relate architecture first to sculpture, among the other arts, yet Wright refers to himself as 'the weaver',[7] indicating the essential nature of this grid system of design and construction in his work. As Kenneth Frampton has noted: 'It is of utmost importance that Wright conceived of himself as a weaver rather than a sculptor and that woven fabric would be the metaphor for all of his architecture.'[8]

In his search for order that would be reinforced and edified in the process of construction and material realization, Wright grappled throughout his life with the one material that proved perfectly 'plastic', able to be formed into any formal or structural shape: reinforced concrete. Wright was often critical of concrete's inherent lack of internal, modular order – the type of 'unit' rhythm evident in brick and standardized wood elements – and, as Frampton has noted, Wright went 'out of his way to classify both terra-cotta and concrete as conglomera; that is, a non-tectonic material'.[9] In 1928, twenty years after the completion of Unity Temple, the first exposed reinforced concrete public building in the US and the masterpiece of his Prairie Period, Wright wrote:

Aesthetically concrete has neither song nor any story. Nor is it easy to see in this conglomerate, in this mud pie, a high aesthetic property, because in itself it is amalgam, aggregate compound. And cement, the binding medium, is characterless. Here in the conglomerate named concrete we find a plastic material that yet has found no medium of expression that will allow it to take plastic form.[10]

While the walls of Unity Temple were cast in repetitively used wooden forms, Wright was nevertheless critical of the inherent lack of constructive order in cast-in-place concrete, and sought a more direct revelation of the construction module and the rhythm of the (necessarily) hidden steel bars – the internal balance between the tensile (steel) and compressive (aggregate) components. It is therefore hardly coincidental that in 1906, the same year that Wright completed the design and began construction of Unity Temple, he designed the project for the Harry E Brown House, which he later titled the 'first block house'.[11] Here his concrete-block system of construction was proposed for the exterior walls and structure, to be built using a mixture of square and rectangular blocks which were evidently intended to be specially cast; the floors and roof were to be cast-concrete slabs, and the interior was to be plastered. The elemental building components, modular construction grid, and revelation of the rhythm of the steel bars of the

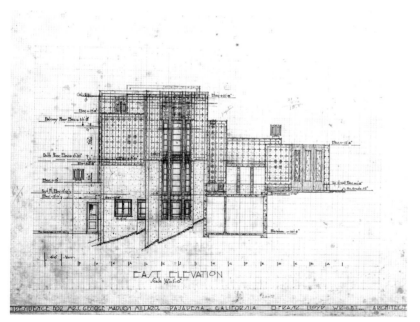

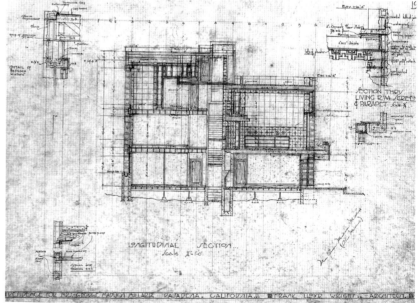

fully developed concrete-block system were thus already achieved in this astonishing and self-critical project of 1906. Concrete had found its character, its means of expression, but it would be another seventeen years before Wright would build using this construction method.[12]

Alice Millard House, 'La Miniatura', Pasadena, California, 1923

Wright's return to this system first conceived in 1906 was likely triggered by the 'ethical' conflict between its massive, uniform, monolithic *appearance* and the stucco-faced, wood-framed, lightweight *construction* of the Hollyhock House, finished in 1921. While the Midway Gardens utilized square blocks of concrete and terracotta, and the Imperial Hotel had in addition employed carved lava stone, in both cases these blocks were not structural, simply acting as cladding – quite similar to Sullivan's use of ornamented terracotta panels in his skyscraper designs. In a series of unbuilt projects, the Shrine for A M Johnson in Death Valley of 1921, the 'House in Textile Block Construction' of 1921 and the 'Little Dipper' Kindergarten of 1921, Frampton notes how Wright finally 'tackled the idea of wire-reinforced, tessellated [concrete] block construction' that he had first conceived while Unity Temple was under construction.[13]

This system of construction, utilizing what Wright called 'textile' concrete block, is first realized in 1923 in 'La Miniatura', the Alice Millard House. Wright described the construction system proposed for this small house by saying:

> We would take that despised outcast of the building industry – the concrete block – out from underfoot or from the gutter – find a hitherto unsuspected soul in it – make it live as a thing of beauty – textured like the trees. All we would have to do would be to educate the concrete block, refine it and knit it together with steel in the joints and so construct the joints that they could be poured full of concrete after they were set up and a steel-strand laid in them. The walls would thus become thin but solid reinforced slabs and yield to any desire for form imaginable. And common labor could do it all. We would make the walls double, of course, one wall facing inside and the other wall facing outside, thus getting continuous hollow spaces between, so the house would be cool in summer, warm in winter and dry always.[14]

When Wright and Millard went to look at a hilltop site without trees in Pasadena, Wright recommended that she purchase a nearby site in a ravine, inexpensive because it was considered undesirable (and therefore 'unbuildable'), where two beautiful eucalyptus trees stood. The house that Wright built on this site consists in plan of two squares, meeting only at one corner, connected by a corridor emerging from the stair behind the fireplace. The rear square, nearer the street, contains the one-storey garage and entrance loggia, while the square set forwards into the

ravine is a three-storey cubic volume containing the dining room, kitchen and servant's room on the lower floor – a terrace off the dining room overlooks a small pond. The double-height living room and guestroom occupy the main floor, and Millard's bedroom occupies the top floor, with a balcony overlooking the living room below and a bridge across to the garage roof terrace; her bedroom is a miniature of the living room, as it is also double-height and overlooked by a small balcony.

The underlying square grid, now for the first time in Wright's work operating in both plan and section (horizontally and vertically), is evident in the beautifully nuanced sketch for the house, showing the plan, section and elevation, as well as details of the perforated concrete-block pattern. It becomes clear in this drawing that the 'textile' and weaving logic of the concrete-block system of construction and design does not only characterize the surface of the individual blocks: the elevation detail of the sixteen-inch-square block pattern extends across neighbouring blocks in all four directions, indicating how this method of making constitutes a knitting together of the surface. The result is a fully integrated building mass, which despite its cubic form and the weight of its concrete construction, imparts an impression of being mechanically fabricated from a lightweight textile: 'Standardization was the soul of the machine, and here I was the Weaver taking

it as a principle, knitting a great future for it. Yes, crocheting with it a free masonry fabric capable of stunning variety, great in architectural beauty. Now here was I, Frank Lloyd Wright, the Weaver.'[15]

The fabric-like quality of construction and spatial definition is even more predominant in the experience of the interior, where upon entering we turn to the right towards the light, stepping out from under the low ceiling into the double-height living room – the front wall facing the ravine appears as a screen, particularly permeable by light. Wright had earlier stated that he was 'working away at the wall as a wall and bringing it towards the function of a screen,'[16] and with the concrete-block system of building he was capable of constructing even the load-bearing walls as perforated screens. At the top of the wall between block piers, each of the concrete blocks is perforated by a cruciform and four small squares, with clear glass cast into the block to make them weather-tight. Below these perforated-block glass doors leading out on to the small terrace are set between the piers, and the door glazing mullions are ordered on the same 16-inch grid. In this way our acts of inhabitation, such as opening a door or looking out of a window, are woven together with the walls through the square-block construction.

A particularly revealing detail occurs at the top of these doors in the living room, where the wood header extends

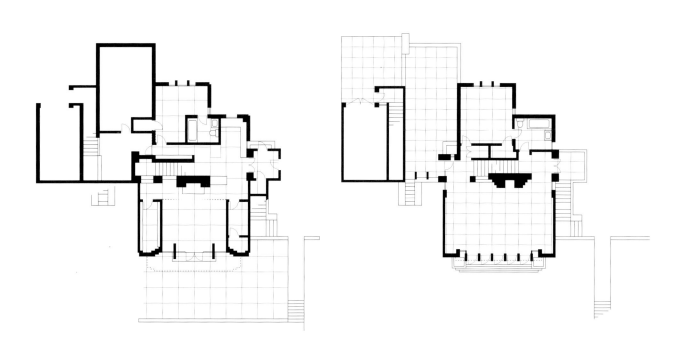

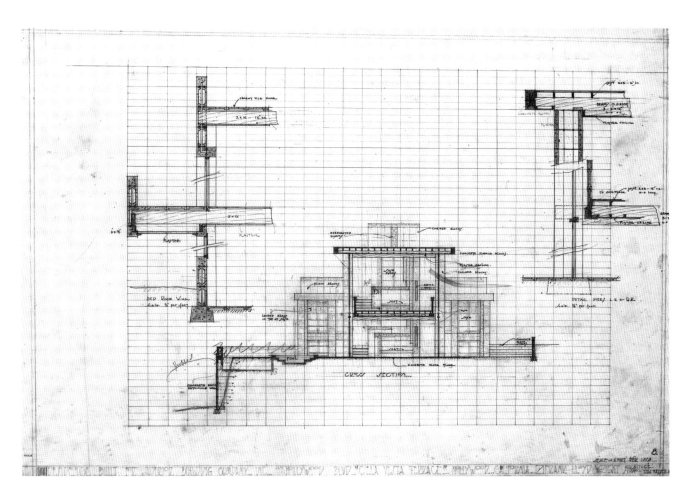

back into the room and carries a sixteen-inch transom glass the full width of the doors, allowing us to look through this transom to see the header course beneath the perforated-concrete blocks. The densely layered enclosure implied in the laminated or layered pattern cast into the surface of the concrete blocks is born out by the layers of glass, and the cruciform perforations in the blocks above are of equal dimension to the mullions in the doors below, fostering a play between grids of light and dark.

Indicative of Wright's insistence that all the elements of the house adhere to the ordering grid is the fact that the working drawings show the wooden-floor joists, though completely hidden beneath wood floors and plaster ceilings in the finished house, they were nevertheless to be placed on the sixteen-inch grid lines originating in the concrete-block joints. Yet Wright is careful to maintain the presence of spaces and elements at several scales – building scale, individual block scale, and the important intermediate scale – so that, like a weaving, there was the whole, the individual stitch, and the pattern that exists between these two scales. In the living room, the vertical piers on the exterior wall that go from floor to ceiling and the horizontal balcony beam over the fireplace that runs all the way across the interior wall exist at this intermediate scale, balancing each other and ordering our experience of the space.

John Storer House, Los Angeles, California, 1923

The plan of the Storer House was developed directly from the G P Lowes House project of 1922, but rather than the stucco finish over wood framing proposed for the Lowes House (as in the Hollyhock House), the Storer House was constructed using Wright's 'textile' concrete-block construction system. The house is T-shaped in plan, its main volume a rectangular double-height block containing the living room over the dining room; on the first floor, the square kitchen is placed on axis off one end of the dining room and a bathroom, with two bedrooms set one on either side, is placed a half-flight up, on axis off the other end. In plan, the volume of the kitchen is projected out of the opening at the end of the primary rectangle, which in turn interlocks with the bedroom block, so that the plan exhibits the nesting and interpenetration of spaces so typical of Wright's earlier work. Wright set this symmetrical plan, open on both of its major sides, against a hillside, designing a series of terraces to accommodate the form to the landscape. Here can be seen the capacity of the omni-directional concrete-block construction system to fit itself to the variety of topographic conditions existing in the hills and canyons surrounding Los Angeles – a landscape very different from that of the flat prairie for which Wright had developed his earlier house types.

As in the Hollyhock House and the Millard House, the fireplace is asymmetrically positioned; here the fireplace is moved off the centre axis and set on the uphill side of the living and dining rooms, turned ninety degrees so as to face downhill, and a built-in inglenook seat is placed only on one side. We face this fireplace upon entry, which is made through one of the five identical doors between six two-storey concrete-block piers, opening on to the terrace at the end of the turning and climbing entrance sequence on the downhill side of the house. The interior is dominated by these two-storey piers that run the full height from dining-room floor to living-room ceiling, tying the rooms together in section and, through the continuous vertical glazing set between them, providing light to the interior. Here, in a way similar to the structural wood posts set between the continuous horizontal window bands of the Prairie Houses, Wright integrated the construction system with the introduction of light into the interior, so that light and structure together give rhythm to the inhabited space.[17]

The ceilings of both the dining and living rooms are structured by exposed wood beams, which carry the joists concealed by the finished floor and ceiling. These beams run across the narrow width of the rooms and are supported by the concrete-block piers, set four feet on centre. Both the dining room, where we enter, and the living room, at the top of the house, are overlooked by the stair, which climbs up along the end wall, partially hidden behind a screen of perforated-concrete blocks. The bedrooms open off this stair at the mid-level between the two primary rooms, and it terminates at the roof terrace over the bedrooms. A smaller roof terrace, over the kitchen, opens off the living room, and two wood beams running along the long axis of the house, framing at ninety degrees into the outer primary beams, cantilever out each end to support the trellis and awnings over both terraces. The piers and beams again produce the important intermediate scale between the individual block and the cubic volume of the house. Within the symmetrical cage created by the piers and beams, the fireplace and stair produce a strong rotational movement pattern, adding a dynamic quality to the space, reminding us that the house itself is set in the diagonal section on the hill.

Right: Storer House, plan.
Far right: View of the entrance terrace; the approach stairs are to the left, and the piers and glass wall of the dining room to the right.
Overleaf: Approach view from the street of the house stepping up the hill.

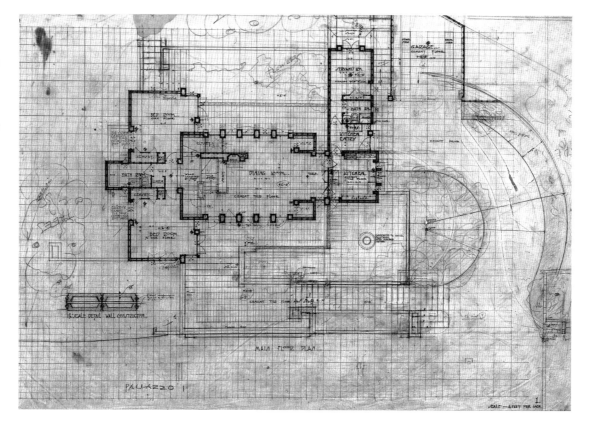

Right: View of the Storer House from the street below.
Below: View of the back garden and pool.
Below right: View of the living room from the stair to the upper terrace, with the fireplace on the left.
Far right: View of the living room, with the fireplace at centre right, the piers and windows rising from the dining room below at left, and the stairs to the upper terrace at the far end.

Charles Ennis House, Los Angeles, California, 1923

The Ennis House was placed at the top of a hill, its primary elevation set on the very edge of its steeply sloping, south-facing side, presenting a formidably defensive, heavy, solid and massive character on the exterior. Indeed, the scale of the exterior seems more related to larger designs, such as the Doheny Ranch Resort project of Los Angeles of the same year, than it does to Wright's other houses. Yet, as Grant Hildebrandt has stated, 'if we switch our attention from the richness of the solids to the configuration of the voids,'[18] we find that inside the concrete-block construction dissolves the massiveness in the play of light and shadow, and the interior space, a series of rooms running along the hillside, is woven together by the variety of openings between rooms and by a loggia running the length of the house.

We enter by first moving into the hilltop, passing under a bridge that leads from the hillside to the pool, emerging in the entrance court framed by the end of the house and the garage; here we first see the view out over the hills and canyons. Turning left, we enter the lower level of the house, behind the enormous retaining wall, moving into the darkness of the cave-like entrance between pairs of low, heavy piers constructed of patterned concrete blocks, with a concrete-block ceiling and stone floor. Ahead our way is blocked by a niche, and we must turn left and then right to start up the stair, drawn upwards by the increasing light

coming from a window, with beautiful diagonal leaded patterns, at the top of the stair. We step out into the loggia – twenty pairs of square concrete-block piers marching down the length of the house – similar to the pergola at the Darwin Martin House of 1903, but rather than connecting isolated and independent buildings, here the loggia forms the inside edge of all the primary rooms, interpenetrating with the living room.

A set of six stairs at the nearest end of the loggia takes us up to the dining room, a cruciform-shaped room projecting out of the main mass of the house towards the view, which is set several feet above and overlooking the living room. The double-height living room is directed away from the view, for its fireplace is positioned on the other side of the loggia, which is lifted to one and one-half storey height in the three bays of the hearth. Delicately leaded square glass clerestory windows are set into the portions of these higher piers between the loggia ceiling and the hearth ceiling, making an interior elevation similar to that at the lobby of the Imperial Hotel. The gilded tiles of the fireplace mosaic gleam out of the shadows of the hearth space in a way that exemplifies how much Wright shared his treatment of light with the Japanese.

Indeed, while the exterior of the Ennis House is starkly lit by the strong sunlight, the interior is dimly lit – a realm of mysterious shadows multiplied by the patterned surface of the concrete blocks. The blocks are cast with a diagonally inflected design of overlapping squares that reinforces the diagonal relation in plan and section between the horizontally proportioned dining room projected out towards the view and the vertically proportioned living room pulled back towards the hill. The diagonal views between spaces, the inability to see all the spaces from any one vantage point, and the sensing of spaces further down the loggia, beyond the space we presently inhabit, all add to the labyrinthine quality of the house – unexpected in such a seemingly simple linear plan – encouraging us to explore its full length.

Samuel Freeman House, Los Angeles, California, 1923

Wright achieves his greatest highest level of resolution of the spatial and constructive forms inherent in his textile concrete-block system in the Freeman House; his plan and elevation drawings are composed over a sixteen-inch-scale square grid completely covering the page, making explicit the woven aspect of the construction of these houses. The concrete blocks are sixteen inches square and four inches deep, with the designed pattern on the flat outside face; the blocks are only two inches thick at any point, the inside face hollowed out to create an insulating airspace between the blocks when they are set back-to-back to make the typical, load-bearing wall. The narrow edges of the blocks are curved to allow the steel reinforcing rods to run vertically and horizontally (making the wall a true woven structure), and to hold the concrete that is poured in these channels to bond the blocks and steel. Small notches allow steel cross-ties to be fitted at each intersection of the rods so as to tie the inside and outside walls of blocks together. The piers and beams are made by spacing the blocks sixteen inches apart around steel reinforcing bars and casting them full of concrete.

The finished double wall, with the cast patterns facing both inside and outside, suggests the monolithic construction that Wright had achieved in cast-in-place concrete, yet allows for greater control of finish, incorporates an insulating and waterproofing airspace, and registers on the interior and exterior faces of the wall the

Right: Ennis House, construction drawings for the dining room: plans, sections and details.

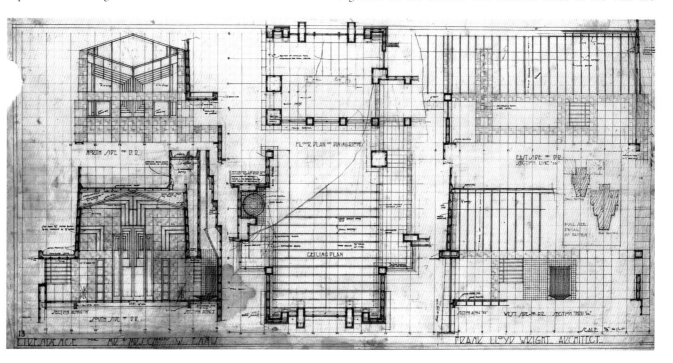

*Right: Ennis House, entrance stair
landing at the main floor.*

rhythm of the steel reinforcing inside. The floor is finished with smooth square concrete blocks throughout the bedroom floor and at the edges of the living room, which has oak-strip flooring in its centre; the wood-board ceiling is divided by V-shaped battens sixteen inches apart, running north–south; and both the floor and roof consist of wood joists, furring strips, flooring and ceiling totalling exactly sixteen inches in depth. The window glazing consists of horizontal steel mullions spaced at sixteen-inch intervals, with the only other natural light coming through the specially cast perforated and glazed-concrete blocks.

The Freeman House is both the smallest and the most beautiful of Wright's concrete-block houses, again occupying the edge of a hillside overlooking the city. The main volume of the house is a cube; a simple square in plan, with the living room on the upper (entrance) level and two bedrooms on the lower level, facing south, with a solid retaining wall housing the fireplaces on the north side. Extended to the east, a short wing houses the kitchen above and bath below, and is anchored at its end by the stair. The garage is set back from this stair, creating an L-shaped entrance court to the north, with an open loggia between, giving a view out before entry, very similar to Wright's own Taliesin.

We enter by turning right in the loggia, opening the front door to face the stairs down, turning right again and edging along the inside of the solid north wall towards the fireplace.

In the living room, two deep beams made of concrete blocks span from piers on either side of the fireplace to matching piers on the other side of the room, dividing the room into three equal spaces, with a small balcony three steps down from the living room (so as not to block the view), opening off the centre bay between the piers. On the north side of the living room, near the fireplace, the ceiling in the centre space is higher, with a row of perforated and glazed-concrete blocks forming a clerestory at its top. The ceiling to either side is slightly lower, and all three sections drop to eight feet in height on reaching the pair of piers set across from each other one-third of the width of the room in from the south side.

At the outside corner in both the living room and bedroom, Wright weaves together the patterned and perforated concrete blocks with the windows, such that the mullions between the glass panes emerge directly from the mortar joints between the blocks. Here Wright makes his first use of the butt-glazed corner window (where the two pieces of glass are butted directly against each other to create the corner, without any corner mullion), a fitting detail to capture the progression from solid-concrete block to perforated block to framed glass to open corner – a dematerialization that appears to us to have been affected by the light which pours into the corners of the living room. At the corner the floor between the living room and bedroom below is cantilevered and bevelled, so that it is less than an inch thick at the point where it meets the glass, allowing the glass to pass by it without interruption.

Inside this wonderful little house, we are held within a woven spatial fabric, the living room enclosed and anchored by the block fireplace and its roof beams, yet opened at its corners to allow freedom of view across the valley. The interior space for living is here produced in an almost mechanical manner and, as might be expected, Wright saw this 'mechanism' of the construction process as a positive aspect of his textile concrete-block system:

> I finally had found simple mechanical means to produce a complete building that looks the way the machine made it, as much at least as any fabric need look. Tough, light, but not 'thin;' imperishable; plastic; no necessary lie about it anywhere and yet machine-made, mechanically perfect. Standardization as the soul of the machine here for the first time may be seen in the hand of the architect, put squarely up to imagination, the limits of imagination the only limitation of building.[19]

Richard Lloyd Jones House, Tulsa, Oklahoma, 1929

After the flurry of construction involved in the four California houses discussed above, Wright incorporated the concrete-block system of construction among his various methods, to be utilized when appropriate over the next thirty-five years. The Arizona Biltmore Hotel, built in Phoenix, Arizona, in 1927, was his next commission to be constructed using concrete block. Albert McArthur, a former apprentice at Taliesin and son of one of his very first Oak

Park clients, laid out and built this project along with his brothers, but he turned to Wright for the designs of the major interior spaces and the system of construction, as is indicated by the series of perspective drawings in the Taliesin archives. The main lobby, with its door-top patterned concrete band, the square corner lights set into the stepped brackets at the top of the concrete-block piers, the mezzanine set asymmetrically down one side of the space, and the dim shadowy light prevalent throughout the whole, all show Wright's mastery of space and detail. For the even larger San Marcos-in-the-Desert Hotel and Resort project of 1928, one of several designs for Alexander Chandler in Arizona, Wright also proposed using concrete block in the construction of both the main structure and the outlying houses.

In the remarkable Richard Lloyd Jones House of 1929, the last concrete-block house of this period, Wright simplified the 'fabric' of construction, eliminating the decorative cast patterns on the surface of the majority of blocks, increasing the size of the blocks (to 15 inches tall by 20 inches wide), bevelling all the concrete-floor slabs to suppress their expression on the exterior, and equalizing the proportion of folded glass and concrete surfaces on the exterior to produce a rhythmic disposition of space across the flat site. As Kenneth Frampton has written, in the Lloyd Jones House 'the hitherto finely woven fabric of the textile block is abandoned in favor of a larger block formation, laid up in piers. Wright's unrealizable Egyptoid

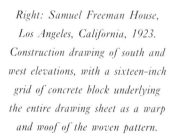

Right: Samuel Freeman House, Los Angeles, California, 1923. Construction drawing of south and west elevations, with a sixteen-inch grid of concrete block underlying the entire drawing sheet as a warp and woof of the woven pattern.

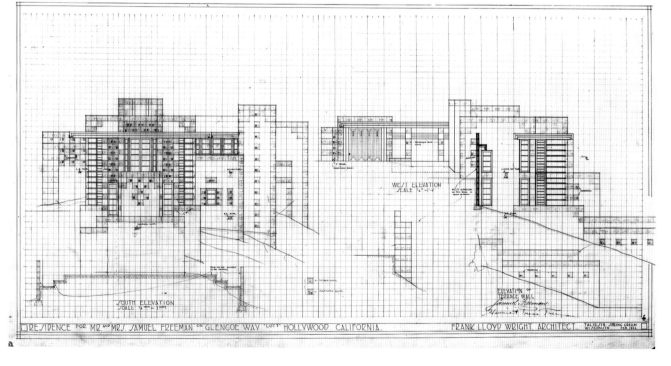

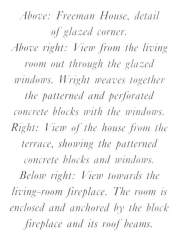

Above: Freeman House, detail of glazed corner.
Above right: View from the living room out through the glazed windows. Wright weaves together the patterned and perforated concrete blocks with the windows.
Right: View of the house from the terrace, showing the patterned concrete blocks and windows.
Below right: View towards the living-room fireplace. The room is enclosed and anchored by the block fireplace and its roof beams.

'ideal' of elevations without windows is now relinquished in favor of an alternating pattern of piers and slots that is as overtly solid as it is void'; utilized in this manner, the increase in the size of the block itself 'produces a paradoxical decrease in apparent mass.' The first block houses did not easily accommodate ventilation ducts and other mechanical services, and part of the reason for Wright's move to the larger block and its use in pier-walls may have been the ability to incorporate 'built-in' ductwork; Frampton has noted that 'Wright was more preoccupied with the tectonic integration of services than any other architect of his generation.'[20]

The Lloyd Jones House is also the first time Wright chose to use an axonometric 'cut-away' drawing to present the house, a series of rooms laid out around a rectangular garden court in a way very similar to Taliesin. The entrance and stair hall, dining room and kitchen are contained in a cruciform volume in one corner with the large living room set behind, its two long sides responding to the differing orientations of their apertures; the east-facing wall low and uncovered, while the west-facing wall is higher and set back in the shade of a loggia. In the other corner behind the living room is the bedroom and study wing, and the garage and maid's quarters anchor the corner diagonally opposite. A swimming pool occupies the courtyard, and there are stairs up to the flat roof terraces at the inside corners.

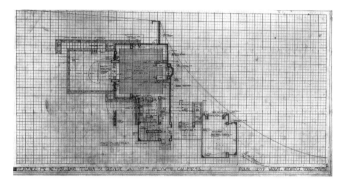

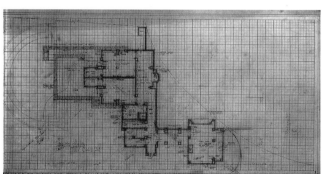

Above: Freeman House, plans.
Above right: Richard Lloyd Jones
House, Tulsa, Oklahoma, 1929,
exterior view.
Right: Axonometric of the Richard
Lloyd Jones House, showing
the floor and walls with the
roof removed.

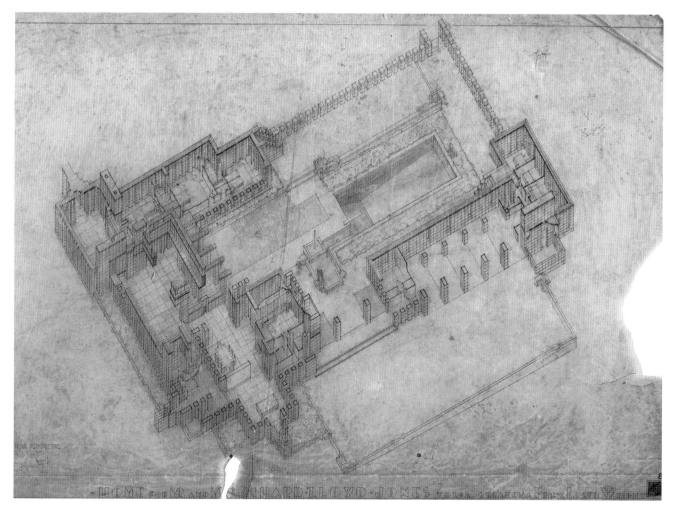

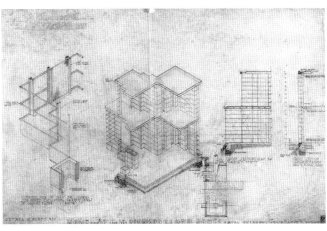

Above: Lloyd Jones House, detail of glass bay and concrete-block piers.
Above right: View into living room. The interior of the house unfolds in all directions, so that we are always aware of the tension between horizontal and vertical, near and far.

The entrance and stair hall is set three steps above the billiard room, both of which have stepped all-glass 'conservatories' projecting from them into the yard, their butt-glazed open corners making them dissolve in reflection when seen from outside; they dissolve in the influx of bright light they allow when seen from within. The dining room is buried deep in the space of the house itself, with no exterior walls, surrounded by openings into the other rooms. Going back up the three stairs we reach the living room, first entering a low space along the east edge, focused on the step-faced fireplace at its end. Moving around to the right under a long, deep concrete beam we arrive in a high bright space ringed by large clerestory windows and defined on its west edge by a row of square concrete-block piers with delicate patterned apertures for their integral lights; these piers are matched by another row set further to the west – originally an exterior loggia shading the glass doors from the living room out to the pool terrace.

The interior of the Lloyd Jones House unfolds in all directions, with precise right-angle corners of concrete and glass, so that we are always aware of the tension between horizontal and vertical, near and far. In a description that could apply to the interiors of all Wright's concrete-block houses, Walt Whitman said, 'every cubic inch of space is a miracle'.[21]

EVEN A cursory examination of the Lloyd Jones House cannot fail to show the rather startling changes made by Wright in his designs for houses following his period of building in California. Though the Lloyd Jones House is back in the familiar confines of the Midwest prairie, it can hardly be called a Prairie House. Gone are the insistent horizontal inflection, the overhanging, hipped, shadow-making roof, and the continuous band of windows running underneath. In their place is a forest of vertical concrete piers with glass running full-height between them, the flat roof almost invisible. The sites in the Los Angeles area where the concrete-block houses are built are deeply fissured with ravines and rock outcrop, the opposite of the Midwest prairie. Wright responded with an architecture that, though based upon plans of the earlier Prairie Houses, articulated the character of these new settings and construction techniques. The houses took shape as geometric abstractions of the rock walls on which they were sited, drawing a vertical monumentality from both the forms of the earth and the concrete blocks out of which they were built, creating a sense of shelter with anchoring walls. The Lloyd Jones House reflects Wright's often hidden fascination with the vertical dimension in architecture, and how the vertical also can anchor us to the earth.

THE CANTILEVERED TOWER

It must be tall, every inch of it tall.

The force and power of altitude must be in it.

It must be every inch a proud and soaring thing,

rising in sheer exultation that from bottom to top

it is a unit without a single dissenting line.

Louis Sullivan, 'The Tall Office Building Artistically
Considered', 1896[1]

Left: First project for the National Insurance Company Building, Chicago, Illinois, 1923. The design is closely related to Wright's concrete-block houses.

While Wright early on established his belief in the horizontal as the appropriate expression of an American space for living, he nevertheless was to return to that realm of pure verticality, the skyscraper, again and again throughout his career. We should remember that in the Chicago of Wright's youth, the skyscraper was considered a uniquely American building form, exhibiting what Thomas van Leeuwen has described as 'the skyward trend of thought'.[2] While still in Sullivan's office, Wright was both present at the initial conception of the classic Chicago frame skyscraper – Sullivan's Wainwright Building of 1890 – and was chief designer on many high-rises such as the Schiller Building, in which he later located his own offices.

Sullivan's principles of skyscraper design were laid out in his article entitled 'The Tall Office Building Artistically Considered', published in 1896. Chief among Sullivan's concerns was the tendency on the part of his Beaux-Arts-trained contemporaries to design the high-rise as an assemblage of classical motifs, stacked one upon another:

'the tall building should not, must not, be made a field for the display of architectural knowledge in the encyclopedic sense. It would seem indeed, as though the 'trained' architect, when facing this problem, were beset at every story, or at most, every third or fourth story, by the hysterical dread lest he be in 'bad form;' lest he be not bedecking his building with sufficiency of quotation ... lest he be not copious enough

in the display of his wares ... he lives, as it were, in a waking nightmare filled with the disjecta membra of architecture.[3]

Wright would follow Sullivan's lead in this rejection of what Wright called the 'psuedo-classical' and its application to the skyscraper, yet he would also ultimately refuse to embrace the steel frame, the greatest innovation of the Chicago School, as the primary generator of space in the high-rise. Colin Rowe has noted in his seminal article on the Chicago frame:

Although we may assert that the architects of the office buildings in the Loop [of Chicago] clarified a basic disposition of twentieth century architecture, yet for the structural skeleton which their achievement exposed, it can only be said that Wright (who might be considered their most illustrious pupil) seems to have shown a most marked distaste ... unlike Sullivan, who had approached architecture primarily with the object of realizing an expressive structure, Wright was from the first abnormally sensitive to the demands of an expressive space.[4]

The expressive character of inhabited space is largely determined, according to Wright, by the plan. Wright believed this so strongly that he was to later make the following assertion: 'To judge an architect one only need look at his ground plan. He is master there, or never.'[5] Wright's *Lieber Meister*, Sullivan, would surely have failed this test; Sullivan's contribution to Wright's formation as an

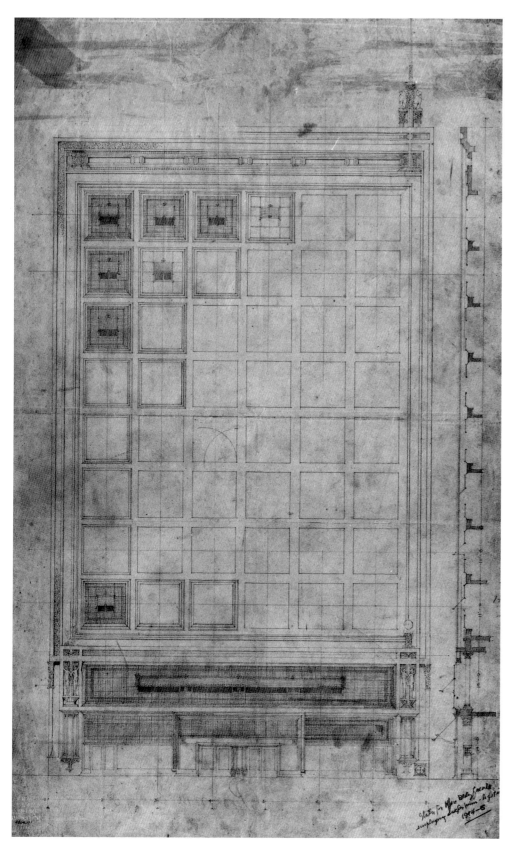

architect did not involve any awareness of the importance of the plan and the space it shaped.

In fact, Sullivan showed remarkably little interest or capacity in the making of plans and the organization of interior space, admitting as much in his discussion of the nature of the skyscraper: 'Only in rare instances does the plan or floor arrangement of the tall office building take on an aesthetic value.'[6] Sullivan accepted the developing logic of commercial high-rise construction – the eight-to-ten-foot-high floors, structural span and window rhythm determined by the economic use of standard steel elements, the building width determined by penetration of daylight to work areas: 'Wanted, an indefinite number of stories piled tier upon tier, one tier just like another tier, one office just like all the other offices – an office being similar to a cell in a honeycomb, merely a component, nothing more.'[7] This soberingly direct presentation of the economic determinism that drove the development of the Chicago-frame building should, as Rowe suggests, do away with that invention of modernist historians, 'the dichotomy between the virtuous Chicago of the Loop and the depraved Chicago of the Fair. Magnificently undisguised, the office buildings of the Loop owe something of their authenticity to their being no more than the rationalization of business requirements.'[8]

For Sullivan, the emphasis was upon the frame and how the elevation and building skin could express (through exposure) this structural skeleton. In the designs examined in this chapter, Wright proposed an alternative to the skyscraper's definition as mere skin and skeleton, pursuing instead the relation between space, plan and structure, characteristically attempting to reinvent the entire concept of the skyscraper rather than merely modifying ideas received from others. In doing this, Wright also rejected the commercial determination of high-rise design, which he sarcastically characterized as 'this glorious patriotic enterprise, space-making for rent, [which] is looked upon as bona-fide proof of American progress and greatness'.[9] He came to feel that the possibility for place-making in the American city was fundamentally threatened by this urge to build higher and higher buildings closer and closer together: 'Space as a becoming psychic element of the American city is gone. Instead of this fine sense is come the tall and narrow stricture. The skyscraper envelope is not ethical, beautiful, or permanent. It is a commercial exploit or mere expedient. It has no higher ideal of unity than commercial success.'[10]

The Tall Building Spatially Considered

Initially, however, Wright attempted to develop the steel frame's spatial possibilities, to determine if indeed this design instrument, which had proved so fertile in the hands of his mentor Sullivan, could be bent to Wright's will. Soon after establishing his own practice, Wright received the perfect opportunity, the commission to design a prototypical office building utilizing the products of the Luxfer Prism Company

Far left: Project for Luxfer Prism Company Building Chicago, Illinois, 1895, elevation and section of street front window wall. The steel frame is a perfect square grid.
Below: 'Romeo and Juliet' Windmill for Hillside Home School, Spring Green, Wisconsin, 1896, plan and view. The windmill was an important precursor to Wright's later high-rise designs.

of Chicago. Wright's design of 1895, shown in a beautifully detailed elevation drawing, is startling in its abstraction, even when compared to Sullivan's efforts. The steel frame is a perfect square grid in elevation, with square prisms projected out of the centre of each bay, and the entire infill surface of each bay – approximately nine feet square – composed of glass divided into a grid of four-inch squares.

The section to the right of the elevation reveals that Wright intended each bay to be fully glazed almost from floor to ceiling, with the windows projecting forward from the structural frame six inches, with a bevelled edge all around. The glass would have constituted the foremost surface or layer of this building, with the frame recessed behind (the opposite of the typical Chicago-frame building where the windows are recessed into the frame), and the Luxfer prisms reaching out into the narrow street to capture the light and bounce it deep into the building. While not a true curtain wall, as it has sometimes been called, this early design established, within each bay, the independence of the glazing system from the underlying structural frame, a development essential to the later realization of curtain walls in Wright's work. But the structural frame itself had proven resistant to even Wright's potent ability to form space into meaningful place.

Wright's 'Romeo and Juliet' Windmill, built in 1896 for his aunts near the Hillside Home School in Spring Green, was his first attempt to utilize natural forms as precedent for a vertical structural design, and was to be an important precedent in Wright's own work for his later developments in high-rise design. The windmill consists in plan of an octagonal volume, four-inch by four-inch wood posts at the corners, with a taller, narrow, diamond-shaped volume penetrating halfway into it; the whole is sixty feet tall and was originally covered with wood shingles and horizontal board battening. Eight steel straps extend six feet out of the solid stone foundations and are bolted to the eight corner posts of the octagon-shaped volume, two of which coincide with the middle corners of the diamond-shaped volume. The whole was an early form of the stressed-skin or tube high-rise structure, and Wright himself accepted the analogy to a barrel's construction, made by his uncles; the windmill looks even more the part after it was given a new skin of board and batten siding in 1939.

The sharply pointed diamond shape (Wright called it the 'storm prow'), has a six-inch by six-inch wood post running its full height at the centre, reinforced and braced every ten feet by diagonal-set wood flooring, carrying the fourteen-foot windmill at the top. While it has been suggested that Wright's later cantilevered skyscrapers, those designed after his extended stay in Japan from 1917 to 1922, had their central 'tap-root' structure derived from the central wooden column typical of Japanese and Chinese pagoda temples, Wright himself made several references to the importance of this little windmill design, with its central wooden post

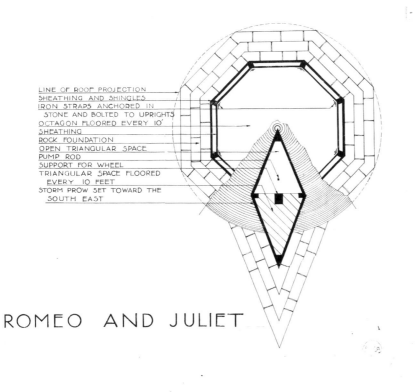

LINE OF ROOF PROJECTION
SHEATHING AND SHINGLES
IRON STRAPS ANCHORED IN
  STONE AND BOLTED TO UPRIGHTS
OCTAGON FLOORED EVERY 10'
SHEATHING
ROCK FOUNDATION
OPEN TRIANGULAR SPACE
PUMP ROD
SUPPORT FOR WHEEL
TRIANGULAR SPACE FLOORED
  EVERY 10 FEET
STORM PROW SET TOWARD THE
  SOUTH EAST

ROMEO AND JULIET

– and to its sustained existence in the face of extensive family doubt about its durability.[11] The dynamic integration of non-rectilinear forms in plan is also an early suggestion of the way in which Wright would engage such geometries much later in his life.

The Larkin Building discussed earlier, seems at first glance to be based quite directly on Sullivan's Wainwright Building, with its brick and terracotta-clad steel frame, its emphasis on the vertical columns, its recessed horizontal spandrels, and its 'Chicago' three-panel windows. Yet the manner in which the central vertical light-filled volume ties all the floors of the building together, spatially and socially, results in a design that rejects the endless horizontal 'pancake' floors of typical high-rise office buildings and instead proposes a place of work that is truly sacred – exactly the opposite of the 'honeycomb' of universal office cells described by Sullivan above.

Rowe has noted that 'Chicago did seem to experience a prevision of two of the major themes of twentieth-century architecture – the frame structure and the composition of intersecting planes.'[12] For Wright, the frame was only a provisional structure for the ordering of interior space: intersecting volumes would prove far more productive. While Sullivan and the other architects of the Chicago School were satisfied to imprint their design ideas on the facade, Wright was intent upon bringing the dynamic,

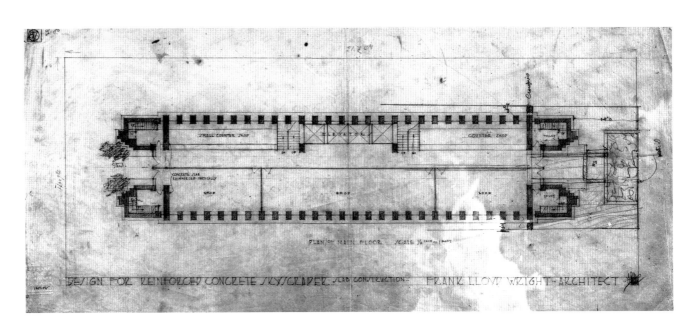

*Far left: Project for San
Francisco Call Building,
San Francisco, California, 1912,
perspective. The cantilevered roof
slabs give precise definition of the
top of the building.
Above: Project for San Francisco
Call Building, plan. Large
concrete corner piers frame the two
narrow ends of the building.*

interpenetrating spatial forms of the Prairie Houses to bear
on public space. As Rowe said, in struggling to clarify his
domestic spatial ideals, Wright's 'Sullivanian training
reasserted itself to demand a rationalization of this spatial
achievement in terms of a generating structure ... a
conviction as to the "organic" unity of space and
structure.'[13] As is already evidenced in the Larkin Building,
Wright was to go far beyond Sullivan in his pursuit of such
an ideal.

Wright's Press or *Call* Building project, proposed for San
Francisco in 1912, was to be built of reinforced concrete,
and takes the form of an elongated twenty-five-storey slab
set on a corner, with a lower block infilling between the
corner slab and the neighbouring building in some of the
perspective sketches – a careful and deferential adaptation
to the context that disappeared when the design was
rendered in the pure white plaster model we see sitting on
the fireplace mantel in the Taliesin draughting room. The
main slab is striated from top to bottom by continuous
concrete piers, the windows and spandrels at the floor lines
recessed behind these piers; the close relation between these
square piers and the square wood slats that Wright used in
his furniture and built-in cabinets can be seen in this
photograph, another example of Wright's nesting of
elements at different scales. Large concrete corner piers
frame the two narrow ends, where the entrances are located,

and which the 'projecting slab' or cornice at the roof
cantilevers far out over. A second slab projects out over the
wider sides two storeys below the roof, so that even in this
tight flat slab Wright achieves his characteristic spatial
weaving through these interlocking cornice slabs with their
crossed trajectories; the interior spaces and the structure
(somewhere between a frame and a wall slab), however, do
not interpenetrate, and it would be over ten years before
Wright was to arrive at his essential fusion of structure and
space in the high-rise.

National Insurance Company Building project, Chicago, Illinois, 1923

In discussing Wright's design of the cantilevered
skyscraper, his pivotal spatial and social contributions to
high-rise design, his rejection of what he termed 'the
tyranny of the skyscraper' and his ideal of making places for
dwelling in the sky, it should first be noted that Wright's
breakthrough to his mature conception of the skyscraper
occurred directly following the Chicago Tribune Tower
Competition of 1922.[14] It is almost impossible to believe that
Wright, by this time the most important architect ever to
have emerged from Chicago, even though away in Japan at
the time of the competition, would not have been appalled
at the results, which seemed to accept the image or purely
formal qualities of the skyscraper, rather than its structure,

189

DING FOR NATIONAL LIFE INSURANCE CHICAGO FRANK LLOYD WRIGHT ARCHITECT W TALIESIN

Left: Second project for the National Insurance Company Building. The curtain wall is here divided into a square grid.

spatial order or social and functional composition, as its most essential and defining feature.[15] Rowe has noted that all other skyscrapers typically had been rendered as solid, single volumes, with static structural frames, while the National Insurance Company Building Wright designed for A M Johnson in 1923–4 is composed of transparent, layered, interlocking volumes, with the dynamic structural solution of the cantilevered slab and curtain wall: 'both its construction and its curtain wall constitute an innovation in the Chicago tradition.'[16]

This is also one of the last of Wright's contextual urban designs – something he is not particularly noted for in his later projects – as it adheres to the street grid in the geometry of its volumes; aligns with the street edge at its base, thus defining the street wall; faces south and utilizes one of the 'alphabet' or E-shaped plan types that constituted the typical gridded American city building forms of this period.[17] Wright developed three versions of this design for its site at Water-Tower Plaza, all utilizing very similar plans and massing, each documented in a separate exterior view.

The first design, seen in an eyelevel perspective drawing, shows what appears to be a concrete and glass base topped by a row of large square apertures, upon which rest the four glass towers. This design seems closely related to the concrete-block houses, and this is confirmed by Wright's publication of an uncaptioned detail photograph of the Millard House at the end of the article where this drawing of the design appeared.[18]

The second design, documented in a delicately and exhaustively detailed axonometric drawing, shows the base, now apparently all glass, cut back so that the corners of the glass towers above cantilever out over the sidewalk below. The curtain wall is divided into a square grid, emphasizing neither horizontal nor vertical, and the formal composition of the elevations that characterized the first design – with the corners at top and bottom turned in towards the centre – is no longer evident.

The third design, documented in an eyelevel perspective drawing taken from the side, shows the true lightness of the building, the ground floor now certainly composed of large sheets of glass, and the transparency of the glass and the curtain-like quality of the tower walls above is beautifully rendered. The square grid of the previous design is here abandoned, replaced by a dynamic weaving of sections of vertically oriented curtain wall, at the centres of the masses, and horizontally oriented curtain wall, at the corners. The contrast with the neighbouring masonry-clad buildings with individually framed windows is direct. Frampton has noted, 'The full implication of the Freeman innovation, the extension of the tessellated semi-solid membrane into mitered glass corners and largely glass surfaces' comes with this design.[19]

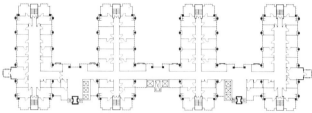

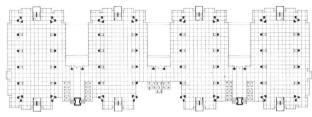

In all three designs, the masses are separated by vertical glazed slots only crossed at the floor lines and the stairs are placed in the centres at both ends of each of the four 'wings', similar to the earlier Larkin Building. As can be seen in the two section drawings, of 1923 and 1924, the structure – pairs of columns set in from the exterior edge of the building wings – are exposed at the top six storeys of the twenty-seven-floor building, where the cantilevered portion of the plan drops away. Each of the four 'wings' or towers acts as an independent building structurally, as indicated by Wright's only drawing in section. The slab-like thin wall at the back of the building that contains the elevators and ties the towers together is supported in sections by spanning between the towers.

Wright drew the section through the structure (rather than through the space, as would be more typical), an unusual choice, but one clearly intended to explicate the cantilevered structure. At basement level, Wright anchors the twin columns with thick reinforced-concrete floors braced against the sides of the foundation walls; interestingly, however, Wright does not show the final foundations for the columns themselves, letting them disappear off the bottom of the drawing in every case. At floors one to sixteen, twenty and twenty-two to twenty-five, the pairs of concrete-clad steel columns support symmetrical sections of cantilevered reinforced concrete and steel floors,

the centre of the plan is a thin floor slab bridging between the inner edges of the cantilevered floors. At ground level, floors seventeen to nineteen and twenty-one, this bridge-slab is left out, producing open central wells not unlike that in the Larkin Building, tying floors together spatially in section, creating vertical connections and potential social interactions within the repetitive floors in a way that is very rare in high-rise buildings.

Almost without exception, the design of high-rise office buildings today eliminates the possibility for place, determined by the character of the building's construction and structure, in favour of universal 'flexible' space; often less flexible in its servicing than Wright's design, but much more flexible in its ability to accommodate the style imposed by the interior decorator, hired separately by each tenant after leasing. Wright's vision of a comprehensive design for building, services, partitions, storage and furnishings, and his emphasis on the creation of vertical social spaces that link the anonymous horizontal office floors, is directly opposed to the endless generation of space for speculative purposes, to be subdivided and decorated according to the latest fashion, that has dominated the recent design and construction of high-rise office buildings, with precious few exceptions.

Wright conceived of the entire building being composed, as Frampton has noted, as a 'woven glass and sheet metal

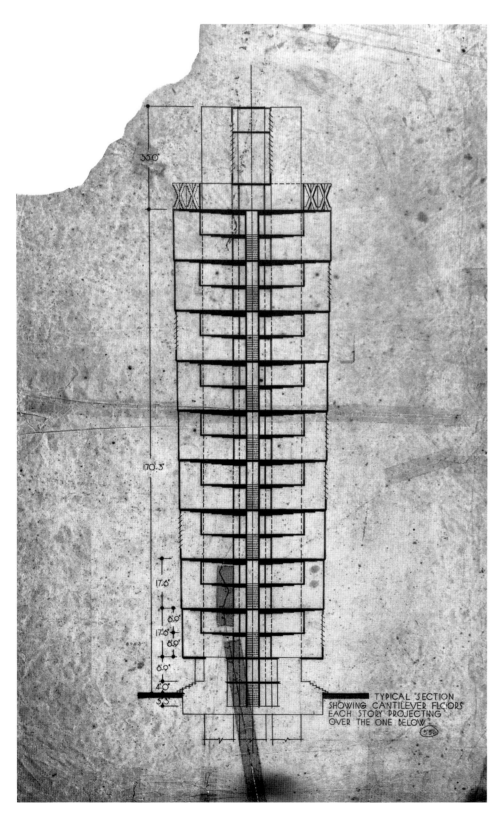

TYPICAL SECTION
SHOWING CANTILEVER FLOORS
EACH STORY PROJECTING
OVER THE ONE BELOW

fabric suspended from a concrete core', constructed almost entirely by prefabrication.[20] Wright wrote:

> The exterior walls, as such, disappear – instead are suspended, standardized sheet-copper screens. The walls themselves cease to exist as either weight or thickness. Windows become in this fabrication a matter of a unit in the screen fabric, opening singly or in groups at the will of the occupant. All windows may be cleaned from the inside with neither bother nor risk. The vertical mullions (copper filled with non-conducting material), are large and strong enough not only to carry from floor to floor and project much or little as shadow on the glass may or may not be wanted. Much projection enriches the shadow. Less projection dispels the shadows and brightens the interior. These projecting blades of copper act in the sun like the blades of a blind.

The edges of the floors are bevelled to the same thin section as the curtain walls they support, appearing:

> in the recessions of the screen in order to bring the concrete structure itself into relief in relation to the screen and well as in connection with it. The [columns] are enlarged to carry electrical, plumbing and heating conduits, which branch from the shafts, not in the floor slabs, but into piping designed into visible fixtures extending beneath each ceiling to where the outlets are needed in the office arrangement. All electrical or plumbing appliances may thus be disconnected and relocated at short notice with no waste at all in time or material. Being likewise fabricated on a perfect unit system, the interior partitions may all be made up in sections, complete with doors, ready to set in place and designed to match the general style of the outer screen wall. These interior partition-units thus fabricated may be stored ready to use, and any changes to suit tenants made overnight. The radiators are cast as a railing set in front of the lower glass unit of this outer screen wall, free enough to make cleaning easy.[21]

We have to remind ourselves that this was written in 1928 about a design completed in 1924, only seven years after the construction of the first true curtain-wall structure in the world, for today few high-rise buildings are as comprehensively and efficiently designed as the Wright's National Insurance Company Building.[22] The perspectives drawn of the interior office spaces exhibit innovative concepts for storage, work stations and integrated services, and yet also show a serene and beautifully proportioned space, similar to traditional Japanese domestic rooms – perhaps not surprising as the design followed his return from five years in Japan. Though he had pioneered air conditioning in the Larkin Building of 1904, Wright here insisted on allowing for individual operation of windows, even many storeys up in the air, rather than the permanently sealed glazing already typical in high-rises. Wright's concern for the mechanical servicing as well as the prefabricated construction of the building was an integral part of his design process, and in these concerns Wright was virtually unique at that time.

In the design of the National Insurance Company Building Wright took into account not only the method of construction of building, fittings and furnishings, but also its operation and maintenance; he planned for simple cleaning of windows, efficient fire exiting, all-glass store-fronts at street level, calculated energy demand, in both heating and lighting, according to the area of glass and insulating copper panels, and – in a comment that suggests just how far in advance of other architects he was at this time – he notes that the building would be 'at least one-third lighter than anything in the way of a tall building yet built – and three times stronger in any disturbance'.[23] This last consideration referred to the cantilevered structural concept first conceived by Wright for the Imperial Hotel, with the load balanced on inset columns, which he here designed for the first time. Sullivan, whose praise for the Hotel after its survival of the earthquake was part of his and Wright's long-delayed reconciliation, was shown the design for the National Insurance Company Building by Wright in 1924, the year of Sullivan's death; Wright remembers Sullivan saying, 'I never could have done this building myself, but I believe that, but for me, you could never have done it.'[24]

St Mark's-in-the-Bouwerie Apartment Tower Project, New York, 1929

It would be twenty years before Wright would actually build a skyscraper incorporating these structural, construction and servicing ideas; while he was commissioned to design a number of high-rise projects during that period, none of them would be built. By far the most important of these was the design for an apartment tower for St Mark's-in-the-Bouwerie, in New York City, of 1929. This departed radically from the design for the National Insurance Company in its urban strategy, for it required the skyscraper to assume a completely independent stance in an open park setting, unrelated to the existing street grid or neighbouring buildings; Wright said, 'this skyscraper planned to stand free in an urban park and thus fit for human occupancy.'[25]

In the St Mark's Tower project, Wright perfected and distilled the structural concept first presented in the National Insurance Company Building, designing a single central cluster of reinforced-concrete core structures, cantilevering the reinforced-concrete floor slabs out in all directions, and tapering them towards the edges where the metal and glass curtain wall was suspended. Wright called the design 'the first expression of a tree-like mast structure', saying it 'is as nearly organic as steel in tension and concrete in compression can make it, doing for the tall building what Lidgerwood made steel do for the long ship. The ship had its keel: this building has its concrete core.'[26] With this design Wright achieved his ideal of a fusion of structural and spatial orders, confirmed in his studies of Japanese pagodas, which he related directly to the organic ideal of the tree with its structural core (trunk), tap-root foundation (roots), cantilevered floors (branches) and nonbearing curtain wall (leaves).[27] Wright wrote that same year:

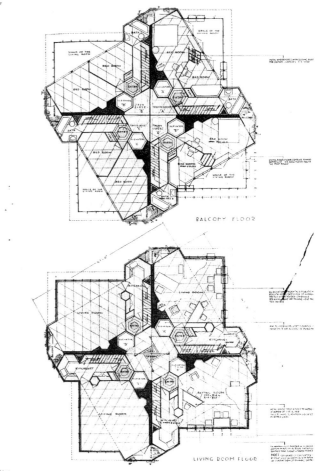

In the steel and glass buildings I have designed there are no walls, only wallscreens. The method of the cantilever in concrete and steel yields best to suspended screens or shells in place of outer walls; all may be shop-fabricated. The spider-web is a good inspiration for steel construction. A slender mechanized fabric for all walls and partitions enters here to give the form and style that is architecture.[28]

The St Mark's Tower is beautifully resolved in its plan geometries, one square appearing to be rotated inside another, with an open centre defined by four triangular fireplace and elevator slabs set in a pinwheel formation, the whole organized on an equilateral triangle grid. In the four double-height apartments on every second floor, the living-dining room and kitchen are overlooked by two bedrooms, the triangular space between the two rotated squares of the building open to below. The living-dining room is a single open space with windows on two sides, looking away from the other apartments, the fireplace housed in one inside wall and the stair, kitchen and entrance built into the other. The rotation of the two squares in plan – the outer square defined by the living-room walls and the inner square defined by the bedroom walls, so that they dominate the volumes of alternate floors, when combined with the largely transparent walls of the living rooms – allows the two volumes to be seen on the exterior simultaneously, slipping in and out of each other,

interpenetrating and interweaving in a highly dynamic spatial composition.

Only the structural and service cores reach the ground, and the apartment volumes stop at the second floor, their corners cantilevering out in all directions. The floors taper as they project out from their central support, stepping out a few inches at each second floor in the final design. Wright explained that this profile would prevent the rain wash of each floor from dripping on to the one below, helping keep the building clean, and that the increase in area towards the top would increase the value of the building, as the upper floors are generally able to bring a higher price per square foot. We should also notice that this stepping out of the floors as they rise both 'corrects' the perspectival distortion evident in the apparent shrinking of high-rise buildings towards the top, and more closely approximates the condition of the foliage of a tree, which varies in width, increasing as it rises; these aspects suggest that Wright, as usual, had reasons for his design decisions that operated simultaneously on a number of levels – technical, material, experiential, analytical and analogous.

WRIGHT CONTINUED perfecting and developing this unique conception of the skyscraper, where the structure is ordered by the spatial experience, designing a series of projects that proposed linking numerous towers like that designed for St Mark's in sequence, joined at their edges and by bridges so as to share elevators and stairs, in such projects as Grouped Towers project for Chicago of 1930 and the Crystal Heights project for Washington, DC, of 1939. These designs incorporated enormous parking garages as their bases, isolating them from other buildings and from contact with the ground or street, so that their urban setting seemed increasingly irrelevant. This antiurban pattern of high-rise design continued in the hypothetical skyscraper Wright designed in 1931 for Chicago's World Fair; though it was ordered on a square grid rather than the triangular one used in the previous projects, and though it is in many ways a considerably enlarged version of one of the four towers of the National Insurance Company Building project, the large plinth-like base made of several floors of terraced parking isolates it from the urban context in a way quite different from the design of 1924.

Wright first realized one of his cantilevered skyscraper designs in 1944, when he built the Johnson Wax Research Tower. This design will be discussed in the context of the buildings Wright constructed for the Johnson Wax Company in a later chapter. Here we should simply note that, despite being designed to house research laboratories, the section of the Johnson Wax Tower is based directly on that of the St Mark's Apartment Tower, right down to its double-height spaces, its 'tap-root' structure, its central mast-like core containing circulation and services, and its outward stepping form. Its only significant difference is in

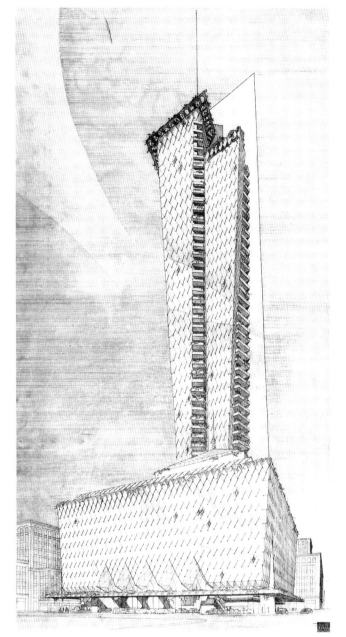

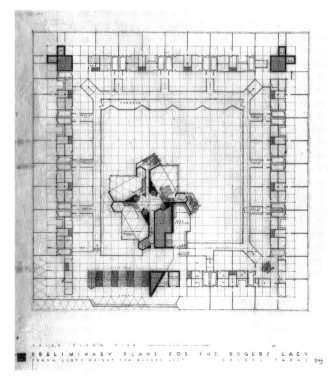

the exterior wall, for the Johnson Wax Tower does not utilize a continuous curtain wall, rather having its glass-tube glazing attached in two-storey segments between exposed, brick-clad upturn concrete walls at the slab edges. Wright said of this design:

So we went up in the air around a giant central stack with floors branching from it, having clear light and space all around each floor. All laboratory space was then clear and in direct connection with a duct-system cast in the hollow reinforced-concrete floors, connecting to the vertical hollow of the stack itself. Cantilevered from the giant stack, the floor slabs spread out like tree branches. All utilities and the many intact and exhaust pipes run in their own central utility grooves, arranged like the cellular pattern of the tree trunk. From each alternate floor slab an outer glass shell hangs firm.[29]

The Rogers Lacy Hotel project for Dallas, Texas, of 1946 is spatially and structurally an extraordinary design which, while not being realized in its original form, has nevertheless affected entire later generations of hotel designs.[30] Wright designed a twelve-storey base building that filled the city block – we should note this adherence to the urban grid – with a pinwheeling tower of the St Mark's type placed in the corner of its square interior top-lit atrium court. As he states, there are no corridors in this building, as the tower rooms open off a central core at each floor and circulation to the atrium rooms occurs as a series of

Right: Project for Rogers Lacy Hotel, section, tower and courtyard atrium.
Far right and Below: Harold C Price Company Tower, section and plans.
Opposite page: Harold C Price Company Tower, exterior view. Office spaces are located behind the angled horizontal fins, while the apartment quadrant is fronted by vertical fins which run the full height of the building.

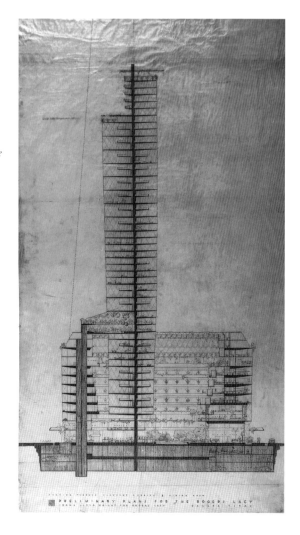

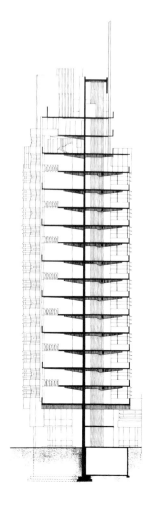

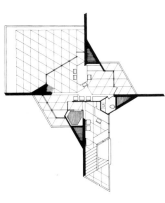

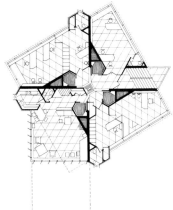

stepped-back mezzanine walkways, open on one side to the central space. The floors of these mezzanine walkways are set two feet below the floors of the rooms they serve, so that the rooms may overlook not only the exterior street, as is normal, but the interior atrium space as well, achieving double exposure and through ventilation without sacrificing the privacy of individual rooms.

The tower section varies as it passes up through the atrium and out the top of the courtyard block, with floors of either single- or double-height rooms, or occasionally both. In plan, one of the tower's four quadrants is given over to service spaces, and is used to anchor the tower to the interior edge of the atrium at the lower levels. Also included in this space is the large air-conditioning intake and exhaust which, above the courtyard block, appears as what Wright called 'the impressive mass:'[31] an angled blade-like wall projecting out of the full height of the tower. This solid concrete mass is in sharp contrast to the rest of the building's skin, which is a kind of quilted fabric of layered glass set on a diagonal grid, suppressing all indications of the structure and floor lines.

H C Price Company Tower, Bartlesville, Oklahoma, 1952

Twenty-three years after its original conception, Wright realized a design directly related in both plan and section to his seminal St Mark's Tower when he built the Price Tower in 1952; he had been sixty-two years old when he conceived this dramatic and innovative design, and was eighty-five years old when he finally built it. The client had requested only a small headquarters for his modest company, but Wright proposed a tower on the prairie, where he had always meant to put it, as called for in his Broadacre City design; the tower alone on the horizontal plain rather than in the vertical urban context with other towers. As the footprint of the Price Tower is considerably smaller than that proposed for the St Mark's design, Wright only provided one stair – as compared to the two in the St Mark's Tower – which has resulted in the Price Tower standing empty for considerable periods, due to its failure to meet the minimum of two fire exit stairs that has more recently been written into law. Though based closely on the St Mark's plan, the Price Tower has apartments in only one quadrant of each floor, for eight double-height apartments in total, with single-height offices taking up the other three quadrants of its pinwheel plan. This makes for a considerably different exterior appearance, in that there exists only one quadrant of the 'second' square, rotated relative to the first in plan, that being the living rooms of the apartments.

We should note that here in a similar way to the Johnson Wax Tower, Wright has abandoned the curtain wall; the

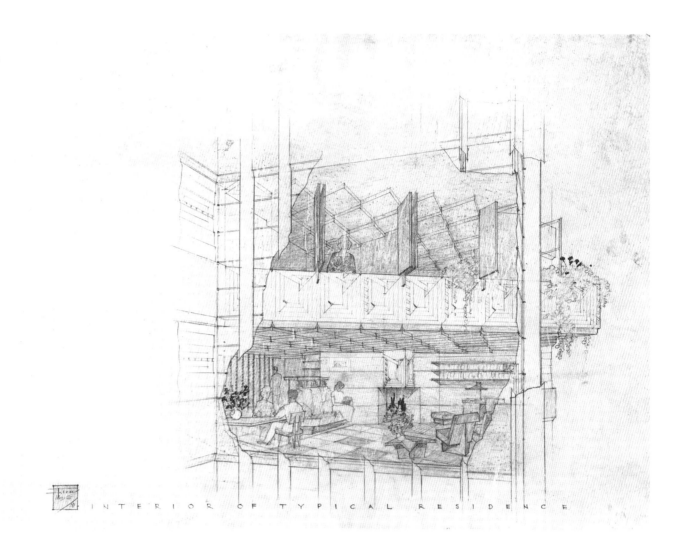

tower looks so much like the St Mark's design that we might not notice this important difference. At both the apartments and, more noticeably, at the offices, the low wall, which on alternate floors is clad in stucco and copper fascia panels, rests on the edge of the floor slab, and the glass in turn rests upon it, so that the tower's skin is not hung like a continuous curtain, as is the case in a true curtain wall, but is instead rendered in structurally and materially independent sections. Yet, in doing this, Wright is still able to clearly indicate the functions housed behind each elevation by his use of the copper fins or sunshades he attached to the windows; in the three quadrants of offices, three angled horizontal fins shade the glass and wrap around the corner, terminating against the projecting bathrooms, stair landing and kitchen; at the apartment quadrant, angled vertical fins run uninterrupted the full height of the building, the double-height floor lines recessed behind the fins and the small balconies off the master bedrooms projecting through them at one edge. One side of the apartments faces south, and on that side we can see both horizontal (office) and vertical (bedroom) elevations. Thus even in this small and compact skyscraper, Wright expresses the functional and spatial differences within on the elevations, suggesting the variety of ways one might live in the sky.

Wright designed custom-made furnishings for the Price Tower, as the small dimensions and triangular planning grid made the use of conventional tables and desks difficult. Wright's designs involve angled edges on desks, triangular end tables and hexagonal chairs; altogether a bit overwhelming when experienced in the close confines of the building, with its triangular grid inscribed in the floor and imprinted in the walls. On the other hand the structural details, such as the hollow reinforced-concrete slab that tapers in gentle steps of the ceiling from twenty inches at the core to only three inches at the edge, articulate the way in which we are being housed and elevated so subtly and effectively as to suggest the tower's origins in natural precedents.

WRIGHT PROPOSED two other skyscraper designs that remained unbuilt, the first being the Golden Beacon Apartment Tower project for Chicago in 1956, a forty-four-storey design that utilized the St Mark's Tower plan and a stretched version of the Price Tower elevation, with a restaurant to occupy the top floors. Wright's 'Mile High' Office Building was also designed for Chicago in 1956, in response to the commission to design a television antenna of that extreme height. At 5,280 feet tall with 528 floors at 10 feet each from grade to top elevator landing, and an

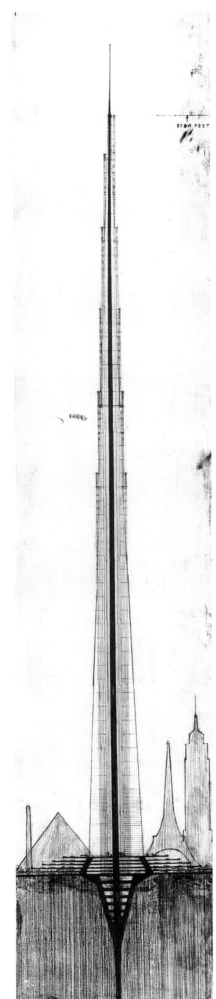

Left: Price Company Tower, cutaway perspective looking into a double-height apartment.
Right: Project for the 'Mile High' Office Building, Chicago, Illinois, 1956, section. For comparison, Wright has drawn at the same scale, from left, the Washington Monument, the Pyramid of Cheops, the Eiffel Tower, and the Empire State Building (the tallest building in the world in 1956).

5280 FEET

antenna above, it dwarfed the other great monuments Wright drew in its shadow – the Pyramid of Cheops, the Washington Monument and the Eiffel Tower – its tap-root foundation extended as far down into the earth as the Empire State Building (then the tallest in the world) extended into the sky.

Wright left us two conflicting arguments behind this rather unlikely proposal, the first revealed when he suggested that only a few would be needed to replace all the density of buildings in New York, and that 'the Mile High is a necessary step in the direction of Broadacre City;'[32] a claim that, if true, would call his great suburban proposal into question. The second reasoning, related to the nature of his conceptual process in designing the cantilevered towers, is his dedication of the Mile High design to innovative builders and structural engineers: Sullivan, Roebling (designer of the Brooklyn Bridge), Lidgerwood (designer of the first modern ship's keel), Coignet and Monier (originators of modern reinforced concrete), Eduardo Torroja (structural engineer), Pier Luigi Nervi (structural engineer) and Robert Maillart (bridge designer). But, unlike the works by these designers and engineers, Wright's Mile High Tower was destined from its inception never to be realized; not because it was technically unbuildable, for it was within that realm of possibility, but because Wright presented it as a purely abstract exercise, not conceiving it as he had his other high-rise designs, as a place scaled to and ordered by human experience.

SULLIVAN HAD engaged the organic metaphor in attempting to give order to the high-rise, and while he succeeded in creating a formidable method of surface articulation or cladding, he failed to bring the structure into his system, employing the traditional post-and-beam, rendered in steel and projected to a scale heretofore unknown. On the other hand, Wright believed that a redefinition of the structure itself, not merely of its cladding, was the key to finding an order for the high-rise. In his most inspired designs Wright engaged the tree as the organic model, deploying the structural cantilevers of the floors from the central mast-like core, letting the curtainwall hang free in the wind. It is indeed ironic that it was Wright, champion of the horizontal and lifelong sceptic as to the merits of the skyscraper, who in the end best answered Sullivan's call for a high-rise that rose 'from bottom to top' as 'a unit without a single dissenting line'.

THE ANCHORED DWELLING

The land is the simplest form of architecture.
It is man in possession of his earth. It is the only
true record of him where his possession of earth
is concerned. While he was true to earth his
architecture was creative.

Frank Lloyd Wright[1]

*Left: Edgar Kaufmann House
'Fallingwater', Mill Run,
Pennsylvania, 1935, detail of stair
from Edgar Kaufmann Sr's study
to west terrace.
Above: Wright and the Taliesin
Fellowship Apprentices, 1937. Bob
Mosher and Edgar Tafel (to the
right) were involved in overseeing
Fallingwater's construction, while
William Wesley Peters (with arms
on desk) developed the concrete
cantilevered structural floors
for the house.*

In 1932, at the end of the Great Depression in America, Frank Lloyd Wright was already sixty-five years old, an age when most people are already well into their retirement years. In the almost forty years since starting his own practice in 1893, Wright had built hundreds of works; it was altogether a long and prodigious career by any reckoning, and one unmatched in America before or since. Wright's practice had all but disappeared in the economic decline of the late 1920s, his last built work being the Richard Lloyd Jones House in 1929. Wright had written his autobiography during those slow years, summing up his seminal contributions to the development of an American architecture. While many chose to see this as the final statement of an illustrious architectural career, Wright intended it to be his means of contacting an entirely new generation of clients.

Wright's place in the evolution of 'modern' architecture was a problem for Henry Russell Hitchcock and Philip Johnson, curators of the highly influential 1932 Museum of Modern Art exhibition entitled 'The International Style', who chose to present Wright's work as the preamble to, rather than the exemplary model of, 'modern' architecture. Wright's themes of regional identity and grounding in the specifics of the site were directly opposed to the 'international' style's emphasis on universal formal models and suppression of regional or national character, and as a result Wright and his ideas were presented as belonging to the nineteenth, rather than the twentieth century.

So it should not be surprising that at the end of the Depression many of the American Public assumed that Wright had retired from active practice, happy to bask in the glory of the new architectural histories that portrayed him as the grandfather of the modern architecture now being built around the world. As Joseph Connors has noted, these histories implied that Wright 'had pointed the way to the promised land that he would never himself enter'.[2]

However, it had never been wise to count Wright out; throughout his life he had repeatedly rebounded from a variety of personal and professional calamities, and was about to do so once again. Pivotal in this resurgence was Wright's marriage in 1928 to Oglivanna Lazovich, born in Montenegro, and a follower of the Russian mystic Georgei Gurdijieff. When in 1932 Wright founded the Taliesin Fellowship, offering apprenticeships to young students willing to work on the farm and in the draughting room, he to a large degree modelled this enterprise – with Oglivanna's guidance – on Gurdijieff's Institute in Fontainebleau. The Taliesin Fellowship was also closely related to contemporary experimental American utopian communities, as well as similar craft-based colonies worldwide.[3]

Opened in the very depths of the Great Depression, the Fellowship succeeded largely because of Wright's continued reputation as the greatest American architect, the popularity of his many works built throughout the country continuing to grow despite the efforts of those defining and defending the 'International Style' to render Wright irrelevant. Students enrolled in the fellowship from all over the United States and the world, coming to Spring Green, Wisconsin, helping to rebuild the dilapidated buildings of Taliesin and the Hillside Home School, which Wright had built for his aunts in 1902, and which he now converted and added to, producing the offices, draughting room and dormitories for the Taliesin Fellowship. The students received no pay for their work in construction, farming, cooking, cleaning and draughting at Taliesin – in fact, they paid Wright for the privilege!

The Fellowship developed as a kind of office-school-monastery, where the young apprentices assisted Wright in every aspect of his practice at Taliesin. Wright's designing rarely ceased at the start of construction, necessitating his regular presence on the often distant construction sites; this had been the rule during the earlier phases of his career. Yet with the rapid nationwide expansion of his practice during the period following the establishment of the Fellowship, Wright relied more and more on his Taliesin apprentices to undertake construction supervision. While Wright had an astonishingly accurate innate sense of materials and their constructive and structural possibilities, he was often unable to pass this on to his apprentices. Wright's judgements made on the construction site were inevitably and unnervingly correct, but his dictates from afar were noticeably less so. However, not following exactly the drawings done under Wright's supervision at Taliesin, or allowing the contractor to make changes not first specifically approved by Wright – even if they seemed clearly called for – would, if discovered by Wright, result in the apprentice being recalled to Taliesin and replaced by another. Wright's apprentices were thus in a no-win situation when alone and facing a dilemma on the construction site, with predictable results.

Edgar Kaufmann House, 'Fallingwater', Mill Run, Pennsylvania, 1935

One of the apprentices who joined the Fellowship in October 1934 was Edgar Kaufmann, Jr, a young art student whose father was Edgar Kaufmann, owner of the Kaufmann's Store in Pittsburgh. At the end of 1934, Kaufmann's parents visited their son at Taliesin, and Wright was commissioned to design a country house on Bear Run, an Appalachian mountain stream in southwest Pennsylvania.[4] After visiting the site, Wright returned to Taliesin, and nine months went by with no discernable evidence that he was designing the Kaufmann House – not even a single sketch. In writing of his design process a few years before, Wright stated that he trained himself to:

conceive the building in the imagination, not on paper but in the mind, thoroughly – before touching paper. Let it live

Right: Preliminary study for the Fallingwater plan, with all three levels of the house superimposed on a site contour map.
Far right: View of Fallingwater from across the stream, showing the integration of the house and the landscape through a careful syncopation of vertical and horizontal, ground-based and air-borne elements.

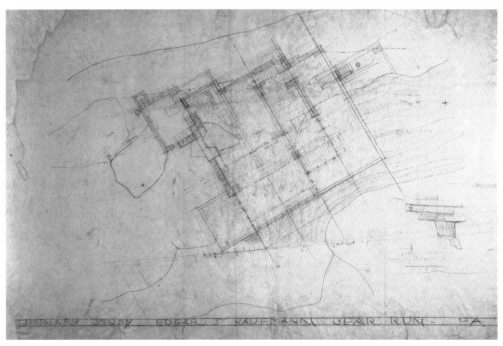

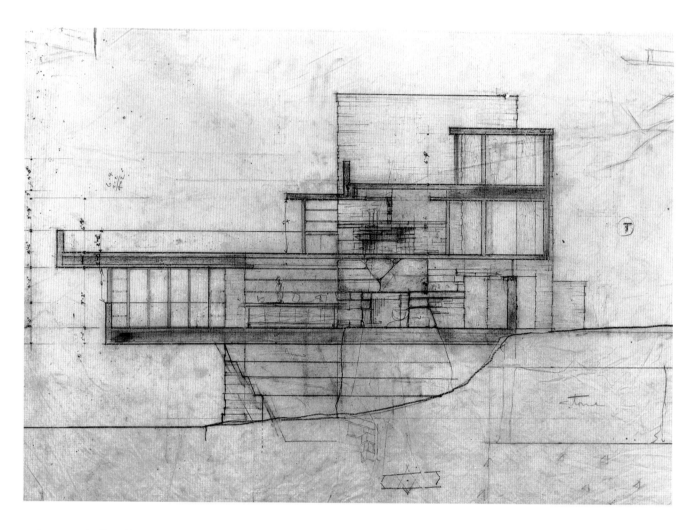

there – gradually taking more definite form before committing it to the draughting board. When the thing lives for you – start to plan it with tools. Not before. It is best to cultivate the imagination to construct and complete the building before working on it with T-square and triangle.'[5]

This description of how a design was conceived and took form in Wright's mind would seem the only explanation in this case, for when Wright received a call from Kaufmann one Sunday morning in late September 1935, inquiring about the design, Wright said, 'Come along, E. J. We're ready for you.'[6] Kaufmann was leaving Milwaukee for Taliesin, a mere two-hour drive, and not a single drawing had been made! The understandable panic of the apprentices did not disturb Wright as he set about drawing plans, sections and elevations for the house; of these drawings Donald Hoffmann has stated, '[Wright's] sketches may have looked a little rough to Kaufmann [who had no idea they had just been drawn], but they turned out to be a remarkably complete presentation of the house as it would be built: the house had been conceived with an awesome finality.'[7]

Historians have often claimed that the design for Fallingwater was inspired by the International Style of architecture that had been canonized in the 1932 Museum of Modern Art exhibition. The close relation of Fallingwater to Wright's earlier work indicates this to be an invention on the part of the historians; Wright was quite specific about this, saying of Fallingwater, 'The ideas involved here are in no wise changed from those of early work. The materials and methods of construction come through them. The effects you see in this house are not superficial effects, and are entirely consistent with the prairie houses of 1901–10.'[8]

The lack of preliminary sketch studies in his design process resulted from Wright's designing buildings in sequence, as variations on a common theme – spatial, constructional or site specific. These sequential designs can be treated as the preliminary studies for Fallingwater, part of the 'constantly accumulating residue of formula' that Wright achieved by designing each building not as a single unique form but as part of the development of spatial types, perfected through a series of designs for different buildings.[9] Wright himself stated that the house for Mrs Thomas Gale, designed in 1904 and built in Oak Park in 1909, with its horizontal planes and balconies projecting from a core of vertical slab-like walls, was the 'progenitor as to general type' for Fallingwater.[10] Following this we could suggest the Robie House of 1909 (cantilevered balcony and diagonal perspective view), Taliesin of 1911 (rough horizontal stonework contrasted with gold-coloured plaster), the Freeman House of 1923 (cantilevered mitered-glass corner), the Elizabeth Noble Apartment Building and St Mark's Tower, both of 1929 (reinforced concrete

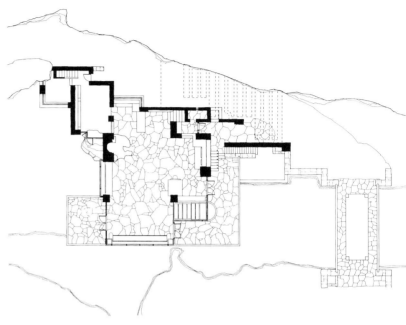

cantilevered floors) and the Malcolm Willey House project of 1932 (balconies cantilevered from central structural core).

As Wright had indicated, the plan of Fallingwater was developed from those of the Prairie Houses; the basic organization of a cruciform interpenetrating a square is to be found here, as is the typical asymmetrical, spiralling, perimeter movement pattern and hidden entrance.[11] In those early houses, Wright's overall symmetrical order in plan allowed the corners to open; here the open corner becomes such a strong spatial element in its own right in that it allows the plan to do without literal symmetry. The house is held together by the diagonal tensions between intimate internal places, so that the outer edges are free to respond to the natural site, as when the rear wall of the house steps along the drive in response to the natural rock wall of the hill behind.

The plan of Fallingwater emphasizes the underlying order of the series of parallel walls and piers which support the main volume of the house. In the main-floor plan, the pier lying under the centre of the living room is not matched, as the others are, by a square stone pier or wall rising through the living room to support the floors above; only the dining table's central position marks this hidden support below. The two piers, fireplace and entrance wall of the living room create a square central volume, off the corners of which open the entrance, stairs, kitchen and balconies. This

'great room' contains in a single volume almost all the rooms – living, dining, library and entrance – typically found in the first floor of Wright's Prairie Houses; only the kitchen remains outside.

Kaufmann had the final plans reviewed by his consulting engineers, who from the start were doubtful about both Wright's competence with a material like reinforced concrete – still considered 'new' in America and atypical for domestic construction – and his decision to place the house on the rock ledge over the waterfall. The reviews were sent to Wright, who immediately told Kaufmann to return the drawings to Taliesin, 'since he did not deserve the house'. Kaufmann quickly apologized and gave his approval for the working drawings; he later had the engineers' reports buried in the stone wall near the dining table.[12]

Wright had absolute confidence in his own structural intuition as well as that of his chief associates in this area: Mendel Glickman, an older structural engineer with the Fellowship, and William Wesley Peters, a brilliant, largely self-taught structural thinker who remained all his life with Wright at Taliesin. Peters and Glickman calculated the loads in the reinforced-concrete, double-cantilevered slab with integral upturned beams that supported the slate floor: an upside-down early version of the 'waffle' slab capable of the eighteen-foot cantilevers out over the stream. This ingenious design placed the flat slab on the bottom, forming

the ceiling of the space below; as the flagstone floor conceals from above the space inside this structural slab, only by studying the section drawing can we discern the integral beams that do the real structural work in this floor.

The most serious mistake in the construction of Fallingwater was made by the contractor and engineer in the pouring of this first-floor concrete slab: at Kaufmann's request the engineers had redrawn Wright's reinforcing plan for the slab, and by their own admission 'put in twice as much steel as was called for on [Wright's] plans'.[13] This excess steel not only added enormous weight to the carefully calculated slab, but was set so close together that the concrete often did not properly fill in between the reinforcing bars, causing an actual loss of strength. In building the wooden formwork to hold the concrete while it was setting, the contractor also neglected to include a slight upward curve or 'camber', to compensate for the structurally insignificant and normal slight settling that occurs over time in reinforced concrete that spans or cantilevers. The result of these blunders, of which Wright was unaware at the time they occurred, are the drooping lines of the main cantilever and the cracks in the concrete that have plagued the house since its completion. That Wright's initial design, refined by Glickman and Peters, has been able to easily sustain these added structural loads and construction weaknesses, argues convincingly for the quality of their structural intuition.

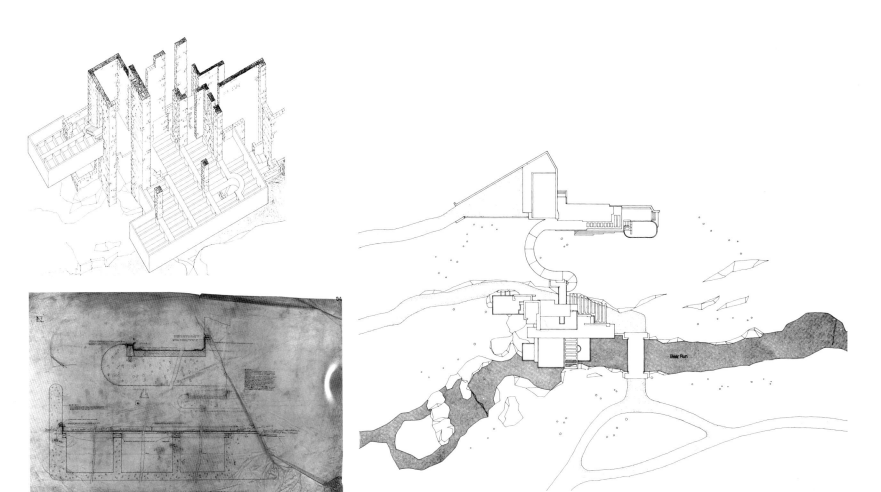

The natural beauty of the extensive site is what we first notice upon arriving at Fallingwater, which is today held in trust by the Western Pennsylvania Conservancy, and may be visited year-round.[14] As we are introduced to the character and natural features of the landscape during our winding approach, we are not aware of the house ahead, for Fallingwater does not dominate its site as country houses have traditionally done, by being placed on the top of the highest point or at the end of a cleared axis. When the house first comes into view, we are somewhat surprised to see across the stream from us a series of horizontal terraces that float without visible means of support. We had expected our first view of the house to be the famous perspective from below the falls; yet the more reserved perspective with which Wright introduces the house is worth considering. As Robert Harrison has said, Fallingwater's 'fame as a masterpiece of architectural design seems strangely at odds with the feature for which it is famous, namely its discretion ... the fact that the house not only comes to rest in its environment but also embodies an extension of the foundation upon which it rests.'[15]

In this house, Wright has created a powerful dichotomy: the natural rock layers are repeated almost exactly, in thickness and random pattern of setting, in the vertical walls that emerge from the boulders above the waterfall, while the lighter coloured horizontal reinforced-concrete

terraces and roof planes exfoliate from this rock wall core, cantilevering both along and across the stream. This opposition reflects the natural condition found in the trees, their roots and trunks anchored to the earth and their limbs and leaves cantilevering out into thin air – a clear conceptual connection between this house and Wright's skyscrapers. The stability of the house, its rooted condition, is unexpectedly emphasized and reinforced by the flow of water under it. Rather than undermining the anchored quality of the house, Harrison notes how 'the dynamic relation between flowing water and solid foundations' imparts to the house a sense of repose on the earth; it appears to have grown from its site.[16] Wright said that 'it is in the nature of any organic building to grow from its site, come out of the ground into the light – the ground itself held always as a component basic part of the building itself'.[17]

'We start with the ground. In any and every case the character of the site is the beginning of the building that aspires to architecture. All must begin there where they stand,' Wright said.[18] He elaborated, 'In the stony bonework of the earth, the principles that shaped stone as it lies, or as it rises and remains to be sculpted by winds and tide – there sleep forms enough for all the ages, for all of man.'[19] What was a small and typical natural event along a stream becomes, with construction of the house, a unique and

211

Above: Early perspective of Fallingwater as seen from the hill across the stream. The floor and ceiling of the living room cross or interpenetrate in space over the stream.

Far right, above: View from the terrace through the living room and out over the waterfall. The terrace is covered by a low roof with trellis-like openings.

Far right: View from the living room through the 'hatch' and down the hanging stairs to the stream below.

habitable space; the house draws all the profiles of the landforms to itself, resolving them within its order.

Yet, here in the forest, thick with trees and fractured by rock walls, Wright also restates the horizontal as the datum of human dwelling, its freedom indicated by the way in which the horizontal concrete planes turn and interlock as they layer one above the other; as Harrison said, 'A house is that which gathers the horizon around itself.'[20] In Fallingwater, Wright creates shelter that is founded on the principle of this horizontal freedom and openness rather than the traditional understanding of closure. Wright built the house into its site, anchoring it to the earth, our only true shelter. In rising from its foundations and opening on to its broad terraces, Fallingwater acts to unfold the sense of shelter latent in the earth itself. Harrison notes how 'Wright reminds us that the earth tends to fold into itself, or to withdraw into its own closure, and that the earth cannot become a shelter unless it is unfolded, or disclosed, by human appropriation.'[21]

As we move around the house, our vantage point changes dramatically in height, from above the house, to even with it, to below it; the horizontal concrete planes and vertical rock walls constantly change position relative to one another, not allowing us to establish any static image of its exterior form. Wright set the house so that it faced thirty degrees east of due south, providing for the dynamic

diagonal views of the house both from the entrance drive and from the flat rock ledge below the falls. 'Thus if the house was photogenic it was not by accident. The picturesque view from the boulder downstream … was built into the design from the start, and to make sure the visitor took it in, a set of stairs was cut into the riverbank leading down to the chosen viewpoint,' Connors has noted.[22]

At the ground floor, the main horizontal volume sits forward of the main vertical set of walls rising out of the back of the house and cantilevers in both directions parallel to the stream above the falls. The main horizontal volume of the first floor, which serves as the ceiling and roof of the floor below, projects perpendicular to the stream bed. These two primary planes cross, one above the other, creating a composite cruciform and capturing the space of the living room at its centre. As is typical in Wright's houses, we are more aware of the undersides than the tops of the horizontal planes; we sense how they cantilever out to cover space, so that the upper portion of the stream above the falls feels as if it has been drawn into the volume of the house. In looking more closely, we notice the glass, set back into the shadows, infilling between the horizontal concrete planes. The red-painted steel mullions only emerge into full view, running in a continuous rhythm up three storeys between the stone walls, when seen from below the waterfall.

On the other side, the view of the house from the bridge is also arresting: the darker vertical rock walls are layered one behind the other, stepping up the side of the hill to the right, while the lighter horizontal reinforced concrete slabs and terraces project far out to the left over the stream. The simple span of the bridge on which we stand, supported at both ends, makes us all the more aware of the extent to which the house cantilevers out from its foundations, supported only at one end. On the bridge, we can hear the waterfall but not see it as the stream disappears over the edge of the rock ledge at the other end of the house. In order to overlook the waterfall from the cantilevered terrace floating in front of us, we cannot enter directly, but must move along the edges of the house, around its perimeter, searching for the entrance which is hidden from the initial view. Utilizing the fact that in architecture the path of the eye can be quite different from the path of the body, Wright lets us catch glimpses of our destination, inviting us to enter the house and rediscover from within what we have first seen or heard from without.

We cross the bridge and turn left, where the concrete trellis over the drive curves dramatically in two places in order to go around the trunks of trees close to the walls of the house. An opening between the layered rock walls to the left lets us into a loggia; ahead is the front door, made like the windows of glass set in red steel frames, deeply

recessed between rock walls, a concrete-slab header forming a low ceiling over the entrance. Opening the door we move into a small foyer; before mounting the three stairs up to the living-room floor, we note that from the level of this lower foyer, our eyelevel is almost exactly at the centre of the space between floor and ceiling. From this perspective, the living room seems to open out in all directions, so that upon passing through the small cave-like entrance, we find, much to our surprise, that we can look out to the trees on all sides. Moving up the three steps, we are struck by the difference our higher viewpoint makes in our perception of the living room: the ceiling (only seven feet and one inch in height) is now very close to our heads and the flagstone floor now dominates our view.

Drawn towards the sound of the waterfall, we walk across the living room and open the glass doors, moving out on to the terrace cantilevered out over the waterfall. Looking out into the trees, the sound of the waterfall now surrounds us and we seem to be a part of it, having been projected out into space directly above it. At this moment we recognize Wright's intention in placing the house where he did: rather than present the waterfall as an object to be looked at, he allows us to feel as if we are part of it, hearing it and sensing it, but rarely seeing it from within the house.

Kaufmann himself had been surprised that the house was to be built above the waterfall, not below it as he had

Above: View of the cantilevered stairs from the east terrace to the master bedroom above.
Far right: View from the east living room terrace; the glazing around the living room 'hatch' can be seen to the left, the east bedroom terrace is at the centre above, and the entry bridge is over stream to the right.
Overleaf: Living room. The continuous glass wall gives views out to the trees, the smooth light ceiling floats overhead, and the polished flagstone floor closely resembles the water of the stream.

expected.[23] Siting the house below the falls would have resulted in the house facing north – an inappropriate orientation for the sun – and the waterfall being present merely as an image to be looked at from the house, neither of which was acceptable to Wright. He told Kaufmann, 'I want you to live with the waterfall, not just to look at it, but for it to become an integral part of your lives', pointing out the critical difference between *hearing* the waterfall (the intimate, nearer experience of daily life), and simply *looking* at it (the formal, distant experience of the perspectival view).[24] The American philosopher John Dewey has noted, 'The eye is the sense of distance' while 'sound itself is near, intimate.'[25] At Fallingwater the waterfall underlies our experience, permeating all of our senses, including most strongly our hearing and our haptic sense – the sense of bodily position and movement in space.

This feeling of being suspended over the waterfall is reinforced as we are drawn back into the living room towards the bright light coming from the trellis skylights opened in the concrete roof directly ahead; under these a low glass-enclosed 'hatch' opens to a concrete stair descending to the stream below. The dark grey colour of the bedrock ledge under the shallow water, and the way light is reflected from the rippling surface of the stream, are matched exactly by the grey flagstone floor upon which we stand. Seen through the hatch, the suspended stairs oppose

the flow of the water in the stream, and the movement down to the water is balanced by the skylight and trellis openings to the sky above. Descending to the stream below, we hover only inches above the water, facing away from the waterfall, hearing its roar behind us, magnified by the hard underside of the living room's enormous cantilevered floor slab that floats over our heads. Kenneth Frampton has written, 'That the rough stone walls and flagged floors intend some primitive homage to the site is borne out by the living room stairs which, descending through the floor to the waterfall below, have no function other than to bring man into more intimate communion with the surface of the stream.'[26]

Ascending the stairs and emerging again into the living room, we turn to the right, where diagonally across the room is the fireplace. This fireplace is not so much set into the wall as it *is* the wall, a half-cylinder cavity running from floor to plaster soffit, the hearth the boulder of the site itself, emerging from the floor. Wright had apparently intended to cut the boulder off flat, even with the slate floor, but – much to Wright's delight – Kaufmann suggested it remain as it was when his family used to picnic upon it before the house was built. Hoffmann has noted, 'Indoors the [flagstones of the floor] were sealed and waxed, but the boulder was not. It came through the floor like the dry top of a boulder peering above the stream waters.'[27] A red spherical kettle is set into a hemispherical niche in the

*Above: The fireplace.
Fallingwater's bedrock boulder
rises up through the polished
flagstone floor as if it were lifting
dry above the surface of
the stream.
Far right: View in the living
room towards the doors to the
east terrace.*

stone to one side, suspended on a steel pivot that allows it to be swung over the fire. The buffet is built-in along the back wall under a high window to the right of the fireplace, and the built-in dining table, centred exactly on the main volume of the living room that projects out across the stream, similarly projects from the back wall into the room.

We are now aware that within the rectangular volume of this room, centred by the two stone piers that make a square with the entrance wall and fireplace, there is a counterpointing pair of strong diagonal axes: that between the stair down to the stream and the fireplace, both vertically oriented (water-sky and rock-sky); and that between the entrance and the terrace over the waterfall, both horizontally oriented. All four points open on the corners of the primary volume of the living room. These two axes between four pivotal 'places' within the house give the cruciform geometric volumes of the whole a diagonal pattern of use or inhabitation. The whole is carefully calibrated to the scale and eyelevel of the inhabitant. The degree to which Wright formed his designs to accommodate and respond to human comfort and the rituals of daily life is rarely acknowledged, despite his statement that 'human use and comfort should not be taxed to pay dividends on any designer's idiosyncrasy. Human use and comfort should have intimate possession of every interior – should be felt in every exterior.'[28]

In the corner between the fireplace and dining table is the door to the kitchen, which is enclosed on almost all sides by the stone walls anchoring the house to its site. The view out from this cave-like kitchen to the terrace floating over the waterfall, set at the same floor level, gives the most succinct experience of the oppositions Wright built into and balanced in this house.

This is again encountered in the stairs which climb up between stone walls to the first floor, beginning across from the kitchen door, behind the entrance foyer. What we might normally expect to find – the heavier falling towards the ground and the lighter rising towards the sky – is reversed when we notice that the heavy stone stairs go *up* into solid stone, while the light concrete stairs at the hatch go *down* into open air. That this is not coincidental becomes evident when we see that the points where the two stairs start their respective ascent and descent from the flagstone floor are aligned along the same edge of the living room, suggesting that Wright intended us to perceive the stairs as the two sides of a single experience of gravitational reversal made possible by the cantilevered, hillside section of the house, grounded by the flagstone floor of the living room. Our penetration down through the stone floor to find light stairs floating over water which reflects the sky overhead, combined with our penetration up through layers of solid stone to finally emerge, unexpectedly, at the tree-tops rather than at their roots, make this one of the most astonishing and richly suggestive movement sequences in all of Wright's work.

The first-floor hall leads to the master bedroom, the fireplace of which exhibits the most dynamic stonework in the entire house; the large rectangular stones of the mantel and adjacent shelves cantilever asymmetrically towards the hearth in a manner similar to the way the house as a whole projects out over the stream. Through glass doors opens a terrace far larger than the bedroom itself. The scale of this terrace demands that it be understood as the second 'great room' of the house; an outdoor room above the living room, with unencumbered views out in three directions. From this vantage point, we can see that the flagstone floors of the house and terraces, so similar to the water's surface, repeat at higher and higher levels the layered planes begun by the two horizontal surfaces of the stream, below and above the falls – just as the rock walls extend the rock layers of the stream-bed outcroppings.[29]

The large volume of the terrace is complemented by the subtlety of Wright's use of wood graining along the opposite wall. The door into the master bedroom has the wood grain running vertically from floor to ceiling, while the built-in closets and cabinets, cantilevered off the wall with four inches left open at top and bottom, have the wood grain running horizontally. This is similar to the ordering of the window mullions in the house, where the operable doors and windows have vertical proportions while the fixed windows have horizontal proportions.

The bedroom used by Mr Kaufmann is over the kitchen, with the same sense of cave-like, rock-walled refuge. Up a few stairs at the back a long terrace cantilevers to the west of the house, anchoring to a freestanding boulder with a series of concrete transverse beams; three holes in the basic structure framed around existing trees to save them and allow them to grow right through the slab when completed. The bedroom used by Edgar Kaufmann, Jr, sits above that used by his father, with which its shares the west terrace.

In both of these small bedrooms and in the kitchen, the stonework of the fireplace wall seems to pass right through the glass from inside to outside, due to Wright's careful provision of a vertical slot between the stones that allows the glass to be set directly into the stone, without any kind of frame. This detail allows inside and outside to merge in a way very similar to the flagstones which are set in the floor so that the joints seem to continue beneath the glass doors out on to the terraces. The pattern of the rock wall, with the slot carefully left between the differing stone patterns on either side, indicates that Wright conceived this detail well before construction; despite this clear evidence, historians have incorrectly described the stone slot as having been cut with a saw. There is no more telling detail in Fallingwater, and Wright's intention 'to bring the outside world into the house and let the inside of the house go

Above: Photograph taken during the construction of Fallingwater showing the west terrace off the study. Beams anchor into rocks behind and voids are framed into the floor structure to allow existing trees to grow through undamaged.
Opposite, left: Project for Desert Dwelling for Frank Lloyd Wright, Mojave Desert, California, 1921, sketch plan. Only the upper rectangular portion of the plan is enclosed by walls and roofs; the majority of the space is a courtyard, open to the sky but walled off from the desert.
Opposite, right: Project for Desert Dwelling for Frank Lloyd Wright, sketch elevation. Concrete walls are topped by canvas tent roofing.

outside' is here given its ideal interpretation.[30] In these rooms he also achieves the perfect open corner, for the corner is made by two small casement windows which, when opened, cause the corner to disappear altogether.

Fallingwater appears to us to have grown out of the ground and into the light, making present the latent power of the boulder on which it sits above the waterfall – the same boulder which emerges from the rippling 'water' of the flagstone living-room floor to provide a place of stability in front of the fireplace. The natural setting is so integrated into this house that in occupying it we are constantly reminded of where we are by the sound of the waterfall, the flow of space and movement inside and outside across the floors and terraces, and the fire burning deep in the bedrock masonry of the house giving a strong sense of refuge; the views and sunlight are framed by the steel windows, which act as spatial 'nets' or 'webs'. The whole provides a true sense of shelter, combining the attributes of refuge and outlook.[31] In describing the ideal relation of landscape, architecture and inhabitation, Dewey provided what could serve as a summary of Fallingwater: 'Through going out into the environment, position unfolds into volume; through the pressure of environment, mass is retracted into energy of position, and space remains, when matter is contracted, as an opportunity for further action.'[32] Fallingwater is perhaps rightly considered Wright's greatest

work, for it is his greatest house, and he was first and foremost an architect of houses.

Dwelling in the Desert

It was while he was living in Los Angeles, working on the Hollyhock House and the Imperial Hotel, that Wright first conceived of a dwelling for himself in the desert. A M Johnson, who would shortly commission Wright to design the National Insurance Company Building for Chicago, approached Wright in 1921 about designing a walled compound consisting of dwellings, a chapel or shrine, and irrigated fields, for a site in the Mojave Desert of California. Wright's design was intended to be built using his concrete-block system, of which it would have been the first built application. After beginning work on this extensive commission, Wright received other commissions for the same region; contemplating moving to the Mojave Desert in 1921 to oversee construction on these various projects, Wright designed a little-known dwelling for himself.

This astonishing design, documented only in a plan and an elevation, shows the living quarters set at the rear of a large octagonal court, the concrete walls of which are stepped out so that the court opens as it rises, roofed by an adjustable canvas awning. The courtyard, entered on axis, is open to the sky at the awning's central oculus, under which a circular pool is set into the ground; behind this a large hearth, directly across from the entrance, is flanked by two stairs that lead to the domestic rooms behind. The whole is almost primeval, suggesting at once a defensive bastion, with its notches cut in the top of the courtyard wall, and, as Neil Levine has suggested, 'a cistern or vessel, protected from, yet receptive to the elements,' open to the sky and yet closed to the desert horizon.[33]

While none of these designs related to the A M Johnson commissions were built, the desert would captivate Wright's interest for the rest of his life. The Arizona desert would be the site for the Arizona Biltmore Hotel of 1927 as well as for the series of designs commissioned by yet another of Wright's 'business mystic' clients, Alexander Chandler, after whom the Arizona town of Chandler is named. Wright's first design for Chandler was the prototypical 'Block House' of 1928, urban dwellings to be constructed, very much like those designed by Irving Gill (whom Wright mentions approvingly in his autobiography),[34] of solid cast-concrete walls with glass infill.

That same year, Chandler asked Wright to design a large resort complex, similar to the one bearing the same name which he operated in Chandler, but to be built in the 'undefiled-by-irrigation desert'; San Marcos-in-the-Desert.[35] In plan this resort hotel consists of two wings of rooms reaching out from a central volume containing public rooms; the whole was ordered on a triangular grid, with the east wing assuming a thirty-sixty-ninety degree angle. The complex wraps around a hillside and is given a delicate woven texture by its concrete-block construction. Numerous outlying individual houses, also to be built using the concrete-block system, were designed by Wright; that for Ralph and Wellington Cudley was closely related in plan and detailing to the first project for the Richard Lloyd Jones House, designed the following year.

Due to these sizable and lucrative commissions in Arizona, and his growing inability at age sixty-two to remain productive in the bitter Wisconsin winters, Wright decided to temporarily move his home and office to the Arizona desert near Chandler in January 1929. Built in six weeks for little more than the cost of renting accommodation nearby, and occupied for only four months, Wright's desert compound and studio, which he called 'Ocotilla', after the ocotilla cactus, is one of his most innovative and site-responsive designs. Ocotilla was composed of fifteen independent pavilions set around the crown of a low hill, joined together by a board-and-batten wall that followed the curving contours of the mounded earthform, abstracting them into a series of angled lines enclosing the compound: 'the one-two triangle [thirty-to-sixty degree] used in planning the camp is made by the mountain angles themselves around about the site.'[36] The angled wood walls were stiffened by triangular bracing folds for strength and painted a rose colour to match the sand of the desert floor; the gables were painted scarlet to match the

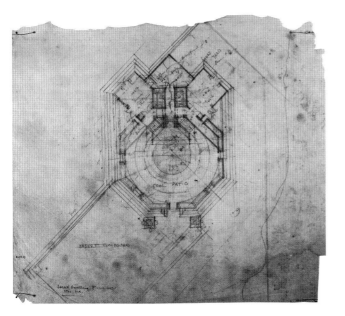

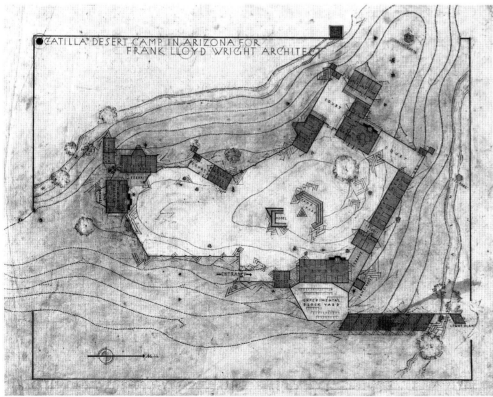

'OCATILLA' DESERT CAMP IN ARIZONA FOR
FRANK LLOYD WRIGHT ARCHITECT

ocotilla cactus bloom. Wright noted that pattern or texture was at least as important as colour in this context, 'every horizontal line in the desert is a dotted line, every flat plane is cross-grained, patterned like the cactus.'[37]

Each of the box-like pavilions was placed against the exterior wall, which formed one or more of each pavilion's walls. Above the wood wall on the shorter sides of the pavilions, thirty-to-sixty-degree gables of hinged wood-framed canvas were set, and each pavilion was roofed with stretched canvas panels. There was no glass anywhere in this design as glass did not belong in the desert, according to Wright; glass being more suited to hothouses than the fabric tents he wished to emulate here. The individual room-pavilions were surrounded by low wood walls, open to the sky and sun only through their luminous canvas roofs, giving a warm light that Wright was to remember long after the little camp was abandoned. Wright did not regret the ruin of this camp (dismantled for its building materials by the local Navajo Indians, on whose land it was built), for it had been intended as temporary from the start, the ideas in it being more important than the permanence of its construction: 'So rather than ponderous permanent blunders in expensive materials, until we learn more of good appropriate building, why not "ephemera" as preliminary study, say? America was given permanent building materials to work with much too soon.'[38]

Above left: Project for San-Marcos-in-the-Desert, Chandler, Arizona, 1928, aerial perspective.
Left: 'Ocotilla' Desert Compound for Frank Lloyd Wright and the Taliesin Fellowship, near Chandler, Arizona, 1929, plan. Wright's quarters are to the left, with the dining room and kitchen at top right, and the draughting room and Taliesin Fellows' sleeping quarters at bottom right.
Above: Period photograph of Ocotilla Compound. This building, built in six weeks and occupied for only four months, is one of Wright's most innovative and site-responsive designs.

Wright's final desert design for Alexander Chandler in this period was his project for the San Marcos Water Gardens in Chandler of 1928, a motor court to have been constructed of low concrete-block walls surmounted by angled wood frames carrying stretched canvas roofs. A continuous loop canal of water is used to order the individual rooms, each a freestanding building ordered by thirty-to-sixty-degree geometry in both plan and section.

Water would again be used by Wright as a primary way of creating place in the arid desert, in his 1931 project for a 'House on the Mesa', shown in the Museum of Modern Art's 'International Style' exhibition the next year. In this design, foreshadowing both Taliesin West and the Usonian Houses, a large rectangular pool of water, labelled by Wright the 'lake' and into which he extends the elevated swimming pool, serves as the focus for the linear house that wraps two sides of a loosely defined courtyard. All the rooms of the house except the living room are on the ground floor, lined up along the solid northeast wall behind a deep loggia facing southwest to the terraced 'lake'-shore; the living room is on the first floor, overlooking the rest of the house.

The house is designed to be built of concrete-block walls, and the primary rooms have extensive glazing set in metal frames that step out as they rise, the horizontal 'bottom' hopper-like sections opening upwards so as to channel the desert breeze up towards the ceilings. Along the northeast

wall at the first floor, the bedrooms are set back behind the deep shadow of the loggia, and the concrete-block wall overhangs its floor slab. Through-ventilation is introduced from this low intake, exiting at the high clerestory windows beneath the ceilings, which also allow light to enter these rooms from over the roof of the loggia. Altogether a remarkable design, this project exhibits Wright's precision in responding to unique characteristics of climate and light quality, constructing space from a carefully selected set of materials, and forming both house and landscape in a powerful yet sensitive manner.

Taliesin West, Scottsdale, Arizona, 1937

Wright returned to the Arizona desert in 1936 on the advice of his doctor due to a bout with pneumonia, but we may suspect that the desert had never really left his memory. He had said, upon driving into the Arizona desert with Alexander Chandler in 1927, 'there could be nothing more inspiring to an architect on this earth than that spot of pure Arizona desert'.[39] When Chandler, whose grand schemes had been devastated by the stock market crash of 1929, discovered that Wright was again in Arizona, he commissioned him to design a project for the Little San Marco Resort Inn outside Chandler. While this also was never to be built, Wright decided to spend his winters in Arizona and build a permanent 'camp' for the Taliesin

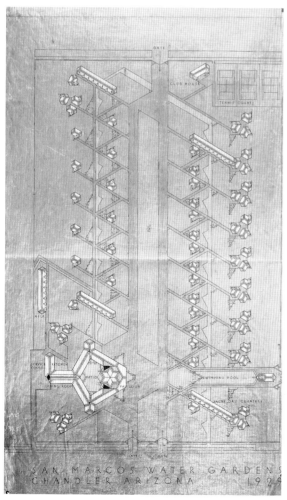

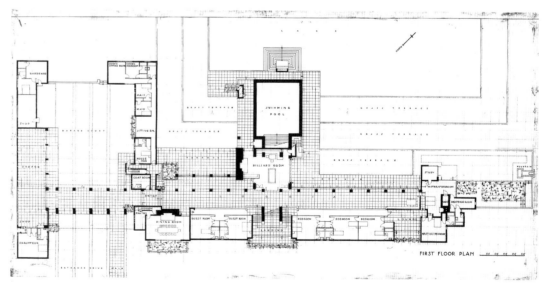

FIRST FLOOR PLAN

SAN MARCOS WATER GARDENS
CHANDLER ARIZONA 1929

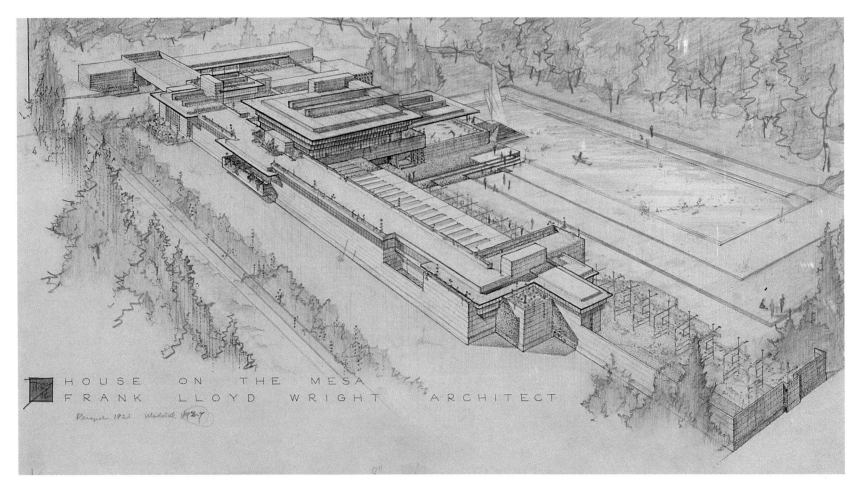

HOUSE ON THE MESA
FRANK LLOYD WRIGHT ARCHITECT

225

Above left: Period photograph, interior of Ocotilla Compound, Wright's quarters. Each room-pavilion in the compound was surrounded by low wood walls, open to the sky and sun through their luminous stretched canvas roof panels.

Far left: Project for San Marcos Water Gardens, Chandler, Arizona, 1928, site plan; a motel, or 'motor court', with individual cabins, continuous loop canal irrigation, dining pavilion and sports facilities.

Left: Project for 'House on the Mesa', 1931, ground-floor plan. This project, exhibited in the Museum of Modern Art exhibition of the 'International Style' of 1932, foreshadowed both Taliesin West and the Usonian Houses.

Above: Aerial perspective, project for 'House on the Mesa', seen from the west.

Fellowship on a several hundred acre site on the Maricopa Mesa at the foot of the McDowell Mountains north of Phoenix.

Upon the arrival of the Fellowship, construction immediately began on a temporary dwelling for Wright, called 'Sun Trap', and completed in 1937. This square, wood-walled design merged the Mojave Desert dwelling with the Ocotilla camp; in plan, a square-walled courtyard, it has small bedrooms placed at the centres of three sides, a fireplace in the centre of the fourth, all projecting towards the centre and supporting a pinwheeling wood-framed canvas roof over it, together creating a cruciform-shaped covered space. Two of the corners are left open to the sky, the others housing the music room and a freestanding toilet; the toilet is related to the other rooms exactly as it is in traditional Japanese houses, and the whole, with its walled gardens, is closely related to that precedent with which Wright was so recently familiar.

Over the next several years, Wright and his apprentices constructed Taliesin West on this spectacular desert site. Though the diagonal space of the garden and pool dramatically alter the experience of the house, its plan is almost exactly derived from the 1911 plan of the original Taliesin. The L-shaped plan, forming an entrance courtyard at its rear and overlooking the desert on its other side, contains the private dwelling in short extensions of each wing, with the bedrooms stretching out to the east and a 'garden room', Wright's translation of the living room to this climate, extending to the south. As at the original Taliesin, an open loggia separates the private dwelling from the draughting room, located along the southern-most edge of the courtyard. At Taliesin West, a smaller court to the northeast houses a small cinema and dwellings of Wright's chief associates. From the start Wright required the younger apprentices to build themselves individual, independent bedroom-houses in the desert surrounding the main complex – these were then criticized as part of the apprentices' design education. The plan is dynamic and asymmetrical, as Wright thought appropriate to the setting: 'Out here in the great spaces obvious symmetry would claim too much, I find, the too obvious wearies the eye too soon. So for me I felt there could be no obvious symmetry in any building in this great desert.'[40]

Approaching the building through the desert, we first see it silhouetted against the low mountains immediately behind, its materials and colours drawn from the desert site itself, and its broken, serrated profile intended to merge with the desert. Wright said, 'The straight line and the flat plane, sun-lit, must come here – of all places – but they should become the dotted line, the broad, low, extended plane textured because in all this astounding desert there is not one hard undotted line to be seen.'[41] The first structure

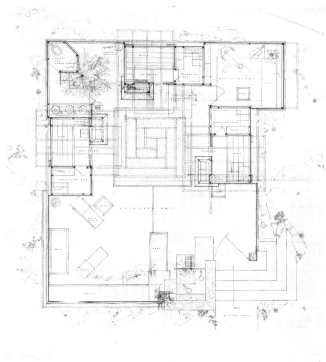

Above: Project for 'House on the Mesa', interior perspective of the living room. The flat bottom panel of stepped glazed wall opens to direct breezes up to the top of the room.

Above right: 'Sun Trap', Wright's temporary dwelling, Scottsdale, Arizona, 1937, plan. The building was constructed on the arrival of the Taliesin Fellowship to Arizona while the design and construction of Taliesin West was carried out.

originally met upon entry would have been the small study on the north, courtyard side of the main building, set on the diagonal of the terraced garden and pool to the south. Here we can see the basic construction and spatial language of this surprisingly simple design: large 'battered' walls, built of large desert boulders set roughly in concrete, supporting thirty-to-sixty degree angled wood-framed, canvas-clad roof and wall structures between them.

A large boulder, found on the site and bearing ancient Indian markings, stands guard at this entrance; as Neil Levine has noted, to the visitor the boulder 'clearly indicated the existence of an earlier, prehistoric occupation of the site, and Wright's reuse of such remains in his design established a continuity with the past.'[42] From this entrance point, we can overlook the desert below, but we must turn away from this view to enter the pergola that leads along the south side of the courtyard; at the far end of the draughting room, the view through the loggia reintroduces the desert and invites us to move out onto the terraced gardens that along with the loggia occupy the geometric centre of the house.

The heavy, primitive stone walls create a strong sense of containment and character, such that Wright recalled Oglivanna saying, 'the whole opus looked like something we had not been building but excavating'.[43] Originally there were small courtyards open to the sky, in one of which Wright placed two Han dynasty funerary urns, floating on

shelves, as if to hint at his conception of enclosure found so richly in this house, which Levine has called 'the building as a lidded pot. Unlike the classic archetype of the hut, the vessel or pot was plastic rather than clastic, spatial rather than structural ... this new model released Wright from almost all ties to traditional structural conventions.'[44]

As it was built and originally inhabited, every room in the house was open on at least one side to the desert; the primary spaces – the garden room and draughting room – were open on both their long sides. All manner of rolling, hinged, stretched and loose canvas allowed an enormous range of adaptability to the daily changes of climate typical in the desert, and created a house where almost every space was simultaneously inside and outside. The canvas roofs, with their wood-framed, canvas-covered flaps at the eaves and gables for ventilation, dominate our experience of the house. The light, coming largely from above, is extraordinary; Wright said, 'I found the white luminous canvas overhead and canvas flaps used instead of window glass afforded such agreeable diffusion of light within, was so enjoyable and sympathetic to the desert, that I now felt more than ever oppressed by the thought of the opaque solid overhead of the much too heavy midwestern houses.'[45]

The original construction of Taliesin West was intended to be both permanent – the stone foundations 'excavated' from the site – and cyclical or seasonal – involving

Right: Taliesin West, Scottsdale, Arizona, 1937. Approaching the building, we first see it silhouetted against the low mountains immediately behind, its materials and colours drawn from the desert site itself, and its broken, serrated profile intended to merge with the desert.

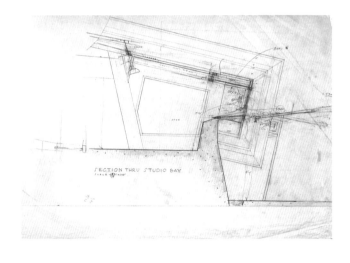

SECTION THRU STUDIO BAY

replacement of the canvas roofs and flaps as part of the Fellowship's annual 'migration' from Wisconsin to Taliesin. In considering the changes and additions that Wright himself made late in his life and those the Fellowship group has made since Wright's death, we should remember that Taliesin West was built by Wright – and used as long as he lived – as a winter residence, with Taliesin 'North' (in Wisconsin) being the Fellowship's summer home. Taliesin West was never intended for summer occupation, being designed to deal with the relatively mild heat of the Arizona desert winter. The retrofitting of the buildings with window air-conditioning units (units designed for the 'guillotine' window Wright so hated), the sealing off from direct exposure to the outdoors of the rooms at Taliesin West (stopping the cross-ventilation and indoor–outdoor movement so critical to the relation with the landscape), and the permanent replacement of the canvas with a plastic roof (denying the seasonal ritual of rebuilding the canvas roof, which was never intended to be permanent, but to record and exhibit the effects of time, sun and weather); all these changes together act to contradict and largely damage Wright's delicate balance of landscape, climate, materials and inhabitation in placemaking.

WITH THESE two astonishing designs, Fallingwater and Taliesin West, Wright re-emerged from the relative obscurity brought about by his lack of work in the previous decade and by his obstinate refusal to embrace the increasingly dominant 'international' definition of modern architecture. In fact, these houses are notable for the degree to which they engage with their respective sites, thereby rejecting the placelessness implicit in the International Style. In Fallingwater, Wright created a dialogue of architecture and nature, with the house growing directly from the earth yet floating out into space as if to deny the gravity of its stony origin. In Taliesin West, Wright recreated the cosmological relationship between landscape and inhabitant first established by the native Americans, employing site lines to surrounding mountain peaks to organize the house and inflecting the geometry of the plan and section to achieve the solar orientations essential for survival in the desert. With these buildings, Wright demonstrated the primary importance of the site in the design of any true modern architecture – an architecture of its time and of all time.

Above far left: Construction detail of the draughting room, one of the few sections of Taliesin West drawn by Wright.
Centre far left: Section of the garden room.
Below far left: Period photograph of the draughting room interior. The canvas roof cuts heat but allows light.
Above left: View of the draughting room today.
Left: Period photograph showing Fellowship apprentices stretching canvas on wood frames for the draughting room roof, a process intended by Wright to be part of the annual winter relocation of the Taliesin Fellowship from Wisconsin to Arizona.
Right: Period photograph of Taliesin West, view of the garden room. Operable canvas flaps, secured with rope ties, opened the room to desert cross-breezes.

THE INHABITED LANDSCAPE
AND THE DISAPPEARING CITY

Measured over great free areas, the living interest
should be educated to lie in the contact of free
individualities in the freedom of sun, light, and air,
breadth of spacing – *with* the ground.

Frank Lloyd Wright[1]

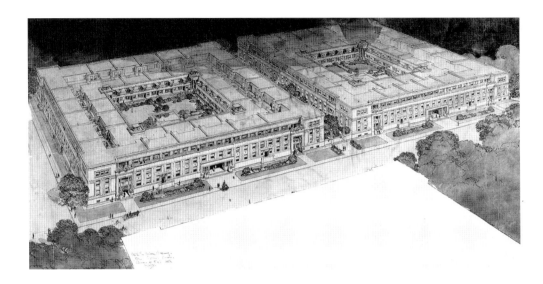

*Left: Low-density urban
townhouse prototype project for
American System-Built House for
Richards Company, Milwaukee,
Wisconsin, 1915, perspective.
Above: Project for Lexington
Terrace Apartments for Edward
Waller, Chicago, Illinois, 1901,
aerial perspective. Wright was
continually involved in developing
prototypes for urban and suburban
housing almost from the beginning
of his practice.*

During a period that would prove to be pivotal in its
development, from 1932 at the end of the Great Depression
to around 1960, the American architectural profession
expressed almost no interest and expended virtually no
effort to help conceive and produce the affordable house for
the emerging American middle class, preferring instead to
focus on residences for the rich and corporate office towers.
Without the direction traditionally provided by the
architects, and with the demand for affordable housing
increasing, contractors were joined by a variety of
newcomers to the field, including home-builders, site-
planners, house-designers, interior decorators and real
estate developers. Together they set about conceiving
housing prototypes, which they tended to cast in stylistic
terms so that economics would be free to drive the market,
building the housing needed by America.

Recently American architects have expressed some dismay
upon realizing that today their involvement is not solicited,
required or needed in the design and construction of
housing, and that they have an insignificant impact on the
market that has for years now been defined by real estate
developers' and home-builders' interests. These architects
have rightly complained about the lack of sensitivity to
landscape or urban context, environment, energy, local
construction methods and regional building materials – as
well as the total absence of appropriate and characteristic

spatial qualities – in contemporary housing developments, yet
their profession was absent during the critically important
period at the inception of the American house and suburb.

Only one American architect constantly insisted on the
importance of the conception and design of affordable
housing for the American middle class during this crucial
period, his innovative and spatially rich urban and suburban
proposals for housing prototypes almost completely ignored
by his own profession: Frank Lloyd Wright. As he said,
'The house of moderate cost is not only America's major
architectural problem but the problem most difficult for her
major architects.'[2] On the other hand, Wright took up this
challenge and was continuously involved in developing
prototypes for urban and suburban housing almost from the
very beginning of his practice.

From as early as 1896 up until his death in 1959, Wright
designed over thirty different comprehensive housing
projects, including more than fifteen complete communities,
several of which involved the design of dozens of new house
prototypes as part of the project. This all in addition to the
hundreds of variations on house design prototypes that were
commissioned from various individual clients. It is important
to understand that all of Wright's house designs were
conceived by him as taking their appropriate places within
his larger concept of the emerging American city and suburb,
conforming to a precisely delineated social and spatial order.

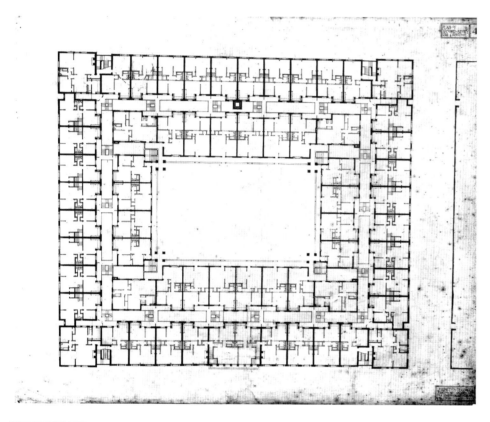

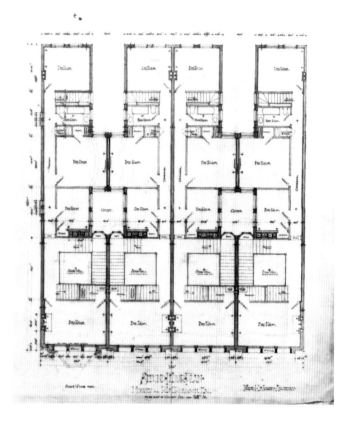

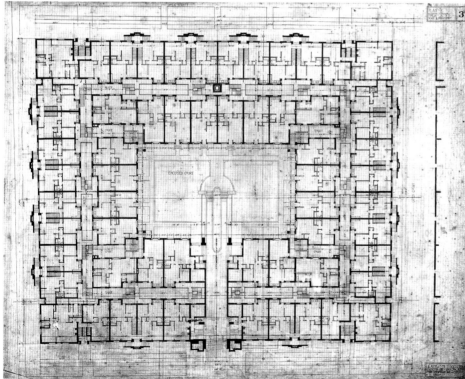

The Existing City: Urban Housing Blocks, 1894-1901

Due to his later rhetoric against the city, Wright is usually portrayed as having no sensitivity to traditional urban space and the social life of the street, but the various 'urban wall' projects discussed in Chapter 7, as well as the housing blocks described here, would indicate that, when appropriate to the context and programme, Wright designed by holding the street line, providing private and semi-public space in the city by using courtyard or rowhouse typologies. Wright's earliest design of this type was for four houses remodelled for Robert Roloson in Chicago in 1894, only one year after starting his own office. Originally designed to have a flat cornice replacing the four steep dormers on the front facade, the plan of the main floor of each apartment is related, as in the McArthur House of 1892, to Wright's interest in having the fireplace stand free of the side walls, allowing light and passage along either edge, as a way of both separating and joining the living and dining rooms – an idea that would eventually achieve its fullest expression in the Robie House. Here the library is built into the central fireplace block, and the edge movement zones are extended into the pair of stairs flanking the living room.

In the Belknap Apartments project, also of 1894, Wright develops two cubic blocks separated by a narrow entrance court, each composed of two L-shaped units wrapped around a central service core, allowing maximum exterior

Far left, above and below:
Lexington Terrace Apartments
project, ground-floor and
upper-floor plans.
Above left: Apartments for Robert
Roloson, Chicago, Illinois, 1894,
first-floor plan.
Above: Francis Apartments,
Chicago, 1895, exterior view.
Above right: Lexington Terrace
Apartments project, perspective
of the courtyard.
Overleaf: Ladies Home Journal
Quadruple Block Houses project,
1900, aerial perspective of
the pinwheel-type.

exposure and light for the main rooms of the apartments. The Francis Apartments, built in Chicago in 1895, indicate Wright's interest in the public aspects of collective housing. He emphasized the entrance floor by cladding it in beautifully patterned terracotta panels set between stone courses, while the rest of the building above is clad in brick. The two entrance pavilions are set in the back inside corners of the small central entrance court, leading diagonally to the square top-lit stair beyond. In the Francisco Terrace Apartments, built in Chicago in 1895 for Edward Waller, these corner entrance pavilions are integrated into the corner stairs, the first-floor landings of which interlock with the inner circulation balcony overlooking the inner courtyard.

This is a particularly early example of this open upper-level entrance balcony or corridor (the concept of the 'street in the air'), which would be utilized in designs considered innovative twenty-five years later, such as the Spangen Quarter housing built in Rotterdam in 1920 by Michiel Brinkman. As Gwendolyn Wright has noted, Wright's early courtyard housing designs 'focused on various combinations of central public spaces – garden courts, hallways, and entrances – which shielded the occupants from the street and dramatized the points where they came together.'[3]

Wright's greatest urban housing-block design, the Lexington Terrace Apartments for Edward Waller of 1901, was to remain unrealized. As Wright noted in the 1910 Wasmuth portfolio publication, this was a development of the Francisco Terrace Apartments built for the same client, but the Lexington Terrace design is far larger and more complex. Consisting of two blocks, each composed of a three-storey perimeter building with a two-storey perimeter building set within it, the design held the street edge and centred on the inner courts. The outer three-storey blocks had their entrances directly off the street, while the inner two-storey blocks had their entrances off the courtyard, either directly for the ground-floor units or from a continuous open balcony ringing the courtyard at the second level. The balcony, created in this case by setting each second-storey unit back, interlocked with stairs in the corners of the courtyard, and each unit had its own covered entrance framed by square columns set in planter boxes.

While the aerial perspective shows a subdued frame around the entrance, other studies show sets of four piers carrying flat projecting roof planes, placed to either side of the entrance, not unlike the later Midway Gardens. Perhaps the most intriguing aspect of all these early courtyard designs was the avoidance of any interior corridors, which in the Lexington Terrace project is complemented by the provision of rear entries and porches in a narrow alley composed of a series of small linked courts between the inner and outer blocks. This type of front-and-back, public-and-private, served-and-service access is generally considered something that is difficult if not impossible to achieve in high-density urban housing, and Wright's handling of this subtly nuanced scheme belies his reputation for disinterest in urban space.

The Emerging Suburb: Quadruple Block Houses, 1897–1903

While he was clearly capable of proposing innovative and contextual designs for his beloved city of Chicago, Wright early on looked to its emerging suburbs as the place where America's future would be built. In 1896, Wright proposed his first suburban housing scheme, a modest set of five houses based on similar floor plans for Charles Roberts. Here Wright was still relying on changes in exterior materials and modifications of the roof line and window pattern to denote difference among the houses in the group. The next year Wright designed another set of prototype houses for Roberts, also to remain unbuilt; in this design he apparently intended the houses to be arranged four on each block, linked by service wings at their back and facing away from one another to assure privacy. In 1900, as we have seen in Chapter 3, Wright arrived at the concept of housing types with the two *Ladies Home Journal* house designs, and from this point forward his proposals for the suburb would concentrate on the creation of a pattern of private and public spaces – a unified, collective texture or fabric of community – with the typical house as its elemental component, rather than attempting to provide a different image for each individual house.

Designed in 1900, the project for a 'Quadruple Block Plan' (published in the February 1901 issue of *Ladies Home Journal*, the same year the two more famous house types were shown in that publication), would be the source for Wright's repeated return to the quadruple-house theme throughout his career. Wright here proposes two siting variants. The first and most typical shows four houses pinwheeling around the corners of a square shared site so that each faces a different direction, and one never sees the same elevations side-by-side. Bound together by low extended walls, the set of four houses each sat on its own square site, four of which were joined to make the larger square shared site, creating a common back yard and individual entries on separate sides. This first scheme was clearly intended for a train-line suburb, as Wright makes no provision for the parking of any kind of transportation, horse or car, and the walkway-entry pattern is clearly only for pedestrians.

The second scheme, while not as directly influential on Wright's later work, proposes a far richer urban space; in this plan, the houses are linked in all directions in a complex *a–b–a* or tartan pattern, relating to and sharing exterior space with four sets of houses rather than one as in the first scheme. The houses in each of the groupings of four are mirror-imaged or reversed in plan rather than rotated relative to their immediate neighbours in all four

directions, which, when combined with the differing distances between houses, produces matching elevations across the street, side yard and back yard. The houses are grouped into sets four times: first, the four that share the largest unbroken site as defined by the streets and driveways; second, the four (two from each of the first groups) that share the walled rear yards centred on the driveways; third, the four that share the segment of the street marked 'court' on the plan; and fourth, the four that are closest together and form a perfect square, even though they are separated by the street and driveways.

The suggestion of multiple spatial and geometrical relationships between the houses in these various clusterings or groupings precisely presents the richness and complexity of urban social relations, and the sharing of space fosters the development of relations on the part of the occupants. The house design used in both of these schemes is a very effective blending of the cruciform and pinwheel Prairie House types, remarkable in that it was developed at the same time. The grouping of these houses into sets of four, or quadruple blocks, creates a paradoxical increase in both density and privacy over the typical freestanding suburban house. This was possible due to Wright's realization that in the suburb designed as a series of house clusters, many elements of the suburban landscape such as streets, sidewalks, service courts, garden walls and back yards could be shared rather than duplicated. His most

productive insight was that as long as views are carefully coordinated (which never happens when each house is designed independently), houses could be spaced much closer together, with the views from each crossing rather than meeting. The second scheme also is carefully organized to accommodate the carriage or car in shared service courts with their own entrances, each house also having a separate front pedestrian entrance. Thus as early as 1901, Wright had designed a fully developed suburb suited for automobile commuter living – simultaneous with the invention of the first mass-produced automobile.

This scheme was given its final development in the Quadruple Block Plan for Charles Roberts, proposed for Oak Park in 1903. Wright's beautifully rendered plans show four variations, three of which use the same house plan – subtly perfected – as the schemes of 1900. The first organizes the houses in a pinwheel configuration, now with a shared garage at the centre of the back yard, and Wright's elegant colours indicate the various shared exterior spaces created by the design. The second, labelled 'B', is the tartan-grid, reversed-plan scheme described above. The third, labelled 'C', is a variation on the previous design, with shared garages set in the spaces between the houses furthest apart, and pedestrian mews running between the closer houses.

The fourth design is quite different from any of the others, in that it utilizes another house plan – the cruciform

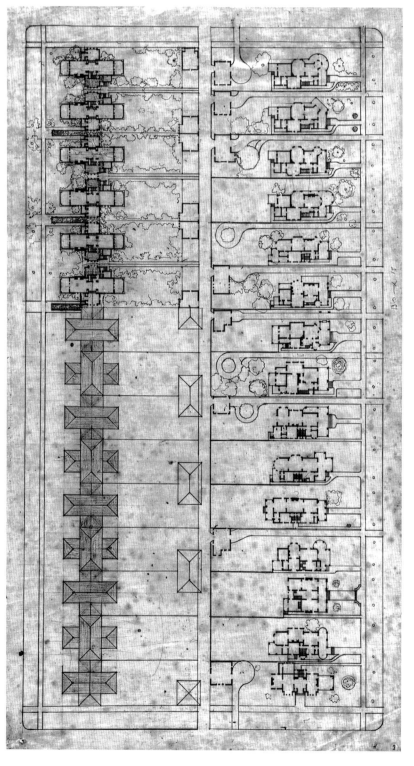

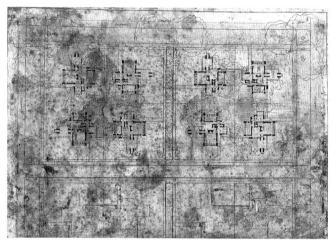

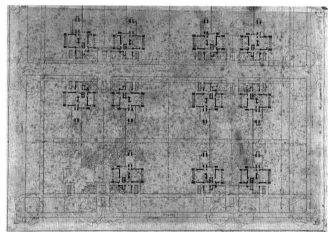

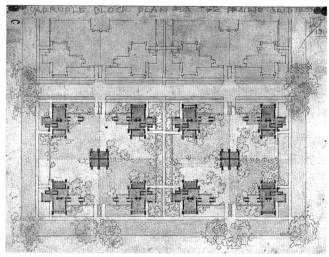

236

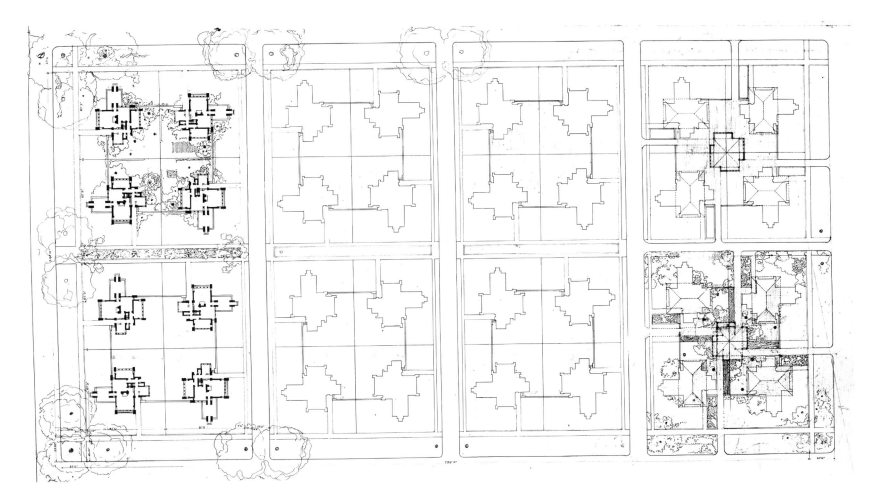

plan used for the Barton House of the same year. These houses are sited so that their shorter wings almost touch – their roofs do connect, leaving space only for a narrow passage for entrance, forming an urban wall; the second-storey bedroom volume alternates its orientation, parallel and then perpendicular to the street; every two houses share a garage located on a back alley; and finally, the design is presented across the alley from a series of carefully drawn existing houses, each displaying its individual, non-repetitive composition of rounded bays, activated volumes, and no doubt variegated roof lines – together highlighting the repose, urban scale, repetitive order and shared service elements (resulting in larger yard spaces) of Wright's design.[4]

Together these plans, with their subtle spatial composition based on the pinwheel and cruciform arrangement of groups of houses to allow sharing of sites, present some of the richest visions of collective space formed by private housing ever proposed for the American way of life.

Integration of Public and Private Realms

Despite its spatial richness, Wright's vision of the appropriate dwelling for a democracy was not yet socially comprehensive, for it was still composed entirely of private houses and did not include the public realm, without which

Wright felt the private realm was impossible to appropriately articulate. All of Wright's early schemes for housing relied on the existence of public services; he only attached his designs to the existing urban planning grid and did not suggest the placement of the public amenities necessary for life, even in the suburb – parks, shops, religious structures, schools, government, sports and cultural spaces. This was even more true of his various 'prototype' house designs of this period, intended to be built on empty sites in existing neighbourhoods, such as the project for Workers' Row Housing for the Larkin Company of 1904, 'A Fireproof House for $5000' of 1906 (examined in Chapter 5), and the E C Waller Housing project of 1909, with its three house types. In these designs, as well as those for the Quadruple Block Houses, Wright assumed the existence of a viable, functioning city fabric into which he wove his housing patterns, and this is reflected in his positive comments about life in the city of Chicago during this period and in his own residence in Oak Park, one of the earliest railroad-line suburbs.

During this period, when commissioned to design resorts sited in the rural countryside, Wright sought to capture in these cities-in-miniature this underlying order given to housing by public spaces. In the Como Orchard Summer Colony project of 1908, proposed for Darby, Montana, Wright composed all the individual wood-framed cabins,

PLATE 97. COMO ORCHARDS SUMMER COLONY, DARBY, MONTANA. GENERAL VIEW

which are clustered in groups of two and four or set in rows, either around a large field of tennis courts, or a long stepped fountain and pool, both of which are centred on and axially aligned with the public clubhouse. The manner in which Wright is able to create an 'urban' space at the centre of this little community, while allowing the houses at the edge to more informally interlock with the surrounding forest, bears comparison with the great gardens of the Italian Renaissance.

While the plans Wright prepared for the new town of Bitter Root in 1909, also near Darby, Montana, are each ordered with a *cardo* and *decumanus* – roads running north–south and east–west, crossing at the town's centre – Wright proposed much looser arrangements for the public buildings of this town than he had for the private houses of the Como Orchard project. The designs for the town's various public buildings – train station, opera house, school, church, hotel and library – are all variations on Wright's cruciform plan, while the houses are a virtual catalogue of his built and unbuilt domestic commissions. The largest buildings, the market and commercial blocks, are oddly enough the least ordered of all, each appearing in both plan and perspective to be only a collection of traditional store-fronts surrounding a service court. While the plans as a whole do not exhibit the geometric precision or spatial order we expect from Wright, they do weave together

public and private structures in an integrated manner – a concept that he would soon return to the city itself.

After 1909, with his own abandonment of Oak Park and definitive removal to the hills and farmlands of rural Wisconsin, Wright began to conceive of prototype house designs, even when they were to be built on existing lots, as belonging to his more comprehensive proposals. For Wright, the public realm could no longer be taken for granted, but had to be created anew with each design. The project for three houses for Honore Jaxon of 1914, the Ravine Bluff Housing Estate constructed in 1915, the Monolith Concrete Houses for Thomas Hardy of 1919, the Prototypical Concrete-Block Houses of 1923, and even the House on the Mesa of 1931 (examined in the last chapter), all contain indications of their being envisioned within Wright's emerging ex-urban concept.

Wright's later houses and housing proposals cannot be conceived independently of their contexts. As is so often the case with Wright, this originated in his rejection of the more instrumental aspects of modernism when they came at the expense of spatial and experiential possibilities. Wright believed the dominant concept of modern urban planning, the zoning or separating of differing functions within the city, to be wholly inappropriate and doomed to failure, as it would not allow the complex weaving of activities, public and private, that he observed in Chicago. Almost every one of Wright's designs, private or public, indicates how much he learned from the integration of functions in the city of Chicago that he loved; the particularly urban characteristic that made possible the kind of local culture he had early on found at Jane Addams' Hull House, the Chicago Architecture Club, the Art Institute of Chicago and the Chicago City Club, where Wright was a charter member of the City Planning Committee beginning in 1908.[5]

Chicago City Club Competition, 1913

Wright's social and spatial vision of an integrated urbanism would be given its most convincing expression in his Chicago City Club Competition entry of 1913, titled 'Model Quarter Section for City Residential Land Development', a proposal for new suburban or ex-urban community first published in 1915. Sited eight miles from the centre of Chicago, which for Wright placed it within the city fabric, the 'established gridiron of Chicago's streets therefore has been held as the basis of this subdivision'.[6] The square quarter is divided into sixty-four smaller square blocks, highly symmetrical and repetitive, yet Wright carefully designed an asymmetrical, pinwheel-based series of primary boulevards centred in two corners by large parks, which take up four blocks each, set diagonally across the quarter from one another, and centred in the other two corners by courtyard apartment buildings set in a pinwheel configuration around the street intersection.

Differing functions are fully integrated in this project, producing a complete and viable neighbourhood or community where public buildings (post office and library), commercial blocks (shops and market), cultural spaces (galleries, cinema and theatre), offices, religious structures, services (heating plant, garbage and garage), and sports facilities are linked to each other and to the dwellings by a series of public parks. The majority of the commercial buildings are organized along the side of the project nearest downtown Chicago, with the public buildings placed in the system of small parks that ties through the entire site, allowing one to walk from edge to edge on grass and under trees. These public buildings and parks are woven into an underlying fabric composed of housing, and the balance between the public and private spaces is carefully developed. The whole is a city-in-miniature, the kind of small-scale quarter for 5,000–7,000 residents, where it would be possible to live and work, and where a true form of democracy could flourish. As Gwendolyn Wright has said, 'Wright believed that place mattered. By this, he implied more than simply natural surroundings; he meant as well urban social life and the public exchange of ideas.'[7]

The blocks given over to housing are composed entirely as quadruple blocks, sixteen houses to the block, four sets of four houses set in pinwheel formation, based directly on those proposed for the Charles Roberts housing project of 1903. Wright said, 'A succession of buildings of any given

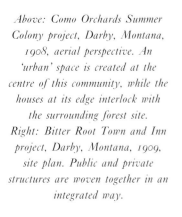

Above: Como Orchards Summer Colony project, Darby, Montana, 1908, aerial perspective. An 'urban' space is created at the centre of this community, while the houses at its edge interlock with the surrounding forest site.
Right: Bitter Root Town and Inn project, Darby, Montana, 1909, site plan. Public and private structures are woven together in an integrated way.

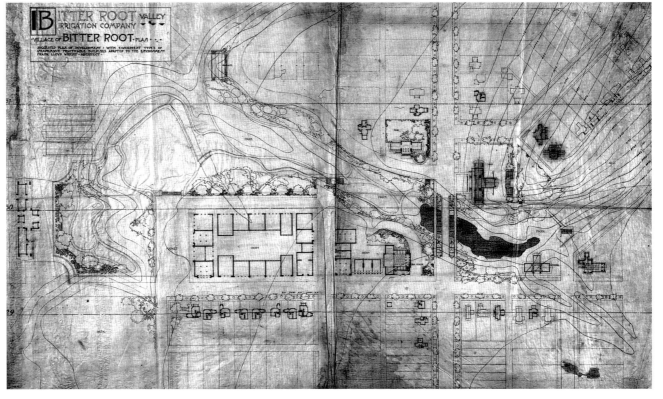

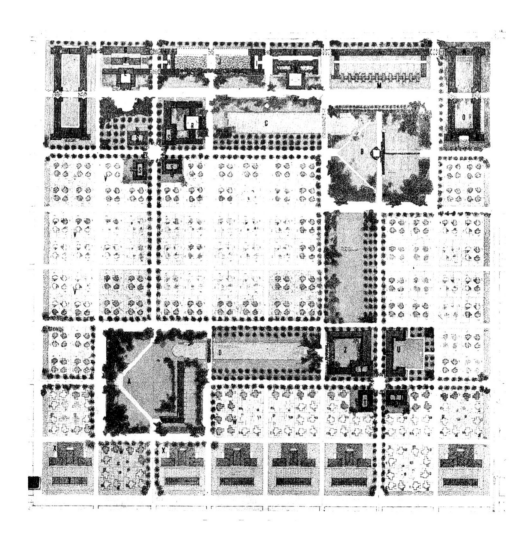

length by this arrangement presents the aspect of well-grouped buildings in a park, of greater picturesque variety than is possible where facade follows facade.'[8] Wright manipulates the square urban grid with ease, as we might expect given his use of the unit grid in his own planning; he points to the fact that though the plan would produce varied and diverse vistas, where 'nowhere is symmetry obvious or monotonous'. It also allows substantial savings due to shared services and greater density, with less length of sewers and sidewalks, and more parks and public spaces than the average suburb. Wright refers to the paradoxical intention that underlies this design in saying, 'Always there is the maximum of building upon a given ground area, [yet] dignity and privacy for all.'[9] This exceptional design for the Chicago City Club Competition is the direct precedent in Wright's work for his Broadacre City proposal of nearly twenty years later.

HAVING ACHIEVED this integrated suburban conception, Wright nevertheless did not cease his involvement in housing projects where such a comprehensive vision was not possible. Throughout his career, Wright had sought to influence the development of low-cost, mass-produced, site-specific housing proposals, resulting in his experimentation with a wide variety of construction methods and housing typologies. Wright's most extensive designs for low-cost,

mass-produced, prefabricated, yet spatially rich urban and suburban housing, called the American System-Built Houses, were developed from 1911 to 1917 for the Richards Company of Milwaukee; an extraordinary project running to almost a thousand drawings – the largest single set in Wright's archives – and numerous constructed houses.[10] Wright's designs presented prototypes for a wide variety of freestanding suburban houses, town houses, attached duplexes, urban rowhouses and apartment buildings. The whole represented a catalogue of his built and unbuilt work to that point in his career, all to be constructed of prefabricated, factory-cut wood wall framing and sheathing, floor joists, roof rafters, windows, doors, frames and trim, finished with stucco outside and plaster inside; interior finishes, trim and furnishings were also designed by Wright for mass production.

The designs are each presented in a perspective view from the street, indicating the basic urban character of the whole project. The closer-spaced buildings tend not only to contain more units but to be more vertical in massing, to use stairs and service spaces to create internal places of meeting (such as shared entrances and rooftop laundry drying pavilions), and to make more gestures towards forming collective shared space (at the entrance, side yard, and garages) than those designed for widely spaced suburban sites. A row of duplex apartments, whose plans are reversed to place their entrances together, was built in Milwaukee by Wright for Arthur Richards, owner of the Richards Company, in 1916.

The same year an apartment building from this project set was built in Milwaukee for Arthur Munkwitz, partner in the Richards Company; now demolished due to the widening of the street, this U-shaped plan has an apartment in each wing, with the living and dining rooms wrapped around central fireplaces, very much like the Bach House of the previous year, and the bedrooms running along the back, away from the street. The entrance court leads to an ingenious set of four stairs that interlock as they run all the way across the centre of the plan, providing two means of exit from each apartment without exterior fire escapes. Here, and in the dozens of other prototypes Wright designed for the Richards Company, even such internal design elements as these stairs make evident Wright's ability to create appropriate housing for the widest possible variety of urban and suburban conditions.

Wright's designs of 1918–20 for Terrace Housing along Hollywood Boulevard, conceived as part of the masterplan for Olive Hill commissioned by Aline Barnsdall, present a uniquely urban character by being linked to produce a continuous street wall of housing with shops below. In this overall configuration and in their individual plans – small cruciform units with their short wings meeting – they may be directly related to Wright's final Quadruple Block House

proposal of 1903 for Charles Roberts, discussed above, and the units themselves were developed as the freestanding Monolith Concrete Houses for Thomas Hardy of 1919.

This wall of houses in Hollywood is related to the San-Marcos-in-the-Desert Resort Housing project of 1929, mentioned in the last chapter. For this project, Wright designed three tiers of small housing units, each stepped back to create a south-facing terrace on the roof of the unit below, with a single-loaded corridor running along the back side against the hill on each floor, leading to the lounge, dining room and dance floor. The units are paired, a smaller one with a larger one, divided by a thick wall containing the fireplace which extends out on to the terrace to assure privacy; each of these pairs are separated from the next by the baths, closets and service elements, which are fronted by terraced gardens. The whole is woven into its undulating site through its folding angled plan and the texture of its concrete-block construction.

The Lake Tahoe Summer Colony of 1922 on Emerald Bay, Lake Tahoe, California, is one of Wright's most extraordinary and beautiful unbuilt works. Various houses and lodges are designed for sites on the steep shore of the lake (called 'shore types'), and for mooring along piers and a floating pontoon bridge stretching from shore to an island (called 'barge types'). While the shore cabins seem intended to have concrete-block retaining walls topped by wood-clad walls and roofs, with names like 'Fir Tree' and 'Wigwam',

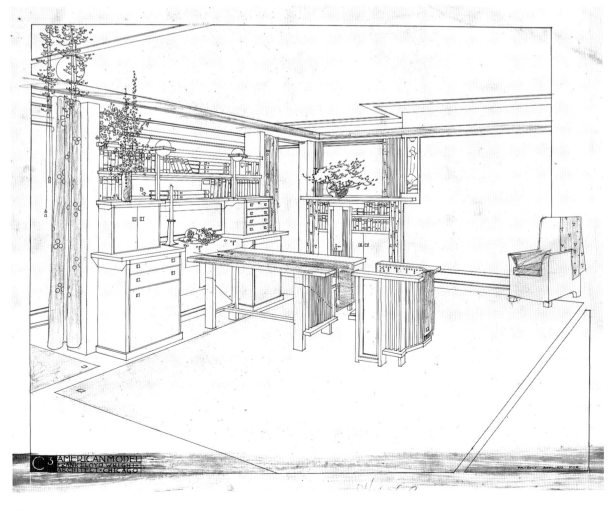

TWO FLAT DWELLING VII·A

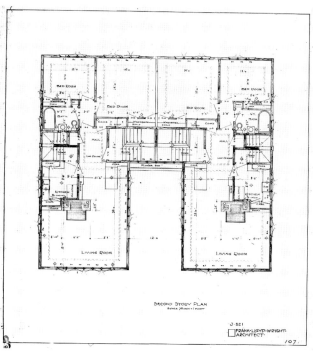

SECOND STORY PLAN

J·521

FRANK·LLOYD·WRIGHT·
ARCHITECT·

107·

the various barge cabins were to be constructed entirely of wood and to float in the lake itself, carrying names such as 'Fallen Leaf'. The smaller floating cabins are of particular interest, each a precise and poetic investigation of geometry, space and wood construction – borrowed equally from home building and ship building.

We can see Wright working his way from the interlocked squares of the 'Catamaran' cabin-barge (similar to the Hardy House of 1905), to the incorporation of the diagonal of the roof into the plan in the 'Family' cabin-barge, to the interlocking of the square and the diamond or rotated square in the 'Fallen Leaf' cabin-barge, and finally to the composition made exclusively with diamonds and hexagons (still based on the two smaller volumes interpenetrating the larger central volume of the Hardy House) of the 'Wigwam' shore cabin and the 'Barge for Two' cabin-barge. The unified composition of plan and elevation (above and below the water line) in these barges results in some of Wright's most geometrically-resolved forms and, given that Wright had only just returned from living in Japan, it should not be surprising that they are also strongly reminiscent of traditional Japanese temples.

Broadacre City, 1934

By the late 1920s, Wright had begun to conceive of a larger, more comprehensive and, he hoped, more influential proposal for the American city of the future; with the opening of the Taliesin Fellowship in 1932, he now had the help necessary to completely present it. That same year, Wright designed a series of hypothetical prototypes needed for such a comprehensive city plan, including the Conventional House (a concrete-block house prepared for a European exhibit of Wright's work), the Standardized Overhead Service Station, and the series of prefabricated sheet-steel projects designed for Walter Davidson, including the Steel House, Roadside Market, Farm and Housing Units. Wright also designed the Malcolm Willey House of 1932 and 1933, which he would call the first Usonian House – the essential ingredient in Broadacre City.

Asked to present his ideas for a 'city of the future' for an exhibition in New York in 1934, and with the financial support of his friend and client Edgar Kaufmann, Wright and his apprentices set about producing a series of drawings and models of individual buildings, and an enormous model over twelve-foot square, representing four square miles of this continuous fabric-city and documenting the complex agricultural, social, cultural, spatial and formal patterns of what Wright called Broadacre City. He would work on this continuously for the rest of his life, constantly incorporating his latest designs for every type of building as new prototypes for use in the plan, producing the most comprehensive plan and perspectives, titled 'The Living City', in 1958, the year before his death.

Immediately evident in an examination of the plan Wright proposed in 1934 is the integration of public and commercial spaces within the fabric of private land and dwellings. Indeed, the acre grid of individual houses and gardens literally underlies the earliest drawings of Broadacre City, forming the fabric into which the public buildings are stitched. Within each four-square-mile unit – based directly upon the Jeffersonian grid of the Louisiana Purchase and understood to be endlessly repeated across the American continent – is a complete community, containing all public amenities as well as a wide variety of housing types. Based upon universal ownership of both the acre of property and an automobile, yet able to be traversed on foot in forty minutes, Broadacre City is organized very similarly to the Chicago City Club Competition project of 1913, divided into nine quarters by a tartan grid of primary roadways. Again the primary office, commercial, manufacturing and transportation elements are organized along one side, buffered from the housing by orchards and vineyards, while the sports, scientific and agrarian elements occur on the opposite edge, along with forest cabins. Cultural and public buildings are woven through the housing across the broad middle, while freestanding towers of the St Mark's-in-the-Bouwerie Tower type are scattered across the landscape to create focal points in the horizontal expanse.

Wright developed a variety of new designs for housing while working on the Broadacre city concept, including the Zoned Houses for City, Suburb and Country of 1935, the All Steel Houses of 1938, the *Life* Magazine House of 1938, and all of the Usonian House types we shall examine in the next chapter. Of particular note, and worthy of further study, are the various designs for four-house clusters produced by Wright, called 'Pinwheel', 'Suntop' (1938) and 'Cloverleaf' (1942) in their various propositions. Each design consists of four houses, sharing a single site, yet backed against a cross-shaped service and structural wall, pinwheeling in plan so they faced away from each other, privacy and views being maintained for all. These designs, developed from Wright's early Quadruple Block designs of 1901 and the St Mark's Tower of 1929, present a unique combination of density and privacy, compactness and spaciousness.

In each unit of the 'Suntop' Homes, built in 1938 in Ardmore, Pennsylvania, the carport and double-height living room share the ground level, separated by the stair, the dining room overlooks the living room on the second floor, the master bedroom occurs on the first floor and the children's bedrooms with a large terrace all around are placed on the second floor. Each house has two exposures that look away from the shared party walls, allowing each unit complete visual privacy from its neighbours as well as visual control over its own L-shaped yard on to which it looks. Built of brick and stepped wood siding, the houses each include slightly offset floors that allow clerestory

Left above: American System-Built Houses for Richards Company, duplex apartment-type built in several locations.
Far left: American System-Built Houses for Richards Company, exterior perspective of the apartment building built for Arthur Munkwitz, Milwaukee, Wisconsin, 1916.
Left: American System-Built Houses for Richards Company, Arthur Munkwitz apartments, plan of top floor.

TAHOE CABIN - White Sand Blocks
Steel Bond (copper liquid sides)
SHORE TYPE

Block Technique
Taliesin

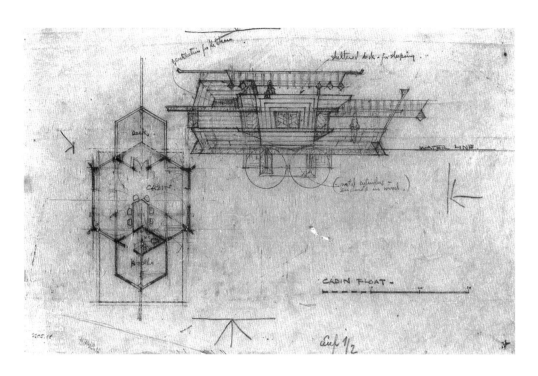

windows, which, along with the ventilating shafts in the shared party walls and at the tops of the stairs, produce cross-ventilation, while the double-height volumes join the clerestories in bringing light deep into the interior.

While much has been written about Broadacre City as an agrarian ideal, a kind of agri-cultural defeat of historical urban culture, it should be noted that the project allowed Wright to present his architectural designs in a coordinated, comprehensive spatial and formal framework, where each design reinforced the other. The whole reflects his belief in the need for a way of relating to the land that was based on inhabitation rather than real estate speculation, and a way of relating to each other that was not possible either in the density of the traditional city or in the isolation of rural agrarian life. Here one could eat the produce from one's own garden and attend a symphony performance of Beethoven the same evening, live in a high-rise apartment and work in the orchards, or live in a woodland cabin and work on the assembly line – all no more than five minutes away.

This was possible because Wright conceived each four-square-mile module as a fully functioning community of a new type, one that intended to foster local identity through the increased capacity of individual mobility.[11] It was meant to engender a new American form of the 'canton' system of small-scale community democracy, and to enrich the typical American citizen's public and private life through

increasing their contact both with the natural landscape and collective culture. Kenneth Frampton has said:

> Broadacre City and the Usonian house shared a similar hypothetical socio-economic basis; Wright's egalitarian vision was one acre reserved for every citizen at birth. Broadacre City may be seen in retrospect as an infinite 'oriental rug,' as a cross-cultural, ecological tapestry writ large, as an oriental paradise garden combined with the Cartesian grid of the occident. This is Wright's textile tectonic literally inscribed into the earth, evoking that Edenic point where culture and agriculture are inseparable, the natural home for the natural economy, the warp and the woof of a transhistorical time.[12]

Broadacre City has rarely been examined as a physical and spatial embodiment of social and cultural ideas.[13] While the relation of Wright's design to the history of America's development as a modern nation – its uneasy movement from agrarian to industrial and from rural to urban – has been exhaustively researched, the spatial characteristics of Broadacre City, and its crucial differences from the typical American suburbs that have developed in the meantime, is less studied.[14] Many later architects and city planners have mistakenly assumed that 'one house on its acre site' was Wright's chief concept in Broadacre City, and thus that Broadacre City is the source and not a possible solution to the suburban sprawl that has occurred across the American rural landscape since Wright's first proposal in 1934.

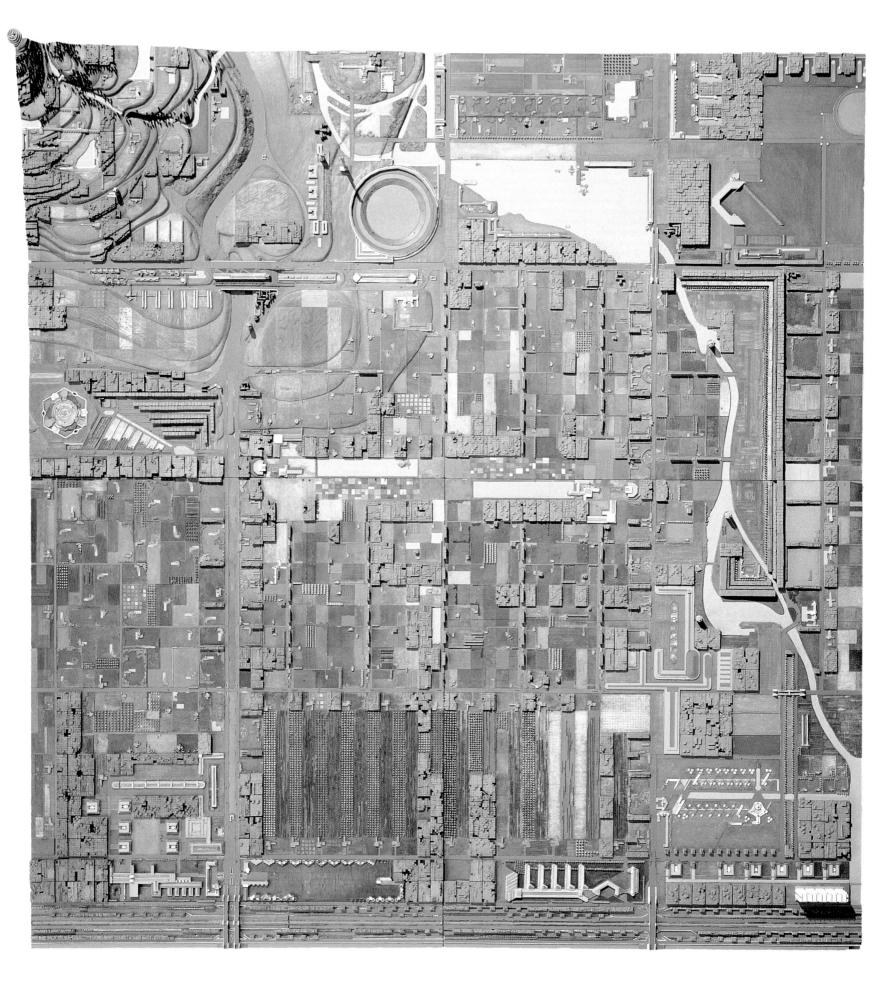

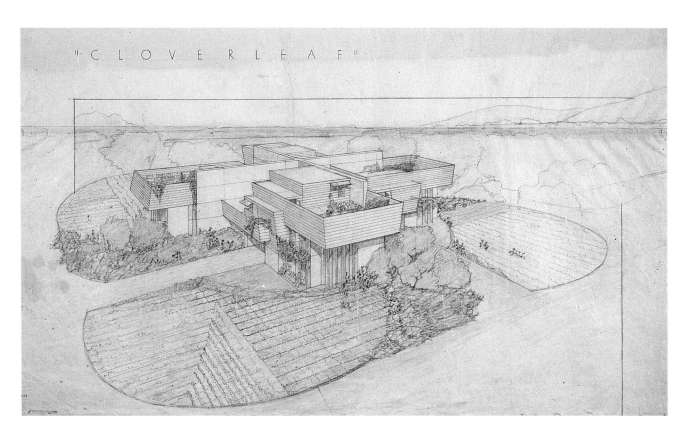

"CLOVERLEAF"

Left: Broadacre City model, 1934. A square mile section of what was proposed to be a continuous fabric of inhabited landscape across the American continent.
Above: 'Cloverleaf' housing, 1942.
Right: 'Suntop' Quadruple Houses for Otto Malley and Todd Company, Ardmore, Pennsylvania, 1938, plan and section. Four houses are backed up to shared cruciform service or 'party' walls, with each house given unobstructed views outward. 'Suntop' and 'Cloverleaf', developed from Wright's early Quadruple Block designs and his St Mark's Tower, present a unique combination of density and privacy, compactness and spaciousness.

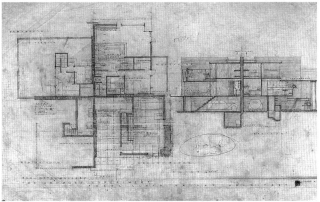

Wright's Broadacre City was intended to be a far more comprehensive construction, providing for both public and private realms, which were to be richly articulated through their relationship as the two necessary and complementary halves of an urban whole. It may be noted that these same attributes are absent from recent American suburban 'developments', where artificial ambience and lonesome lifestyle are the direct result of the fact that the suburb's primary reason for being is the generation of real estate profit not the creation of urban amenities.

IT IS interesting to note that while he was designing Fallingwater, the most celebrated individual 'natural' house, Wright was also designing Broadacre City, composed of thousands of small Usonian Houses, each on its acre of land, the whole a woven fabric of public and private functions that makes virtually impossible the kind of land speculation and speculative home building that would become so common in the American suburb. Wright is absolutely clear about this aspect, noting how in the typical American suburb 'architecture and its kindred, as a matter of course, are divorced from nature in order to make of [architecture] the merchantable thing. It is a speculative commodity.'[15] Broadacre City was Wright's greatest and most comprehensive counter-proposal to the traditional city, to the isolation of agrarian life and, finally, to the developer's speculative suburb. The consequences of not employing this visionary proposal – not giving the developing American suburbs an appropriate and precise spatial and social definition – is certainly now being fully felt across America.

THE USONIAN HOUSE

Whether people are fully conscious of this or not,
they actually derive countenance and sustenance from
the 'atmosphere' of the things they live in or with.
They are rooted in them just as a plant is in the soil.

Frank Lloyd Wright[1]

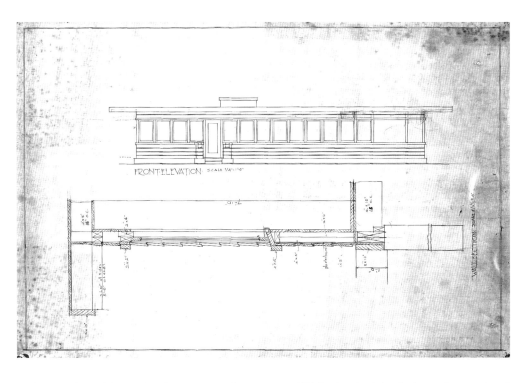

FRONT ELEVATION

As Wright himself endeavoured to make evident, despite the length and diversity of his career, his architectural designs were a continuous reinvention or rediscovery of the same fundamental principles; the 'periods' and 'stylistic' variations upon which historians have focused were less important to Wright than this continuity of ordering principles. As Kenneth Frampton has noted, the Usonian Houses, while spatially and functionally different from his earlier work, are in other ways a return to the construction logic underlying Wright's 'Board and Batten' cottages of the turn of the century, more than thirty years before; here 'once again the generic prototype was conceived as having woven walls'. In this a direct link can be seen in the 1911 project for a summer cottage for Sherman Booth, which shared with the later Usonians its single-storey, gridded plan, flat roof with cantilevered eaves, continuous south-facing windows and horizontal wood cladding. Frampton suggests the fact that the conception of the Usonian House 'comes with Wright's literal return to the Midwest should remind one of the regional inflection that was always latent as a creative impulse in Wright's work.'[2]

This is confirmed by Wright's utilization of the Prairie Houses as the source for his Usonian Houses. The plan of the Darwin Martin House hung in the Taliesin draughting room for fifty years, representing both the perfection of plan-making Wright always sought and serving as a

generative source. While he had looked to the work of others early in his career for models to perfect, for the vast majority of his life Wright returned to his own work as the source for spatial prototypes: 'I would watch sequences fascinated, seeing other sequences in those consequences already in evidence. I occasionally look through such early studies as I made at this period, fascinated by implications. They seem, even now, generic.'[3] It is perhaps not surprising, then, that close approximations of the Usonian House plans may be derived by folding the plan of the Martin House along its symmetrical axes, suggesting that Wright saw the Usonian Houses as asymmetrical quadrants of the larger symmetrical Prairie Houses.

Wright had experimented with the smaller, more dynamic spaces characteristic of the Usonian Houses in earlier designs, such as the Walter Gerts House project of 1906. In comparison to his other designs of this period, this small house is rather startling in its asymmetry, its L-shaped plan set directly on the ground, its dynamic living-dining room space composed of overlapping incomplete geometries, its long walls extended from inside out into the garden, and its enclosure of a small court at the rear – with its first floor bridging the drive very similar to the Coonley House of the next year. This project is perhaps related to the somewhat mysterious 'House for an Artist', an asymmetrical pinwheeling design of indeterminate date,

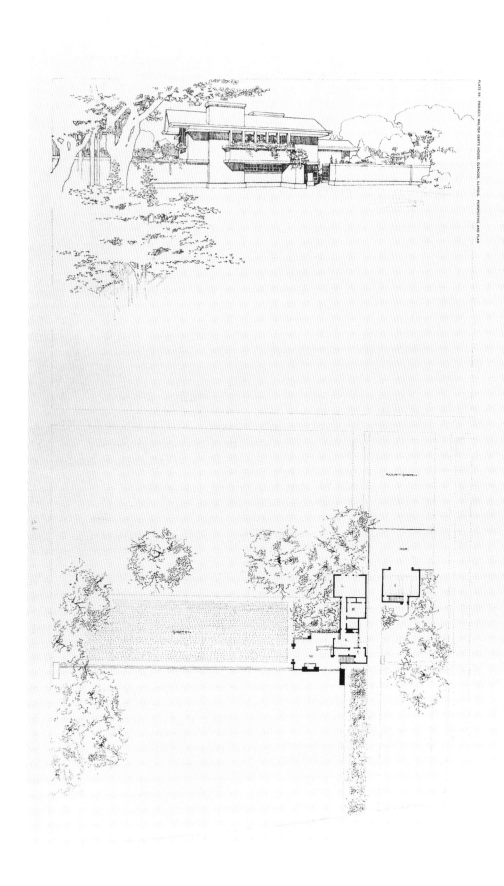

likely intended for Wright himself (as mentioned in Chapter 6), published in the Wasmuth portfolio of 1910. In this design the fireplace, created by four piers set in cruciform configuration, with its corners opening into three different rooms, acts to centre the dynamic spaces of the plan. In these small designs, the 'systematic' production of space so typical of the larger Prairie Houses is less evident, replaced by a series of focal elements set in an asymmetrical order. In this they are crucial to the transition wherein the diagonal, edge-movement experience of the Prairie Houses became the primary space-making order of the Usonian Houses.

Wright's Usonian Houses may best be understood as an integrated design development that began with his transformation of the symmetrical, cruciform and pinwheel Prairie House plan into the courtyard plan. As we have seen, the courtyard typology appeared as a recurring transitional development in Wright's house plans; Wright's own Taliesin of 1913 enclosed the land on three sides to form a garden which was the focus of the interior spaces, yet was composed of L-shaped primary volumes, producing an asymmetrical order in the whole. Wright had first proposed this type of plan as early as 1904 with the Frank Thomas House built in Oak Park. This L-shaped plan is wrapped around a raised terrace and walled flower garden, and is related to the W E Martin House of 1902, mentioned in Chapter 3 for its dynamic, interlocked relationship with its garden. The ground-floor plan of the Herbert Angster House of 1911, since demolished, is a direct precedent for a number of the later Usonian Houses; the fireplace is set off-centre in the living room, interlocking with the entrance hall, and dining takes place along the garden edge of the living room on the other side of the fireplace.

Wright's Prairie Houses typically developed as an expansion of interior space into the landscape, with axes crossing inside the house, at the fireplace core, and the main rooms focusing along the expansive (longitudinal) axes, their spaces not directed laterally. The Henry Allen House of 1916, its L-shaped plan joining with its pergola, garden house, and perforated brick wall to enclose a pool and courtyard, completes a reorientation of the Prairie House; the main rooms now focusing laterally towards the court, with entry at the intersection of the house's two wings. While the Malcolm Willey House of 1932–3, its spaces lined up along a brick back wall, opening to the south-facing terrace, is often considered the first Usonian House, it was with the C R Hoult House project of 1936 that Wright proposed the Usonian as a fully developed type; a single-storey, wood and brick-walled, flat-roofed, L-shaped house framing a garden. In the Robert Lusk House project of the same year, the house was joined with a freestanding wall to enclose its garden, the longitudinal volume inside anchored at its ends by solid brick walls so that the interior space is redirected laterally towards the garden – the new centre of the composition. In all these designs, Wright's reorientation

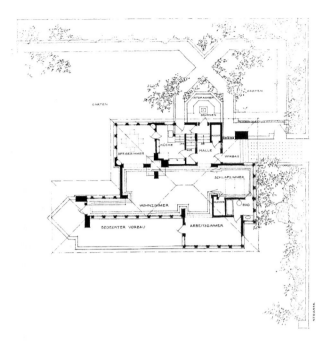

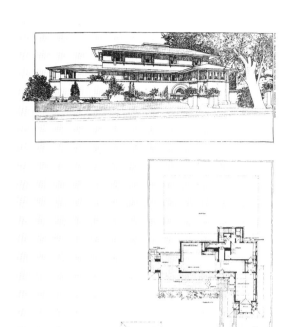

*Far left: Walter Gerts House
project, Glencoe, Illinois, 1906,
site plan and perspective.
Above: 'House for an Artist',
before 1907; probably intended for
Wright himself.
Above right: Frank Thomas
House, Oak Park, Illinois, 1904,
perspective and plans.*

of the focus of interior domestic space is complete; rather than being directed along the long interior axis as in the Prairie House, the inhabited spaces of the Usonian House focused laterally towards the garden it enclosed or defined.

The name of 'Usonian' which Wright gave this modest type of house first designed in 1936 has never been fully explained, and like many architectural titles, was intended to set Wright's proposals apart from the various other contemporary house styles then emerging and to give his work a distinctive identity in its public perception. While 'United States of North America' (USONA), as a more accurate name for the United States of America, may be the most precise source, John Sergeant notes that Wright soon made the name Usonian his own, defining it within his vocabulary of design principles as he had earlier done with Sullivan's 'organic'.[4] Usonian was first the name of the houses, but soon after it referred as well to the larger context of Broadacre City in which they were to be built, and finally to the 'integrated society which was to flourish there.

Herbert Jacobs House, Madison, Wisconsin, 1936
Wright's plan of the first Jacobs House (Wright was later to build a second house for the same client, discussed in Chapter 16) reveals his underlying intentions for the Usonian Houses quite clearly. The garden takes up the geometric centre of both the actual site and the plan drawing, and is

the focus of the entire spatial composition; only the brick walls of the house are darkened, appearing to stand free in the field of lighter, thinner lines denoting the other features of the house, which is set along one side of its suburban lot. The house itself is L-shaped in plan, folding inwards to make a corner, anchoring its site without completely enclosing it, and the garden is woven together with the interior space of the house. The two wings of the plan are carefully organized to articulate the relationship between public and private spaces inherent in the domestic realm.

From the carport at the outside corner, the entrance opens into the living room, and the secondary service or private entrance leads to the bedroom wing. The kitchen and bathroom form the solid masonry core at the juncture of the L-shaped plan, and the dining area – on to which the kitchen opens – is fitted into the inside corner, serving as the transition between public and private spaces. The brick walls are placed only within the living-room wing of the house and at the entry, and are utilized to demarcate and indicate the public nature of these spaces. The spatial and movement axis of the living room is blocked in its expansive (longitudinal) direction, and the space focuses sideways or laterally, reoriented and folded in towards the garden. Lateral apertures – rows of tall windows and doors – from public and private wings direct space such that it crosses in the garden defined by the L shape of the house.

RESIDENCE FOR MR·MRS MALCOLM
MINNEAPOLIS MINNESOTA
FRANK LLOYD WRIGHT
ARCHITECT

Above: First project for the Malcolm Willey House, Minneapolis, Minnesota, 1932, perspective.
Right: Herbert Angster House, Lake Bluff, Illinois, 1911, ground-floor plan.
Far right: Robert Lusk House project, Huron, South Dakota, 1936, aerial perspective and plan.

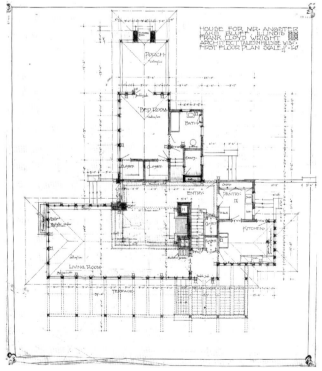

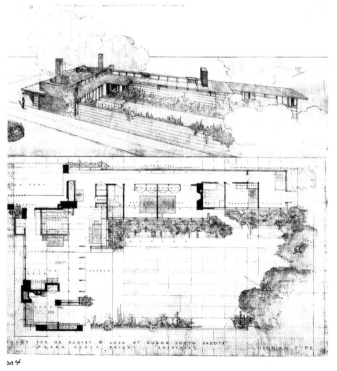

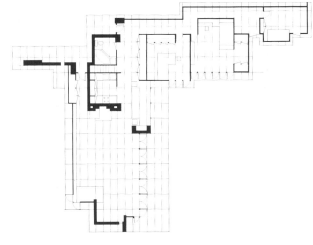

In the site plan, Wright utilizes two 'hemicycles' of planting, similar to that constructed at the Darwin Martin House (another indication that this earlier house served as the origin of the Usonian designs), centred on the ends of the two wings and creating smaller spaces titled 'lawns'. We should note that the semicircle is complete at the living-room wing while it is incomplete at the bedroom wing, another subtle differentiation of the public and private spaces. The garden, enclosed and defined by the two wings, is drawn with furrowed agricultural rows and is titled 'garden', with an area specified for vegetables, and an evenly spaced line of trees placed along one edge. Wright's agricultural vision for the American suburb, with each family sustaining itself to at least some degree on the produce from its own garden, is here explicitly planned and presented.

In the Jacobs House, Wright defined the Usonian House as emphasizing the topographic, and including in that the natural landform and the history of previous human occupation of the site – in most cases through agriculture. Wright's work acknowledges and makes experiential the close relationship between agriculture and architecture; he understood architecture (to build and edify) and agriculture (to care for and cultivate the land) as related activities on the earth – tending and transforming the landscape. The American landscape was for Wright unique and in need of integration into American daily domestic life. Here the total

place – site and building – has been designed as one, and the form of this house would be unbalanced if its interlocked landscape was removed; the house and its spaces of inhabitation are incomplete without its garden.

Examination of the paired perspectives Wright drew of the Jacobs House reveals the reading of inside and outside he intended for the site itself. The street view is seen against the foreground of the empty front yard, with no indication of path or means of inhabitation. This is clearly the exterior view, as the house itself is closed, composed of continuous horizontal wood boards and recessed battens, small clerestory windows set high up the wall under the roof overhang, with only the cantilevered carport offering the possibility for entry. Most important, the perspective is taken from an elevated viewpoint, off the ground – as he stated in his criticism of photographs of the Larkin Building taken from that same position, this view does not capture the experience. In the case of the Jacobs House, we are clearly outside the habitable realm of the house, looking at it as an object in the landscape.

Compare this to the matched garden view, taken from eyelevel at ground, where we feel as if we are standing in the garden itself, enclosed by the wings of the house. Here the house is seen against the expanse of the sky, and the elevations are composed largely of vertical glass doors, many of which stand open, letting us see into the rooms. This is

the interior view, and we are now inside the space of the house, even as we stand in the garden. With its garden walls sliding off each edge of the drawing, we see the house as anything but an object in the landscape – we understand that we are within its most important room, the garden.

Protecting the garden as its 'interior', the Jacobs House presents a closed facade to the street. The brick wall defining the carport at the corner shields a brick-lined walk, moving along the edge of this wall, under the carport's cantilevered roof, we enter the masonry core of the house. Having entered at the left end of the elevation, we turn right, opening the door, and move into the foyer, a narrow space between a brick inside wall and the closet at the exterior. At the ceiling small clerestories run the length of the living room along this outside or back wall, and the closets are pushed through the exterior wall so that the one foot depth remaining inside aligns exactly with the front face of the bookshelves that line the back wall of the living room. The bookshelves are spaced on the vertical grid of one-foot boards and one-inch recessed battens that constitutes the exterior and interior surface of the wood walls of the house, and the shelves' front edges match the one-inch wide, dark wood battens used in the walls, so that it seems as if the bookshelves were pulled out of the walls.

The ceiling above is also constructed of these one-foot lighter boards and one-inch darker recessed battens, and

these lines now pull us forwards into the living room. Ahead the wood wall and clerestory band on the right turns and ends in a brick wall, which itself turns and ends in a set of small stacked windows, their mullions spaced on the same horizontal grid as the walls, seeming to pass through a brick pier to reach the wall of glass doors that open to the left. This continuous set of vertical wood-framed glass doors reorients the room towards the garden, and Wright reinforces this by reorienting the wood bands of the ceiling from being parallel to the back wall over the side of the living room nearest the street to perpendicular over the garden side of the room – the change takes place at the exact middle of the space.

Turning to face the garden, we see the fireplace which we passed upon entry; the brick fireplace registers the rotation and reorientation of the living room by its asymmetrically placed brick seat, set on the left side nearest the entrance. The dining room is to the right of the fireplace, projected out into the garden, yet not enclosed by vertical glass doors but by horizontal wood walls, with high windows allowing views out for those standing in the kitchen – enclosed on three sides by brick walls and behind the fireplace – but blocking views and directing the gaze inward for those seated at the table. Past the dining room and the pantry we turn to the right along the corridor leading to the bedrooms, bending to delineate the master bedroom and study at the end from the other bedrooms; to the outside of this hallway is a horizontal wood wall solid except for the high clerestory windows along its top below the ceiling. The two outer walls of the L-shaped plan are made of horizontal wood boards, closed except for the thin clerestory band running continuously between wall and roof, while the two 'interior' garden walls are made largely of vertical glass doors – the whole carefully scaled to the human figure.

The proportions of the house are quite low, opening outwards rather than upwards, and Wright detailed the roof soffit to step upwards in stages from twelve inches in typical structural depth to four inches at its eaves, so that the roof presents an appropriately thin profile at its outer edge. For Wright, the horizontal orientation of the house was essential in 'perceiving the horizontal line as the earth line of human life (the line of repose)'.[5] The low, oversailing, layered roof planes produced a strong horizontal release of space, giving spatial presence to Wright's intended relationship between house and landscape: 'I see this extended horizontal line as the true earth line of human life, indicative of freedom. Always.'[6] Most important for Wright was the way in which the emphasis on the horizontal acted to ground the house, making it a true foundation for the life within: 'the planes parallel to the earth in buildings identify themselves with the ground, do most to make the buildings belong to the ground.'[7]

The construction of this and the other Usonian Houses may be related, as Frampton has noted, to that of both the traditional Japanese house and the four primal elements identified by the German architect and theorist Gottfried Semper in 1852: 'One would first cast the floor slab and build the masonry chimney core and thus arrive at the first two elements of Semper's architectural hypothesis, the earthwork and the hearth. This was followed by Semper's third element, the framework and roof. The whole was concluded with the application of a screen-like infill wall [Semper's fourth element].'[8] Wright fused the first two elements of floor (earthwork) and hearth (heating) by casting a network of small pipes into the concrete slab itself, which carried steam or hot water, so that the floor itself became the source of heat – an idea he had apparently first encountered in the Tokyo home of his client for the Imperial Hotel.

As Frampton has again noted, Wright exploited the thermal 'flywheel' effect of the concrete slab and brick walls of the core, which due to their mass retain either heat or cold.[9] Heated in the winter by the sun angling in through the south-facing glass doors and kept cool in the summer when they were shaded by the carefully calculated roof overhangs, the concrete floor and brick core walls moderated the temperature of the house, combining with the cross-ventilation in summer and heat from the fireplace in winter to make these Usonians extremely energy efficient long before this was an issue for other architects. Yet in the

Left: Jacobs House, view from the street showing the carport and entry on the left. The house is composed of horizontal wood boards and recessed battens.
Below: View from the living room to the dining alcove, with the fireplace to the left.
Below right: Living room, with doors to the garden at left and the built-in shelves and table to the right.

Jacobs House, as in all his designs, Wright sought a comprehensive synthesis of construction and experience, and in describing this floor slab he emphasized how it anchored the house to its site, so that it seemed to grow from the earth: 'the feeling that the house should look as though it began there at the ground put a projecting base course [of brick] as a visible edge to this foundation where, as a platform, it was evident preparation for the building itself and welded the structure to the ground.'[10]

In adopting planning modules (the vertical one-foot and one-inch grid and horizontal two-foot or four-foot grid) that corresponded to standard mass-produced material dimensions (such as the four-by-eight-foot plywood sheet that served as the core for the standard one-foot wood-board walls), Wright related the Usonian Houses more closely to the material-based grid of the early Board and Batten Cottages than to the universal sixteen-inch plan and section grid possible in the concrete-block houses, where the materials were literally custom-made to fit the grid. In the Jacobs House, the whole is developed as a woven horizontal composition of wall and roof layers; the Usonian House consisted of a three-dimensional matrix with interlocking horizontal layers. Frampton notes that this 'is borne out by Wright's provision of three separate plan cuts: one at the floor level, one at door-head or clerestory height [which was the roof height for the bedroom wing], and one at [living room] roof level.'[11]

With its integral built-in bookshelves, storage, door and window heads and sills, perimeter seating and furniture aligned to the one-foot one-inch vertical grid of the wood-board walls, the Jacobs House demonstrates Wright's statement that 'furniture, pictures and bric-a-brac are unnecessary except as the walls can be made to include them or be them'.[12] In his essential study on the Usonian Houses, John Sergeant noted that the 'elements of [wood] millwork were interwoven like basketry so that the upper battens were aligned through the head of the door frames, while the boards overlapped their jambs'.[13] The door and window openings (including the high clerestories), built-in cabinets and closets are positioned on the horizontal two-by-four-foot grid inscribed into the concrete floor slab during construction. As the floor is constructed first, all subsequent building is keyed to its planning grid, eliminating the need for long strings of dimensions; each element in the plan was either located on or dimensioned back to the nearest grid line.

Though it is often overlooked in studies on Wright, he oriented the Usonian Houses – as he did all his houses – so that each of their rooms would receive sun at appropriate times during the day: 'Proper orientation of the house, then, is the first condition of the lighting of that house. The sun is the great luminary of all life. It should serve as such in the building of any house.'[14] Wright insisted on a southern orientation for the living-room elevation which

HOUSE FOR HERBERT JACOBS
MADISON WISCONSIN

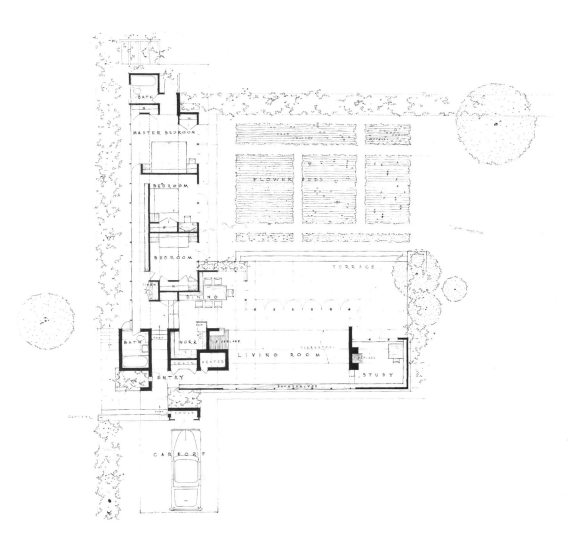

faced the garden; Wright would push the house to the rear of the lot, rotate it or mirror it if needed to attain this proper exposure for the main room. Wright constructed the Jacobs House around its garden or sun court; flooded with southern sun, this court or garden became the focus of the house and the life that went on within it. Wright strove for what he called free association with the earth: 'And with the integral character of extending vistas gained by marrying buildings with ground levels, or blending them with slopes and gardens; yes, it is in this new sense of earth as a great human good that we will move forward in the building of our new homes.'[15] Wright emphasized the importance of natural (sun)light in this marrying of building to garden and to landscape, 'This dawning sense of the Within as reality when it is clearly seen as Nature will by way of glass make the garden be the building as much as the building will be the garden, the sky as treasured a feature of daily indoor life as the ground itself.'[16]

In the Jacobs House, as in all the Usonians, the spaces of the site are experienced as being 'interior', so that both exterior and interior space were conceived by Wright as being 'inside'. Wright said that 'in integral architecture the room space itself must come through. We have no longer an outside and an inside as two separate things. Now the outside may come inside, and the inside may and does go outside. They are of each other', and 'The materials of the

outside walls came inside just as appropriately and freely as those of the inside walls went outside. Intimate harmony was thus established not only in the house but with its site.'[17] For Wright, the concept of boundary was made not by a literal 'edge' but by the construction and inhabitation of place. Wright stated that 'terminal elements are most important as to form. Nature will show this to you in her own fabrications. Take good care of the terminals and the rest will take care of itself.'[18] This is an extraordinarily open-ended design logic for an architect usually presented as being obsessed with control, yet it is perfectly exemplified in the asymmetrical positioning of piers and walls as terminal elements simultaneously defining and anchoring both the rooms and the gardens in Usonian House plans.

Daily life taking place in direct contact with nature was what Wright sought to make possible through his Usonian House designs, and he was therefore opposed to many typical aspects of contemporary suburban-housing construction, including the flattening or grading of landscape contours, the failure to provide proper solar orientation and siting, and the mechanical control of climate: 'To me air conditioning is a dangerous circumstance. I think it far better to go with the natural climate than to try to fix a special artificial climate of your own. Climate means something to man. It means something in relation to one's life in it.'[19] Wright believed – as did Emerson – that the forms, construction, materials and the relation to nature of domestic spaces directly affected those who lived in them, indicating his deeper understanding of the relation between *cultivation* and *inhabitation*: 'Whether people are fully conscious of this or not, they actually derive countenance and sustenance from the "atmosphere" of the things they live in or with. They are rooted in them just as a plant is in the soil.'[20]

OF THE later Usonians with L-shaped plans closed to the street, the Stanley Rosenbaum House, built in Florence, Alabama, in 1939, is perhaps the most beautiful. The street elevation is layered in plan, with windowless wood and brick walls running parallel to the street, and in section, with three roof projections woven together above the walls, the thin clerestory windows set deep in their shadows; the sense of protection of the inner realm is palpably present. The plan again indicates an enclosed garden to the south that completes the square defined by the house's two wings, and here Wright built this garden up to become a raised, plinth-like space set above the rest of the site. In the Rosenbaum House the integration of living room and garden is accomplished by the extension of the living room's concrete slab, marked with the two-by-four-foot grid, out beyond the dining-room projection at the inner corner. Smaller floor slab extensions link the bedrooms to the garden, but this

terrace is not connected to that of the living room, being separated by the planter at the dining room, so that even the outdoor spaces of the bedroom and living-room wings are carefully articulated as private and public, respectively.

This provision of what Frampton has called 'nuanced zones of microspace throughout the house for every conceivable activity' characterizes all the Usonians.[21] It extends not only to the careful delineation of spaces-within-spaces in the primary rooms – such as the typical fireplace alcove, library with reading table, and dining room, all set in the living room – but to the detailing of highly functional service elements, such as the 'thick wall' with continuous storage and high clerestory windows above that edges both the entrance and the bedroom hallway. In this way no space in the house is given over solely to circulation, but provides access to service elements so they do not encroach upon or interfere with the primary spaces.

Loren Pope House, Falls Church, Virginia, 1939

In achieving his preferred orientation for the Pope House – the living-room glass doors face due south, opening on to the garden – Wright placed the entrance and carport of the L-shaped plan on the bedroom-wing side of the outer corner. This allowed him to open the living room in both directions, and he placed a screened porch on the north side, diagonally opposite the south-facing dining-room projection in the inner corner, which is in this case enclosed

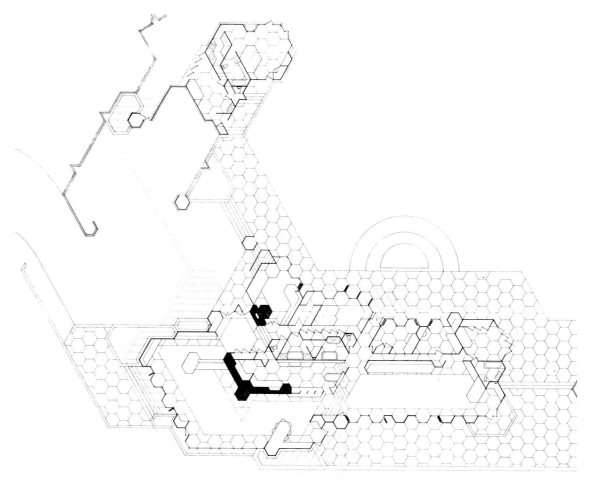

Left and above: Paul and Jean Hanna House, Stanford, California, 1936, plan and view from the street. The floor plan is patterned on a module of hexagons, giving rise to the name 'Honeycomb House'.

by full-height glass doors. The site drops from the entrance, which is unusually formal for the Usonian Houses, with a pair of glass doors set between full-height windows, the entrance defined above by the cantilevered carport roof and below by the brick floor slab. After passing through this symmetrical entrance, we discover that no other elevation or volume in this house is symmetrical, and space is continuously moving around a corner into the next, unseen space, drawing us through the house and thus through the landscape it occupies and makes present.

Rather than defining a garden in its inner corner, the living-room wing of the Pope House is projected out into the woods, standing among the large existing trees of the sloping site, like a pavilion set in the woods. At the end of the living room is a closed wall of horizontal wood boards housing the bookshelves inside. Wright projected the roof farther than any other place in the house, cutting openings into this cantilevered roof slab to create a trellis which casts long shadows on to this solid facade – apparently to be seen only by those walking in the woods, as this effect is visible from nowhere within the house.

From the entrance we take five steps down on to the concrete floor of the foyer, defined by the 'workroom'-kitchen on the right and the dining space open to the landscape on the left. This space opens directly into the living room, one of Wright's most effective small spaces,

opened diagonally in both plan and section and thereby seeming far larger in experience than it is in measurement. Light comes from all directions, through tall glass doors and high clerestory windows, the latter framed by cut-out wood panels of Wright's geometric design. The fireplace occupies the corner of the kitchen block, and its wraps the corner in interlocking brick masses that follow our movement as we enter – as in the Prairie Houses, this re-entrant corner condenses, focuses and captures the dynamic qualities of these spaces of living. The rooms of the house open to one another in a diagonal sequence: entrance/gallery opening diagonally to the kitchen, which in turn opens to the dining area, which opens to the screened porch, which opens to the built-in seating along the south wall, which finally opens to the library alcove at the end of the room; all together suggesting a kind of zig-zag pattern of occupation for these volumes.

Of this folded space-making Wright said, 'If you will take paper and fold it and bend it, or cardboard sheets and cut them and fit them and arrange them into models for buildings, you will see the sense of the new structure in its primitive aspect. And then, after this superficial external view, get inside and make the whole line as one plastic entity.'[22] The floors, walls and ceilings are constructed out of a series of horizontal layers of wood, brick and glass, so that the daily rituals of inhabitation are set within

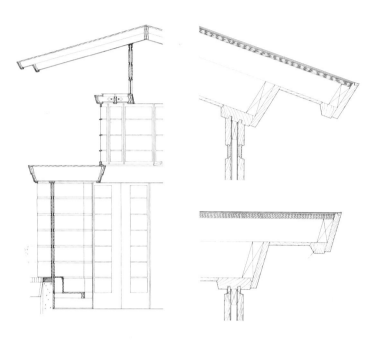

overlapping and layered spatial definitions, that not only creates flue-like cross-ventilation of all spaces due to the series of high clerestories, but insinuates the spaces of living into the forest landscape so that outside and inside merge in our experience. Here again we are made aware that Wright felt these two aspects of dwelling, the practical and the poetic, were in no way contradictory; indeed, his intention was always the simultaneous achievement of both, as either alone was insufficient to allow dwelling to take place.

Paul and Jean Hanna House, Stanford, California, 1936
Despite being considerably larger, more complex and expensive than the typical Usonian House, the Hanna House is usually grouped with the Usonians for Wright employed many of the same planning and construction procedures developed for the Usonians in its design. The Hanna House is wrapped around the brow of a low hill to form a small courtyard centred on a pool and large oak, similar to Wright's own Taliesin. The plan is a variation on the L-shaped Usonian plan, but with significant differences; with little threat to privacy from the street at the bottom of the hill to the south, the living room is placed on the outer corner, with views opening in all four directions. The main wing contains the northwest-facing bedrooms and southeast-facing playroom, while the minor wing spans the carport and is anchored at its end by the guest suite.

Most importantly, the whole house is planned on a thirty-to-sixty-degree angle grid, the floor patterned with a module of hexagons – thus giving rise to the name 'Honeycomb House'.[23] All the walls of the house are ordered on this grid, the typical corner a 120-degree angle, much more open than the 90-degree corner typical of the square-grid houses. Wright had described this crystalline concept of geometry he used in his designs, saying, 'All things in nature exhibit this tendency to crystallize – to form and then conform, as we may easily see. There is a fluid, elastic period of becoming, as in the plan, when possibilities are infinite. New effects may, then, originate from the idea or principle that conceives.'[24]

We enter from the small court focused on the loggia between the main house and the guest wing, through which we can see the hilltop garden within. A low soffit reaches across this loggia, and we turn to the right to enter; again, very much like Taliesin. We enter into a raised masonry element with clerestory windows under a pitched roof set at the inside corner of the plan. In the Hanna House Wright developed a layered series of low hipped roofs and flat soffit 'decks', which when combined with the stepped floor slabs, produces a wide variation of ceiling height within the house. At the entrance foyer and kitchen, the ceilings, clerestories and door-top decks reach a level of complexity and articulation of space similar to the early Darwin Martin

House, but in this case much more literal in its implication and formation of diagonal space and movement.

Over the kitchen and bathroom, Wright actually provided a double roof, allowing breezes to pass through the house to create a flue-like ventilation, drawing air from the top of the kitchen and bathroom through operable ceiling vents. The kitchen – here labelled 'laboratory' – is not only the tallest space in the house but is at its very centre, behind the entrance and fireplace, with openings allowing visual and acoustic connection with the public rooms of the house, reflecting Wright's much earlier redefinition of the domestic hierarchy within the home. The Hanna House shares this characteristic with the other Usonian Houses, and in general Wright's liberatory spatial and functional ideas were rarely limited by existing social norms.

Wright incorporated indirect lighting in the top of the decks or soffits, allowing light to be reflected up on to the ceiling, giving a sense of open, floating lightness overhead, emphasizing the overlapping ceiling planes at the edges of spaces. In the walls of the Hanna House, the horizontally interwoven woodwork and brickwork are exceptionally beautiful, particularly the interlocked corners of the brick walls. Large portions of the elevations are composed of full-height folded walls of glass, horizontally divided by wooden mullions spaced to match the one-foot one-inch board siding, used inside and out. These horizontal window mullions are set to the outside of and overlap the vertical posts, strengthening the horizontal dominance and the impression that the house weaves its various materials together, giving the whole house a distinct quality of folded space, continually wrapped around the hilltop. Wright incorporated sliding *shoji* panels made of insect screen, heightening the distinctly Japanese quality of the house. The view out of the folded glass wall of the living room, with the landscape seen through both the geometric mullions and the knurled oak limbs, is particularly indicative of Wright's capacity to compose views outwards that subtly act to return our attention to the space within.

Lloyd Lewis House, Libertyville, Illinois, 1939

Developed from the first Willey House project of 1932, the Lewis House exemplifies the linear type of Usonian House plan Wright developed for more open sites – in this case a linear form set along the top of a ridge paralleling the river at the bottom of the site, with rows of garden planting emerging out from under the raised living room, connecting house to river. The house has a closed north side and open south side, as if the L-shaped plan of the Jacobs House was 'straightened'. In the living room the fireplace is placed in the solid masonry wall, facing the glass wall which opens to the terrace overlooking the river-front site, while in the bedroom wing the 'thick-walled' gallery, lined with storage shelves, aligns with the fireplace wall of the living room and the bedrooms open onto a narrow

RESIDENCE FOR
MR AND MRS LLOYD LEWIS
FRANK LLOYD WRIGHT ARCHITECT

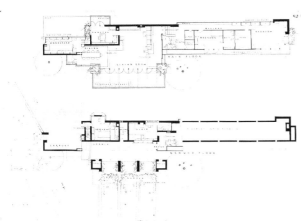

balcony, similar to that at the living room. The house acts as a kind of wall in the landscape, dividing the private garden on the river side from the more public entrance drive and yard on the street side. The entrance or north elevation is composed of a series of closed brick and lapped wood-board clad volumes, overlooked by the porch of the study or 'sanctum', the long wall's only aperture being the shaded carport cantilever.

To enter, we must go around the end of this extended wall, where Wright placed the boat landing at the river edge, and move along the other side, into the loggia under the living room. In the Lewis House, all the primary rooms are lifted on to the first floor, the entrance and secondary spaces are set on the ground – similar to the earlier Robie House. The entrance stair, rising at the far end of the loggia, forms the joint and connection between the higher living wing and the lower bedroom wing, set a half-level apart, so that upon entry we are immediately introduced to the hierarchy of public and private within the house; in this the entrance functions exactly as it does in the L-shaped plan of the Pope House. Across the living room the brick-clad 'sanctum' or study intrudes into the living room, protecting the alcove for the dining room, behind which is the spacious kitchen, prominently positioned at the front end of the linear plan – and with its own small service stair leading to the carport.

The diagonal nesting of the kitchen, dining room, study, raised living room (up two steps from both entrance and dining room) and exterior covered terrace create a richly layered space of living, unfolding towards the landscape. This is subtly counterpointed by the pattern of the wood-ceiling boards, which creates a slight peak at the centre and is edged by a band of clerestories, overlapping to join the dining room and entrance foyer to the living room. Upon entering the living room, we see ahead a linear light, recessed behind slotted ceiling boards, which passes in front of the fireplace and through the open transom over the study door and into the brick-walled 'sanctum', linking the two rooms without sacrificing the privacy of the latter. We cannot move directly towards the fireplace or study door upon entry, as we are on a lower level and are blocked by the low wood bookshelf wall that makes us turn and move to the left before stepping up on to the living-room floor. In this way Wright requires us to face the river view before turning to face the fireplace, condensing the concept of the house in that experience.

Bernard Schwartz House, Two Rivers, Wisconsin, 1939
The Schwartz House was directly based on Wright's 1938 'House for a Family of $5000 a Year Income', designed for *Life* Magazine.[25] In that design, Wright produced a variation on the plan of the earlier Storer House, with a

Right: Bernard Schwartz House, view from the terrace towards the dining room; the kitchen is to the left and the living room to the right.
Centre: Perspective of 'House for a Family of $5000 a Year Income', designed for Life *magazine, 1938.*
Below right: Axonometrics and plan of the ground floor of the 'House for a Family of $5000 a Year Income'. With the exception of the swimming pool shown here, this served as a model for the Schwartz House of the following year.

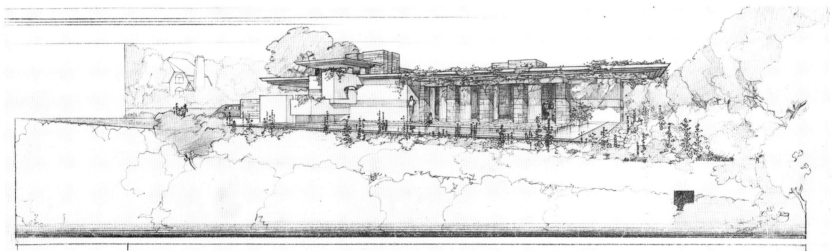

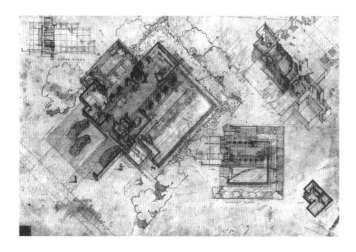

primary rectangular volume opened on both long sides with piers, the whole penetrating into a two-storey cross-block, containing the bedrooms, kitchen and carport, and protecting the large open living room from the street behind. In the *Life* House project, Wright proposed a swimming pool on the south side, wrapped around the dining room and terrace, and a sunken walled garden to the north. Except for the swimming pool, the Schwartz House is in every other way very close to the *Life* House design, the storey-and-a-half living room nestled in the two-storey bedroom block, the carport continuing the level of the living-room roof so that the house is read as the interlocking of two rectangles, a truncated cruciform. The two sets of brick piers on the north and south sides of the living room are shifted, producing alternating open sides and a diagonal movement of space not unlike that found in the Pope House.

The entrance does not place us on the axis of symmetry of the living room; rather we enter it along the edge nearest the shadowed sunken garden. The brick-clad kitchen and stair is passed upon entry, and the fireplace anchors the other end of the room; the library, with its low ceiling and patterned clerestory, wrapping around behind it. The living room, apparently a simple rectangle in plan, is experienced as a complex and subtly nuanced space: at the southeast glass doors the light is brighter yet the ceiling is lower,

while at the northwest glass doors the light is dimmer yet the ceiling is higher. The clerestory windows that ring the room catch direct sunlight as well as that bounced from the roof, making them far brighter than any other aperture in the room – their geometric patterned wood panels are thrown in sharp relief.

Three wood ceiling levels create three layers of overlapping space: the lowest has boards that run across the narrow dimension of the room and begins at entry, defines a space in front of the southeast windows, and wraps around behind the fireplace to cover the library; the wood boards of the intermediate ceiling run parallel to the long dimension of the room and cover the space at the centre and along the northeast glass wall; the highest is a section of the latter lifted to allow a view of the living room from the first-floor balcony and stair landing. Like the Pope House, the position of the street relative to the house allows both long sides of the living room (significantly enough entitled 'recreation room' by Wright) to be opened, so that in the Schwartz House we again feel we are in a pavilion projected into the landscape.

Alma Goetsch-Katherine Winckler House, Okemos, Michigan, 1939

In the Goetsch-Winckler House, Wright placed the house on the end of a ridge and its entrance at the rear so that

the main space was able to be open on both of its long sides, similar to the Schwartz House and the Robie House.[26] The plan is a sophisticated series of points and counterpoints, starting with the simple rectangular volume set in the landscape, defining very different spaces on its southeast side (where the land falls away and the room projects out over it) and on its northwest side (where the land is flat and is developed as a garden court). Entry is from the end on the northwest side, and the shadowed space of the cantilever-roofed carport is mirrored in plan by the walled grass lanai that projects from the diagonally opposite corner. The bedroom block sits next to the lanai and is mirrored in plan by the large fireplace alcove that is placed next to the carport in the diagonally opposite corner. The living-room volume itself – the ground for these various spaces clustered around it as their centre – is Z-shaped, the alcove and gallery sliding out of the main volume at each long side, and the built-in dining table is the pivot around which this entire room rotates; the whole is here titled 'studio' as Wright searched for new definitions for traditional rooms.

The resulting interior space is of great complexity, richness and subtlety, especially in the ways in which light and views are introduced. The brick fireplace, behind which the kitchen is nestled, appears to be the origin for the two primary ceiling planes that reach out to cover the living area. The simple plywood surfaces separate just enough to house the rows of narrow clerestories that illuminate the underside

of the higher ceiling, which defines the space that projects down the hill. The walls of the kitchen and alcove are also topped by clerestory bands, so that the house seems to open in all directions, with light entering every room from several sides, and the roofs appear to float lightly over the spaces of the house. This is surely one of Wright's most astounding interior spaces, and it is significant that it is to be found in a house of such modest budget and dimensions. This reflects Wright's Usonian ideal, exemplified in the set of seven house designs for 'Usonia', a proposed suburban enclave of which the Goetsch-Winckler House was the only one realized. Each of the other house designs proposed a different yet equally rich interior realm for domestic experience.

IN HIS Usonian Houses designed for steeply sloped sites, Wright developed some of the dynamic and integrated interpretations of the domestic landscape first designed for Fallingwater, building them into affordable houses for the American middle class. The earth form itself, particular to each place, was the starting point for Wright's house designs; as he said, 'the source of inspiration, the ground'.[27] The plan of the John Pew House, built in Madison, Wisconsin, in 1938, with its ground-floor rectangle pinned down by the square off-centre first floor, is derived from the Robie House of 1906. Yet, unlike the Robie House in its urban setting, Wright designed the Pew House so that it acts to pull the landscape at the bottom of the hill under

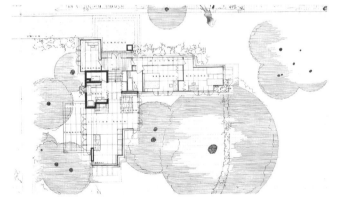

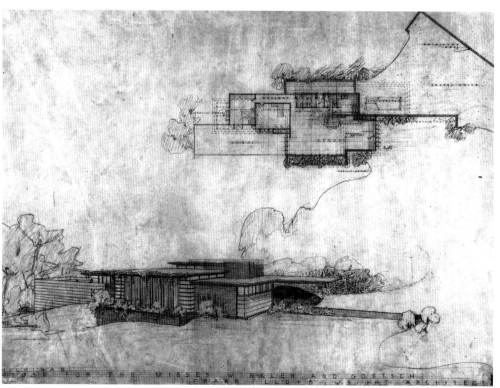

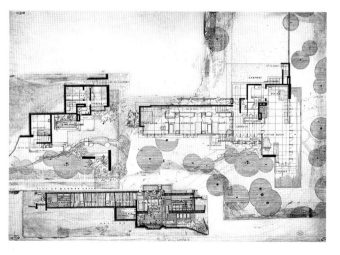

Left: Goetsch-Winckler House, Okemos, Michigan, 1939, view from the entry drive.
Below far left: Goetsch-Winckler House, plan and aerial perspective.
Below left: John Pew House, Shorewood Hills, Wisconsin, 1939, perspective from the lake.
Bottom left: Gregor Affleck House, Bloomfield Hills, Michigan, 1940, plans and section.
Below: Goetsch-Winckler House, view from the living room looking towards the dining room; the kitchen is to the left and the library alcove to the right.
Below right: Skiney Newman House project, Lansing, Michigan, 1939, perspective. The house is exemplary of Wright's 'anchored' Usonian Houses, related to Fallingwater.

the house and to pull the landscape at the top of hill over the house, building the place for dwelling in-between – on the slope of the hill. In the Gregor Affleck House, built in Bloomfield Hills, Michigan, in 1940, Wright again folds the house into the section of the hill, and in so doing he constructs spaces deep inside the house that remain directly related and connected to the landscape and the sky.

Perhaps the most dramatic of these houses on sloping sites is the George Sturges House, built in Brentwood Heights, Los Angeles, California, in 1939, where Wright places a wall of brick at the edge of a steep slope and projects the entire volume of the house out beyond it, wrapping a continuous terrace around the cantilevered spaces, so that the house seems to leap out over the canyon below. In all of these houses Wright develops and concentrates the habitable volume in the middle of the elevation or section such that the upper and lower edges of the house are allowed to merge with the sky and ground, respectively; again this is similar to Wright's own house, Taliesin.

THE USONIAN HOUSES are perhaps Wright's most important designs, for he never before or after achieved both such economy and such spatial richness in the same spaces. It is incomprehensible that these experientially extraordinary, yet entirely practical house designs, have been so completely ignored in the efforts to house the American middle class to whom they were directed. This situation dismays not only architects but observers from other fields, such as Robert Harrison, who has written:

Wright conceived of housing as the basis of American democracy, not as the privilege of the rich. That is why he spent so much time developing models for the so-called Usonian homes – low-cost single-family houses. In the wondrous simplicity of the Usonian home one lives in the unfolding of space, in the exteriority of its 'broad open shelter', in the freedom of space as such. Why is housing still governed by intolerable models when poets have shown, down to the last tangible detail, how to build even the most modest dwelling in accordance with the means of dwelling? It suffices to compare a model of the Usonian home to what today falls under the rubric of 'affordable housing' to wonder why the nation as a whole invariably and systematically ignores its poets. No amount of running water or safe wiring can of itself turn a house into a home, for when a nation ignores its poets it becomes a nation of the homeless.[28]

THE SACRED
SPACE OF WORK

This great building is as inspiring a place to work in as
any cathedral ever was in which to worship.

Frank Lloyd Wright[1]

*Left: S C Johnson and Son
Company Building, Racine,
Wisconsin, 1936–44. Courtyard
and base of the Research Tower,
with a sculpture of a native
American. Wright was determined
that his commission from the
Johnson Company should be made
to completely embody his ideal of
the disappearing city.
Above: View of Johnson Company
Buildings. The Administration
Building (1937) is to the right
and the Research Tower (1944)
to the left.*

Establishing the workplace as a public space equal in importance to the places of worship, government and culture was Wright's intention from the very start of his independent career. In his Oak Park Studio of 1895, Wright constructed the plan type for the consecrated place of work, utilizing his own practice as the model. His intention was confirmed by the progressive, Emersonian ideals of the Larkin Company management; in the Larkin Building of 1904, with its introverted, top-lit central court, its inspirational inscriptions at the entrance fountain and around the top of the court, and its collective dining room placed at the top of the building with the roof garden, Wright achieved the sacred place of work. As Kenneth Frampton has noted, it was 'Wright's lifelong desire to transform the workplace into a sacramental structure'; this is further evidenced in both the Larkin Building and the Johnson Wax Building by his elevating the office cafeteria to the top of the building, thereby creating an almost theatrical space of public appearance, and in his efforts in both buildings to incorporate a pipe organ into the mezzanine overlooking the main workroom floor.[2]

Taliesin Fellowship Draughting Room,
Spring Green, Wisconsin, 1932

After founding the Taliesin Fellowship in 1932, Wright had the newly arriving apprentices begin work on the much-

needed renovation and additions to the Hillside Home School buildings he had designed for his aunts in 1902, and which, though owned by Wright himself for a number of years, had nevertheless remained empty and fallen into decay during the previous decade. Wright's plan of 1932 included numerous wings, courtyards and independent pavilions opening off the rear of the original building; only the large draughting room and sixteen dormitory rooms were finally built during this period. The Taliesin Fellowship draughting room is unlike anything Wright had designed up to this time, and at first seems totally different from his other places of work. But closer examination shows both how essentially related this space is to the earlier work spaces, as well as how thoroughly Wright had transformed the type in this extraordinary design.

Upon entering the draughting room, our first impression is of a horizontal space, without the vertical emphasis of the earlier public designs. We seem to have entered a literal forest of trunks and limbs, for the wood trusses leaping across the space are thickly woven in the air over our heads, and the light drifts down through them; with its low-flying wood structural elements, this space reminds us somewhat of the draughting room in Oak Park. The trusses, at first proposed as consisting entirely of simple equilateral triangles, were modified during construction so that the triangles are now interwoven with slightly angled secondary

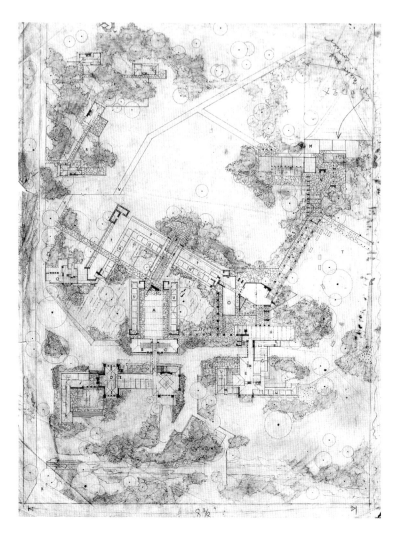

members, resulting in the thickening of certain triangular members where the two systems overlap.

The various purely structural explanations for these inserted members, which add significant complexity to the initially simpler truss, may be technically correct; nevertheless they do not address what for Wright was the paramount purpose of construction and structure in architecture – to make present the nature of the space. The truss as originally drawn would have produced a flat space with no emphasis on the centre, whereas the final built truss contains both the uniform grid of the equilateral triangles and the focus on the centre produced by the rise of the secondary members. The interwoven character of the final trusses therefore should not be interpreted as a compromised design, but as an intentionally more complex design, one that allows the space to be experienced in at least two ways: as a uniformly gridded volume and as a centred space, both characteristic of Wright's public spaces such as Unity Temple.

This experience is confirmed when we examine the draughting room in more detail. We notice that the light comes from above, and that the walls at the side are solid, without apertures or views out; this was true of all Wright's public buildings, but here this toplight is interlocked with the structure in a far more complex manner. The trusses each support secondary angled pairs of joists which lift the roof in sections to produce a row of north-facing

clerestories above each truss. At the two longer sides of the room the trusses bear on inverted equilateral wood triangles set on low stone-pier footings. The sidewalls are thus free of structural load from the main roof, and Wright emphasized this by running clerestory windows just under the ceiling down the entire length of the room on both sides. Wright inserted red-painted reinforcing braces made of flat wood board at the joints in the truss, in the angled joists at the ceiling, and in the legs of the draughting tables; these are echoed in the red-painted trim pieces set into the infilled webs of the bearing triangles and in the red squares painted on their metal bases. As at Unity Temple, Wright utilizes these painted trim elements to delineate and emphasize the integrated nature of the space.

The centre of the room is filled with draughting tables facing the enormous fireplace at the north end, and Wright utilizes the hearth as an 'altar' in creating the sacred space, as he had done in Unity House and in his own Oak Park Studio. The draughting room is entered around the edges of the fireplace, just as one enters Unity Temple around the edges of the altar. The nave-like quality this gives to the space is reinforced by the wood floor set in the centre, upon which stand the draughting tables, surrounded at its perimeter by a flagstone floor, one step higher than the wood floor, on the inner edge of which the truss footings bear. The sacred quality of the space is further suggested

275

in plan, as the draughting room itself is flanked by the sixteen dormitory rooms – it is these which produce the low blank wall at its sides. The dormitories relate to the central draughting room as the monks' cells relate to the central courtyard in a monastery, complete with the flagstone perimeter walkway.[3]

Our experience of this room is most strongly characterized by the manner in which the trusses make the space: skeletal and open, they allow a place to come into being under their forest-like canopy.[4] Both forest grove and monastic courtyard, the central top-lit draughting room is clearly intended as a consecrated space that combines natural and man-made prototypes – both would be necessary to arrive at the design for the Johnson Wax Building. In what seems like a most atypical understatement, Wright confirms the public, identity-giving qualities of the draughting room as place of work with the simple inscription carved into the fascia panel set into the truss at the end of the room opposite the fireplace: 'What a man does – *that* he has.'[5]

S C Johnson and Son Company Buildings, Racine, Wisconsin, 1936, 1944

In 1936 the corporate officers of S C Johnson and Son, a manufacturing company specializing in wax and paint products, determined that they needed to expand their administrative offices. Yet it was only after commissioning an undistinguished design from another architect that Herbert F 'Hibbert' Johnson, the company president and grandson of its founder, was directed to Wright.[6] In retrospect the match seems obvious: the Johnson Company had established a reputation of enlightened management and provision of a humane working environment for its employees very similar to the Larkin Company, for whom Wright had designed the most progressive office building in the country over thirty years before.

Here again we are reminded to what degree Wright had vanished from the public mind in the years before the construction of Fallingwater, which was undertaken at the same time as the design for the Johnson Company. It is hard to believe that Hibbert Johnson did not know of Wright, as the Hardy House had been built in 1905 very near his family home in Racine. Nevertheless, it was the company officers Jack Ramsey and William Connelly who recommended that Johnson consider hiring Wright, even as construction was set to start on the earlier design. After a meeting at Taliesin where the two headstrong men seemed unable to agree on anything except their taste in automobiles – they both owned new streamlined Lincoln Zephyrs – Johnson was nevertheless finally convinced to abandon the earlier design and commission Wright to construct his new administration building.

The concept underlying Wright's design for the Johnson Wax Administration Building was first developed in his

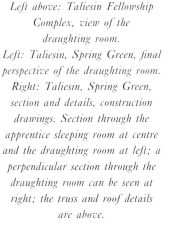

Left above: Taliesin Fellowship Complex, view of the draughting room.
Left: Taliesin, Spring Green, final perspective of the draughting room.
Right: Taliesin, Spring Green, section and details, construction drawings. Section through the apprentice sleeping room at centre and the draughting room at left; a perpendicular section through the draughting room can be seen at right; the truss and roof details are above.

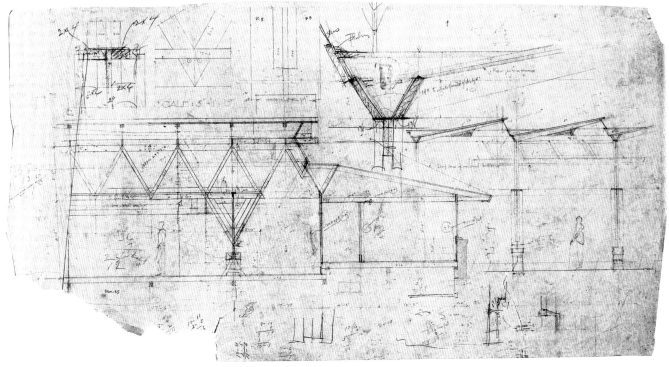

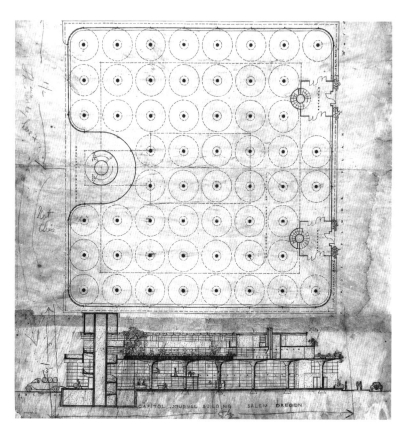

project for the Capital Journal Office Building of 1931. This design proposed a double-height printing plant on the ground floor, surrounded by an open office mezzanine, with a first floor of housing for employees surrounding a rooftop garden, the whole supported by a grid of 'mushroom' columns set twenty feet-on-centre in both directions, bearing on the printing plant floor. The building was to be wrapped in a glass and sheet-metal skin similar to that proposed for the National Insurance Company Building project of 1924, and the design as a whole represents an extraordinary synthesis of ideas from many of Wright's earlier designs.[7]

Though the Johnson Company was already decentralized in organization and headquartered in the small Midwestern town of Racine, Wright was determined that this commission should be made to completely embody his ideal of the disappearing city. While the site next to the Johnson Wax factories in Racine was perhaps 'unimpressive', as Wright would later characterize it, the scattered wooden homes and small businesses were not as grim as one might expect given the intensity of Wright's efforts to convince the company to build its headquarters and move its factories out of town.[8] Wright saw this as his first chance to realize Broadacre City as a new company town in the Wisconsin prairie, and he was so determined to achieve this that he argued at length with Johnson and his officers at

several meetings, coming close to losing the commission. Only his wife Oglivana, upon hearing his account of these meetings, could dissuade Wright: 'Give them what they want, Frank,' she recalled saying, 'or you will lose the job.'[9]

It is interesting to speculate what kind of administration building would have emerged had Wright got his wish for a new company town in which to place it. The design for the Johnson Wax Administration Building that emerged in 1936 is very similar in its organization to Wright's earlier public buildings in urban settings, involving the common themes of the primary volume set directly on the ground floor, surrounded by open mezzanines or walkways, with solid exterior walls blocking views outwards and light coming from clerestories and skylights overhead. Frampton has indicated that Wright's difficulty with opening his buildings to urban sites, even in smaller towns such as Racine, was not due to the quality of the specific context, but to the fact that 'Wright, Romantic Emersonian to the last, could never bring himself to accept the often provisional and ugly reality of the late-nineteenth-century American city, the open-ended grid of which was usually too speculative in nature to provide any convincing sense of civic continuity.'[10]

While this is certainly true – being directly reflected in the anti-speculative character of Wright's Broadacre City design – does it follow that Wright would have built so

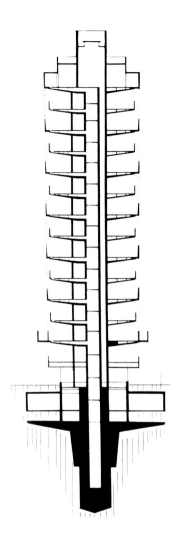

different a building in the open landscape? Wright had created an introverted, top-lit, viewless monastic courtyard as his own place of work in his beloved Wisconsin hills, leading us to suspect that his ideal of the sacred workplace transcended either urban ugliness or rural beauty, and that he would have built a very similar building even in Broadacre City. It was the consecrated character that Wright endeavoured to achieve, whatever the context, and Frampton has noted that like all of Wright's other public spaces, the Johnson Wax Building is 'a totally hermetic citadel; a compensatory semipublic realm within which the new industrial democracy could be brought to realize its essentially secular Protestant ethos through the daily sacrament of work.'[11] We are reminded of the 1904 perspective of the Larkin Building, labelled by Wright, 'Grammar of the Protestant'.

The design Wright developed for the Johnson Wax Administration Building was of 'great simplicity', as he said; an exacting type of simplicity that called for an astonishing level of precision in every detail.[12] On the 245-foot-square site, Wright placed a double-height 'great workroom' measuring over 120 feet by 200 feet, with columns spaced at twenty feet in both directions, surrounded by a seventeen-foot deep mezzanine and a solid brick wall at the outer edge. Air conditioning is introduced into this workroom through ceiling plenums, while the floor is a concrete slab containing heating pipes similar to the Usonian

Houses. The bathrooms are in the basement underneath the workroom, easily accessible by four small circular stairs.

As it had been at the Larkin Building and Unity Temple, the entrance way was brought in between this main volume and a smaller service annex, with the actual entry occurring only after we have reached the centre of the site. Two circular stairs, each housing a circular elevator at its core, are set to either side just inside the entrance, and Wright opened up a narrow triple-height lobby between them through which we pass to enter the workroom. These stairs and lobby rise first to the mezzanine, where they open to a theatre-cafeteria, and then to the 'penthouse', linking the two parts of the building at the roof, where the executive offices and conference room are located; Wright developed this penthouse level directly from the plan of the backstage service area of the New Theatre of 1931 (discussed along with the mezzanine-level theatre in Chapter 7). In the entrance sequence Wright takes us from the garage portico, its columns only 8 feet and 6 inches tall, to the lobby, its columns rising to over thirty feet, and finally into the workroom, where the forest of columns rise to twenty-five feet in height.

The brick-clad exterior walls are separated from both the mezzanine floors and the workroom roof by glass 'cornices', continuous bands glazed with a double layer of horizontally stacked Pyrex tubes – the type used to make laboratory test tubes. With the exception of the plate-glass entrance doors,

Left: Detail of Research Tower and its adjacent support structures.
Above: Research Tower, section. The tower provided Wright with the first opportunity to build the cantilevered high-rise ideal he conceived in 1923 with the National Insurance Company Building project.
Right: Research Tower seen from the sidewalk, with the administration office building to the right.

all the glazing in the building consists of this tubing, set in steel racks, secured by wire wrapping, and sealed originally by sealant and later by rubber gaskets laid in the joints between them. This unique form of glazing results in the absence of all views out, as the tubing distorts light passing through it, resulting in a 'woven' quality of light not unlike that produced by Wright's earlier leaded-glass windows.

The columns are the most extraordinary feature of the building; starting from a nine-inch diameter base set in a steel cup-shaped footing at the floor, and tapering out to produce an eighteen-and-a-half-foot diameter disk at the top, each is joined to the neighbouring columns by small beams spanning the eighteen-inch gap. Wright called these slender, hollow concrete columns 'stems and petals', alluding to their origin in his studies of the hollow structure of the staghorn cholla cactus in Arizona. Wright drew the extraordinarily thin profiles of these columns and specified their dimensions without using any structural calculations. Other than a slight thickening of the collar at the petal base to accommodate the punching shear, Wright's apprentices Mendel Glickman and William Wesley Peters needed to make no substantial changes to Wright's intuitive design – another indication of Wright's astonishingly accurate grasp of structural principles.

The two-to-three-inch thickness of the hollow shaft and petal were constructed using expanded steel mesh reinforcement and newly developed high-strength concrete. The latter required vibration, steel formwork, continuous mixing and application through a pumping system – all of which were innovative at this time. This resulted in strengths as high as 7,000 pounds per square inch, though Wright's design only required 4,000 psi in the petal and 6,000 psi in the shaft. As Jonathan Lipman has noted, the thinness of these hollow columns and petals makes them qualify as what are now called 'shell structures – though they were designed before that term was invented' by structural engineers.[13]

As was becoming typical of Wright's structural innovations, professional engineers and inspectors not only did not understand these columns, they felt they did not possess the formulas necessary to calculate the indeterminate loads. They therefore opposed their use when Wright submitted the construction drawings to obtain a building permit – this despite Glickman and Peters's provision of calculations showing that the columns could sustain the relatively light loads. The majority of the workroom roof does not carry any floor above, so that each column is only required to carry 400 square feet of roof (a square twenty feet on each side), and any snow likely to accumulate on it. Anchored at the floor and connected in all four directions into the neighbouring petal tops above, Carl Condit has noted that together the columns are 'in effect a continuous multi-support rigid frame. The resulting absence of bending in the column makes possible the use of an extremely narrow, virtually hinged bearing at the column foot.'[14]

However, in 1937 the Wisconsin State Building Commission was utilizing a building code that could not be applied to Wright's design. As a compromise, Wright proposed casting a single column and test loading it. The maximum anticipated load was six tons; the typical structural engineering 'safety factor' required doubling this load, thus arriving at twelve tons as the weight the column would have to carry if Wright was to gain approval for his structure.

The scene that resulted was the most amazing confirmation of Wright's structural genius. The column was poured on 26 May 1937, the formwork stripped and the petal braced by four wood beams, similar to the four braces to neighbouring petals in the complete design. The test took place on 4 June, the concrete having cured for only one week. Johnson, the contractor Ben Wiltscheck, Wright, the state and local engineers and building inspectors, the concrete and steel manufacturers, national news reporters, two car loads of Wright's apprentices and a steadily growing crowd gathered to view what Wright clearly saw as a performance, with himself at centre stage. A wooden platform was built on the top of the column petal and sandbags were hoisted and set in a ring around the perimeter. As the weight was loaded on, Wright explained the structural principles of the column to interested spectators.

At twelve tons, the state building inspectors and engineers were satisfied – the test was a success. But Wright was not finished yet, wanting to discover the real strength of his invention. He directed that more weight be placed on the column top; at thirty tons, Herbert Jacobs, a journalist and client of Wright's, recorded Wright saying, 'Keep piling'. Next a crane deposited loose sand in the centre of the sandbag ring, and when that filled the space, the contractor had heavy pig-iron loaded on to the mound of sand. At this point, Wright walked over and stood directly beneath the column, kicking it and striking it with his cane. By late afternoon no more material could be fit on the top of the column, now piled high with over sixty tons of material – ten-times the design load and five-times the doubled safety factor. Wright ordered a crane to pull out one of the wood braces; the column broke only at the collar between shaft and petal, though the impact of the load's fall smashed a drainpipe ten feet underground.[15]

While the columns of the 'great workroom' are unique in Wright's work, they may nevertheless be related to the always-present square-planning grid and the forest metaphor we found more subtly evident in the Darwin Martin House and the Taliesin draughting room. As structural elements, they were unprecedented and, as Frampton noted, these hollow thin-shell columns 'introduced an entirely new tectonic and spatial discourse into twentieth-century architecture', one that inspired the

Left: View of the glazed entry doors to the administration office building as seen from the covered entry drive.
Right: View of the covered walkway from the entry drive to the base of the Research Tower.

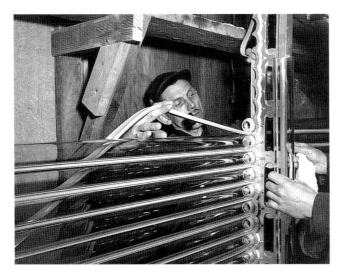

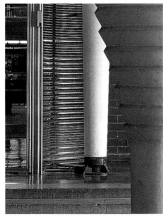

Left: Detail of Pyrex glass tubing at the theatre wall.
Top: Construction photograph showing a worker installing a weatherproofing gasket in the Pyrex glass tubing wall of the Research Tower, 1950.
Above right: Period photograph looking into the main workroom clerestory, constructed of two layers of Pyrex glass tubing.
Above: View of Pyrex glass tubing and carport column at the front entry doors to the administration building.

later structural determination of space in the work of Louis Kahn.[16] Wright said of the great workroom, 'By way of a natural use of steel in tension, weight in this building appears to lift and float in light and air; miraculous light dendriform [columns] standing up against the sky take on integral character, plastic units of a plastic building construction, emphasizing space instead of standing in the way as mere inserts for support.'[17]

The columned 'great workroom' is one of Wright's most astonishing spaces, surrounded by the light bands in the brick enclosing walls and opened by a series of tubular glass skylights that fill in between the curved tops of the column petals; as Wright said, the effect is that of being 'among the pine trees, breathing fresh air and sunlight'.[18] The toplight, and the refractions of the curved glass tubing in general, impart a certain sense of distance, so that we feel we are in a world apart from the everyday. The detailing, particularly of the glass tubing (the result of over a year of experimentation with various glass blocks, sheet plastics and tube profiles), everywhere reinforces the simple, smooth lines of the space and the introverted, almost magical quality of the workroom itself. Wright placed electrical lighting in the air space and the two layers of glass tubing in the 'cornices' and skylights, so that after dark the artificial lighting mimics the effect of the sunlight during the day.

The essential aspect of the great workroom consists in the relation between the columns and light, as Lipman has noted: 'one element of the universe outside entered his forest [of columns] – light, which poured in, bathing every surface and silhouetting the columns above. So rich that it appeared to have substance, the light seemed to be the matter of which the great room was made. This quality of light, enveloping the columns, lends a greater reality to the enclosed space. The columns generate the space; the light makes it tangible. Space, the stuff of architecture, is nowhere more available to human experience than it is in this building.[19]

The Wright-designed furniture reinforces the curved profiles of the columns, glass tubing, walls and the workroom's horizontal layers of space, though the three-legged chairs, which have a propensity to fall over – even when Wright himself sat in them – are not informed by the same structural genius that inspired the columns. The 'great workroom' is used not only for the daily administrative tasks, but could originally accommodate the company's entire workforce from the nearby factories for occasional meetings, during which Hibbert Johnson would address the crowd from the narrow bridge between the lobby and the workroom. Over the years, Wright's building has not only resulted in increased productivity and satisfaction on the part of the office workers, but in the

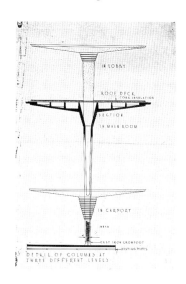

company being able to recruit the most creative people in the field.[20]

Even in the earliest sketches, Wright considered a tower essential to balance the predominantly horizontal composition of the Johnson Wax Building. But it was not until 1944 that Johnson could convince the directors of its necessity, now programmed to hold the company's research laboratories. The Johnson Wax Research Tower provided Wright with the first chance to build the cantilevered high-rise ideal he conceived in 1923 with the National Insurance Company Building project, and perfected in 1929 with the St Mark's-in-the-Bouwerie project. He incorporated the double-height section from the latter tower's apartments, making the square lower levels the laboratories proper, while reserving the circular upper levels for offices. The central structural and circulation spine accommodated the necessary ventilation and services, while the single layer of horizontal glass tubing provided light without views resulting in a tower, by its nature extroverted, that paradoxically matches the introverted, sacred experience of the workroom.

The tower is set within an open courtyard, similar to Japanese temple compounds, and in the workroom Wright utilized the precedent of the Egyptian hypostyle hall and what he himself called 'dendriform' columns – the name applied to Egyptian columns. Noting these hardly

coincidental aspects, Lipman states that 'the main elements of Wright's Johnson complex, a great columnar hall and a narrow tower, are two of the most commonly recurring forms in ecclesiastic architecture'.[21]

THE S C Johnson and Son Company Buildings stand today as one of Wright's greatest designs, still serving admirably as the headquarters of a successful corporation and providing an environment for daily office work far superior to anything built before or since. Frampton has written that the workroom 'is at one and the same time both *res publica* and unspoilt nature, both corporate cathedral and the original domain of God', a similar dichotomy to that which we noted earlier in the Taliesin draughting room, where Wright joins the forest grove and the monastery courtyard. At the age of seventy, Wright achieved a public masterwork which, together with Fallingwater of the same year, projected him once again into the central position in American architectural practice he had held years before. Pointing to the extraordinary and unprecedented level of creativity exhibited by Wright in this building, Frampton has said, 'It may be argued that Wright's Administration Building for Johnson Wax is not only the greatest piece of twentieth-century architecture realized in the United States to date but also, possibly, the most profound work of art that America has ever produced.'[22]

THE SACRED SPACE OF WORSHIP

Architecture is life; or at least it is life itself
taking form and therefore it is the truest record of
life as it was lived in the world yesterday, as it is
lived today or ever will be lived.

Frank Lloyd Wright[1]

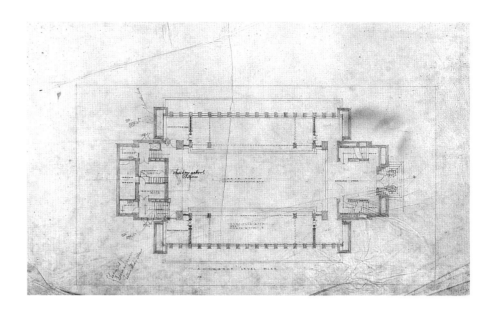

Left: Beth Sholom Synagogue, Elkins Park, Pennsylvania, 1954, detail view of exterior corner. Wright once said that he belonged to no specific religious sect because he attended 'the greatest of all churches', nature.

Above: Project for Christian Catholic Church, Zion, Illinois, 1911, plan. The rectangular volume is divided into a central nave, with high ceiling, and side aisles, up two steps under lower ceilings.

The continuity of principle in the designs of Frank Lloyd Wright throughout his seventy years of practice is nowhere more evident than in his religious buildings, and this is all the more remarkable given the wide range of religions and denominations for which he designed. Wright once said that he belonged to no specific religious sect because he attended 'the greatest of all churches', nature.[2] Dedicated to none in particular, yet his own principles related to all, Wright believed he could thereby be an effective designer for all religions. This was a natural result of the transcendentalist philosophy that structured Wright's own values and moral interpretation of architecture, which also allowed him to draw inspiration from other cultures distant in both space and time. Wright's sanctuaries, while sharing their characteristic top-lit, introverted, sacred qualities with his other public buildings, invariably utilize inset corner piers to establish both the boundaries and structure of the communal space – similar to the majority of centralized buildings of worship throughout history.

In Wright's early work, this often assumed the form of four enormous pillars, creating an aedicula-like volume with four re-entrant corners, as we have seen in the Abraham Lincoln Center project of 1897–90 and the Unity Temple of 1904. In the design of the sanctuary for the Christian Catholic Church project of 1911–15 for Zion, Illinois, the rectangular volume is divided into a central nave, with high

ceiling, and side aisles, up two steps under lower ceilings. The foyer and altar, flanked by the stairs, are projected from the narrow ends of the building, while continuous windows run high up above solid lower walls at the sides. The early sections show a balcony over the entrance, and the plan indicates that school rooms would overlook the sanctuary from above the side aisles – later Wright removed them to the lower floor. The vocabulary of the Christian Catholic Church's directional piers and brick construction is more closely related to the Larkin Building than to Unity Temple, though its central entrance is to be found in neither.

We should here take note of the remarkable similarity between Wright's Christian Catholic Church design and the First Congregational Church, designed and built in 1908 – at least three years earlier – by William Drummond, while he was still employed at Wright's Oak Park Studio. In this design Drummond also utilized the forms and materials of the Larkin Building, for which he had been the chief draughtsman, as well as incorporating its corner stairs and the stained-glass ceiling of Wright's Unity House.[3]

Anne Pfeiffer Chapel, Florida Southern College, Lakeland, Florida, 1938

In 1938, Wright was commissioned by Dr Ludd Spivey, president of a small Methodist college in central Florida, to design both a masterplan for the campus and the most

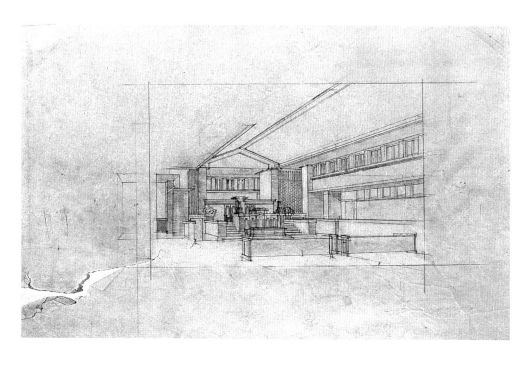

important buildings there. While the chapel is without
doubt the best building of the series Wright designed for
the Florida Southern College campus, the masterplan
should be briefly examined, as it is one of Wright's most
fascinating designs, and its realization one of his most
disappointing. Historians have spent considerable energy
attempting to convince their readers that Wright based his
masterplan for Florida Southern College on the plan of
Hadrian's Villa, an enormous ancient Roman domestic
complex outside Rome. Familiarity with Wright's work up
to 1938 indicates, however, that Wright already possessed a
command of complex geometries and their manipulation,
and that he tended to use his own earlier work, rather than
specific historical monuments, as the source for his
organizational schemes. In this case, his design for Taliesin
West of 1937, with its diagonal landscape plan, and, even
more directly, his plan for the expansion of the Hillside
Home School at Taliesin of 1933, are the more likely
origins of the Florida Southern College masterplan.

What has been overlooked by historians, but which is
nevertheless of far greater importance than this question of
the possible 'sources' for Wright's design, is the difference
between the masterplan Wright proposed and the campus
that was in fact built in Lakeland. The beautiful aerial
perspective drawing in pencil captures the essence of
Wright's vision for the campus; it shows a collection of

independent buildings standing in a dense grove of trees,
joined by a series of covered arcades, the whole linking the
top of the hill to the lake at its base, culminating in the
amphitheatre and boat pier projecting into the water. Two
critically important aspects of this inspired design are
absent from the final built work, the first being the
connection of the campus to the lake.

Wright had initially proposed bridging the road that runs
around the lakeshore, with the primary movement axis of
the masterplan ending in the pier. In 1947 he designed a
swimming pool and outdoor theatre as the culmination of
this axis, the circular pool – half in land and half in water
– is an extraordinary merging of the two. Both designs
would have built the daily promenade out on to the water
into the pedestrian structure of the campus; as with
Kaufmann and his waterfall at Fallingwater, Wright wanted
the inhabitants of the campus not simply to *look* at the lake,
but to move out into it, to *occupy* it.

The second element of the masterplan missing from the
final constructed campus is even more essential to Wright's
vision, that being the dense grove of trees into which the
buildings were to be set. The hillside upon which the
campus is built was originally a citrus-tree grove, and
Wright took into account in his design not only the trees'
particular size and density, but the rhythm of their rows –
which he utilized to set his planning grid. Every building

Right: Anne Pfeiffer Chapel,
Florida Southern College,
Lakeland, Florida, 1938, exterior
view. The cast concrete blockwork
is exposed at the base, with smooth
rendered concrete finish above.

Wright designed for the campus relates directly to the specific height of the canopy of citrus trees, and the arcades are precisely scaled to meet the underside of this canopy. The original trees were removed during construction, and today both the buildings and the arcades stand forlornly in open grass fields under the hot Florida sun.

This is exactly the opposite of Wright's original intention, in which the low arcades, whose pier supports were set on the grid of the tree rows, were intended to make a path through the dense foliage, with views out under the shade of the citrus-tree canopy. In Wright's perspective drawing, the campus as a whole appears as a series of linear circulation spaces, including arcades and porches attached to the buildings, ordered on the module of the tree rows and set into their dense foliage, out of which the main centralized volumes of the college were carefully designed to rise.[4] The importance of the citrus-tree grove to Wright's original vision for the college can be seen in the unbuilt 'water dome' surrounded by terraced rows of trees that he designed to be placed at the top of the hill, condensing the essential qualities of the site – rows of trees stepping down to the water's edge.

We must also bear in mind this disparity between Wright's intentions for a campus in the citrus grove and what actually exists in Lakeland after the destruction of the original trees – a series of isolated buildings and arcades that appear somewhat alien to the landscape they inhabit – when examining the Anne Pfeiffer Chapel, the first building Wright constructed on the campus. The Chapel is banded on the exterior at the ground floor by custom-cast and patterned concrete block of a tan colour, made from local aggregate; this ground-floor 'base' of exposed-concrete blocks is to be found on all the buildings built on the Florida Southern College campus while Wright was alive.[5] Above this concrete-block band the building steps outwards in section, the upper walls constructed of unadorned reinforced-concrete block, finished inside and out with a layer of smooth-stucco plaster.

This distinctive break in material and section between the lower and the upper levels of the elevations of the Chapel originally corresponded exactly to the canopy height of the trees. As we walked in the shadows under the canopy and arcades, we would have seen only the intricately patterned and shadowed, tan-coloured concrete-block walls set upon the ground. The smooth, white, plastered walls and tower would have risen into the sky above the canopy, visible in the bright sunlight from a great distance. If the citrus trees were still standing in their original rows on the hillside above the lake, entry to the Pfeiffer Chapel would be a variation on Wright's theme of moving from a low, horizontal, small and dark passage into a high, vertical, large and bright central space, in this case wonderfully

adapted to bring out the unique characteristics of Florida's geography, landscape and climate.

The section of the Chapel indicates the importance of the low, horizontal, shadowed space under the tree canopy; Wright brings it into the Chapel by placing deep balconies around three sides of the space, under the low ceilings and in the shadows of which we must walk to reach the centre. Here the section suddenly turns and heads straight up, a tall hollow tower rises overhead, its only function being to introduce light into the sanctuary and announce the building at a distance. Near the base of the tower, an angled red steel-framed skylight hovers over the centre of the sanctuary; as we look through it we see an astonishing series of angled and patterned concrete walls framing diamond-shaped openings to the sky, the whole capped by another steel-framed skylight. As we emerge from the relative darkness of the entrance, the light falling down through this complex shaft of space is rarely direct, being bounced off surfaces and broken into intricate shadow-patterns by the angled geometries of the tower.

The delicacy of the filigree-like steelwork in the skylight is somewhat compromised by the clumsily scaled and detailed concrete choir screenwall running all the way across the width of the sanctuary, which also partially obscures our view of the structural piers as they rise from the floor. Yet, taken as a whole, the interior space is masterfully balanced; in section the low mass is centred by the tower, while in plan the larger rectangle stretching out to either side is counterpointed and crossed by the smaller rectangle of the tower, the 30-120-30 degree prow-like walls at front and rear gathering and fusing these disparate volumes.

Wright's first sketch-plan for the Chapel is a direct development of the early balcony plan for the Hillside Playhouse at Taliesin, designed in 1933: a cruciform-shaped plan with a rectangular volume centred within it. The final plan of the Chapel as built is closely related to that of Unity Temple, with its four concrete piers set in a perfect square, their hollow interiors used as ventilation ducts, and the four stairs positioned behind the piers in the outside corners of the plan. Entry to the Pfeiffer Chapel is possible from all four corners, coming in between the piers and stairs, and like the Johnson Wax Building of two years before, the restrooms and service spaces are placed in the basement. In these last aspects, the Chapel does not conform precisely to the plan type identified earlier as characterizing Wright's public buildings, but it may be understood as a transitional step to the separation of service and served in section, rather than in plan, that would be fully present in the later public buildings.[6]

In the Pfeiffer Chapel, space is articulated more precisely and shaped more powerfully in section than in plan, and the plan is remarkably simple, by the standard of Wright's other buildings. This exemplifies how Wright created a balance between plan and section such that when one was strongly modulated, the other was reciprocally moderated.

Left: Anne Pfeiffer Chapel, interior view. One enters under a dark shadowing horizontal plane to emerge in a vertical toplit central volume.
Below: Anne Pfeiffer Chapel, plans.
Below right: Florida Southern College, 1938, aerial perspective, site plan. The existing citrus tree groves are clearly shown, with Wright's proposed new buildings integrated into the grid of the trees.

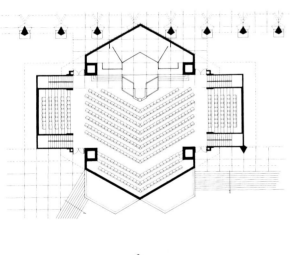

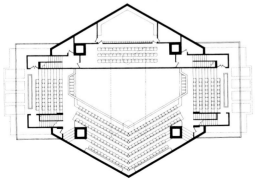

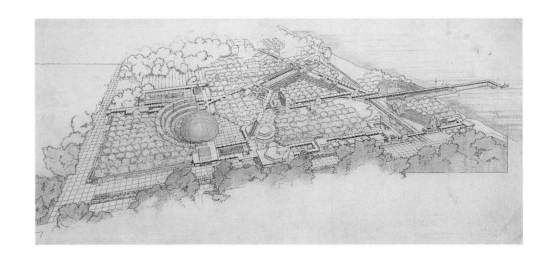

As in so many of Wright's buildings, in order to fully appreciate the subtle and yet all-encompassing aspects of Wright's design intentions, we must imagine what our experience of the spaces would be if elements now destroyed – in this case the landscape composed of linear rows of citrus trees – were still remaining.

IN EXAMINING his commissions for religious buildings, which steadily increased in number towards the end of his life, it becomes clear that, for Wright, light and a prismatic and geometric type of space were the architectural characteristics that allowed a place to achieve the sacred quality particular to worship. This is already evident in the Unity Temple which, though it shared its organizational scheme with other non-religious public structures such as the Larkin Building, alone employed the perfect cubic volume and the crystalline geometries that together produced what might be called a prismatic quality of space. Wright's later conception of this quality appeared, fully formed, in his extraordinary Steel Cathedral project of 1926, proposed for New York City (thus the often-used subtitle, 'Cathedral for Six Million'), commissioned by William Norman Guthrie, who would later have Wright design the tower for St Mark's-in-the-Bouwerie.

The visionary design of the Steel Cathedral, for which Wright made a plan and two elevations, proposed an enormous interior volume that was to rise 2,100 feet from floor to peak, housing a cathedral at its centre, called 'The Hall of the Elements', and six churches of different denominations arranged like chapels within its pyramidal glass and steel canopy. The whole was to be supported primarily by three steel legs or girders forming a tripod joined at the centre, the secondary structure being in the form of suspended steel elements not unlike those of a suspension bridge. A continuous ramp was woven into the exterior skin, allowing access to the suspended gardens, and at night the entire volume would have been illuminated from within as well as supporting spotlights that, as indicated in his sketches, would have criss-crossed the night sky of New York City with lines of light.

Typical of Wright's sacred designs, the plan is quite closely related to both the plans of similarly centralized churches from the Baroque period of the 1600s and Islamic hexagonal patterns illustrated in Owen Jones's *The Grammar of Ornament*.[7] At the same time the structure and section, which this plan was translated into as it rose, are like nothing that had ever existed before – the only 'precedent' again being from Wright's own work: the 'butterfly' stained-glass hanging lamps of his 1900 Dana House. The Steel Cathedral project was to be the source for a variety of later designs by Wright, including the Twin Suspension Bridges for Pittsburgh Point Park project of 1948, the Beth Sholom Synagogue of 1954 and the Arizona State Capital project of 1957.

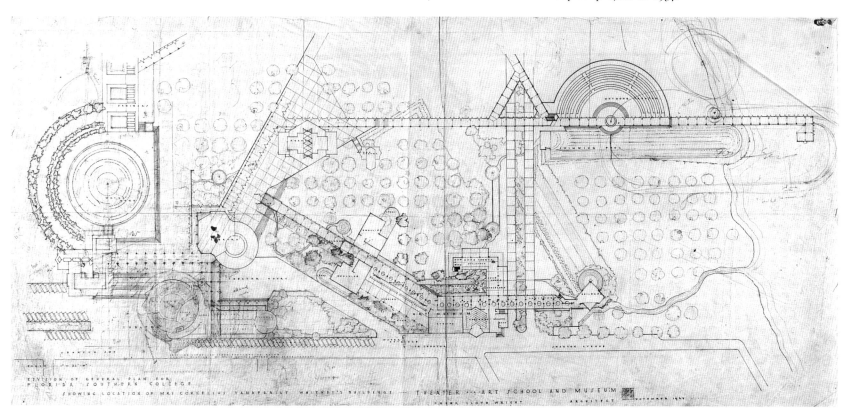

Below left: Florida Southern
College, site plan from 1944
showing Pfeiffer Chapel, the
Library and various other
buildings; again, the existing citrus
tree grid is clearly evident.
Below: Steel Cathedral project,
sketch plan.
Right: Steel Cathedral
('Cathedral for Six Million')
project for William Norman
Guthrie, New York, 1926,
elevation/partial section. The
client later commissioned Wright
to design the tower for
St Mark's-in-the-Bouwerie
(discussed in Chapter 9).

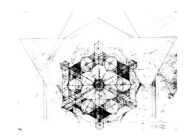

Wright's first opportunity to build a place of worship employing the ideas proposed in the Steel Cathedral project was in the Unitarian Church he designed for Shorewood Hills, Wisconsin, in 1947. Wright descended from a long line of ministers, including those who had founded the Unitarian sect, and for this church near his home at Taliesin, Wright said he 'tried to build a building here that expressed the over-all sense of unity. The plan you see is triangular. The roof is triangular and out of this triangulation, or aspiration, you get this expression of reverence without recourse to the steeple. The roof itself, covering all … says what the steeple used to say, but says it with greater reverence, I think, in both form and structure.'[8] Wright here refers to his lifelong endeavour to translate intentions not into expressive or referential form (such as the steeple) but into space (such as that found under this folded copper roof), so that the idea can be inhabited, thereby literally becoming the present experience itself. Oglivanna Wright's later attempts to characterize the roof form as being 'like the hands together in the attitude of prayer' is therefore equally as inappropriate as the steeple Wright worked to rid from the church.

Both the plan and section of the Unitarian Church are related to the Steel Cathedral project of twenty years before, but only the angled horizontal wood mullions of the glass 'prow' behind the pulpit, where the roof reaches its highest point, directly derive from the earlier design. The plan is composed of two equilateral triangles set back-to-back; the rear triangle, where the ceiling is at its lowest, is given over to entry from the lobby, garden and classroom wing, and a kitchen and fireplace opening directly on to this informally furnished space. A soffit angled down from the main ceiling is all that delineates this space from the sanctuary, which occupies the front triangle, and whose ceiling rapidly rises from both the back and sides, all light entering from the glass wall surrounding the pulpit. The plan of the church is contained by low stone walls similar to those at Taliesin, and is covered by a broadly sweeping copper roof. Both the plan, at the front 'prow' window, and the section, at the peak of the striated roof, are folded to produce the space of worship, creating a prismatic volume that maximizes the spatial implications of its diamond-shaped plan and section.

Beth Sholom Synagogue, Elkins Park, Pennsylvania, 1954

The year before receiving the commission for the Beth Sholom Synagogue, Wright designed the small 'Rhododendron Chapel' for the Kaufmann family, intended to be built upstream from Fallingwater. The lower walls were to be of stone similar to the house, but the roof or 'dome' was to be a prismatic pyramid made of triangular glass and copper panels. The interior volume of this

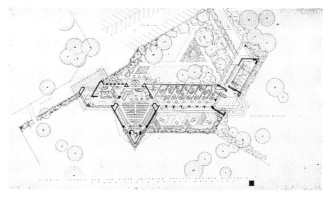

miniature version of the Steel Cathedral is another example of a 'lidded pot', as Neil Levine characterized Wright's later works; as in all Wright's religious structures, large or small, the lower portion is a solidly walled vessel set into the earth, covered with a woven crystalline top, light falling into the space from above.[9]

In the design for the Beth Sholom Synagogue, Wright returned to the Steel Cathedral in an even more direct manner, utilizing the section almost exactly and modifying the plan only to eliminate the six smaller chapels. Like the Rhododendron Chapel, the synagogue is anchored to the ground, in this case by a series of complexly folded concrete walls that incorporate the foundation buttresses for the three steel tripod girders or legs which support the steeply inclined walls. These woven walls of metal, glass and plastic are as tent-like as anything Wright had designed, and remind us of his canvas roofs at Taliesin West, built as a climactic response, but also directly related to typical tented structures often utilized by those who live in the desert.

The congregation's rabbi, Mortimer Cohen, asked Wright to design a building that would incorporate elements of both the American and Jewish experience, and the synagogue may thereby be related to both the steep-walled tepee tents of the Native Americans and the 'travelling Mount Sinai' requested by Rabbi Cohen (the 'mountain of light' where Moses received the Torah from God during the time in which the Israelites wandered in the desert).[10] In the building Wright constructed for the Beth Sholom congregation, he combined these two intentions to achieve a synthesis in which both are essential to the final experience. The night-time perspective Wright drew of the synagogue, with the building illuminated, sending out beacons of light, clearly portrays a 'mountain of light'. During the day, the light of the interior, entering through the woven translucent walls overhead, is exactly like that found within a tent.

In plan, both the lower and the upper walls between the three steel tripod legs are folded and bevelled out, making a modified hexagon. We enter the synagogue from the west, at an opening in the concrete wall located at one of the three prow-like folds in the wall midway between two of the

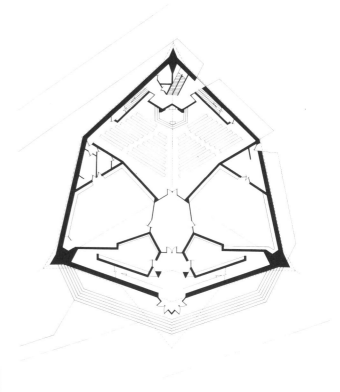

steel-beam columns and their angled corner foundations. Directly ahead, under a low ceiling, the floor steps down, leading to the lounges and a small chapel at the base. The taller ceiling of the vestibule draws us towards gently sloping ramps to either side, where we can see up into the main sanctuary. We are brought out into the open at the top of these ramps; standing next to the concrete buttress at the base of one of the tripod legs, we gaze up at the pyramidal room, 100 feet high, into which we have entered. The woven walls of the sanctuary are composed of layers of wire glass and plastic with an air space inbetween to allow the heat entering through the exterior glass to be captured and vented, either to the outside in summer or to the inside in winter. The structure of the steel tripods is set largely to the outside, reinforcing for those inside both the walls' lightness and mystery; as Lipman has said, 'One gazes up into an expansive, palpable space, whose bounding surfaces are so luminous and abstract as to be otherworldly.'[11]

The synagogue develops the relation of servant and served spaces in section rather than plan, as first proposed in the rest rooms set below the floor of the main workroom at the Johnson Wax Building. In the synagogue the services are all removed to the basement, surrounded by the concrete base wall of the building, allowing the sanctuary above to occupy the entire volume defined by the woven translucent glass and plastic walls. The concrete walls at the

ground, and the spaces they contain, thus literally support the luminous sanctuary above, both structurally and functionally. In developing this section Wright freed the sanctuary floor from the ground, allowing him to fold and shape the floor plane so that it gently slopes from all sides towards the centre, creating, as he said, 'a kind of building that people, upon entering it, will feel as if they were resting in the very hands of God'.[12]

The structural and decorative elements of the building are designed by Wright to reinforce its relation to Jewish ceremony; the three steel tripod beams, the seven projecting lanterns that march up each of them on the outside, and the triangular, multi-coloured, winged lamp hanging inside at their centre all relate to various ritual elements and events of the Jewish faith. Together, these unique, astonishing, yet convincing qualities of the Beth Sholom Synagogue sanctuary demonstrate Wright's unmatched capacity to translate ritual into space and experience.

IN LATE 1955 Wright was hired to design the Annunciation Greek Orthodox Church in Wauwatosa, Wisconsin. The building committee did not consider him for the commission until after they interviewed a number of other architects, one of whom said, 'I'll give you a perfect Byzantine'. Wright was interviewed late in the search after one committee member stated that 'the most prominent

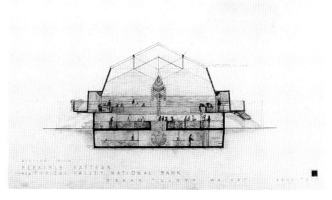

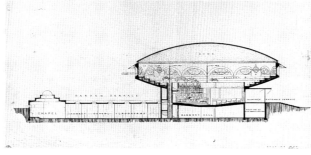

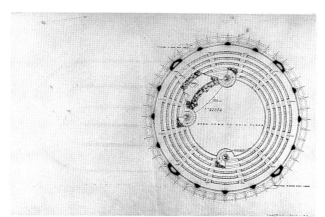

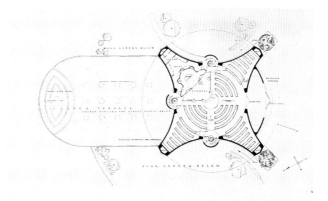

Above: Annunciation Greek Orthodox Church, Wauwatosa Wisconsin, 1957–62, exterior view. Right, right centre, and right below: section, plan at upper balcony level and plan at ground or entry floor. Light is introduced into the sanctuary at the dome's outer edge through a frieze of small glass globes and arched stained-glass windows. Far right: 'The Daylight Bank', Valley National Bank, 1947, section.

architect of our generation, living here in Wisconsin', must be considered for the project.[13]

Wright's design for the Annunciation Greek Orthodox Church, completed in 1957–62, is related to the project for 'The Daylight Bank', designed ten years before for Valley National Bank of Tucson – but with interesting differences.[14] The bank consisted of a double-height circular room with a mezzanine around its perimeter at the second level, with a small aperture looking into the basement, where the vault was placed below ground. This cylindrical volume was to be roofed by a dome-like structure, hexagon-shaped in plan, filled with wireglass skylights. The Greek Orthodox Church, however, is not top-lit,[15] but, instead, defined by the continuous unbroken surface of its blue-tiled, thin-shell concrete dome; light is introduced into the sanctuary only at the dome's outer edge through a frieze of small glass globes and arched stained-glass windows.

In section, the double-height sanctuary, with the mezzanine extending out beyond the edge of the main floor below, is the only room visible as we approach; the services and classrooms are placed below ground, as in the Beth Sholom Synagogue. The balcony or mezzanine level, which contains far more seats than the central main floor, forms a downward-sloping concave curve matching the dome's lifting curve overhead, resulting in the building's startling

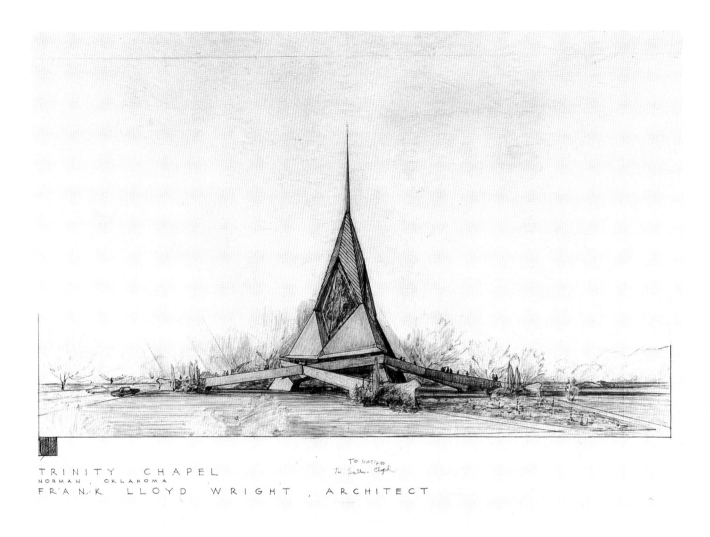

TRINITY CHAPEL
NORMAN, OKLAHOMA
FRANK LLOYD WRIGHT, ARCHITECT

Above: Project for Trinity Chapel, Norman, Oklahoma, 1958, perspective. The building's hexagonal sanctuary, enclosing a tall pyramidal space, shoots towards the heavens.

and otherworldly exterior appearance. This church is more detached from the ground than perhaps any other of Wright's works, suggesting that in his later years – he was now aged ninety – Wright may have himself lost contact with some of the fundamental principles upon which his architecture had always been founded; we shall explore this possibility in the last chapter.

On the other hand, the plan of the Greek Orthodox Church is one of Wright's most geometrically pure and precise: a circle over a cruciform or Greek cross, the latter constructed of four circle segments, so that the convexity of the large circle above is counterpointed by the concavity of the four circle segments below. The whole is locked together in section by the smaller circular opening of the main floor at the centre, and the three spiral stairs at its edges. This plan of Wright's is almost an exact match for the plan of the drum of S Andrea delle Fratte, designed in 1653 by Francesco Borromini, the greatest architect of the Baroque period; Borromini's plan is in turn closely related to those of ancient Roman buildings. Once again we see that Wright's work is related to much that has preceded it in history, but always through the universal power of geometry to form space.

IT IS no coincidence that Wright's first and last churches – Unity Temple and the Annunciation Greek Orthodox Church – designed and built fifty years apart, are both composed in plan of a static form (square or circle) interpenetrated by a dynamic form (cruciform). Wright's later projects for religious structures include the Christian Science Church project for Bolinas, California, of 1956, with its circular sanctuary set within the square walls, and the Trinity Chapel project for Norman, Oklahoma, of 1958, with its hexagonal sanctuary enclosed on a tall pyramidal space that shoots towards the heavens, the whole held above the ground by its angled concrete-ramp outriggers like a diamond in its setting. In these designs, as much as in his extraordinary Beth Sholom Synagogue, Wright completed his career as an architect as he had begun it, fascinated by the timeless power of pure geometries such as the triangle, circle and square.

N R GUGGENHEIM

THE SACRED SPACE OF ART

Architecture not alone as form following function,
but conceived as space enclosed. The enclosed space
itself might now be seen as the reality of the building.
The sense of the within, or the room itself, I now saw
as the great thing to be expressed as architecture.
This interior conception took architecture entirely
away from sculpture, away from painting.
The building now became a creation
of interior-space in light.

Frank Lloyd Wright[1]

Left: Solomon Guggenheim Museum, New York, 1943–56, exterior view. The building itself has become an artwork of the highest order.
Above: Spaulding Gallery project, Boston, Massachusetts, 1919, section/perspective.

Wright's designs of spaces for the viewing of art, though widely separated in time and remarkably few in number, are nevertheless consistently defined by two conceptions – the creation of a hermetic and introverted space lit from above, and the transformation and fusion of that space through the movement necessary to view the art objects. Exemplifying the first of these is the project for the Spaulding Gallery for Japanese Prints of 1919 for Boston.[2] Very few of Wright's designs define his method of constructing public spaces as laconically and yet powerfully as this small scheme, and one senses the respect Wright had for the essential qualities of these small Japanese prints, which, he wrote, presented a 'stringent simplification by elimination of the insignificant and a consequent emphasis of reality'.[3]

In plan, a thick-walled, single-storey, square volume is placed in the centre of a rectangular double-height space, creating the entrance vestibule and office at either end. This vault-like volume set within the space is the gallery itself, in effect an enormous piece of furniture with flat-file storage up to around four feet off the floor and a continuous bevelled wall above for the easel-like display of the Japanese prints. This square gallery room is illuminated by a square grid of skylights, with lamps hanging down from its corners, similar to Unity Temple. The rectangular ceiling of the space, while matching the edge of the gallery on the sides, sails over the two ends to the exterior walls beyond,

creating a layered, protective space that further reinforces the sense of the value of that held within it. Variations on this scheme, where bevel-walled display elements are inserted to create top-lit and introverted rooms within a room, were employed by Wright in designs for Thurber's Art Gallery of 1909 and the S Mori Japanese Print Shop of 1914, both built in the Fine Arts Building, Chicago.

The second of Wright's ideas for the display of art – the transformative effects of the inhabitant's movement on space and form – may be seen as early as 1906 and 1908 in the astonishing display furniture Wright designed for exhibitions of Japanese prints at the Chicago Art Institute. In the 1906 exhibit, a series of freestanding vertical display panels are folded out at waist height to produce a tilted horizontal surface; the vertical panels are anchored at either end by perpendicular bookend-like panels that reach the floor, and a single print is mounted on a portion of the vertical panel cantilevered out either end, beyond the supports – following our own movements upon exiting each aisle of the exhibit.

In the 1908 exhibit, Wright indicated even more directly the transformative effect of the occupants' movement by designing display panels and stands that ran right through existing doorways, hiding a portion of the doorframe and placing exactly half of the display element in each room. In this way one was discouraged from reading the separation implied by the (now partially hidden) doorframe and encouraged to read the fusion of the two spaces implied by the display panel's smooth, unbroken surface and the symmetrical positioning of the paired terminal stands; the whole acting to join rooms that were normally experienced separately – again, as if to follow and reinforce the actual movements of the visitor.

In a quite different scale and manner, the shaping of space to fit the dynamic quality of movement also forms the generative concept for Wright's Automobile Objective and Planetarium project, designed in 1924 for Sugar Loaf Mountain, Maryland. As its name implies, this design was entered by driving the automobile up the spiral ramp that, along with its matching down-ramp underneath, constituted the building's exterior. The series of design sketches indicate that Wright first envisioned a cylindrical volume at the centre of the design, open to the sky and containing a radio tower.[4] Next he replaced the tower with a domed volume set at the bottom of the cylindrical interior court, which still produced steadily increasing depths in the surrounding floors as they came down to the ground, these deep spaces filled with an auditorium, restaurant and gallery.

In the final design Wright created a large semispherical planetarium dome that closely follows the sloped sides of the building, producing only shallow curved spaces at the edges of floors, inside the automobile ramps, for services. Due to the occupation of the entire centre of this man-made mountain by the planetarium, this final scheme required all vertical pedestrian circulation to be removed to a separate stair and elevator tower, compromising the purity of this design but also establishing the method of solving a similar problem in the Guggenheim Museum, for which this design is clearly a precedent. However, the scaling of the Automobile Objective and Planetarium to accommodate automobile movement, as opposed to the pedestrian movement typical within a museum or gallery, would also prove to be a challenge for Wright in employing this concept for the Guggenheim Museum.

V C Morris Gift Shop, San Francisco, California, 1948

Though the design for the Guggenheim Museum was started five years earlier, the V C Morris Shop was completed long before construction of the museum was even begun, so that the smaller design allowed Wright his first opportunity to build the internal spiral concept the two schemes share. Though it is rarely studied, the V C Morris Shop is one of Wright's most beautiful and accomplished designs, combining as it does both the introverted, top-lit building-within-a-building (similar to the Spaulding Gallery) and the transformative effect of movement on spatial form (as in the Automobile Objective). In both plan and section it is also closely related to the Daylight Bank project of the year before, with its double-height, mezzanine-ringed, top-lit circular space. Yet in the Morris Shop there is a

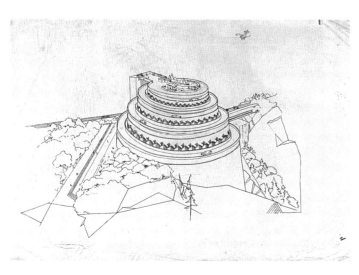

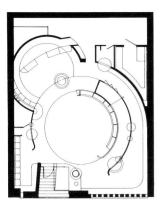
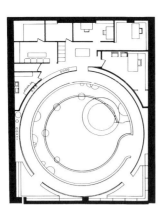

rectangular outer 'box' in which the precious circular inner volume is contained, defined to a large degree by the site itself, a party-wall lot on a narrow downtown street.

The circular inner volume of the Morris Shop is hidden behind a simple, almost solid wall of the finest brickwork, an exterior street elevation almost unique among Wright's works. Two layers of brick, one set slightly in front of the other, are woven together by a horizontal line of square lights inset along the bottom edge near the sidewalk and a vertical grille created by removing every other brick from the left edge of the front surface – this is also backed by recessed lights. Where these come together in the lower left corner, Wright placed the entrance, a beautiful arch composed of four stepped, concentric layers of brick springing from the stone string course above the horizontal lights, which extends halfway into the space of the arch, and landing on the sidewalk at the other side.

When the owner questioned the lack of traditional store-front windows in the shop, Wright indicated once again his understanding of the part played by that which is obscured or hidden from view in our desire to enter and occupy a building:

> We are not going to dump your beautiful merchandise on the street, but create an arch-tunnel of glass, into which the passers-by may look and be enticed. As they penetrate further into the entrance, seeing the shop inside with its spiral ramp

and tables set with fine china and crystal, they will suddenly push open the door, and you've got them!'[5]

In the interior of the Morris Shop, Wright inserted a circular mezzanine with a spiral ramp climbing up inside it – both made of smooth white reinforced concrete – within the rectangular volume defined by the site. The off-centre position of the entrance archway, and the intrusion of the low wall into the arch itself, prepares us to enter the circular interior volume along its edge, as is appropriate to the spiralling circulation pattern. There could not be a greater difference between the outside and the inside of this building: we move through the restrained, severely flattened, dark, ribbed surface on the street to reach the sensuous, expansively curved, light, smooth surface of the interior – it is almost as if we have entered another world. Inside, the light falls from a grid of interlocked translucent globes suspended at the top of the space; as we ascend the ramp we pass small circular openings containing illuminated objects which are scattered around the curved wall. The various built-in wood and glass furnishings are also composed of circle segments, interlocking with the geometries of the larger space. A large shallow bowl of plants hangs from the ceiling where, seen upon entry, it floats mysteriously in the centre of the volume, encouraging the appropriate suspension of disbelief that seems to be called for by this design.

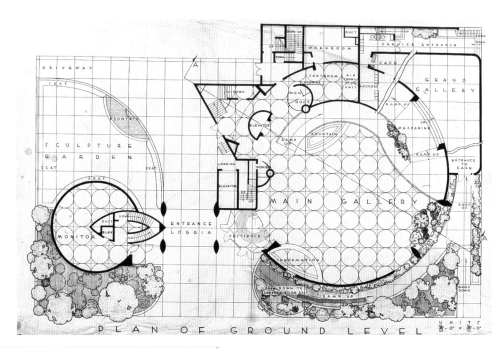

P L A N   O F   G R O U N D   L E V E L

Solomon R Guggenheim Museum, New York, 1943–56

In 1943, at the age of seventy-six, Wright was commissioned to design what was then called the Solomon R Guggenheim Collection of Non-Objective Painting, a museum to house one of the most comprehensive collections of modern painting in the world. Construction of the building did not start until 1956, and the Guggenheim Museum remained unfinished at Wright's death in 1959. The collection Wright was commissioned to house, including paintings by early twentieth-century avant-garde artists such as Wassily Kandinsky, was owned by the Guggenheim family, famous for their patronage of the arts. Baroness Hilla Rebay von Ehrenweisen, the director of the collection, proposed that Wright design what she called a 'Temple of Non-Objectivity', and while Wright's scheme of a singular, top-lit, introverted volume shaped by the dynamic pattern of the viewers' movements was similar to his earlier public buildings for art, it was exceptional among all his works for the degree of its plasticity and sculptural power, inside and out. Where the V C Morris Shop, hiding its dynamic ramp behind a flat and solid brick street wall, uses its small party-wall site and narrow street as foil, the Guggenheim Museum uses the entire densely built and gridded fabric of Manhattan.

The scheme for the Guggenheim Museum was developed by Wright soon after receiving the commission, but none of the sites selected for consideration by the clients provided what either they or Wright considered an appropriate context. Wright's initial designs are for a downtown corner site, empty save for a narrow building at one end, and surrounded by brick warehouses and commercial buildings. In 1949, after considerable efforts, a site on Fifth Avenue was secured; Wright now had the entire end of a standard 200-foot-wide New York block between 88th and 89th Streets, facing directly west to Central Park and free of party walls on three of its four sides. Wright's design for the museum created a virtually freestanding plastic form relating to the park that was nevertheless able to play off against the dense, straight street wall of Fifth Avenue.

Reminding us of the design's origins in his 1924 Automobile Objective, Wright designed a drive-through drop-off that allowed cars to enter the museum from Fifth Avenue, between the main spiral gallery to the south and the smaller 'monitor' to the north, exiting onto 89th Street. Thus entry and movement of automobiles, pedestrians and visitors all penetrated in to the interior of the museum, carving into the thickness of the urban block. Lipman has noted that this entrance sequence matches that of Unity Temple, Johnson Wax and all of Wright's public buildings, occurring as it does between the main volume and a service annex.[6] The floor plans Wright drew for the Guggenheim Museum show a consistent development of these paired

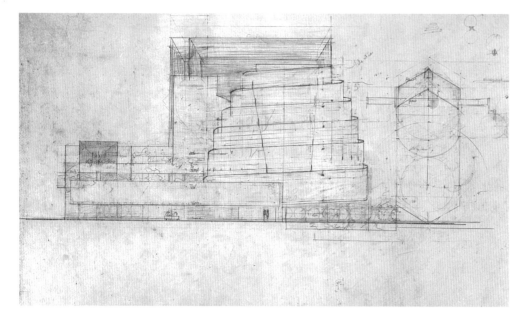

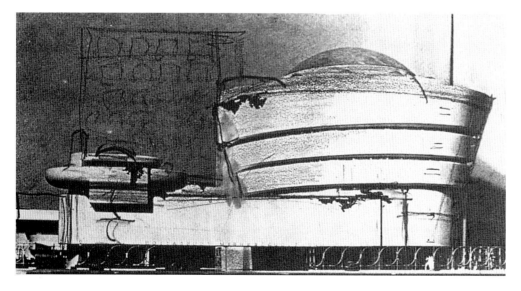

circular volumes, a larger spiral and a smaller monitor, both set up against Fifth Avenue, a stair and elevator tower placed behind and between them.

Wright's sequence of perspective design drawings for the museum is breathtaking in its formal audacity and colourful exuberance. The order of these perspectives has not been definitively established, but we can presume that Wright began with the form closest to his own model for this design: the Automobile Objective of 1924.[7] Therefore what we shall consider the first perspective and elevation of the sequence shows a spiral that grows smaller, moving inwards as it rises, like a man-made mountain, very similar to the earlier project. Yet we are astonished at the colour – a bright pink-red that is shown glistening as if it were enamelled. A white concrete tower-like volume, bevelled at its top and side, cuts into the large spiral at its rear; this clearly houses the stair, and is glazed extensively with glass tubing like the Johnson Wax Buildings.

Wright's second scheme is probably represented in the perspective of a hexagonal gallery volume, its aqua-blue walls bevelled out slightly and topped at each floor by continuous bands of glass tubing, the whole capped by a concrete top and seated on a concrete base. This scheme apparently does not incorporate the spiralling ramp, as the floor lines do not climb as they move around the hexagonal volume; behind again is the bevelled stair tower.

Wright's third perspective scheme presents the space that would be found in the museum's final design: a spiral that grows larger, moving outwards, as it rises, with bands of glass-tube glazing recessed in-between the stepped sections of the spiral. In this scheme the bright pink-red glossy colour has returned, producing an image sure to get the attention of even the most jaded New Yorkers. Yet the form lying under this red colour is that of the final design, revealed in the final perspective of the sequence, a pure-white spiral lifting off the sidewalk, leaving its brown blocky neighbours behind as it ascends to the sky. A cylindrical stair tower now emerges behind the spiral, and a dome glazed with the same glass-tubing as the bands between the ramping floors peeks out of the top. In this perspective drawing, the spiral again glistens as if enamelled, and the lines drawn later in pencil over the white exterior indicate that Wright was considering cladding the whole in thin marble – an idea soon abandoned, like his notion of gold-leafing the concrete slab at Fallingwater; in both cases we have the client's discretion (and budget!) to thank for saving Wright from these inappropriate propositions.

While Wright's Guggenheim Museum is unique in many ways, being based on his 1924 Automobile Objective, it is interesting that other architects of the period also turned to the spiral when designing a museum. Le Corbusier, who used a square spiral plan in the design of several museums, chose the spiral for its open-ended quality. In his Museum of the Twentieth Century project of 1929, time, represented

by the museum's collection, did not stop, and thus neither could the space of the linear museum, which Le Corbusier proposed as continuously expanding, like a seashell, wrapping new galleries around the old.

Wright's Guggenheim Museum has a beginning and an end, and extension or expansion of the spiral itself never appeared to figure in Wright's design concept. Yet the organic growth metaphor, best seen in the seashell, which the museum's spiral recalls, clearly is meant to come to mind in the experience of this building. Wright sought not the literal extension of growth, but the spatial fusion implied in the continuously unfurling ramp and the space it defines; as Wright said, the Guggenheim Museum is 'one great space on a single continuous floor. The eye encounters no abrupt change, but is gently led and treated as if at the edge of the shore watching an unbreaking wave ... one floor flowing into another instead of the usual superimposition of stratified layers. The whole is cast in concrete more an eggshell in form than a crisscross stick structure.'[8]

We enter the Guggenheim Museum between the spiral and the monitor, under a horizontal single-storey-deep concrete bar that runs the length of the street front. As in all of Wright's works, this entrance space is both low and dark, yet here it is unusually obvious – not a 'front door' to be sure, but nonetheless more directly accessible than is normal in Wright's designs. This low, dark entrance takes

us, as in the Johnson Wax Buildings, to the middle of the plan; here the original open loggia, where cars could enter and drop off passengers, has since been glazed, and the original drive-through and sculpture garden behind has been enclosed to house the bookstore. A circular glass vestibule projects from the right, opening to the loggia and towards the sidewalk; we move under its low ceiling and out on to the floor of the main gallery, the concrete walls of the ramping floors spiralling up to the enormous skylight high overhead, which pours pure white light down into the space.

Once again Wright has brought us through a small, low, dark entrance sequence and released us into a large, high, bright interior volume – this last a true world unto itself, defined by its own astonishing spiral geometry, its means of support not visible upon entry, seeming to grow up from the ground in one continuous curve. While we recall that the spiral expands as it rises on the exterior, inside we find that it diminishes as it rises, not only producing the largest floors at the top but creating a perspectival effect that makes the central space seem even taller than it actually is, hindering our efforts to understand its structure and dimension. The skylight, circular in plan and divided into twelve segments, is the width of the lowest spiral floor, allowing copious light to cascade into the space from above, washing the sides of the concrete ramp walls and emphasizing the darker voids or slots between them.

The twelve thin concrete piers set in a radial pattern in plan, which support and structure the spiral in its rise towards the skylight, were carefully retracted by Wright from the inner edge of the central volume and placed along the outer wall of the spiral, reappearing to view only when they reach the top, where they bend inwards to become the skylight's structuring ribs. This both requires circulation up and down the ramp to occur at its inner edge, so that the visitors can overlook the main space, and withdraws the vertical structural supports from the view upon entry, allowing us to believe for at least a moment that the concrete spiral may in fact be self-supporting. These thin concrete piers act to frame the view of the paintings hung on the outside wall, dividing the continuous ramp space into rooms defined on three sides and open to the movement zone at the inner edge of the ramp on the fourth.

Wright produced a rather astonishing series of perspectives showing how these various spaces on the ramp were to be used for the display of art; labelled 'The Watercolor Society', 'Average Painting and Sculpture', 'Middle of the Road' and, finally, 'The Masterpiece', showing the ramping display spaces from the widest space and largest number of artworks (at the top of the ramp) to the narrowest space and the single artwork (near the bottom of the ramp), respectively.

Light is introduced into the space and on to the paintings in two distinctly different ways: the main volume, lit by the skylight, is ringed by the ramp-gallery, whose inner circulation zone is illuminated from the central space while its outer wall, where the artworks are hung, is lit by a continuous band of horizontal clerestories that separate each level of the ramp from the one above it, both inside and out. These were originally labelled 'skylights' on Wright's section, and are indeed carved in a V shape into the ramp space to drop light down onto the wall which bevels out below it. Wright first proposed that these clerestory bands be made of a double layer of horizontal glass tubing, exactly as he had done in the 'anti-cornices' of the Johnson Wax Building; as was typical with Wright, this detail also included an air duct and floor heating. The detail of the clerestories as built was simplified to an angled flat skylight outside, with integral gutter at the top of the concrete spiral

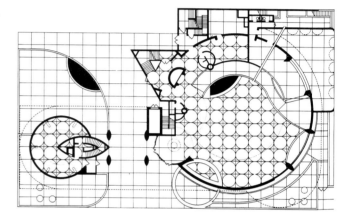

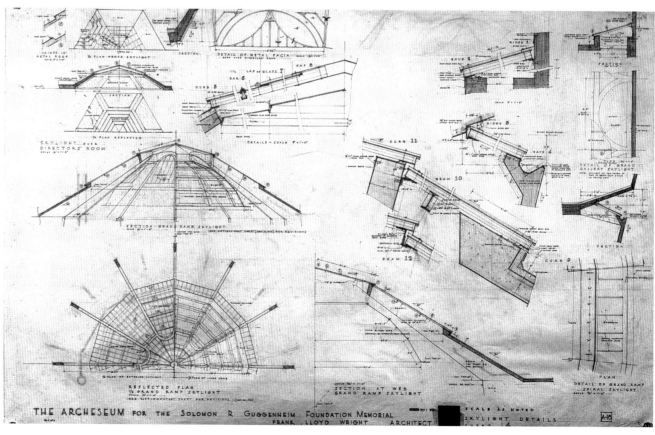

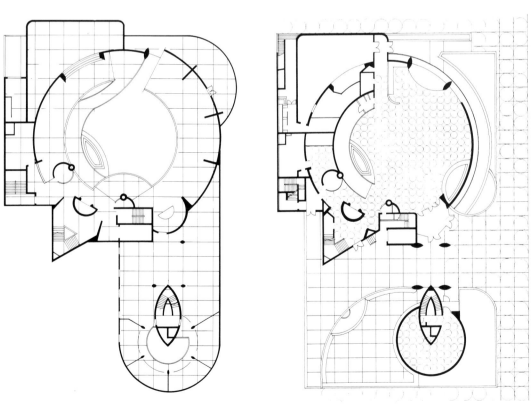

wall, set over a translucent panel inside, with an electric light and reflector fitted into the space between them.

At some point after the building's completion, the museum staff closed these clerestories, inserting continuous fluorescent lighting behind the translucent panels and mounting fluorescent bands and spotlights to the ceilings, so that daylight no longer enters the individual ramping gallery spaces and the pure smooth surface of the ramp ceilings – into which Wright had recessed triangular downlights – is compromised.

Critics and historians have attempted to justify another curatorial decision, that of not allowing visitors entering the museum to do what seems most natural and expected, and what Wright clearly intended – that is, to begin their visit by walking up the ramp that opens so invitingly ahead. Indeed, some writers have even criticized Wright's design for this 'feature'. In order to ensure compliance with this illogical 'one-way' circulation system imposed by the curators (first go up the elevator and then walk down the ramp), a museum guard must be assigned to the entrance area solely to keep visitors from ascending the ramp, directing visitors instead to stand and wait to enter the tiny elevator in a small cramped space at the very foot of the generously-sized ramp. The currently required rapid ascension to the top, where the ramp holds the largest volume, does not produce the experience Wright intended – the unfolding and expansion of the volume as we slowly climb towards the light – but rather its opposite – arrival at the largest and brightest space followed by a descent into those which are increasingly darker and smaller.

Given the care with which Wright handled the section and vertical view upon entry, we certainly would be surprised if he did not handle the plan in a similar manner. In fact, we find that the ramp meets the floor of the main space only after passing the elevator door, its outer wall creating a small space in front of the elevator, totally unsuitable for waiting. The large triangular stair that is placed behind the much smaller elevator is, unlike the elevator, scaled to the dimension of the entire spiral volume, and suggests most strongly that Wright intended the building to be experienced primarily on foot, whether ascending or descending, whether by circular ramp or triangular stair – both complete geometries, it should be noted, as compared to the incomplete geometry of the semicircular elevator. Referring to the plan, we note that the ramp meets the floor of the main space at the fountain pool, which acts to anchor the ramp to the floor, and which is the only intrusion on to the main-floor space – a precise and inviting announcement of the intended beginning of our journey.

The ramp and floor, both made of reinforced concrete, are finished with a layer of terrazzo-concrete flooring with

a grid of inlaid brass circles. The interior walls are finished with a layer of plaster and painted, while Wright's original intention of applying a thin layer of marble to the exterior was abandoned in favour of a gunned concrete sprayed against exterior forms with a PVC coating as a finish.

The Guggenheim was completed after Wright's death, and like many of his later works, it seems to be lacking his final touch in the details, producing a somewhat vacuous quality in the spaces, an imprecise sense of scale and an uncertainty about how intentional some of the more disturbing effects are that it has on its occupants. The ramp walls, like the terrace parapet walls at Fallingwater, are set so low as to make many visitors uncomfortable in approaching the edge. Yet Wright's design clearly calls for us to move to the inner ramp edge and overlook the central volume, thus providing opportunities for both traditional and innovative views of the artwork. This central volume allows a continuous sense of orientation stronger than that found in any other modern museum, and the ability to view the artworks both up close, in the almost private dimension of the ramp, and from the other side of the central volume, across the entire width of the space, produces a most comprehensive and rewarding experience of both art and architecture.

Wright's design for the Guggenheim Museum was clearly intended to place the 'new' art of the collection in an appropriately innovative type of space. Yet from the very beginning of the design process to the opening of the museum after Wright's death – a span of almost twenty years – the artists and art historians of this 'new' art were noticeably uncomfortable with the undeniably new kind of museum space Wright proposed to house the new art. During this time, Wright expressed considerable amusement at what he saw as the architectural and spatial conservatism of the self-proclaimed 'avant-garde' artists and their collectors and interpreters. While, according to the new artists, Wright's design compared unfavourably to the traditional white rectangular box as a space for the display of the new art, Wright wondered why this new art, which purported to represent space and form in a new, fully integrated manner, would not be most appropriately displayed inside exactly such a 'plastic' space as he proposed? Wright, of course, has had the last word in this debate, and today not only is his museum enormously popular with the public, but his design is credited by many artists with engendering profound reinterpretations of the perceived boundaries and bonds between painting, sculpture and architecture.

THE RECENTLY completed restoration and addition to Wright's Guggenheim Museum by the architectural firm of Gwathmey Siegel is a careful, modest and deeply respectful design. Basing the location, dimensions and tartan-gridded facade of their tower addition exactly on Wright's own tower-annex drawings of 1949, the architects have, in addition, freed up many spaces within the museum long filled with ineptly conceived storage and office renovations made by the museum's curators. This is most notable at the seventh floor, where the top of the ramp for many years was used for storage and was therefore closed to the public, interrupting and crudely terminating the graceful ascent of the ramp. Today, we may once again ascend to the very top of the museum, to that important space where the ramp ends and the skylight supports arch up out of the radial piers; we are able to experience through our occupation what was clearly intended by Wright to be the complement of the entrance space below, where we began. The museum today, after the renovation, is without question much closer to what Wright envisioned in his original design.

It is astounding that this intelligent and necessary renovation was opposed so vociferously by so many, particularly those who appear to have little understanding of Wright's original intentions for this museum and for his architecture in general. Those who would argue that no changes should ever made to Wright's buildings – that they should be frozen in time and, as would almost always be made necessary by this, emptied of the activities they were intended to house – operate under a misguided concept of preservation which does not acknowledge Wright's vision of architecture as essentially the framework for daily life; the life without which architecture has no meaning and no reason to exist.

IT WAS Wright's lifelong propensity to transform all building tasks entrusted him – whatever their purpose – into the creation of sacred spaces, thereby reconnecting to the ancient understanding of building itself as a sacred act. This is nowhere more evident than in the Guggenheim Museum, which through this process may be understood to have become itself an artwork of the highest order. The aspects common to all Wright's public buildings which give them their sacred character – introverted, vertically-oriented volumes lit largely or solely from above – are in turn complemented by the articulation within the interior space of ritual circulation patterns particular to the building's use. In the Guggenheim Museum, it is the movement of the spectator to the art that orders the building's space and form. The spiral ramp becomes the unifying architectural experience, bringing the art and the spectator together, bathed in a cascade of light and suspended in a ceaselessly moving space.

Above left: View from the top of the Guggenheim Museum to the floor below, the whole a dynamic and flowing yet integrated space. Right: View at the turn of ramp, the beginning of the continuous vertical ascent.

INTEGRATION
AND DISINTEGRATION
IN THE LATE WORK

Time is the test that discriminates the imaginative
from the imaginary. The latter passes because it is
arbitrary. The imaginative endures because, while at
first strange with respect to us, it is enduringly familiar
with respect to the nature of things.

John Dewey[1]

Left: Marin County Civic Center, San Rafael, California, 1957. As Wright said, the hills are a feature of the design and the building is a bridge between them.

In the last twelve years of his life, after the age of eighty, Wright was busier than he had ever been, undertaking nearly four hundred projects all over the world, seemingly unable to turn down a commission, no matter how small or large. Perhaps the memory of the lean years before, when he had very little work to sustain him and his apprentices, drove him to take on everything that was offered, whether or not he could give it the appropriate attention. Wright's apprentices were rarely capable of effectively assuming responsibility for his designs, and as a result many of Wright's works in this late period consisted of either repetitive schemes, often adapted to neither their sites nor programmes, or extravagant and overscaled forms, usually given only superficial design development.

Since founding the Taliesin Fellowship in 1932 at the age of sixty-five, Wright had been surrounded by those who literally worshipped him; the increasingly ritualistic daily life at Taliesin had long been guided by Oglivanna Wright, who effectively assumed the guise of the high priestess.[2] Certainly there can be no question that Wright had, through his extraordinary works, earned both the admiration of the world and his reputation as the greatest living architect – the greatest architect ever to emerge from America. Yet the effect of his increasingly isolated situation (physically, intellectually and socially), the vast increase in the amount of work coming into the office, and the absolute ban Oglivanna

imposed on any kind of criticism of Wright's ideas, no matter how inappropriate or superficial they might be, led inevitably to the decline in quality of many of Wright's designs. During this period, Wright often seems to have lost his previously innate grasp of the imaginative, as defined by Dewey above, falling instead into the realm of the purely imaginary – abandoning the poetic for the preposterous.

It is interesting to compare this situation to Wright's early Oak Park practice, which had been organized as an atelier where Wright's designs were discussed and critiqued during their development by architectural colleagues whose talents he respected, such as Griffin, Mahoney and Drummond. In the Oak Park Studio, Wright was clearly the best designer and the principal of the practice, yet his work was not above constructive criticism. The Taliesin Fellowship, on the other hand, was composed not of experienced designers of Wright's generation, but largely of untrained highschool-aged beginners who would spend their entire adult lives as part of the Fellowship. The fact that the associates of the Oak Park Studio went every evening to their own homes and families, and did not live in a communal, almost cult-like atmosphere as did the Taliesin apprentices, should not be overlooked.

At Taliesin there was 'the Master and the apprentices', and everyone – apprentice, family member or guest – was required to address and refer to Wright only as 'Mr

321

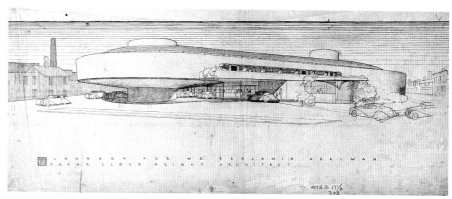

Above left: V C Morris House project, San Francisco, California, 1945, perspective from the ocean – an incredible cliff-top site.
Above right: Adelman Laundry project, Milwaukee, Wisconsin, 1945, perspective; here a service building has been elevated to the status of a public monument.

Wright', even after his death. Criticism of any sort was simply not allowed, and therefore every sketch from the Master's hand was, by definition, a stroke of genius. Genius of this sort does not feel compelled to explain itself, nor is it accountable or responsible to anything except its own whims. Wright could not have avoided being affected by the ritualized lifestyle that developed at Taliesin, where he was the centre of all attention, revered almost as a god.[3] However, it is also certain that architecture of quality cannot emerge in the absence of constructive criticism – whether self-criticism or the criticism of respected colleagues.

Integrity, or integration of space, function, construction and site, had always been Wright's unifying and primary principle of design, and the disintegration that occurred in certain later works can be registered precisely in the distance they are removed from those very aspects which Wright had earlier considered fundamental to his architecture. The project for the V C Morris House, designed in 1945 for an incredible site in San Francisco on a cliff above the ocean, was intended to be built of reinforced concrete. As in all Wright's cast-in-place concrete buildings, the scale that is given by modular building materials is absent, making the scale of the house difficult to grasp. Wright's intuitive sense of the minimal needed to achieve an appropriate richness of experience is here abandoned as the small, slab-like house plan is poised atop an enormous concrete abutment. The multistorey telescoping cylindrical buttress supporting the comparatively diminutive room above seems almost absurdly exaggerated when we remember the subtle yet powerful buttresses lurking in the shadows under the living room at Fallingwater.

A similarly inappropriate and unnecessary exaggeration occurs in the project for the Adelman Laundry, also of 1945, where a service building is elevated – literally, as it is lifted clear of the ground – to the status of a public monument. This concept would eventually be built as the Annunciation Greek Orthodox Church, previously discussed; the scheme for a laundry, complete with concrete dome, clerestory ring and main floor detached from the ground, was adopted for a church. This project exemplifies how, during this late period, Wright turned from developing differing spatial 'types' for each programme type, as he had done earlier, to merely modifying a previous design to accommodate whatever programme had been commissioned. The equality implied in Wright's early motto 'form and function are one' (adapted from Sullivan and Greenough's 'form follows function') is here overturned, with preconceived form now dictating to function.

Some of Wright's most beautiful renderings depict the 1947 project for a Play Resort, Hotel and Sports Club, commissioned by Huntington Hartford, and intended for

COUNTRY CLUB FOR HUNTINGTON HARTFORD HOLLYWOOD
FRANK LLOYD WRIGHT ARCHITECT

Above: Huntington Hartford Resort project, Hollywood, California, 1947, perspective. A beautiful rendering, but a denial of all of Wright's fundamental design principles.
Right: Arizona State Capital project, Phoenix, Arizona, 1957, perspective of exterior arcade.

Hollywood, California. The design consisted of luxury 'cottages' terraced up the hillside, the site plan culminating in the Sports Club, a collection of concrete disks cantilevered off an enormous triangular, canted, rock-clad tower or abutment. The saucer-shaped volumes contain a cabaret, bar, restaurant, tennis court and swimming pool, the water of the latter spilling over the rim and falling to the canyon below in a crude display of wealth in this arid, water-starved region. It would seem Wright intended to deny all of his fundamental principles in this design, for he systematically dismisses space, function, structure,

materials, scale, landscape and inhabitation, appearing in this design to be interested only in the unrestricted play of his imagination.

Very similar comments could be applied to Wright's 1947 project for the Pittsburgh Point Civic Center, a hugely overscaled parking garage modelled on the 1924 Automobile Objective; the 1955 project for Leukurt Electric Company, a vast over-extension of the Johnson Wax Building; the uncommissioned '*pro bono*' project of 1957 for the Arizona State Capital, where a huge greenhouse canopy covering the entire complex is edged by a colonnade with abstract-classical column capitals, an indication of the degree to which Wright had lost his way; the series of projects for the King of Iraq, designed for Baghdad in 1957, including a opera house, museum, art gallery, post office, bazaar and spiral monument – this last an almost direct copy of Borromini's cupola for SIvo Sapienza in Rome, here with camel riders climbing up to a statue of the caliph; and the 'updated' perspectives for Broadacre City, renamed 'Living City', now incorporating not only all the unbuilt projects listed above, but Wright-designed cars, boats and helicopters, all streamlined to match the buildings.

As may already have become apparent, in Wright's designs from this period that are based primarily on the curve or circle, he has an unsettling propensity to ignore all his earlier discoveries related to siting, structure and space. The David

Wright House of 1950, built by Wright for his son in Phoenix in the form of an unfurling spiral, is lifted up off the ground, the only source of coolness in this hot, dry climate. With this design Wright also lost contact with the earth as the fundamental foundation for the act of building, which had so effectively anchored his earlier designs.

The increasingly unreal quality of the spaces within these designs, caused by their lack of any discernable attention to the nature of materials, is well illustrated by Wright's perspective of the living room in the 1957 project for the Arthur Miller House. A concrete-shell dome similar to that of the Greek Orthodox Church, is placed directly upon a series of cylindrical-stone columns; Wright's suppression of structure, used in his earlier works to produce the visually inspired psychological effects noted by Joseph Connors, here has little if any effect, as the columns and dome simply run into each other, imparting neither structural tension nor resolution.[4]

The project of 1959 for the 'Donohue Triptych' House, sited on a clifftop in Paradise Valley, Arizona, employs the forms of the Marin County Civic Center, a public building, in the design of a private house, albeit an expensive one. The bombastic overtones of this design are born out by Wright's statement that he wished to 'put the top back on the mountain' – a long way indeed from his earlier idea of building around, not on to, the top of the hill at Taliesin.[5]

The unbuilt design for the Iraqi Opera House, part of the Plan for Greater Baghdad, is recycled in the Grady Gammage Memorial Auditorium, built in 1959 at Arizona State University. In both cases a circular auditorium is surrounded by a structurally unnecessary colonnade of ludicrously thin columns – so thin as to advertise their lack of any meaningful structural load – which nevertheless appear to support thick puffy arches. Those aspects of Wright's earlier work which increased our sense of being experientially grounded through the manner in which the buildings were constructed have, in these late works, all but disappeared.

Marin County Civic Center, San Rafael, California, 1957

During his first visit to the site for the Marin County Civic Center, the clients apparently told Wright that if he felt the steeply rolling, grass and oak tree-covered hills were an obstacle in his designing, 'we can easily flatten them out, and give you a more suitable building ground that way'. Wright said he replied, 'To the contrary, those hills will be the feature of the design, and the building will be a bridge between them.'[6] The building that resulted is perhaps Wright's most disappointing design, for the potential expressed in that initial concept is indeed powerful. The building does bridge from hill to hill in the form of a viaduct, pivoting around the circular council chamber at the centre,

Right: Opera House project, Baghdad, Iraq, 1957, aerial perspective.
Far right: David Wright House, Phoenix, Arizona, 1950, perspective of courtyard.
Below right: Perspective for 'The Living City', reworked version of Broadacre City, 1958; the boats, cars, helicopters, infrastructure, landscape and buildings were all designed by Wright.
Below far right: Arthur Miller House project, Roxbury, Connecticut, 1957, perspective of the living room.

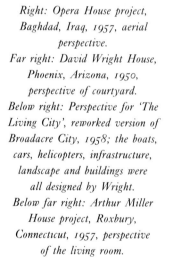

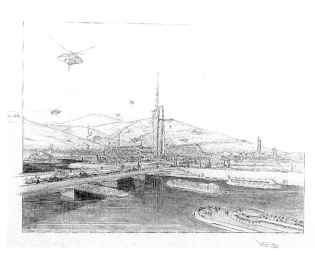

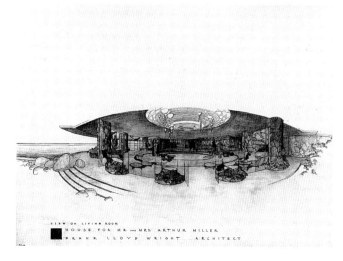

but the manner in which the civic centre is constructed, and the spaces to be found inside, do not allow us to experience the initial concept in the final design that was built.

The exterior would seem to be related to Roman aqueducts, yet the arches are not structural, being steel-framed stucco panels hung from the concrete-floor slabs hidden behind. The barrel-vaulted and domed concrete thin-shell roof is covered with a plastic waterproofing membrane of a penetrating blue colour, referring far too literally to the sky overhead. The roofs are edged with gold anodized aluminum fascia panels, complete with small arch-and-ball details, and the building is illuminated with globular light fixtures of various dimensions – all contributing to the impression that the building is somehow unreal. Perhaps the oddest feature of the exterior is the radio antenna Wright designed in the distinctive form of a steeple; after working to eliminate it from the church, he brings the steeple to the civic centre to represent his frighteningly accurate notion of the manner in which electronic media would replace the public realm in the American democracy of the very near future.

This loss of the habitable, spatial public realm, where we meet face to face to discuss those things we hold in common, is even more evident inside the civic centre, which is the only one of Wright's public buildings where the central space – here given the telling title of 'mall' – is in fact unimportant, 'because no activity essential to the nature of the building occurs in it', as Jonathan Lipman has noted.[7] This mall is in fact little more than an oversized corridor and lightwell, neither housing the primary function of the building nor providing a focus or collective identity for the occupants, as did the central spaces in the Larkin Building and the Johnson Wax Building. Given the natural beauty of this originally rural site, Wright appeared to be uncertain where to direct the attention of the occupants; here eyelevel views outward are allowed, and the mall of the civic centre is certainly not the introverted, top-lit, sacred and spiritual space typical in Wright's earlier public buildings.

Like many of Wright's late works, this design for the Marin County Civic Center seems to have been developed without any significant constraints, limitations or even goals, and is merely an exercise of the unfettered imagination. Wright had warned of this exact tendency as early as 1930, stating:

> Architecture is abstract. Abstract form is the pattern of the essential. Strictly speaking, abstraction has no reality except as it is embodied in materials. Realization of form is always geometrical ... as the rug-maker weaves the pattern of his rug upon the warp. Yet, all architecture must be some formulation of materials in some actually significant pattern. *Building is itself only architecture when it is essential pattern significant of purpose* (my emphasis).[8]

Above: Marin County Civic Center, view at ground level. Above right: Interior 'mall' or central space of the Center. Far right: View from the upper level offices; note the numerous uses of the circle as a decorative motif.

Rappel à l'Ordre: Limits and the Imagination[9]

It was these pompous public buildings and the spectacularly extravagant private commissions that received the vast majority of the publicity given to Wright's work of the 1950s, both in the professional and popular press. As a result many architects who had begun their careers admiring the material and spatial precision and daring of such buildings as the Robie House, the Larkin Building, Fallingwater and the Johnson Wax Building, now turned away from the more recent designs coming out of Taliesin, seeming as they did entirely unrelated to the discipline so amply evident in Wright's earlier works.

This almost total lack of order, scale and formal control of Wright's late public buildings and more extravagant private commissions is unquestionably related to the unlimited formal capacity and lack of modular order of the reinforced-cast concrete used in their construction. At the same time, the balance of invention, order and scale maintained by Wright's Usonian Houses designed in the same period must be related to the modular order characteristic of their major materials: block, brick and wood. Only when he combined cast concrete with modular materials was Wright able to attain the same balance in larger buildings that he continually maintained in the Usonian Houses. In addition to the use of brick and glass tubing, the excellence of the Johnson Wax Building originates in the fact that its concrete

columns were themselves cast as *modular* elements rather than as part of a *monolithic* mass.

Here we can see the importance of limitations in Wright's work: the tight economic and spatial limits imposed on the Usonian Houses are the reason that they remain more true to Wright's own principles than did his larger commissions. Wright himself spoke of the positive power of economy, the beauty of the minimal, and their relation to the imagination: 'the human race built most nobly when limitations were greatest and, therefore, when most was required of imagination in order to build at all. Limitations seem to have always been the best friends of architecture.'[10]

(Second) Herbert Jacobs House, Middleton, Wisconsin, 1944

The second house Wright designed for his journalist friend Herbert Jacobs was located on the open prairie, and in this brilliant design Wright distilled the energy-efficient siting concepts of the Usonians into an almost perfect construction, which he labelled the 'Solar Hemicycle'. The two-storey plan is curved to create a semicircle, its inner side opened by continuous full-height glazing to the warm south sun, and its outer edge closed by solid rock walls and an earth berm to the cold north winds. In the winter, the double-height glazing allows the south sun to heat the concrete slab and rock walls during the day, radiating heat

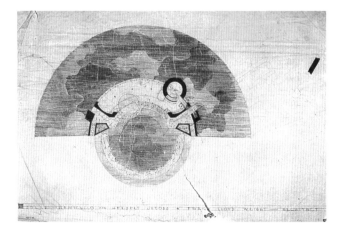

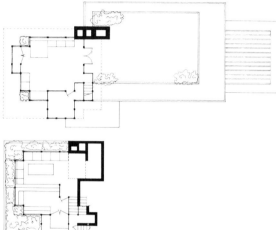

Top left: Second Herbert Jacobs House, Middleton, Wisconsin, 1944, site plan; subtitled 'Solar Hemicycle', the land is bermed up to the north (above) and sculpted out to make a circular garden to the south (below).
Above left: View of the living room, with the stone retaining wall to the north at left and the two-storey glazed wall to the south at right.

up into the house at night. This combines with the heat from the fireplace carved into the back stone wall and, when necessary, may be augmented by the typical heating system of piping cast into the concrete-slab floor. In the summer, the roof overhang to the south is carefully calculated to block the hot south sun, allowing the concrete-slab floor and rock north walls, both set into the earth, to remain cool. As the heat rises during the day within the open, double-height house, it is vented out through the high clerestories that run along the very top of the space, above the earth berm at the back of the house.

Wright mounded the earth up behind the house so that from the north only the cylindrical utility volume and the narrow band of clerestories is visible above what appears to be a grass-covered hill. We enter the house through a rock-walled tunnel that goes into the side of this hill, emerging not in the house interior but in the sun-drenched sunken circular court, defined half by the glass wall of the house and half by a row of plantings. The mounded hill cradling the carved garden creates a powerful sense of place on the flat prairie.

We turn and enter the house through the double-height glass wall, finding a matching narrow space inside, defined by the balcony parapet on the bedroom floor above which follows the curve of the window, so that we can see the roof above and the floor below moving from outside to inside.

This merging with the south-facing garden is reiterated in the circular pool set into the living-room floor, the glass wall cutting right through it so that half is inside and the other half outside. This is both one of Wright's simplest and yet most moving designs, indicating that when limitations – the best friends of architecture, as he said – were imposed upon him, the disintegrative tendencies often present in his circular designs could be easily and almost effortlessly tamed.

Raymond Carlson House, Phoenix, Arizona, 1950

The Carlson House is without doubt one of Wright's greatest works, and this is in no way mitigated by its absence from all the standard studies on Wright. Wright himself thought enough of this extremely inexpensive house to publish six illustrations of it in his book on the Usonians, *The Natural House*. The house is split-level in plan and section, with entry into the one-and-one-half storey living room occurring at the middle level, the dining and kitchen areas being a half-level below, the bedrooms a half-level above, and a penthouse study opening onto the large roof terrace at the top of the house. In the construction of the Carlson House, Wright returns to the simplicity of the four-inch-by-four-inch wood frame used in the plans of the Board and Batten Houses of the turn of the century. But in the Carlson House he employed the redwood elements in both plan and section, forming a four-foot-four-inch grid horizontally and vertically, so that the four-inch-by-four-inch wood members are utilized as both columns and beams.

This wood structural grid is exposed on both the exterior and interior, painted with a turquoise enamel paint so as not to dry out in the arid desert climate, with white insulated cement asbestos panels and glass infilling between. Wright subdivided this grid into two-foot-two-inch and one-foot-one-inch grids, creating a highly flexible planning module, much more easily manipulated to express the appropriate horizontality or verticality than the fixed sixteen-inch-square grid of the concrete-block houses; panels or windows varied from two feet wide by ten feet tall to four feet wide by one foot tall. This may also be seen in the similarly constructed W L Fuller House of 1951, built in Mississippi and destroyed by a hurricane in 1969.

Every space inside the Carlson House was ordered by the grid of enamelled wood elements infilled by glass or white panels, making the interior, in both construction and experience, closer to traditional Japanese houses (with their polished wood elements) than any other of Wright's designs. In its skilful weaving of horizontal and vertical within a gridded system of construction, the Carlson House also strongly reminds us of the Prairie Houses, indicating how similar the underlying ordering principles were for the Usonians and their predecessors.

Harold Price Summer House, Paradise Valley, Arizona, 1954

For the client of the Price Tower, Wright designed and built a summer house that both adds to the beauty of the desert setting and takes advantage of the subtleties of the climate. In plan, the house is centred by a double-height, open-air, covered outdoor atrium, open on two sides to the desert views and breezes. The atrium is defined by four concrete-block piers on each side, each pier stepping out as it rises, and a fireplace is set diagonally opposite the living-room doors; in the centre of the atrium is a fountain with a matched aperture in the roof opening to the sky overhead. Two long wings extend from this atrium: that stepping up towards the east contains the bedrooms, while that projecting towards the west houses the living-dining room and kitchen.

On the exterior, the edges of the roofs are trimmed with a stamped and punched copper fascia which casts delicate staccato shadow patterns on to the concrete-block walls – the kind of broken pattern Wright felt was natural to the desert. On the interior, the roofs of the house are layered one over another, and they all seem to float over the concrete-block walls and piers, supported by thin steel pipe-columns painted turquoise that emerge from the anchoring concrete elements. Rarely did Wright so clearly articulate and construct his concept of dwelling defined as life taking place in the shadows, the walls falling away so that we feel we are in a simple roofed pavilion terraced into the desert floor.

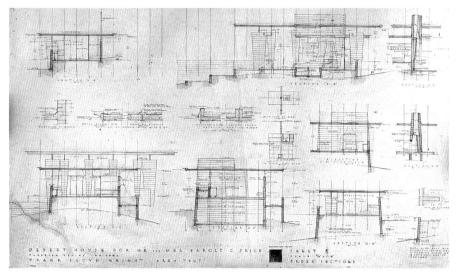

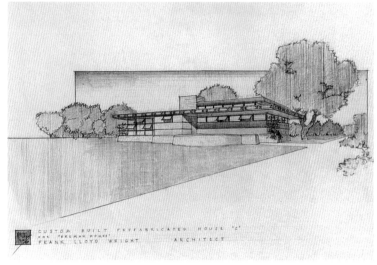

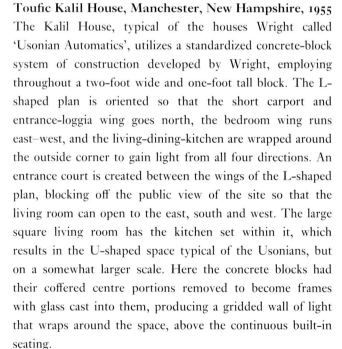

Above left: Harold Price Summer House, Paradise Valley, Arizona, 1954, construction drawing sections.
Above right: Perspective of 'Prefab #3' for Erdman and Associates, 1959 – a typical example of Wright's ongoing efforts to design housing affordable to the average American family.
Centre left: Toufic Kalil House, Manchester, New Hampshire, 1955, entry court of one of Wright's so-called 'Usonian Automatics' late concrete-block houses.
Centre right: James Gutierrez House project, Albuquerque, New Mexico, 1958, view from the north.
Right: Toufic Kalil House living room with glass cast into concrete blocks.

Toufic Kalil House, Manchester, New Hampshire, 1955
The Kalil House, typical of the houses Wright called 'Usonian Automatics', utilizes a standardized concrete-block system of construction developed by Wright, employing throughout a two-foot wide and one-foot tall block. The L-shaped plan is oriented so that the short carport and entrance-loggia wing goes north, the bedroom wing runs east–west, and the living-dining-kitchen are wrapped around the outside corner to gain light from all four directions. An entrance court is created between the wings of the L-shaped plan, blocking off the public view of the site so that the living room can open to the east, south and west. The large square living room has the kitchen set within it, which results in the U-shaped space typical of the Usonians, but on a somewhat larger scale. Here the concrete blocks had their coffered centre portions removed to become frames with glass cast into them, producing a gridded wall of light that wraps around the space, above the continuous built-in seating.

The fireplace and kitchen volume are constructed of the exposed, smooth-faced block, while other interior walls are often finished with two-foot wide vertical polished plywood panels, matching the doors and cabinetry. The ceilings of the one-storey house are constructed of two-foot-square concrete blocks, coffers facing down into the rooms; at the edges of the rooms, where the ceilings met the walls, the

Above: Harold Price Summer House, Paradise Valley, Arizona, 1954, view of the central open-air loggia. The house gives the inhabitant the feeling of being in a simple roofed pavilion terraced into the desert floor.

blockwork was thickened to deal with structural shearing, exposing the smooth block face. All the surfaces of the rooms, therefore, including the polished concrete floor which was scored with the two-foot-square grid, were bound together by the construction module of the blocks, producing a tightly woven space of inhabitation.

THE EXTRAORDINARY series of late Usonian Houses culminated Wright's lifetime effort to make available to the public his discoveries in low-cost housing. Wright vigorously published these 'do-it-yourself' house designs in popular magazines, complete with interviews with contractors and clients about the utility and pleasure of building and living in a Usonian House.[11] Outstanding designs among these include the project for the Joe Monroe House of 1946, the Robert Sunday House of 1955, the project for the James Gutierrez House of 1958, and the project for the Gilbert Wieland House of 1959. The series of concrete-block houses, which included the Benjamin Adelman House of 1951, the Gerald Tonkens House of 1954, and the T A Pappas House of 1955, were called the 'Usonian Automatics' by Wright, indicating that these houses were intended to be so modular and logical in their design that they could be assembled by the clients themselves a task several of them found to be not nearly as easy as the 'automatic' name implied. It is indeed fitting

to note that Wright's last project, which he was working on when he died in 1959, was not a resort or museum or church or civic centre, but a simple and affordable prefabricated concrete-block house.

All of these houses exhibited a material and structural integrity and economy intended to critique the lifestyle and 'developer' construction Wright saw evolving in the American suburb. As he said:

> What is needed most in architecture today is the very thing that is most needed in life – integrity. Just as it is in a human being, so integrity is the deepest quality in a building; but it is a quality not much demanded of any building since very ancient times when it was natural. It is no longer the first demand for a human being, because 'success' is now so immediately necessary. The Usonian House, then, aims to be a natural performance, one that is integral to site, integral to environment, integral to the life of the inhabitants.[12]

CONCLUSION

Discoveries made about the structure of space
and time always react on the structure of the mind.
Other kinds of discovery enrich human knowledge
without affecting its basis. However, anything to
do with conceptions of space will suggest very
different ways of constructing knowledge.

Gaston Bachelard[1]

Left: Frank Lloyd Wright at the lobby balcony of the Johnson Wax Administration Building.

The Countenance of Principle

The question of Wright's importance and necessary influence on the future of architecture centres not around issues of style or form, as most of Wright's so-called followers would seem to believe, but on the aspect of expanded experiential possibilities made evident in Wright's works. As the primary method he used to order and construct spatial experiences, Wright stated early in his career that the *floor plan* was of pre-eminent importance in his conception of architecture; the building was conceived as being generated from the plan, which gave form and order to the space within to be lived in.

For Wright, the only reason to shape space in plan was for the experience of man; architecture was first and foremost concerned with the presentation of man. Architecture gave order to man's experience, and thus made him present in the world – in space conceived and formed as being occupied; as Wright said, 'Architecture is man's great sense of himself embodied in a world of his own creation.'[2] It was this basic principle that led Mrs Avery Coonley, a client of Wright's for several projects and built works, to say that she and her husband selected Wright as their architect because his works bore 'the countenance of principle'.[3]

Wright understood buildings to be the background or framework for human existence; architecture gave dignity to daily life. Wright's system of design was measured by, scaled by, and calibrated precisely by the human body and its experience; as he later said, in referring both to his own system of design and to the Froebel training that he had studied, 'form became feeling'.[4] Wright's architecture appealed at a fundamental level to the occupant's sense of embodied presence and bodily movement. While the geometric rigour of Wright's planning is well known, the esteem in which he held the concepts of *use* and *comfort* is not as widely understood. The intellectual and formal order of Wright's plans was balanced by the physical and spiritual engagement of the inhabitant; for Wright concept and experience were one and the same.

Wright understood that man inhabits architecture through movement, so that space and material are woven together to become the setting for the repeated rituals of daily life; as the ancient Chinese philosopher he quoted had said, 'In emptiness alone motion becomes possible.'[5] Space gives us the possibility to be, to dwell, to live, to move, to act; as John Dewey said, architecture forms space 'as opportunity for movement and action. It is a matter of proportions qualitatively felt.'[6] The dynamic spatial development of Wright's architecture originated in this understanding of inhabitation and experience as nonstatic events. As Henri Bergson had said in 1888, 'We attribute to the motion the divisibility of the space which it traverses, forgetting that it

333

is quite possible to divide an object, but not an act.'[7] Or as Dewey said, 'We unconsciously carry over this belief in the bounded character of all objects of experience … into our conception of the experience itself. We suppose the experience has the same definite limits as the things with which it is concerned. But any experience, even the most ordinary, has an indefinite total setting.'[8]

Yet space in infinite extension, 'universal space', as defined by Heidegger, has no ability to make place – indeed does not recognize the validity of place-definitions. Wright's buildings, on the other hand, are places *par excellence*. The definition of boundless space given by the physicist A S Eddington in 1928 is here suggestive: 'Space is boundless by re-entrant form, not by great extension.'[9] Wright's use of re-entrant forms throughout his life leads us to propose that the space of his designs is not space in infinite extension, but space made boundless by re-entrant form – space folded to produce boundless place. Study of Wright's designs indicates that space can be simultaneously systematic and uniquely formed, simultaneously boundless and precisely formed. A *system of places* was what Wright was engaged in making with his ideal of spatial continuity.

Wright's Legacy of Spatial Experience

'Principles are not invented by one man or one age', Wright said, and his principles of place-making are important for reasons other than their interest to art historians and architects bent on formal imitation.[10] Wright's principles comprise a comprehensive system of space formation determined by ethical values and an understanding of the nature of things; his work is founded on architecture understood as a discipline – a history of principled place-making. It could be argued that Wright's contribution is almost unique in our century, which has produced a rich assortment of new forms but few systematic conceptions that link spatial form and order to human occupation and experience. It is the systematic nature of Wright's work that makes it exceptional and worthy of further study. Yet Wright's spatial legacy is today in danger of being lost altogether, for several reasons that may at first appear unrelated.

First, because we have forgotten that inhabited space is founded on ethical intentions. Wright stated that for him architecture was a 'conservative' discipline, dedicated to the creation of a framework for the life of man based on fundamental principles. Wright's vision was essentially ethical in nature – space was to be created for the dwelling of man; as Wittgenstein said, 'Ethics and aesthetics are one.' The loss of this legacy of Wright's – his system for place-creation and the principles that underlie it – is thus not just a matter of academic or historical interest. Today the absence of any ethical meaning or intentions in architecture considered fashionable, the absence of even the belief that contemporary architecture is intended to 'edify' (*aedificare*)

in the sense of inspiring and housing an ethical life, and the open aversion to such terms as 'ethical' and 'moral' being linked to architecture are indications enough of the spiritual vacuousness prevalent in current architectural practice. Wright's principles of place-making are absolutely opposed to this spiritual absence, and it is for this reason alone, if for no other, that we should endeavour to study and develop them today.

Second, because we have forgotten that architectural design, like the human actions that go on within it, cannot be subdivided. Wright's definition of his work as the synthesis of interior space, construction and landscape is the absolute opposite of the contemporary disintegration of architecture into specialized professions of interior design, landscape architecture, building construction, structural and mechanical engineering and, finally, architecture; as he said, 'Nothing could be more external than an interior decorator. Nothing could be more irrelevant than the external architect. Nothing could be more remote from life at the moment than citizens content to live in what either of them produces.'[11]

Wright, as indicated earlier, was opposed to the instrumental aspects of modernism and the Enlightenment when they resulted in a diminishment of spatial experience. The tendency for modern professions to divide and subdivide themselves endlessly into ever smaller areas of specialization was of particular concern to Wright, and he operated his own practice as a model of opposition and resistance to such tendencies, maintaining a coherence and unity among inhabited space, construction and landscape.

Third, because architects have forgotten how to appropriately follow his example. The copying of forms was always anathema to Wright; how can there be those today that assume it is an appropriate way to learn from him?[12] In addressing this issue after the break-up of his Oak Park Studio, Wright said, 'I still hope to see these basic principles more comprehended, therefore the effects imitated less. No man's work need resemble mine. If he understands the working of the principles behind the effects he sees here, with similar integrity he will have his own way of building.'[13]

I would argue that the only architect in America to continue the work of Wright was Louis I Kahn. Kahn was Wright's only true disciple in that he understood the principles upon which Wright's best work was based, and did not simply copy his forms. Though Kahn never directly admitted such an influence, it is evident in his work and in his search for fundamental beginnings; the Larkin Building of 1904 and Unity Temple of 1906 were tremendous inspirations for Kahn's own endeavours to give modern form to fundamental principles of architectural order. The distinction between 'servant' and 'served' spaces; the development of different structures for each different type and scale of space; the room as the generator of all architecture; the need for the spaces allowing unplanned meetings; construction and detail as the concretization of architectural experience; and the understanding of history as a source of principles, not forms – all these attributes of Kahn's work can be traced back to Wright. Yet, given the often absurd designs that Wright was producing for public buildings in the 1950s, just when Kahn was reaching his maturity as an architect, it is not surprising that Kahn would not admit the deep debt he owed to Wright's earlier work.

Fourth, because we have forgotten that Wright's spaces exist as complete experiences, they cannot be dismantled without being lost altogether. This particular danger is due in large part to the recent resurgence of Wright's popularity; many of his remaining buildings are being plundered so as to feed the ever-expanding appetite of the art market, their spaces are now represented only by photographs of objects in exhibition catalogues and auction house listings. As an example of this dismemberment, the extraordinary stained-glass windows of the Coonley Playhouse are now scattered between the Metropolitan Museum in New York and the Domino's Pizza Collection in Ann Arbor, far indeed from their original site in Riverside, Illinois.

In addition, we have also pointed in this text to the numerous important buildings designed by Wright that have been destroyed, usually to accommodate the dictates of 'real estate development'. Wright was totally opposed to financial speculation that utilized either architecture or landscape, and it is bitter irony indeed that so many of his most beautiful designs, such as the Larkin Building, the Martin House, the Little House, Midway Gardens and the Imperial Hotel, have fallen victim to it. The complete space of inhabitation is Wright's legacy; its dismemberment is its extinction.

Finally, Wright's spatial legacy is in danger of being lost because, dazzled by the contemporary determination of our life-world by economic and legal definitions, we have forgotten what it means to dwell poetically on the earth, to rediscover the many ways of experiencing space, and to inhabit architecture in all its simple beauty and emotional power. Yet, 'where the danger exists, there too grows the saving power', as the poet Friedrich Hölderlin wrote.[14] It is precisely in this universal loss that Wright's place-making work may prove capable of saving us – if we open ourselves to Wright's work and allow his buildings to remind us of the ways of spatial experience.

Without question, Frank Lloyd Wright was the greatest architect of modern times. Still, we can only truly know him through his works, through the precisely articulated, experientially determined spaces for inhabitation he has left us. Wright's legacy is in our hands, to be cultivated, explored, and even extended by each of us. In so doing, we may hope to repay our enormous debt of love for the wonders found in the space within.

NOTES

Introduction

1 Ludwig Wittgenstein, *Culture and Value* (Chicago: University of Chicago Press, 1980), p22.

2 I have in this opening paragraph both paraphrased and quoted the beautiful and inspiring ideas on the nature of critical writing defined by George Steiner, one of this century's most insightful and perceptive thinkers, as they seem to perfectly capture what is intended in this book; George Steiner, *Tolstoy or Dostoevsky*, (New York: Vintage/Random House, 1959), p3.

3 Josef Albers, quoted in Mary Emma Harris, *The Arts at Black Mountain College* (Cambridge, MA: MIT Press, 1987), p17.

4 The built works are carefully documented in two outstanding catalogues by William Allin Storrer, *The Frank Lloyd Wright Companion* (Chicago: University of Chicago Press, 1993) and *The Architecture of Frank Lloyd Wright: A Complete Catalog* (Cambridge, MA: MIT Press, 1974, 1978). Many of Wright's works may be visited, and in this Arlene Sanderson's *Wright Sites: A Guide to Frank Lloyd Wright Public Places* (River Forest: FLW Building Conservancy, 1991), is immensely helpful. Recent publication efforts have bravely attempted to undertake the staggeringly large task of documenting all available drawings and buildings by Wright; a selection of the drawings held in the Frank Lloyd Wright Archives, along with new photographs of the existing buildings, have been published as *Frank Lloyd Wright Monograph*, Volumes 1–8, *Frank Lloyd Wright Preliminary Studies*, Volumes 9–11, *Frank Lloyd Wright in His Renderings*, Volume 12, and *Frank Lloyd Wright Houses*, Volume 1–8, Yokio Futagawa, with texts by Bruce Brooks Pfeiffer (Tokyo: ADA Edita, 1985–1992). These and the other publications 'sanctioned' (and copyrighted!) by the Taliesin Fellowship, represent only a fraction of Wright's drawings, however, and sales of original drawings to private collectors by the Fellowship and FLW Foundation in the 1980s dispersed other equally essential material, making it unavailable for any future study (see note 11 in Chapter 4). Photographs of all drawings by Wright and his apprentices still remaining in the FLW Archives (originally numbering over 22,000) have been placed in the Getty Center in Los Angeles, increasing access to the material. The photographs have not been able to capture all the information on the drawings – particularly the design sketches in light pencil – and therefore are a completely inadequate substitute for greater and wider access to the original drawings themselves; this also would suggest the need for an immediate and permanent ban to the Fellowship's sales of Wright's drawings to private collectors.

5 *In the Cause of Architecture*, the title of a series of articles by Wright published in Architectural Record, starting in 1908.

6 It is interesting to note that Steiner also felt compelled to follow his poetic definition of the criticism of persuasion with a summary of other 'escapist' criticism which had dominated writings on the subject, as has I believe also been the case in the field of architecture.

Chapter 1

1 Horatio Greenough, 'Form and Function' (1852), reprinted in *Roots of Contemporary Architecture*, ed Lewis Mumford (New York: Dover, 1972), p33.

2 Meryle Secrest, *Frank Lloyd Wright* (New York: Knopf, 1992), pp19–50.

3 Wright, *An Autobiography* (1932), (New York: Horizon Press, 1977), p31. See also Wright's extensive ode to his summers on his uncle's farm, included in his autobiography as poetic introductions to each 'book' or section.

4 Ibid, p33.

5 Grant Carpenter Manson, 'Wright in the Nursery: The Influence of Froebel Education on the Work of Frank Lloyd Wright', *The Architectural Review* no113, February 1953. See also Richard MacCormac, published at full length as 'Froebel's Kindergarten Training and the Early Work of Frank Lloyd Wright', *Environment and Planning B* (Great Britain: Pion, 1974) and as 'Form and Philosophy' in *Frank Lloyd Wright: A Primer on Architectural Principles*, ed Robert McCarter (New York: Princeton Architectural Press, 1991); shorter versions were published as 'The Anatomy of Wright's Aesthetic' in *Architectural Review*, no143, February 1968 and in *Writings on Wright*, ed H Allen Brooks, (Cambridge, MA: MIT Press, 1981).

6 This and all other Froebel quotes that follow are from Frederich Froebel, *Selected Writings*, ed, I M Lilley (New York, 1898).

7 Wright, *In the Cause of Architecture*, (1908), ed F Guthiem (New York: McGraw-Hill, 1975), p230.

8 Transcendentalism was the idealistic philosophical school of thought prominent in New England from 1830 to 1880, and best represented in the writings of Emerson. The use of the term in the United States originated with the founding of the Transcendentalist Club by Emerson in 1836. Transcendentalism included philosophical, theological, social and economic aspects, and was intended to concretely affect everyday life, rather than be the subject of abstract speculation. Despite the transcendentalist philosophy being a particularly American origin for Wright's design philosophy, it has been consistently recognized for its true importance only by European critics. Of particular note is Fabrizio Brunetti, *Le Matrici di una Architettura Organica, F. Ll. Wright* (Florence: Alinea, 1974); also see Marcello Angrisani, 'The Architectural Innovations of Frank Lloyd Wright', in *Frank Lloyd Wright Drawings, 1887–1959* (Florence: Centro Di, 1976). These two Florentine examples indicate the enormous influence Wright's work has had on Europeans, and Italians of the 'Florentine School' from 1960–80 in particular; see also the excellent Heidi Kief-Niederwohrmeier, *Frank Lloyd Wright und Europa* (Stuttgart: Karl Kramer, 1983).

9 All Emerson quotes that follow are from Ralph Waldo Emerson, *Emerson: Essays and Lectures* (New York: Library of America, 1983).

10 Kenneth Frampton, 'The Text-tile Tectonic: The Origin and Evolution of Wright's Woven Architecture' in *Frank Lloyd Wright: A Primer on Architectural Principles*, ed McCarter, pp124–149.

11 Charles Olson, *Call Me Ishmael* (San Francisco: City Lights, 1947), pp11–12.

12 Wright, *In the Cause of Architecture*, p123.

13 Agrisani, 'The Architectural Innovations of Frank Lloyd Wright', p13.

14 Henry David Thoreau, *Walden and Other Writings*, ed B Atkinson (New York: The Modern Library, 1937).

15 This and all Horatio Greenough quotes that follow are from 'Form and Function'.

16 This and all Louis Sullivan quotes that follow are from *Kindergarten Chats and Other Writings* (New York: Dover, 1979).

17 Ibid, p179.

18 For an excellent discussion of the relation of Sullivan and Wright to Owen Jones, and connections to the 'woven wall' concepts of Semper, see Frampton, 'The Text-tile Tectonic', pp126–31.

19 Otto Graf, 'The Art of the Square' in *Frank Lloyd Wright: A Primer on Architectural Principles*, ed McCarter, p221.

20 Joseph Connors, *The Robie House of Frank Lloyd Wright* (Chicago: University of Chicago Press, 1984), p41. This deceptively small book is packed with large insights into this house and Wright's work in general, including perhaps the only attempt by an architectural historian to analyse Wright's design process.

21 Wright, *An Autobiography*, p93.

22 Wright, *In the Cause of Architecture*, p59.

23 Connors, *The Robie House of Frank Lloyd Wright*, p45.

24 Wright, *An Autobiography*, p132.

25 Wright, *An Autobiography*, pp128 and 132.

26 Wright, *An Autobiography*, p126.

27 See Werner Seligmann's analysis of the massing and detail of the Charnley House in his 'Evolution of the Prairie House' in *Frank Lloyd Wright: A Primer on Architectural Principles*, ed McCarter, pp66–9.

28 Wright, *An Autobiography*, p132.

29 Ibid, p147.

30 See Patrick Pinnell's excellent account of Wright's early period in his 'Academic Tradition and Individual Talent: Similarity and Difference in the Formation of Frank Lloyd Wright' in *Frank Lloyd Wright: A Primer on Architectural Principles*, ed McCarter, p33.

31 James F O'Gorman makes this point, using Sullivan's own writings on the subject; 'The Tall Office Building Inconsistently Considered' in his *Three American Architects* (Chicago: University of Chicago, 1991).

32 See the excellent discussion of the relationship between the German émigré community of Chicago, Root, Semper and the engineer Frederick Bauman (who developed the isolated pier foundation necessary for high-rise construction in Chicago's marshy soil) in Frampton, 'The Text-tile Tectonic', pp125–6.

33 Pinnell, 'Academic Tradition and Individual Talent', p36.

34 Wright, *An Autobiography*, p147.

35 Frampton, *Modern Architecture: A Critical History* (London: Thames and Hudson, 1980), p57.

36 All following quotes are from Victor Hugo, *Notre-Dame de Paris*, (1832) (New York: Penguin, 1978), pp188–202.

37 Wright, 'The Art and Craft of the Machine', *Frank Lloyd Wright Collected Writings*, Volume 1, ed Bruce Brooks Pfeiffer (New York: Rizzoli, 1992), p61.

38 Wright, *An Autobiography*, p152.

Chapter 2

1 Emerson, *Essays*, p424.

2 Grant Carpenter Manson, *Frank Lloyd Wright to 1910: The First Golden Age* (New York: Van Nostrand Reinhold, 1958), p1.

3 This is pointed out in appropriately tart terms by Seligmann, 'Evolution of the Prairie House', pp59–60. I have also noted elsewhere that in this art historical process of implying influence, 'The reliance on one-to-one correspondence between the individual work and its historical "source" is based on a superficial visual "reading" of architecture – one conveniently accomplished within the confines of the university library. It is therefore not surprising that these studies seem strangely disengaged from the physical reality of the building and its experience,' in 'Abstract Essence: Drawing Wright From the Obvious', in *Frank Lloyd Wright: A Primer on Architectural Principles*, ed McCarter, p7.

4 Wright, *An Autobiography*, p153.

5 In much of the following I am indebted to Pinnell's 'Academic Tradition and Individual Talent', and Seligmann's 'Evolution of the Prairie House'. While the two articles use different methods of research and analysis, and sometimes come to conflicting conclusions, I am convinced that a full understanding of this early period of Wright's work is only possible by taking them both into account.

6 Henry Russell Hitchcock, 'Frank Lloyd Wright and the "Academic Tradition" of the Early Eighteen-Nineties', *Journal of the Warburg and Courthauld Institutes* VII (January–June 1944); he opened this important but still little-known article with the story of the Burnham offer, first written about by Wright in 1932 in the first edition of his autobiography. Hitchcock had made much the same point two years before in his 'approved' monograph on Wright, *In the Nature of Materials*.

7 It should here be noted that Wright not only had a lifelong tendency to 'backdate' his drawings – resulting in his designs seeming even more 'ahead of their time' – but even to pull old drawings out of his files years later and begin to change them, 'improving' them, much to the dismay of historians such as Hitchcock who wished the drawings to be treated as historical artefacts for the museum.

8 Seligmann, 'Evolution of the Prairie House', p66.

9 Ibid, p73.

10 Pinnell, 'Academic Tradition and Individual Talent', p26.

11 Manson, *Frank Lloyd Wright to 1910: The First Golden Age*, p44.

12 In fact, the plan is incorrectly redrawn in Manson, *Frank Lloyd Wright to 1910: The First Golden Age*, fig 38. Manson does go into significant and informative detail about the exceptional woodwork and glasswork in the built-in cabinets Wright had installed in the MacArthur House, but his own illustrations show that his plan is incorrect in not indicating that the walls of the dining room and entrance hall are aligned (the wall in fact being a bearing wall that runs straight through the length of the house), as is indicated in the working drawing; Futagawa (ed), Pfeiffer, *Frank Lloyd Wright Monograph, 1887–1901*, Volume 1, (Tokyo: ADA Edita, 1986), fig 14.

13 H Allen Brooks, *Writings on Wright* (Cambridge, MA: MIT Press, 1981), p88.

14 Wright, *In the Cause of Architecture*, p56.

15 In the McAfee plan, Wright would also seem to have used the Winn Memorial Library of 1877 by Richardson as its 'model' for reinterpretation. Pinnell, 'Academic Tradition and Individual Talent', sees another five years passing – until the Husser House of 1899 – before Wright was to turn to the libraries of Richardson for inspiration, but the differences between the McAfee and the Husser Houses are not that significant; see my somewhat different reading of the part played by Richardson's library as 'type' further on in this chapter, and note 19.

16 Meryle Secrest, *Frank Lloyd Wright*, p168. This can also be found in a number of sources other than Wright, including the memories of Wright's various children, such as Lloyd Wright (1977, questions asked by Edgar Kaufman, Jr) in *Frank Lloyd Wright Remembered*, ed P Meehan (Washington: Preservation Press, 1991), pp221–2; Edgar Kaufman, Jr, 'Crisis and Creativity', in his *Nine Commentaries on Frank Lloyd Wright* (Cambridge, MA: MIT Press, 1989), p94; and Manson, *Frank Lloyd Wright to 1910: The First Golden Age*, p48. In later years Wright was to describe the Froebel system's 'gifts' too precisely and comprehensively, and his own philosophical statements were to paraphrase its instructional texts too closely, for his recollections to be based solely on childhood memories.

17 Wright, *In the Cause of Architecture*, p55.

18 Ibid, p60.

19 It was this re-exposure to the Froebel training that allowed Wright to perceive the typological approach of Richardson in designing libraries as a series of variations on a theme, and to engage this in his own work. Pinnell, 'Academic Tradition and Individual Talent', makes an excellent case for the direct influence of Richardson's libraries (as an example of type) on Wright's design method, but in this the Froebel training was not only more familiar and explicit, but was there first.

20 Richard MacCormac, 'Form and Philosophy', p102.

Chapter 3

1 Greenough, 'Form and Function', p54.

2 See the excellent diagrams in Pinnell, 'Academic Tradition and Individual Talent', pp49–54.

3 Colin Rowe, 'Chicago Frame', (1956), *Mathematics of the Ideal Villa and Other Essays* (Cambridge, MA: MIT Press, 1976), p92.

4 First said in Wright, *In the Cause of Architecture*, p61.

5 Wright, *An Autobiography*, pp156–162.

6 This includes Bruce Pfeiffer of the Fellowship; yet even a less careful scrutiny of the working drawing held in the Taliesin Archives clearly reveals – in Wright's use of open walls for the original house and solid walls for the new construction – the plan and extent of the old house in the new.

7 Robin Evans, 'Figures, Doors and Passages', in *Architectural Design*, April 1978, p278. Wright's work would appear to be directly opposed to what Evans calls 'the general lobotomy performed on society at large, obliterating vast areas of social experience', which he maintains has occurred in most architecture of the last two hundred years; as was often the case, we find that Wright was opposed to the more instrumental aspects of modernism and the enlightenment, particularly when they resulted in a truncation of experiential possibilities.

8 Futagawa (ed), Pfeiffer, *Frank Lloyd Wright Monograph 1902–1906*, Volume 2, (Tokyo: ADA Edita, 1987), p96.

9 Wright, *In the Cause of Architecture*, p155.

10 Edward Ford, *The Details of Modern Architecture* (Cambridge, MA: MIT Press, 1990), p183.

Chapter 4

1 Wright, *In the Cause of Architecture*, p53.

2 Europeans, living every day with the best examples of Renaissance and baroque architecture, appear to see through Wright's claims that history had nothing to do with his architecture. While Europeans understand the deeper relation between the architect and the living history of built space, most Americans continue to seek in Wright's work European 'influences', as defined by art historical methodologies; see the recent efforts of Vincent Scully who, in entirely losing his early understanding of Wright's more complex relation to history, has led a generation of American art historians down the same path.

3 Wright, *In the Cause of Architecture* (1914 edition), p123.

4 John Dewey, *Art as Experience*, William James Lectures given at Harvard, (1932) (New York: Putnam's, 1980), p265. Though Wright never credits Dewey as an inspiration, many of Dewey's ideas are remarkably similar to Wright's own philosophy of design, as shall hopefully be made evident in my later use of quotes from Dewey.

5 Jonathan Lipman, 'Consecrated Space: The Public Buildings of Frank Lloyd Wright', in *Frank Lloyd Wright: A Primer on Architectural Principles*, ed McCarter, p195.

6 Ibid. This excellent study was the first to examine Wright's public buildings as the development of a common spatial 'type', derived from Wright's own studio of 1895.

7 David van Zanten, 'Schooling the Prairie School: Wright's Early Style as a Communicative System', in *The Nature of Frank Lloyd Wright*, ed Bolon, Nelson and Seidel (Chicago: University of Chicago Press, 1988), p80.

8 Futagawa (ed), Pfeiffer, *Frank Lloyd Wright Monograph 1887–1901*, Volume 1, p63.

9 Throughout this section I am indebted to the superb study by Jack Quinan, *Frank Lloyd Wright's Larkin Building, Myth and Fact* (Cambridge, MA: MIT Press, 1987). This book, an extraordinary example of sustained and meaningful research, brings the building to life again, and makes its destruction seem all the more tragic.

10 Ibid, p100.

11 In the late 1980s the Taliesin Fellowship and FLW Foundation, in an attempt to raise funds to pay back taxes and to support the (unaccredited) FLW School at Taliesin, sold, through the Max Protetch Gallery in New York, numerous important early sketches by Wright. Among these were sketches of the Larkin Building with the only known documentation of this moment where the stairs are pulled to the corners; the actual moment of design is seen in faint pencil plans and axonometrics in the margins of a perspective. Unfortunately, these drawings are no longer available for study, having been purchased for more than $15,000 by private collectors. The FLW Foundation claimed these were 'unimportant', but what they apparently meant was they were design sketches, as they held on to the finished renderings which were generally not from Wright's hand, letting the far more important design sketches be sold. This was a serious failure on the part of the Taliesin Fellowship and FLW Foundation, which is charged with preserving, not selling off, Wright's drawings.

12 Wright, *An Autobiography*, p175.

13 Ibid.

14 Wright, 'The New Larkin Administration Building', in *The Larkin Idea*, 6, (1906), pp2–9; quoted in Quinan, *Frank Lloyd Wright's Larkin Building*, p33.

15 Wright, *In the Cause of Architecture*, p65.

16 Wright's rebuttal to Russell Sturgis's criticism in the April 1908 edition of *Architectural Record* took him to task for using photos 'taken with a wide-angle lens from the third story window of the factory opposite – not a normal point of view' and for writing his criticism of the building based only on a viewing of photographs and not a site visit; Wright, 'Reply to Mr. Sturgis's Criticism', in Quinan, *Frank Lloyd Wright's Larkin Building*, p165.

17 Quinan, *Frank Lloyd Wright's Larkin Building*, p108.

18 Ibid, p63.

19 Graf, 'The Art of the Square,' in *Frank Lloyd Wright: A Primer on Architectural Principles*, ed McCarter, pp228–237.

20 Quinan, *Frank Lloyd Wright's Larkin Building*, p108.

21 Ibid, p119. My description of the Larkin Building's last years is based upon a chapter of Quinan's book entitled 'The Demolition'.

22 This and all other quotes on the design of Unity Temple in this section are from Wright, *An Autobiography*, pp177–184.

23 Walt Whitman, 'Chanting the square deific', *Leaves of Grass*, in *Walt Whitman, Poetry and Prose* (New York: Library of America, 1982), p559.

24 An appropriately exhaustive geometric analysis of Unity Temple is not possible here, as it would take many pages even to begin to suggest the richness that we discover in visiting the building and studying the plans. A wonderful analysis (with over a thousand diagrams) has been made by Otto Graf, *Die Kunst des Quadrats, Zum Werk von Frank Lloyd Wright*, Volume 1 (Unity Temple) (Vienna:Verlag Bohlau, 1983).

25 Wright, *The Japanese Print – An Interpretation*, (1912), (New York: Horizon, 1967), p12.

26 Wright, *In the Cause of Architecture* (1908 edition), p54.

27 Wright, *An American Architecture* (New York: Horizon, 1955), pp208–10.

Chapter 5

1 Martin Heidegger, 'Building Dwelling Thinking,' (1951), in *Basic Writings* (New York: Harper and Row, 1977), p332.

2 Wright, *An American Architecture*, p146.

3 Wright, *An Autobiography*, p166.

4 Ibid, p164.

5 Ibid, p166.

6 Ibid.

7 Connors, *The Robie House of Frank Lloyd Wright*, p57.

8 Leonard Eaton has given us a profile of these clients, and in particular of Robie, in 'Mr. Robie Knew What He Wanted,' in his *Two Chicago Architects and Their Clients* (Cambridge, MA: MIT Press, 1969), p128.

9 Ibid.

10 Donald Hoffman, *Frank Lloyd Wright's Robie House* (New York: Dover, 1984). The dates and other facts of commission and construction noted here are from this definitive monograph on this house.

11 Wright, *An American Architecture*, p84.

12 Connors, *The Robie House of Frank Lloyd Wright*, p25.

13 Louis I Kahn, who in this instance was certainly *not* a follower of Wright, would later say, 'I asked the brick, what did it want to be? And the brick answered, I want to be an arch.' Only when placed in an arch can brick span without other supporting structures. Kahn's work would present perhaps the most articulate and powerful argument for a 'moral' reading of structure, one that required its exposure to avoid falsehood of any sort. For Kahn, this exposure of structure was also necessary to give character to the space of dwelling.

14 Hoffman, *Frank Lloyd Wright's Robie House*, p61.

15 Wright, *An Autobiography*, p167.

16 Rudolph Schindler, quoted in Esther McCoy, *Vienna to Los Angeles: Two Journeys* (Santa Monica, 1979), p131.

17 While we have seen Wright utilize the square as the main proportioning device in his designs, we might remember that the Gothic architecture which Wright admired is based on diagonal geometries and rotated squares.

18 Reyner Banham in his seminal study, *The Architecture of the Well-Tempered Environment* (Chicago: University of Chicago Press, 1969, 1984), p120.

19 Ibid, p121.

20 *Chicago Sun-Times*, 18 November 1958, p18.

21 The house is owned, and was beautifully renovated, by the Steelcase Corporation, a furniture manufacturer.

22 Wright, *An Autobiography*, p165.

Chapter 6

1 Okakura Kakuzo, *The Book of Tea*, (1906); (Tokyo: Tuttle, 1956), p45. Wright paraphrased this quote in his own writings and lectures starting around 1938, though this astonishing little book was given to him by the Japanese ambassador to the US in the early 1920s, after he had designed the Imperial Hotel in Tokyo. He apparently was unaware of it before then, despite having visited Japan several times, starting in 1905. As was typical with him, Wright's analysis of Japanese architecture and culture began as a spatial understanding, and only later found verbal representation.

2 While these square-patterned stucco panels in the Coonley House are clearly the formal, geometric and modular precursors of Wright's later terracotta panels and concrete blocks – both formed with integral patterning – they are not made of either terracotta or concrete, as has sometimes been presumed. This understandable misinterpretation apparently arises from examination of the photographs, for in a visit to the house itself the nature of the material and construction of these panels is amply evident.

3 David van Zanten, 'Schooling the Prairie School', *The Nature of Frank Lloyd Wright*, ed Bolon, p71.

4 Barry Byrne, 'On Frank Lloyd Wright and His Atelier', *AIA Journal*, no39 (1963), pp109–12.

5 These biographical aspects of Wright's life have been fully and repeatedly covered in the various biographies; refer to the chapter 'A House Divided', Meryle Secrest, *Frank Lloyd Wright*.

6 Wright, *An Autobiography*, p131.

7 This period of Wright's life, the production and distribution of the Wasmuth publications, and the general importance of Europe in Wright's development, are exhaustively researched by Anthony Alofsin in his *Frank Lloyd Wright: The Lost Years, 1910–1922* (Chicago: University of Chicago Press, 1993), and his dissertation, *Frank Lloyd Wright: the Lessons of Europe, 1910–1922* (Ann Arbor: UMI, 1989).

8 Wright, *In the Cause of Architecture*, pp121 and 125.

9 Several studies of the Prairie School exist: the best is H Allen Brooks, *The Prairie School: Frank Lloyd Wright and His Midwest Contemporaries* (New York: Norten, 1972); see also Mark Peisch, *The Chicago School of Architecture: Early Followers of Sullivan and Wright* (New York: Random House and Columbia University, 1964).

10 These two Wasmuth volumes, *Ausgefuhrte Bauten und Entwurfe von Frank Lloyd Wright* (1910) and *Frank Lloyd Wright, Ausgefuhrte Bauten* (1911), remain perhaps the best way to be introduced to Wright's work of the Prairie Period. It is interesting to note that, without exception, the perspective drawings of the built works shown in the former volume were traced from photographs, many of which were published in the second volume.

11 Wright, *An Autobiography*, p192.

12 Narcisco Menocal has also shown how the domestic room cluster at Taliesin was related to the O'Shea and Gilmore Houses, only the latter of which was built in 1909: 'Taliesin, the Gilmore House, and the Flower in the Crannied Wall', *Taliesin 1911–1914*, Wright Studies, Volume 1, ed Menocal (Carbondale: Southern Illinois University Press, 1992), pp66–97.

13 Neil Levine makes a case for the 'delayed effect' of Taliesin on Wright's work, which only showed its influence twenty-five years later, as being a reaction to the disaster that took place there, which I will outline shortly: 'The Story of Taliesin: Wright's First Natural House', *Taliesin 1911–1914*, ed Menocal, pp20–4.

14 Connors, *The Robie House of Frank Lloyd Wright*, p60.

15 Levine, 'The Story of Taliesin: Wright's First Natural House', p8. Levine credits David van Zanten with pointing out this aspect during a visit to the house they made together.

16 Wright, *An Autobiography*, p195.

17 Ibid, p194.

18 This room has similar traits of allowing supervision of the courtyard and overlooking the entrance that Klaus Herdeg has analysed as being essential features of Alvar Aalto's Villa Mairea: *The Decorated Diagram: Harvard Architecture and the Failure of the Bauhaus Legacy* (Cambridge, MA: MIT Press, 1983), p30.

19 Those wishing further information on the Hollyhock House and other projects for Aline Barnsdall should refer to the exhaustive study by Kathryn Smith, *Frank Lloyd Wright: Hollyhock House and Olive Hill* (New York: Rizzoli, 1992). Appearing as this text was being completed was Donald Hoffmann, *Frank Lloyd Wright's Hollyhock House* (New York: Dover, 1992), a comprehensive and insightful study. A more brief but no less insightful overview, accompanied by outstanding photographs, is made by James Steele, *Barnsdall House* (Architecture in Detail) (London: Phaidon, 1992).

20 Steele, *Barnsdall House*, gives a synopsis of this speculation in the section entitled 'Mayan Influences' (no page numbers).

21 Henry Russell Hitchcock, *In the Nature of Materials* (New York: Hawthorn, 1942), p71.

22 Wright, *In the Cause of Architecture*, p201. Hitchcock apparently conducted his 'research' without visiting many of the built works. Wright also perpetrated this myth that Hollyhock was built of concrete or concrete block in the final edition of his autobiography:

'the unit-block system I first used in Hollywood, 1920', Wright, *An Autobiography*, p329.

23 See Kathryn Smith's perceptive description of Wright's use of water in his designs; Smith, *Frank Lloyd Wright: Hollyhock House and Olive Hill*, pp58–9 and 66–71.

24 This house was destroyed – due to the unwillingness of a locality to 'grandfather' it into a revised zoning code – and the living room was dismantled and reconstructed in the Metropolitan Museum of Art in New York; a sad statement indeed if this is the only way to save an important Wright design.

Chapter 7

1 Wright, *An American Architecture*, p80.

2 Wright, *An Autobiography*, p201.

3 Ibid, p200. Jonathan Lipman recognizes the consecrated space called for in this desire for a 'garden in the wilderness' as being Wright's primary motivation in his public work: Lipman, 'Consecrated Space: The Public Buildings of Frank Lloyd Wright', *Frank Lloyd Wright: A Primer on Architectural Principles*, ed McCarter, p202.

4 Lipman, 'Consecrated Space: The Public Buildings of Frank Lloyd Wright', p202.

5 Incorrectly stated as '200-square-foot block' in David Hanks, *The Decorative Designs of Frank Lloyd Wright* (New York: Dutton, 1979), p116. The correct site dimension – 300 *feet square* – may be easily obtained by adding the dimensions given on the working drawings; a 200-*square-foot* space would only measure fourteen feet on a side.

6 Wright, *An Autobiography*, p203.

7 Lipman, 'Consecrated Space: The Public Buildings of Frank Lloyd Wright', p202. Lipman's article identifies and analyses the shared organizational scheme or *parti* Wright utilized for all his public buildings.

8 While clearly one of Wright's greatest achievements, Midway Gardens has had surprisingly few progeny since its completion in 1914; one exception is the Oakland Museum of 1961–8, designed by architects Roche and Dinkeloo and landscape-architect Dan Kiley.

9 Wright, *An Autobiography*, p208.

10 Ibid, pp204–5.

11 Ibid, pp208 and 214.

12 Lipman, 'Consecrated Space: The Public Buildings of Frank Lloyd Wright', p202.

13 Wright, *An Autobiography*, p216.

14 Wright, *An Autobiography*, pp217–9. Extensive information on Wright's relation to Japanese culture is to be found in the excellent *Frank Lloyd Wright and Japan* by Kevin Nute (New York: Van Nostrand Reinhold, 1993).

15 Lipman, 'Consecrated Space: The Public Buildings of Frank Lloyd Wright', pp204–5, argues that this promenade, which opened into the more typically used entries at the sides and separated the auditorium and dining room, operates in the same way as the cross-axial entrance at Wright's Studio, Unity Temple, and all of his other public buildings.

16 Frampton, *Modern Architecture: A Critical History*, p62.

17 This model of Imperial Hotel was not 'lost in transit to the US', as Wright incorrectly states in his caption for its illustration in his *An American Architecture*, p155 – in fact it never left Tokyo; students from the University of Tokyo School of Architecture who attended my classes on Wright at Columbia University in 1986–91 have shown me recent photographs of this model, which is on display in their former school.

18 All the quotations by Wright on the design of the Imperial Hotel are from his chapter, 'Building Against Doomsday', *An Autobiography*, pp237–45.

19 Wright indicates that he understood the structural 'friction' that results from such foundation systems, which were prevalent in conditions where no bedrock or other appropriate bearing strata were available near the surface.

20 Lipman, 'Consecrated Space: The Public Buildings of Frank Lloyd Wright', p206.

21 Wright, *An Autobiography*, p237.

22 Louis Sullivan, 'Reflections on the Tokyo Disaster', in Wright's *The Life-Work of Frank Lloyd Wright, Wendigen*, (1925) (New York: Horizon, 1965), p131.

23 Quoted in Norris Kelly Smith, *Frank Lloyd Wright: A Study in Architectural Content* (Watkins Glen: American Life, 1979), p180.

24 Wright, *An Autobiography*, pp229–31.

25 'The Imperial Hotel, with its indirect lighting, is on the whole a pleasant place, but in summer even it might be a bit darker.' Jun'ichiro Tanizaki, *In Praise of Shadows*, (New Haven: Leet's Island Books, 1977), p38. This small book, despite its reiteration of traditional Japanese chauvinism towards women, is the best example of an alternative to the continuous and deadening praise of light – ever more light – in Western literature.

26 Tanizaki, *In Praise of Shadows*, p30.

27 See the excellent photographic documentation in Cary James, *The Imperial Hotel* (Vermont: Tuttle, 1968, recently reprinted by Dover Publications); this book was published in memory of Wright's great lost work.

28 In order to begin to understand the richness of this ornamented world of Wright's making, we must turn to the exceptional analysis, with over 5000 diagrams, by Otto Graf, *Die Kunst des Quadrats, Zum Werk von Frank Lloyd Wright*, Volume 2 (Imperial Hotel) (Vienna: Verlag Bohlau, 1983).

29 Wright, *An Autobiography*, p246. Brendan Gill makes the baseless charge that Wright did not receive this telegram from Baron Okura, but instead sent it to himself! Gill claims this because the telegram has 'Spring Green, Wis' above the message, which was received by Wright at the Hollyhock House construction site. Yet the telegram clearly states in the first line that the original cable was sent first *to* Spring Green, and relayed *from* there to Los Angeles, resulting in the Spring Green heading. It is difficult to understand why historians feel compelled to question any confirmation of Wright's intuition, structural or otherwise. Gill, *Many Masks: A Life of Frank Lloyd Wright* (New York: Putnam's, 1987), p264.

30 The question of the part played in this design by Norman Bel Geddes, whose ideas on the modern theatre were essential to Barnsdall's conception of her theatre company, is carefully investigated in Kathryn Smith, *Frank Lloyd Wright: Hollyhock House and Olive Hill*.

31 Futagawa (ed), Pfeiffer, *Frank Lloyd Wright Monograph 1951–59*, Volume 8, (Tokyo: ADA Edita, 1988), p206.

Chapter 8

1 Valéry, 'Introduction to the Method of Leonardo da Vinci', (1894), *Paul Valéry: An Anthology*, ed J R Lawler, (Princeton: Princeton University Press, 1956), p82.

2 Wright, *An American Architecture*, pp96 and 196 respectively.

3 Wright, *The Future of Architecture* (New York: Horizon, 1953, 1981), p162.

4 Wright, *Frank Lloyd Wright, Writings and Buildings*, (1929), ed E Kaufmann Jr and B Raeburn (New York: New American Library, 1960), p101.

5 Wright, *In the Cause of Architecture*, p153.

6 Wright, *The Life-Work of Frank Lloyd Wright, Wendigen* (1925) (New York: Horizon, 1965), p57.

7 Wright, *Frank Lloyd Wright, Writings and Buildings*, p220.

8 Frampton, 'Introduction', *Frank Lloyd Wright Collected Writings*, Volume 2, ed Pfeiffer (New York: Rizzoli, 1992), p9. Frampton has almost single-handedly brought attention to Wright's 'woven' construction logic, and its relation to the ideas of Gottfried Semper, the work of Louis Sullivan and Oriental origins. He also shows how both Wright and Sullivan's 'tattooing' of the wall surface is related to Islamic 'writing on the wall' and Owen Jones's theory of ornament as primary place-maker; see Frampton's 'The Text-tile Tectonic'.

9 Frampton, 'Introduction', *Frank Lloyd Wright Collected Writings*, Volume 1, ed Pfeiffer (New York: Rizzoli, 1992), p14.

10 Wright, *In the Cause of Architecture*, pp205–8.

11 Futagawa (ed), Pfeiffer, *Frank Lloyd Wright Monograph 1902–1906*, illustration 463. This is described in Frampton, 'The Text-tile Tectonic', p137; the author pointed out this project and its hardly coincidental timing to Frampton when soliciting the article in 1989.

12 The suggestion by both H Allen Brooks and Edward Ford that Walter Burley Griffin invented the concrete block system of construction in 1917, and therefore before Wright, is doubtful; the Brown House project of 1906 ('first block house') was designed by Wright while Griffin was in his employment, and obviously was the source for the concrete-block system Griffin patented six years before Wright was to build his own first block house: Brooks, *The Prairie School*, p262 and Ford, *The Details of Modern Architecture* (Cambridge, MA: MIT Press, 1990), p325.

13 Frampton, 'The Text-tile Tectonic', p138.

14 Wright, *An Autobiography*, (1932), in *Frank Lloyd Wright: Collected Writings*, Volume 2, ed Pfeiffer, pp282–83.

15 Ibid, p270.

16 Ibid, p166.

17 This house has been recently restored to its original condition by its current owner, Joel Silver, and Eric Wright, architect and grandson of Wright.

18 Grant Hildebrandt, *The Wright Space: Pattern and Meaning in Frank Lloyd Wright's Houses* (Seattle: University of Washington Press, 1991), p85.

19 Wright, *Frank Lloyd Wright, Writings and Buildings*, p225.

20 Frampton, 'The Text-tile Tectonic', p141. This same ideal of building without glass, which Frampton traces to Egyptian architecture, is also shared by Louis I Kahn, who found his glass-less ideal in ancient ruins of all types, particularly Roman.

21 Whitman, *Leaves of Grass*.

Chapter 9

1 Louis Sullivan, 'The Tall Office Building Artistically Considered', in *Kindergarten Chats and Other Writings*, p206.

2 Thomas A P Van Leeuwen, *The Skyward Trend of Thought: The Metaphysics of the American Skyscraper* (Cambridge, MA: MIT Press, 1988)

3 Sullivan, 'The Tall Office Building Artistically Considered', p207.

4 Colin Rowe, 'The Chicago Frame' (1956), *The Mathematics of the Ideal Villa and Other Essays*, pp93 and 98. It is indeed unfortunate that this remains Rowe's only writing on Wright, for it is lucid and full of insight. Rowe's own theories for the design of increasingly historicist buildings were developed after this initial article was written, so that by 1982, when he was approached by Jonathan Lipman about reviewing a manuscript on the Johnson Wax Buildings, Rowe responded, 'I don't like Frank Lloyd Wright', a statement that conflicts directly with the praise for Wright contained in the earlier essay. Lipman, 'Postscript', in McCarter, p290.

5 Wright, *In the Cause of Architecture*, p153.

6 Sullivan, 'The Tall Office Building Artistically Considered,' p203.

7 Ibid.

8 Rowe, 'The Chicago Frame', p104.

9 Wright, 'Modern Architecture: The Tyranny of the Skyscraper', The Princeton Lectures, 1930, *The Future of Architecture*, p167.

10 Ibid, p180.

11 M F Hearn, 'A Japanese Inspiration for Frank Lloyd Wright's Rigid-Core High-Rise Structures', *Journal of the Society of Architectural Historians*, Vol L, No 1 (March 1991), p70. In reference to the Johnson Wax Research Tower, Jonathan Lipman had earlier made this suggestion of the Japanese pagoda inspiration for Wright's central mast, tap-root structures – even placing a photo of the Horyu-ji Temple at Nara in his main text: *Lipman, Frank Lloyd Wright and the Johnson Wax Buildings* (New York: Rizzoli, 1986), pp130–1.

12 Rowe, 'The Chicago Frame', p92.

13 Ibid, p99.

14 Only rarely followed since that time, most notably in Norman Foster's recent high-rise, the HongKong Shanghai Bank, which is possibly the only true descendent of the Larkin and National Insurance Company Buildings by Wright, in that it attempts to create a hierarchy of public and private spaces within its volume. Other examples, where the architects claim their designs to be descendants from those of Wright, should be carefully examined. Paul Rudolph's Yale Art and Architecture Building, while claiming heritage to the Larkin Building, shows through a comparison of construction and, most tellingly, *finish*, the steady decline in our collective capacities since the time of the Larkin Building – the battered, ribbed concrete of Rudolph's building is astonishingly coarse in comparison to the elegant roman brick and concrete trim of Wright's building, and Rudolph is not able to achieve the same coherence between structure and space that Wright produced so admirably. Rudolph's building may be said to exemplify the particularly American manner of 'learning' from history – that is, its debt to the Larkin Building is above all *formal* and not *spatial*, *structural*, *material* or *experiential*. The subtly nuanced and beautifully detailed spaces of the Larkin Building, were it still existing today, would lay any such inappropriate genealogical claims to rest.

15 There are a number of interesting studies of this competition, most of them far too positive, in this author's opinion; one of the more balanced, insightful and exhaustive is Manfredo Tafuri, 'The Disenchanted Mountain: The Skyscraper and the City', *The American*

City: From the Civil War to the New Deal, Cucci, Dal Co, Manieri-Elia, and Tafuri (Cambridge, MA: MIT Press, 1979), pp389–528.

16 Rowe, 'The Chicago Frame', p94.

17 These are documented in Steven Holl, *Alphabet City: Pamphlet Architecture No. 5* (New York: Pamphlet Architecture, 1980).

18 Wright, 'In the Cause of Architecture: VIII. Sheet Metal and a Modern Instance', *Architectural Record*, October 1928; in the Gutheim reprint, the illustration of the tower appears on p218, while the uncaptioned Millard House photo appears on p221.

19 Frampton, 'The Text-tile Tectonic'.

20 Frampton, 'The Text-tile Tectonic'; the second version of this essay is a chapter in *Studies in Tectonic Culture* (Cambridge, MA: MIT Press, 1994).

21 Wright, *In the Cause of Architecture*, pp217–19.

22 The first true curtain wall structure was Willis Polk's Hallidie Building in San Francisco, 1915–17.

23 Wright, *In the Cause of Architecture*, p219.

24 Ibid, p221.

25 Wright, *Writings and Buildings*, p276.

26 Wright, *Writings and Buildings*, pp292 and 276 respectively.

27 Hearn, 'A Japanese Inspiration for Frank Lloyd Wright's Rigid-Core High-Rise Structures', *Journal of the Society of Architectural Historians*, Volume L, No 1 (March 1991), p70; 'a feature in the pagoda that had been consciously adopted from China to help the tower withstand the shock of earthquakes; a rigid central member, or "heart pillar", acting as a mast'.

28 Wright, *Writings and Buildings*, p225.

29 Ibid, p291.

30 I am referring to the hotels of John Portman and various other illegitimate offspring, all of which utilize (without reference, usually) Wright's tower set in an interior toplit atrium, with its mezzanine circulation. Nothing designed or built since, however, has come close to the plastic dynamism of Wright's Lacy Hotel plan and section.

31 Futagawa (ed), Pfeiffer, *Frank Lloyd Wright Preliminary Studies, 1933–1959*, Volume 11, (Tokyo: ADA Edita, 1987), p144.

32 Futagawa (ed), Pfeiffer, *Frank Lloyd Wright Monograph, 1951–1959*, Volume 8, (Tokyo: ADA Edita, 1988), p269.

Chapter 10

1 Wright, *The Future of Architecture*, p41.

2 Connors, *The Robie House of Frank Lloyd Wright*, p63.

3 Gill, *Many Masks: A Life of Frank Lloyd Wright*, p326.

4 Edward Kaufmann, Jr, *Fallingwater: A Frank Lloyd Wright Country House* (New York: Abbeville Press, 1986), p36. The younger Kaufmann, never having intended to be an architect, went on to become an important art historian, and one of Wright's chief interpreters. This beautifully illustrated book gives his own recollections of the history of the house with which he was so closely associated.

5 Wright, *In the Cause of Architecture* (1928), p153.

6 As remembered by Bob Mosher and Edgar Tafel, both of whom would serve as on-site supervising apprentices during Fallingwater's construction; for their version, as well as Tafel's memories of the construction, see Edgar Tafel, *Apprentice to Genius: Years with Frank Lloyd Wright*, (1979) (New York: Dover, 1985), pp1–9.

7 Donald Hoffmann, *Frank Lloyd Wright's Fallingwater, The House and Its History* (New York: Dover, 1978), p17. Most of the factual information on the site, design and construction of Fallingwater used here is drawn from this book, which is the definitive historical study of this house. Hoffmann's exhaustive investigation of the history of Fallingwater is essential reading for those desiring the full story of this extraordinary building.

8 Wright, *Frank Lloyd Wright: On Architecture*, ed F Gutheim (New York: Grosset and Dunlap, 1941), p232.

9 Wright, *In the Cause of Architecture* (1908), p61. This is quoted in Connors' insightful study of the Robie House, where he finds three precedents within Wright's own work for the Robie House – for which again we have no surviving sketch studies.

10 Hoffmann, *Frank Lloyd Wright's Fallingwater*, p73. In 1936 Wright had his apprentice John Howe add a roof trellis similar to those at Fallingwater to the original perspective for the Gale House, even though this detail did not exist on either the working drawings or the house as built.

11 Documented and analysed in Paul Laseau and James Tice, *Frank Lloyd Wright: Between Principle and Form* (New York: Van Nostrand

Reinhold, 1992), p34. Werner Seligmann has written an unpublished essay giving a full analysis of Fallingwater and its relation to the earlier Prairie Houses.

12 Hoffmann, *Frank Lloyd Wright's Fallingwater*, p24.

13 Ibid, p33.

14 The house and 1,543 acres of land was donated by Edward Kaufmann, Jr, to the Western Pennsylvania Conservancy on 29 October 1963. For tours of Fallingwater, reservations and information are available from the Conservancy at P O Box R, Mill Run, Pennsylvania, 15464; telephone 412-329-8501.

15 Robert P Harrison, *Forests, The Shadow of Civilization* (Chicago: Chicago University Press, 1992), p232. Harrison's discussion of Fallingwater's relation to the forest and to the landscape is far more inspiring and accurate, I believe, than the continuing efforts to see Fallingwater as yet another country house or villa in the classical tradition.

16 Ibid, p232.

17 Wright, *The Natural House* (New York: Horizon, 1954), p44.

18 Wright, *The Future of Architecture*

19 Wright, *In the Cause of Architecture* (1928), p177.

20 Harrison, *Forests, The Shadow of Civilization*, p233.

21 Ibid, pp234–5. In this analysis, Harrison is indebted to Martin Heidegger's various essays that address dwelling and architecture.

22 Connors, *The Robie House of Frank Lloyd Wright*, p61.

23 Blaine Drake, an apprentice, recalls this in a letter quoted in Hoffmann, *Frank Lloyd Wright's Fallingwater*, p15.

24 Bob Mosher, in a 1974 letter quoted in Hoffmann, *Frank Lloyd Wright's Fallingwater*, p17.

25 John Dewey, *Art as Experience* (1932) (New York: Putnam's, 1980), p237. This distinction between the experience of *nearness* and *distance* is fully developed by the philosopher Martin Heidegger; see his *Basic Writings* (New York: Harper and Row, 1977).

26 Frampton, *Modern Architecture: A Critical History*, p189.

27 Hoffmann, *Frank Lloyd Wright's Fallingwater*, p56.

28 Wright, *An Autobiography*, p169.

29 Refer to Kathryn Smith's insightful discussion of Wright's use of water; 'Reacting to gravity, on a flat plane, [water] can be still; or in a line, it can ripple and move; from a height, it picks up speed and falls with a rush of energy. Water is essential to life, and it connects the earth with the heavens': *Frank Lloyd Wright: Hollyhock House and Olive Hill*, p59.

30 Wright, *An Autobiography*, p166.

31 Categories necessary for a sense of dwelling to unfold, according to the theory of landscape proposed by Jay Appleton in his *The Experience of Landscape* and extensively utilized by Grant Hildebrandt in his *The Wright Space*.

32 John Dewey, *Art as Experience*, p213.

33 Levine, 'Frank Lloyd Wright's Own Houses and His Changing Concept of Representation', in *The Nature of Frank Lloyd Wright*, ed Bolon, et al, p42.

34 Wright, *An Autobiography*, p249.

35 Ibid, p330.

36 Ibid, p335.

37 Ibid, p339.

38 Ibid, p337.

39 Ibid, p331.

40 Ibid, p333.

41 Ibid, p333.

42 Levine, 'Frank Lloyd Wright's Own Houses and his Changing Concept of Representation', p50.

43 Wright, *An Autobiography*, p480.

44 Levine, 'Frank Lloyd Wright's Own Houses and his Changing Concept of Representation', pp43–8.

45 Wright, *An Autobiography*, p335.

Chapter 11

1 Wright, *The Future of Architecture*, p195.

2 Wright, *The Natural House*, p68.

3 Gwendolyn Wright, 'Architectural Practice and Social Vision in Wright's Early Designs', *The Nature of Frank Lloyd Wright*, ed Bolon, et al, p104.

4 Though to my knowledge never admitted by the designers, this scheme of Wright's is clearly the source for the linked cruciform housing built by Elizabeth Plater-Zyberk and Andreas Duany at Charleston Place – the parallels are too close to be coincidental.

Perhaps they cannot name their source because Wright, in his later promotion of the individual freestanding house on the acre lot, is considered by these new 'town planners' as a chief cause of our current problem with suburban sprawl.

5 Gwendolyn Wright, 'Architectural Practice and Social Vision in Wright's Early Designs', p114.

6 Wright, 'Plan by Frank Lloyd Wright', (1916), *Frank Lloyd Wright Collected Writings*, Volume 1, p139.

7 Gwendolyn Wright, 'Architectural Practice and Social Vision in Wright's Early Designs', p98. She notes that Wright proposed a minimum of 1,032 families and 1,550 individuals for this quarter; her source is Wright, 'Non-Competitive Plan', in *City Residential Land Development: Studies in Planning. Competitive Plans for Subdividing a Typical Quarter Section in the Outskirts of Chicago*, ed A B Yeomans (Chicago: University of Chicago Press/Chicago city Club, 1916).

8 Wright, 'Plan by Frank Lloyd Wright', p141.

9 Ibid, p142.

10 Further information on the built works may be found in Shirley duFresne McArthur, *Frank Lloyd Wright, American System-Built Homes in Milwaukee* (Milwaukee: North Point Historical Society, 1983). This is the documentation assembled to have these buildings, rarely even acknowledged to have been designed by Wright, designated as landmarks for preservation.

11 This is noted by Wright's client for the first Usonian House, Malcolm Willey, in his paper 'Communication Agencies and Social Life', quoted in Lionel March's third radio broadcast on the BBC, January 1970, 'Frank Lloyd Wright: An Architect in Search of Democracy'; it is referenced in John Sergeant, *Frank Lloyd Wright's Usonian Houses* (New York: Whitney Library of Design, 1976), p133.

12 Frampton, 'The Text-tile Tectonic', p149.

13 Noted most recently by Donald Johnson in his *Frank Lloyd Wright versus America: The 1930's* (Cambridge, MA: MIT Press, 1990): 'much has been written about Broadacre City by many people who focused on planning or economic or political or social considerations ... [yet all exhibit] the absence of a proper analysis of the physical form of the proposed city', pp108–9. An insightful exception would be Sergeant, *Frank Lloyd Wright's Usonian Houses*, pp121–6; others include George Collins, 'Broadacre City: Wright's Utopia Reconsidered', *Four Great Makers of Modern Architecture* (New York: Columbia University, 1970), and Lionel March, 'An Architect in Search of Democracy: Broadacre City', in *Writings on Wright*, pp195–206.

14 Giorgio Ciucci, 'The City in Agrarian Ideology and Frank Lloyd Wright: Origins and Development of Broadacre City', *The American City*, Ciucci, et al, pp293–388.

15 Wright, *The Future of Architecture*, p69.

Chapter 12

1 Wright, *The Natural House*, p123.

2 Frampton, 'The Text-tile Tectonic', p143.

3 Wright, *An American Architecture*, p206.

4 Sergeant, *Frank Lloyd Wright's Usonian Houses*, p4.

5 Wright, *The Natural House*, p16.

6 Ibid, p58.

7 Ibid, p16.

8 Frampton, 'The Text-tile Tectonic', p147. The relation to traditional Japanese domestic construction is also noted by Sergeant, *Frank Lloyd Wright's Usonian Houses*, p19.

9 Frampton, ibid, p146.

10 Wright, *The Natural House*, p16.

11 Frampton, 'The Text-tile Tectonic', p145.

12 Wright, in an issue of *Architectural Forum* dedicated entirely to his work, (January 1938), p79.

13 Sergeant, *Frank Lloyd Wright's Usonian Houses*, p19. This exceptional study of the Usonians stands alone, as no other book has been written on these astonishing and still-timely designs; as Sergeant points out, these small energy-efficient houses are superior to all typical housing built since.

14 Wright, *The Natural House*, p150.

15 Ibid, p46.

16 Ibid, pp46–47.

17 Ibid, pp44 and 106 respectively.

18 Wright, *An American Architecture*, p61.

19 Wright, *The Natural House*, pp175–9.

20 Wright, *The Natural House*, p123.

21 Frampton, 'The Text-tile Tectonic', p146.

22 Wright, *In the Cause of Architecture*, p142.

23 See Paul and Jean Hanna, *Frank Lloyd Wright's Hanna House: The Client's Report* (Carbondale: Southern Illinois University Press, 1981), a rather remarkable document produced by the clients, indicative of the dedication Wright's clients typically felt for their houses. The house is now owned by Stanford University, donated by the Hannas.

24 Wright, *In the Cause of Architecture*, p163.

25 This sum seemed to hold an unusual fascination for Wright; recall the earlier Fireproof Concrete House for $5,000 and other projects titled as costing $5,000. In this case Wright was not going to promise that the house would only cost $5,000 – an insufficient amount by this time, perhaps – but that a family with a $5,000 yearly income could afford it.

26 See Susan Bandes (ed) *Affordable Dreams, The Goetsch-Winkler House and Frank Lloyd Wright* (East Lansing: Kresge Museum and Michigan State University, 1991).

27 Wright, *The Future of Architecture*, p42.

28 Harrison, *Forests: The Shadow of Civilization*, p237–8.

Chapter 13

1 Wright, *An Autobiography*, p498.

2 Frampton, 'The Johnson Wax Buildings and the Angel of History', introduction to Jonathan Lipman, *Frank Lloyd Wright and the Johnson Wax Buildings* (New York: Rizzoli, 1986), pxiv.

3 The exhibition gallery at the south end of the draughting room is separated from the former by a circulation spine, similar to that between the main and annexe blocks of the Larkin Building; the draughting room would appear to be another example of Wright's public building plan type identified by Lipman in 'Consecrated Space', in *A Primer on Architectural Principles*, ed McCarter.

4 It seems likely that E Fay Jones's extraordinary series of chapels sited in woodland settings are all variations on the exposed wooden truss structure of Wright's 1932 Taliesin draughting room, where Jones sat for a year while serving as an apprentice to Wright. See McCarter, 'Without the Space Within: The Work of Frank Lloyd Wright's Followers in America', *Architektur & Bauforum* (Vienna No. 145, 1991), pp39–44.

5 Also in Wright, '1935: Organic Architecture', first published in *Architect's Journal* (August 1936); reprinted in *Frank Lloyd Wright, On Architecture*, ed F Gutheim (New York: Grosset and Dunlap, 1941), p177.

6 The primary source for study of the Johnson Wax Buildings is the exceptional study by Jonathan Lipman, op cit. This book was also the basis of an exhibition of the same title curated by Lipman which toured the US in the later 1980s.

7 It is interesting to compare this glass-walled and columned volume to Le Corbusier's Villa Savoye of 1929, as Lipman has suggested, for Wright has here moved into another realm far in advance of the canonical modern movement: Lipman, *Frank Lloyd Wright and the Johnson Wax Buildings*, p9.

8 Wright, *An Autobiography*, p498.

9 From an interview Lipman conducted with Oglivanna Wright; Lipman, *Frank Lloyd Wright and the Johnson Wax Buildings*, p15.

10 Frampton, 'The Johnson Wax Buildings and the Angel of History', pxi.

11 Ibid, pxi.

12 Wright, *An Autobiography*, p495.

13 Lipman, *Frank Lloyd Wright and the Johnson Wax Buildings*, p56.

14 Carl Condit, *American Building Art. The Twentieth Century* (New York: Oxford University Press, 1961), p174. Also quoted in Lipman, *Frank Lloyd Wright and the Johnson Wax Buildings*, p56.

15 Lipman, *Frank Lloyd Wright and the Johnson Wax Buildings*, p62.

16 Frampton, 'The Johnson Wax Buildings and the Angel of History', pxii.

17 Wright, *An American Architecture*, p165.

18 Oglivanna Wright, in interview with Lipman: *Frank Lloyd Wright and the Johnson Wax Buildings*, p41.

19 Ibid, p51.

20 Ibid, p173.

21 Ibid, p127.

22 Frampton, 'The Johnson Wax Buildings and the Angel of History', pxii.

Chapter 14

1 Wright, *An American Architecture*, p18.

2 From an interview with Mike Wallace in 1957, quoted in Bruce Brooks Pfeiffer, *Frank Lloyd Wright Drawings* (New York: Abrams, 1990), p87.

3 For a discussion of Wright's relation to Drummond and other followers, see McCarter 'Without the Space Within: The Work of Frank Lloyd Wright's Followers in America' (translated as "Ohne den Innenraum"), *Architektur & Bauforum* (Vienna), Number 145, 1991, pp39–44.

4 Discerning this crucial difference between Wright's design intention and the built fact has not been helped by the Frank Lloyd Wright Archives insisting on dating all the drawings of the masterplan to 1938 – this despite the date of '15 September 1955' quite clearly seen on the plan that shows no trees. By that late date Wright would have incorporated the fact that the orange groves recorded in his first sketch plan no longer existed, having been removed at some point during construction; Futagawa (ed), Pfeiffer, *Frank Lloyd Wright Monograph 1937–1941*, Volume 6, fig 144.

5 Many of the buildings at Florida Southern College were done either late in Wright's life or after his death by the Taliesin Fellowship, and do not exhibit Wright's capacity to construct well-articulated and scaled space and form, nor his unerring sense of how to relate architecture to the landscape.

6 This sectional development, which displaced the plan type of service annexe and served main volume that was exemplified by Unity Temple and the Larkin Building, is identified by Lipman in 'Consecrated Space', p213.

7 For baroque churches see in particular St Ivo Sapienza in Rome by Francesco Borromini, the Shrine of St John Nepomuk at Zdar by Johann Santini Aichel and the Visitation Chapel at Vallinotto by Bernardo Vittone.

8 Wright, in interview with Hugh Downs in 1953; Futagawa (ed), Pfeiffer: *Frank Lloyd Wright Monograph 1942–50*, Volume 7, p172.

9 Levine, 'Frank Lloyd Wright's Own Houses and his Changing Concept of Representation,' in *The Nature of Frank Lloyd Wright*, ed Bolon, et al, pp43–8.

10 Wright, *Architectural Forum* (June 1959), 123. Also quoted in Vincent Scully, *Frank Lloyd Wright* (New York: Braziller, 1960), pp31–2.

11 Lipman, 'Consecrated Space', p214.

12 Futagawa (ed), Pfeiffer, *Frank Lloyd Wright Preliminary Studies 1933–59*, Volume 11, p203.

13 John Gurda, *New World Odyssey, Annunciation Greek Orthodox Church and Frank Lloyd Wright* (Milwaukee: Milwaukee Hellenic Community, 1986), pp50–1.

14 This relation has been established by Lipman, among others: Lipman, 'Consecrated Space', p213.

Chapter 15

1 Wright, 'In the Realm of Ideas', (1931 lecture at the Art Institute of Chicago), *Frank Lloyd Wright Collected Writings*, Volume 2, ed Pfeiffer, p89.

2 Wright bought numerous Japanese prints for the Spauldings while living in Japan working on the Imperial Hotel; this design was the outcome of this partnership. For more information on Wright's involvement in the purchase and collection of Japanese prints by Americans, see Julia Meech-Pekarik, 'Frank Lloyd Wright's Other Passion', in *The Nature of Frank Lloyd Wright*, ed Bolon et al, pp125–53.

3 Wright, 'The Japanese Print: An Interpretation', in *Frank Lloyd Wright Collected Writings*, Volume 1, ed Pfeiffer, p119.

4 This radio tower, drawn in the early section of 1924, bears a striking resemblance to recent towers by Santiago Calatrava and Norman Foster, indicating once again Wright's amazing structural intuition and foresight.

5 Wright, *Frank Lloyd Wright Monograph 1942–50*, Volume 7, ed Pfeiffer, p228.

6 Lipman, 'Consecrated Space', pp210–12. This drive-through has since been closed to both cars and pedestrians, being filled in with a bookshop and other services, so that the museum no longer conforms to the plan type and entrance sequence Wright intended.

7 As with many of Wright's designs, though numerous drawings exist in the Taliesin archives for the Guggenheim Museum (almost 800), few of his followers have been willing to engage in the task of ordering the various sketches in anything like a design sequence. This has led to the arbitrary numbering system of the archives, which should not confuse any serious effort to put the drawings into an order of conception.

8 Wright, *An American Architecture*, pp216–17.

Chapter 16

1 Dewey, *Art as Experience*, p269.

2 The cult-like atmosphere Oglivanna created around Wright and herself apparently led her to believe she was above the law, as indicated by the following. After Wright's death in 1959, he was buried in the Wisconsin Valley of the Lloyd Jones, as he had requested, near his family chapel and next to Mamah Cheney, the early love of his life taken from him in the 1914 Taliesin tragedy. Oglivanna was not pleased with this arrangement, and her last instruction to Wright's former apprentices before passing away in 1985 was supremely selfish, intended to assure her own fame after death: the Fellowship was told to exhume Wright's body, have it cremated, and take the ashes to Arizona to rest next to her own ashes. Amazingly, the Fellowship members were unable to disobey Oglivanna, even after her death, and Wright's ashes were moved illegally one night across state lines from Wisconsin to Arizona, where they remain a cause of considerable contention between the two states that claim Wright as their own.

3 This directly referenced in the title of his son John Lloyd Wright's book, *My Father Who Is On Earth*, and Wright's own revealing title for his last book, published in 1957, *A Testament*.

4 Connors, *The Robie House of Frank Lloyd Wright*, p25.

5 Futagawa (ed), Pfeiffer, *Frank Lloyd Wright Monograph 1951–59*, Volume 8, p372.

6 Ibid, p320.

7 Lipman, 'Consecrated Space', p216.

8 Wright, 'Modern Architecture', (The Princeton Lectures, 1930), *The Future of Architecture*, p60.

9 I am here indebted to Kenneth Frampton, '*Rappel à l'Ordre*: The Case for the Tectonic', in *Constancy and Change in Architecture*, ed M Quantrill and B Webb (College Station: Texas A&M University, 1991), and to Robin Evans's last lecture, entitled 'Perils of the Imagination', given at the University of Florida Department of Architecture in January 1993.

10 Wright, *The Future of Architecture*, p62.

11 See the chapter titled 'Popularizing the Usonian House', in Sergeant, *Frank Lloyd Wright's Usonian Houses*, pp137–58.

12 Wright, *The Future of Architecture*, pp121–3.

Conclusion

1 Bachelard, *L'Experience de l'espace dans la physique contemporaine*, quoted in Mary McAllester Jones, *Gaston Bachelard, Subversive Humanist* (Madison: University of Wisconsin Press, 1991), p3.

2 Wright, *An American Architecture*, p44.

3 Wright, *An Autobiography*, p185.

4 Ibid, p34.

5 Okakura Kakuzo, *The Book of Tea*, p45.

6 John Dewey, *Art as Experience*, p209.

7 Henri Bergson, *Time and Free Will* (1888; reprint, New York: Harper and Row, 1960), p112.

8 Dewey, *Art as Experience*, p193.

9 A S Eddington, *The Nature of the Physical World*, (New York: MacMillan, 1928), p83.

10 Wright, *In the Cause of Architecture*, p54.

11 Wright, *The Future of Architecture*, p69.

12 In the case of the Taliesin Fellowship, whose inept copying of Wright's designs has led to the general degradation of his reputation, this is Wright's own fault. Perhaps he should have done something similar to the great Finnish architect Alvar Aalto who, when on his deathbed, was told that the clients had stopped all the projects in the office, refusing to continue without Aalto's personal involvement; Aalto was reported to have told his distressed apprentices, "This is as it should be, for, after I am gone, who will do the work?"

13 Wright, *An American Architecture*, p17.

14 Friedrich Hölderlin, quoted in Martin Heidegger, *The Question Concerning Technology* (New York: Harper and Row, 1977), p28.

FRANK LLOYD WRIGHT COMPLETE LIST OF WORKS

Compiled by
Bruce Brooks Pfeiffer

Key The work is grouped according to the year of the project's initial design.
PR#number: project record number of the Frank Lloyd Wright Archives; followed by name, type and address.
PJT project
EXE executed
DMD demolished
( ) italicized line in parentheses: editorial explanation of the work;
 – italicized line without parentheses: a name or remark by Frank Lloyd Wright;
 – italicized line with and without parentheses: part in parentheses is editorial, the part outside: a name or remark by Frank Lloyd Wright
#1 first version
#2 second version of same client and project

1885 PR#8501
Civil Engineering Drawings
Engineering Drawings
WI, USA
PJT
(Class Assignment, University of Wisconsin)

1886 PR#8601
Unity Chapel/Hillside
Religious
County T/Near Route 23
Spring Green, WI 53588,
USA EXE
(Joseph Lyman Silsbee, Architect – FLLW Interior Ceiling)

1887 PR#8704
Country Residence
Residence
Hillside, WI, USA
PJT

PR#8701
Drawing shown to Louis Sullivan
Residence
IL, USA
PJT
'Drawing shown to Lieber-Meister when applying for a job' FLLW

PR#8703
Hillside Home School 'Home Building'
Educational
Route 23, Taliesin
Spring Green, WI 53588,
USA
DMD

PR#8702
Unitarian Chapel
Chapel
Sioux City, IA, USA
PJT

1888 PR#8801
Auditorium Drawing
Ornament
Michigan Ave
Chicago, IL, USA
EXE
(Chicago Auditorium, Adler and Sullivan, Architects, FLW Designer)

1889 PR#8901
FLLW Oak Park House
Residence
951 Chicago Ave
Oak Park, IL 60302,
USA
EXE

1890 PR#9001
Charnley, James
Residence/Summer
509 East Beach
Ocean Springs,
MS 39564, USA
DMD

PR#9004
Cooper, Henry
Residence
La Grange, IL, USA
PJT

PR#9002
Macharg, W S
Residence
Chicago, IL, USA
DMD

PR#9003
Sullivan, Louis
Residence/Summer
100 Holcomb Blvd
Ocean Springs, MS 39564
EXE

1891 PR#9001
Charnley, James
Residence
1365 Astor St
Chicago, IL 60610, USA
EXE

1892 PR#9201
Blossom, George
Residence
4858 Kenwood Ave
Chicago, IL 60615, USA
EXE
(Joseph Lyman Silsbee, Architect – FLLW Interior Ceiling)

PR#9209
Clark, W Irving
Residence
211 S La Grange
La Grange, IL 60525,
USA
EXE

PR#9202
Emmond, Robert
Residence
109 S 8th Ave
La Grange, IL 60525,
USA
EXE

PR#9203
Gale, Thomas
Residence
1027 Chicago Ave
Oak Park, IL 60302,
USA
EXE

PR#9204
Harlan, Dr Allison
Residence
Chicago, IL, USA
DMD

PR#9205
McArthur, Warren
Residence
4852 Kenwood Ave
Chicago, IL 60615, USA
EXE

PR#9206
Parker, Robert
Residence
1019 Chicago Ave
Oak Park, IL 60302,
USA
EXE

PR#9210
Roberts, C E Res
Residence
Oak Park, IL, USA
PJT

PR#9207
Sullivan, Albert
Residence
Chicago, IL, USA
DMD

PR#9208
Victoria Hotel
Hotel
Chicago Heights, IL,
USA
DMD
(Adler and Sullivan, Architects: FLLW Designer)

1893 PR#9309
Fisherman and the Genie
Mural
951 Chicago Avenue
Oak Park, IL 60302,
USA
EXE

PR#9307
FLLW Oak Park Playroom
Playroom
951 Chicago Avenue
Oak Park, IL 60302,
USA
EXE

PR#9302
Gale, Walter
Residence
1031 Chicago Avenue
Oak Park, IL 60302,
USA
EXE

PR#9301
Lamp, Robert
Residence/Summer
Governor's Island
Madison, WI, USA
DMD

PR#9306
Library and Museum
Library
Milwaukee, WI, USA
PJT

PR#9304
Lake Mendota Boathouse,
Boathouse
Madison, WI, USA
DMD

PR#9308
Lake Monona Boathouse,
Boathouse
Madison, WI, USA
PJT

PR#9305
Winslow, William
Residence
515 Auvergne Place

River Forest, IL 60305,
USA
EXE

PR#9405
Wooley, Francis
Residence
1030 Superior Street
Oak Park, IL 60302,
USA
EXE

1894 PR#9413
Bagley Baptismal Font
Sculpture
Chicago, IL, USA
EXE

PR#9411
Bagley Co. Communion Rail
Sculpture
Chicago, IL, USA
PJT

PR#9401
Bagley, Frederick
Residence
121 County Line Road
Hinsdale, IL 60521, USA
EXE

PR#9402
Bassett, Dr H W
Residence
Oak Park, IL, USA
DMD

PR#9410
Belknap Apartments
Apartments
Austin, IL, USA
PJT

PR#9409
Candlesticks in cast metal
Candleholder
USA
PJT

PR#9406
Goan, Orrin
Residence
La Grange, IL, USA
PJT

PR#9403
Goan, Peter
108 S 8th Avenue
La Grange, IL 60525,
USA
EXE

PR#9407
McAfee, A C
Residence
Kenilworth, IL.,
USA
PJT

PR#9408
Monolithic Concrete Bank
Bank
USA
PJT
(See PR# 0113, A Village Bank in Cast Concrete)

PR#9412
Orb Flowerholder
Vases
USA
EXE

PR#9404
Roloson Houses
Apartments
3213–19 Calumet
Chicago, IL 60616,
USA
EXE

PR#9414
Weedholder
Vases
USA
EXE

1895 PR#9508
Baldwin, Jesse
Residence
Oak Park, IL, USA
PJT

PR#9504
Flat Building
Apartments
2840–2858 W Walnut St
Chicago, IL 60612, USA
EXE
(For E C Waller)

PR#9506
FLLW Oak Park Studio
Studio
951 Chicago Avenue
Oak Park, IL 60302,
USA
EXE

PR#9501
Francis Apartments
Apartments
Chicago, IL, USA
DMD

PR#9502
Francisco Terrace Apartments
Apartments
Chicago, IL, USA
DMD

PR#9512
Hanging Vases, Bronze
Vases
USA
PJT

PR#9509
Luxfer Prism Office Building
Office Tower
Chicago, IL, USA
PJT

PR#9513
Luxfer Prisms
Prisms
Chicago, IL, USA
EXE
(For Luxfer Prism Company)

PR#9503
Moore, Nathan
Residence
333 Forest Avenue
Oak Park, IL 60302,
USA
DMD

PR#9503
Moore, Nathan
Stables
325 Forest Avenue
Oak Park, IL 60302,
USA
EXE

PR#9505
Williams, Chauncey
Residence
530 Edgewood Place
River Forest, IL 60305,
USA
EXE

PR#9510
Wolf Lake Amusement Park
Amusement Park
Chicago, IL, USA
PJT
(For E C Waller)

PR#9507
Young, H P
Remodelling
Residence
334 N Kenilworth
Avenue
Oak Park, IL 60302,
USA
EXE

1896 PR#9604
Devin, Mrs David
Residence
Chicago, IL, USA
PJT

PR#9612
Eve of St Agnes
Graphics
Auvergne Press
River Forest, IL, USA
EXE
(With William Winslow,
Auvergne Press)

PR#9601
Goodrich, H C
Residence
534 North East Avenue
Oak Park, IL 60302,
USA
EXE

PR#9611
Grandfather Clock
Furniture
Oak Park, IL, USA
EXE
(For CE Roberts)

PR#9606
Heller, Isadore
Residence
5132 S Woodlawn
Avenue
Chicago, IL 60615, USA
EXE

PR#9609
The House Beautiful
Graphics
Auvergne Press
River Forest, IL, USA
EXE
(With William Winslow,
Auvergne Press)

PR#9605
Perkins Apartments
Apartments
Chicago, IL, USA
PJT

PR#9602
Roberts, C E
Stables
317 N Euclid Avenue
Oak Park, IL 60302, USA
EXE

PR#9608
Roberts, C E
Housing
Ridgeland, IL, USA
PJT

PR#9610
Roberts, C E
Residence/Summer
USA
PJT

PR#9603
Roberts, C E
Remodelling
Residence
321 N Euclid Avenue
Oak Park, IL 60302, USA
EXE

1897 PR#9702
All Soul's
Religious Club
Chicago, IL, USA
PJT
(For Jenkin Lloyd Jones,
V Abraham Lincoln
Center)

PR#9701
Factory for the Chicago
Screw Company
Factory
Chicago, IL, USA
PJT

PR#9701
Furbeck, George
Residence
223 N Euclid Avenue
Oak Park, IL 60302, USA
EXE

PR#9706
Gale, Thomas
Residence/Summer
5318 South Shore Drive
Whitehall, MI, USA
EXE
PR#9705
Roberts Block Plan
Block Plan
Oak Park, IL, USA
PJT
(For CE Roberts)

PR#9607
Romeo and Juliet
Windmill Tower
Route 23, Taliesin
Spring Green, WI 53588,
USA
EXE
(For Jane and Ellen Lloyd
Jones, Hillside Home
School)

PR#9703
Wallis, Henry
Boathouse
Lake Delavan, WI, USA
DMD

1898 PR#9801
Furbeck, Rollin
Residence
515 Fair Oaks Avenue
Oak Park, IL 60302, USA
EXE

PR#9804
Mozart Gardens
Restaurant
Chicago, IL, USA
PJT
(For David Meyer)

PR#9802
River Forest Golf Club
Clubhouse
River Forest, IL, USA
DMD

PR#9803
Smith, George
Residence
404 Home Avenue
Oak Park, IL 60302, USA
EXE

PR#9806
Vases and
Flowerholders
Vases
USA
PJT

PR#9805
Waller, E C
Residence
River Forest, IL, USA
PJT

1899 PR#9903
Cheltenham Beach
Resort
Amusement Park
Chicago, IL, USA
PJT
(For E C Waller)

PR#9906
Eckhart, Mrs Robert
Residence
River Forest, IL, USA
PJT

PR#9901
Husser, Joseph
Residence
Chicago, IL, USA
DMD

PR#0205
Ornamental Features
Sculpture
Chicago, IL, USA
PJT
(For E C Waller)

PR#9904
Residence
Residence
USA
PJT
(For Architectural Review,
June, 1900)

PR#9902
Waller, E C
Remodelling
Residence
River Forest, IL, USA
DMD

1900 PR#0010
Abraham Lincoln
Center
Religious Club
Chicago, IL, USA
PJT
(For Jenkin Lloyd Jones)

PR#0011
Adams, Mrs Jessie W
Residence
9326 S Pleasant Avenue
Chicago, IL 60620, USA
EXE

PR#0002
Bradley, B Harley
Residence
701 S Harrison Avenue
Kankakee, IL 60901, USA
EXE
Glenlloyd

PR#0003
Foster, S A
Residence
12147 Harvard Avenue
Chicago, IL 60628, USA
EXE

PR#0004
Hickox, Warren
Residence
687 S Harrison Avenue
Kankakee, IL 60901, USA
EXE

PR#0102
Hills, E R
Residence
313 Forest Avenue
Oak Park, IL 60302, USA
EXE

PR#0007
A Home in A Prairie
Town,
Residence
Curtis Publishing Co
February 1901
PJT
(Ladies Home Journal)

PR#0016
Jones, Fred B
Boathouse
Lake Delavan, WI, USA
DMD

PR#0014
McArthur, Warren
Garage
4852 Kenwood Avenue
Chicago, IL 60615, USA
EXE

PR#0015
McArthur, Warren
Remodelling
Residence
4852 Kenwood Avenue
Chicago, IL 60615, USA
EXE

PR#0005
Pitkin, E H
Residence/Summer
Desbarats
Sapper Island, ON, Canada
EXE

PR#0019
Quadruple Block Plan
Block Plan
Curtis Publishing Co
February 1901, USA
PJT
(Ladies Home Journal)

PR#0013
Residence for Oakland,
California
Residence
Oakland, CA, USA
PJT

PR#0008
Small House with Lots
of Room In It
Residence
Curtis Publishing Co
June 1901, USA
PJT
(Ladies Home Journal)

PR#0006
Wallis, Henry #1
Residence
Lake Delavan, WI, USA
PJT

PR#0114
Wallis, Henry #2
Residence
3409 South Shore Drive
Lake Delavan, WI 53115,
USA
EXE

1901 PR#0101
Davenport, E Arthur
Residence
559 Ashland Avenue
River Forest, IL 60305,
USA
EXE

PR#0201
Fricke, William
Residence
540 Fair Oaks Avenue
Oak Park, IL 60302, USA
EXE

PR#0112
Hebert, Dr A W
Remodelling
Residence
Evanston, IL, USA
DMD

PR#0104
Henderson, F B
Residence
301 S Kenilworth Avenue
Elmhurst, IL 60126, USA
EXE

PR#0103
Jones, Fred, B
Residence
3335 South Shore Drive
Lake Delavan, WI 53115,
USA
EXE
Penwern

PR#0111
Lexington Terrace
Apartments
Apartments
Chicago, IL, USA
PJT
(For E C Waller)

PR#0115
Lowell, MH
Residence/Studio
Matteawan, NY, USA
PJT

PR#0209
Metzger, Victor
Residence
Sault Ste Marie, MI,
USA
PJT
(In association with
Webster Tomlinson)

PR#0105
River Forest Golf Club
Additions
Clubhouse
River Forest, IL, USA
DMD

PR#0106
Thomas, Frank
Residence
210 Forest Avenue
Oak Park, IL 60302, USA
(Rogers was father of the
bride; the house was his
wedding gift to her)

PR#0017
Universal Portland
Cement Pavilion
Exhibition
Buffalo, NY, USA
PJT

PR#0113
Village Bank in
Cast Concrete
Bank
USA
PJT
(Monolithic Bank)

PR#0108
Waller, E C
Gatehouse
River Forest, IL, USA
DMD

PR#0109
Wallis, Henry
Gatehouse
3407 South Shore Drive
Lake Delavan, WI 53115,
USA
EXE

PR#0110
Wilder, T E
Stables
Elmhurst, IL., USA
DMD

1902 PR#0107
Children of the Moon
Sculpture
301 E Lawrence Avenue
Springfield, IL 62703,
USA
EXE

PR#9905
Dana, Susan Lawrence
Residence

301–327 E Lawrence
Avenue
Springfield, IL 62703, USA
EXE

PR#0220
Lake Delavan
Clubhouse
Clubhouse
Lake Delavan, WI, USA
PJT

PR#0217
Lake Delavan
Yachtclub
Boathouse
Lake Delavan, WI, USA
DMD

PR#0218
Dial Office Remodelling
Office Remodelling
Fine Arts Building
Chicago, IL, USA
PJT

PR#9907
Flower in the
Crannied Wall
Sculpture
301 E Lawrence Avenue
Springfield, IL 62703,
USA
EXE
(Sculpture for Dana House)

PR#0202
Gerts, George
Residence/Summer
5260 South Shore Drive
Whitehall, MI 49461, USA
EXE

PR#0203
Gerts, Walter
Residence/Summer
5260 South Shore Drive
Whitehall, MI 49461, USA
EXE

PR#0204
Heurtley, Arthur
Residence
318 Forest Avenue
Oak Park, IL 60302, USA
EXE

PR#0214
Heurtley, Arthur
'Les Cheneux Club'
Residence/Summer
Marquette Is, MI 49754,
USA
EXE

PR#0216
Hillside Home School
Educational
Route 23, Taliesin
Spring Green, WI 53588,
USA
EXE
(For Jane and Ellen
Lloyd Jones)

PR#0009
Little, Francis W
Residence
1505 W Moss Avenue
Peoria, IL 61606, USA
EXE

PR#0215
Little, Francis W
Residence/Summer
Wayzata, MN, USA
PJT

PR#0304
Martin, W E
Residence
636 North East Avenue
Oak Park, IL 60302, USA
EXE

PR#0210
Mosher, John
Residence
USA
PJT

PR#0213
Residence, Board/Batten
Residence
Oak Park, IL, USA
PJT

PR#0206
Ross, Charles
Residence/Summer
3211 South Shore Drive
Lake Delavan, WI 53115,
USA
EXE

PR#0219
Skyscraper Vase
Vases
USA
EXE

PR#0207
Spencer, George
Residence/Summer
3209 South Shore Drive
Lake Delavan, WI 53115,
USA
EXE

PR#0219
Terracotta Flowerholder
Vases
USA
EXE

PR#0212
Waller, EC #1
Residence/Summer
Charlevoix, MI, USA
PJT

PR#0208
Willits, Ward W
Residence
1445 Sheridan Road, High-
land Park, IL 60035, USA
EXE

1903   PR#0010
Abraham Lincoln
Center
Religious Club
700 E Oakwood Blvd
Chicago, IL 60653, USA
EXE
(Executed by Dwight Heald
Perkins; Wright's sketches
much altered in execution)

PR#0311
Artist's Studio-
Residence
Residence/Studio
Oak Park, IL, USA
PJT

PR#0301
Barton, George
Residence
118 Summit Avenue
Buffalo, NY 14214, USA
EXE

PR#0313
Cement Vase
Vases
USA
EXE

PR#0401
Cheney, Edwin H
Residence
520 North East Avenue
Oak Park, IL 60302, USA
EXE

PR#0312
Freeman, W H
Residence

Hinsdale, IL, USA
EXE
(Altered in execution)

PR#0307
Lamp, Robert
Residence
Madison, WI, USA
PJT
(House for Investment)

PR#0403
Larkin Company
Administration Building
Office Building
Buffalo, NY, USA
DMD
(For Darwin D Martin)

PR#0303
Prairie House Type D
Residence
USA
PJT

PR#0308
Railway Stations (3)
Transport
Chicago Suburbs, IL, USA
PJT

PR#0309
Roberts Quadruple
Block Plan
Block Plan
Oak Park, IL, USA
PJT
(For CE Roberts)

PR#0305
Scoville Park Fountain
Sculpture
Lake Street at Oak Park
Oak Park, IL 60302, USA
EXE

PR#0310
Waller, EC #2
Residence/Summer
Charlevoix, MI, USA
PJT

PR#0306
Walser, J J
Residence
42 N Central
Chicago, IL 60644, USA
EXE

1904   PR#0406
Baldwin, Hiram #1
Residence
Kenilworth, IL, USA
PJT

PR#0513
Barnes, Charles
Residence
McCook, NE, USA
PJT

PR#0407
Clark, Robert
Residence
Peoria, IL, USA
PJT

PR#0417
Hanging Lamp
Lamp
USA
PJT
(Moved to Bogk file, 1602)

PR#0302
Lamp Post in Concrete
Lamp Post
USA
PJT

PR#0402
Lamp, Robert
Residence
22 N Butler Street

Madison, WI 53703, USA
EXE

PR#0408
Larkin Workmen's
Houses
Housing
Buffalo, NY, USA
PJT
(For Darwin D Martin)

PR#0405
Martin, Darwin D
Residence
125 Jewett Parkway
Buffalo, NY 14214, USA
EXE

PR#0416
Martin, Frank
Residence
Buffalo, NY, USA
PJT

PR#0404
Owens, O D
Remodelling
Residence
USA
PJT

PR#0412
Residence Wood and
Plaster
Residence
Highland Park, IL, USA
PJT

PR#0409
Scudder, J A
Residence
Desbarats, ON, Canada
PJT

PR#0410
Smith Bank #1
Bank
Dwight, IL, USA
PJT
(For Frank L Smith)

PR#0413
Soden
Residence
Riverside, IL, USA
PJT

PR#0414
Study for Brick and
Concrete
Study
USA
PJT

PR#0411
Ullman, H J
Residence
Oak Park, IL, USA
PJT

1905   PR#0524
Adams, M H
Remodelling
Residence
USA
PJT

PR#0501
Adams, Mary
Residence
1923 Lake Avenue
Highland Park, IL 60035,
USA
EXE

PR#0503
Brown, Charles A
Residence
2420 Harrison Street
Evanston, IL 60201, USA
EXE
(Also called Evanston
Model Home)

PR#0529
Buckingham, Clarence
Office Remodelling
Chicago, IL, USA
PJT

PR#0519
Chair
Furniture
USA
EXE
(Later adapted for Frank
Lloyd Wright's Taliesin)

PR#0702
Cummings, E A
Real Estate Office
Office Building
River Forest, IL, USA
DMD

PR#0528
Darrow, Mrs
Residence
Chicago, IL, USA
PJT

PR#0526
Double Residence
Board & Batten Type
Residence
Oak Park, IL, USA
PJT

PR#0504
E-Z Polish Factory
Factory
3005–3017 W Carroll Ave
Chicago, IL 60612, USA
EXE
(For Darwin D Martin
and WE Martin)

PR#0523
Gale, Mrs Thomas
Residence/Summer
5380 South Shore Drive
Whitehall, MI 49461, USA
EXE

PR#0522
Gale, Mrs Thomas
Residence/Summer
5370 South Shore Drive
Whitehall, MI 49461, USA
EXE

PR#0521
Gale, Mrs Thomas
Residence/Summer
5324 South Shore Drive
Whitehall, MI 49461, USA
EXE

PR#0514
Gilpin, T E
Residence
Oak Park, IL, USA
PJT

PR#0505
Glasner, W A
Residence
850 Sheridan Road
Glencoe, IL 60022, USA
EXE

PR#0506
Hardy, Thomas P
Residence
1319 S Main Street
Racine, WI 53403, USA
EXE

PR#0507
Heath, William R
Residence
76 Soldier's Place
Buffalo, NY 14222, USA
EXE

PR#0518
House on a Lake
Residence

USA
PJT

PR#0508
Johnson, A P
Residence/Summer
3455 South Shore Drive
Lake Delavan, WI 53115,
USA
EXE

PR#0509
Lawrence Memorial
Library
Library
Laurel St/At first
Springfield, IL 62704,
USA
EXE

PR#0530
Martin, D D
Residence/Gardener
285 Widward Avenue
Buffalo, NY 14214, USA
EXE

PR#0520
McArthur Concrete
Apartment Building
Apartments
Chicago, IL, USA
PJT
(For Warren McArthur)

PR#0531
Moe, Ingwald
Residence
669 Van Buren
Gary, IN 46402, USA
EXE

PR#0527
Moore, Nathan Pergola
Garden Feature
Oak Park, IL, USA
PJT

PR#0510
River Forest Tennis
Club
Clubhouse
615 Lathrop Avenue
River Forest, IL 60305,
USA
EXE

PR#0511
Rookery
Office Remodelling
209 S La Salle Street
Chicago, IL 60604, USA
EXE

PR#0512
Smith Bank #2
Bank
122 West Main Street
Dwight, IL 60420, USA
EXE
(For Frank L Smith)

PR#0415
Study 1905
Study
USA
PJT

PR#0516
Sutton, Harvey #1
Residence
McCook, NE, USA
PJT

PR#0525
Sutton, Harvey #2
Residence
McCook, NE, USA
PJT

PR#0710
Sutton, Harvey #3
Residence
602 Norris Avenue

McCook, NE 69001, USA
EXE

PR#0611
Unity Temple
Religious
875 Lake Street
Oak Park, IL 60301, USA
EXE

PR#0515
Varnish Factory
Factory
Buffalo, NY, USA
PJT

PR#0211
Yahara Boathouse
Boathouse
Madison, WI, USA
PJT
(For Cudworth Bye,
University of Wisconsin)

1906   PR#0601
Beachy, PA
Residence
238 Forest Avenue
Oak Park, IL 60302, USA
EXE

PR#0625
Blossom, George
Garage
1322 E 49th Street
Chicago, IL 60615, USA
EXE

PR#0701
Blossom, George
Garage Additions
1322 E 49th Street
Chicago, IL 60615, USA
EXE

PR#0612
Bock, Richard
Residence/Studio
Maywood, IL, USA
PJT

PR#0622
Brown, Harry #1
Residence
Genesco, IL, USA
PJT

PR#0623
Brown, Harry #2
Residence
Genesco, IL, USA
PJT

PR#0803
Coonley, Avery
Residence
300 Scottswood Road
Riverside, IL 60546, USA
EXE

PR#0602
Derhodes, K C
Residence
715 W Washington Street
South Bend, IN 46601,
USA
EXE

PR#0613
Devin, Mrs Aline
Residence/Summer
Eliot, ME, USA
PJT

PR#0614
Fireproof House
Residence
Curtis Publishing Co
April 1907, USA
PJT
(Ladies Home Journal)

PR#0624
Frazer

346

Residence
USA
PJT

PR#0603
Fuller, Grace
Residence
Glencoe, IL, USA
PJT

PR#0615
Gerts, Walter
Residence
Glencoe, IL, USA
PJT

PR#0604
Gridley, A W
Residence
637 N Batavia Avenue
Batavia, IL 60510, USA
EXE

PR#0605
Hoyt, P D
Residence
318 S Fifth Avenue
Geneva, IL 60134, USA
EXE

PR#0616
Ludington, R S
Residence
Dwight, IL, USA
PJT

PR#0606
Millard, George Madison
Residence
1689 Lake Avenue
Highland Park, IL 60035, USA
EXE

PR#0607
Nicholas, Frederick
Residence
1136 Brassie Avenue
Flossmoor, IL 60422, USA
EXE

PR#0619
Pettit Memorial Chapel
Chapel/Mortuary
Harrison at Webster
Belvidere, IL 61008, USA
EXE

PR#0608
River Forest Tennis Club Rebuilding
Clubhouse
615 Lathrop Avenue
River Forest, IL 60305, USA
EXE

PR#0908
Robie, Frederick C
Residence
5757 Woodlawn Avenue
Chicago, IL 60637, USA
EXE

PR#0620
Early Rug Designs
Carpets
USA
PJT

PR#0621
Seidenbecher, Joseph
Residence
Chicago, IL, USA
PJT

PR#0617
Shaw, C Thaxter
Residence
Montreal, QU, Canada
PJT

PR#0610
Shaw, C Thaxter Remodelling
Residence
Montreal, QU, Canada
DMD

PR#0618
Stone, Elizabeth
Residence
Glencoe, IL, USA
PJT

1907 **PR#0801**
Boynton, EE
Residence
16 East Blvd
Rochester, NY 14610, USA
EXE

PR#0716
The Breeze
Graphics
Oak Park, IL, USA
EXE
(Graphics by Maginel Wright – FLLW's sister)

PR#0802
Browne's Bookstore
Shop
Fine Arts Building
Chicago, IL, USA
DMD

PR#1103
Coonley, Avery
Residence/Coachouse
336 Coonley Road
Riverside, IL 60546, USA
EXE

PR#0715
Lake Delavan Cottage
Residence/Summer
Lake Delavan, WI, USA
PJT

PR#0703
Fabyan, Col George
Residence
1511 Batavia Road
Geneva, IL 60134, USA
EXE

PR#0704
Fox River Country Club
Country Club
Geneva, IL, USA
DMD

PR#0705
Hunt, Stephen M B
Residence
345 7th Avenue
La Grange, IL 60525, USA
EXE

PR#0706
Larkin Company Exhibition Pavilion
Exhibition
Norfolk, VA, USA
DMD
(For Darwin D Martin)

PR#0707
Martin, Emma
540 Fair Oaks Avenue
Oak Park, IL 60302, USA
EXE
(Additions to Fricke House)

PR#0713
McCormick, Harold
Residence
Lake Bluff, IL, USA
PJT

PR#0708
Pebbles-Balch Shop
Shop
Oak Park, IL, USA
DMD

PR#0709
Porter, Andrew
Residence
Route 23, Taliesin
Spring Green, WI 53588, USA
EXE
Tanyderi

PR#0714
Porter, Andrew #1
Residence/Summer
Spring Green, WI, USA
PJT

PR#0711
Tomek, F F
Residence
150 Nuttall Road
Riverside, IL 60546, USA
EXE

PR#0712
Westcott, Burton
Residence
1340 East High Street
Springfield, OH 45505, USA
EXE

1908 **PR#0810**
Baker, Frank #1
Residence
Wilmette, IL, USA
PJT

PR#0811
Brigham, E D
Stables
Glencoe, IL, USA
PJT

PR#1002
Como Orchards Summer Colony
Resort
469 Bunkhouse Road
Darby, MT 59829, USA
EXE

PR#0812
Copeland, Dr W H #1
Residence
Oak Park, IL, USA
PJT

PR#0804
Davidson, Walter V
Residence
57 Tillinghast Place
Buffalo, NY 14216, USA
EXE

PR#0805
Evans, Ray W
Residence
9914 Longwood Drive
Chicago, IL 60643, USA
EXE

PR#0806
Gilmore, E A
Residence
120 Ely Place
Madison, WI 53705, USA
EXE

PR#0813
Guthrie, William Norman
Residence
Sewanee, TN, USA
PJT

PR#0807
Horner, L K
Residence
Chicago, IL, USA
DMD

PR#0814
Horseshoe Inn
Resort
Estes Park, CO, USA

PJT
(For Willard Ashton)

PR#0800
Japanese Print Exhibit
Exhibition
Art Institute
Chicago, IL, USA
DMD

PR#0815
Little, Francis W
Residence/Summer
Wayzata, MN, USA
PJT

PR#0818
Martin, D D
Residence/Summer
Lake Erie, NY, USA
PJT

PR#0817
May, Meyer
Residence
450 Madison Ave, SE
Grand Rapids, MI 49503, USA
EXE

PR#0816
Melson, J G
Residence
Mason City, IA, USA
PJT

PR#0808
Roberts, Isabel
Residence
603 Edgewood Place
River Forest, IL 60305, USA
EXE

PR#0809
Stockman, Dr G C
Residence
First St, NE @E Street
Mason City, IA 50401, USA
EXE

1909 **PR#0901**
Baker, Frank #2
Residence
507 Lake Street
Wilmette, IL 60091, USA
EXE

PR#0502
Baldwin, Hiram #2
Residence
205 Essex Street
Kenilworth, IL 60043, USA

PR#0926
Bitter Root Inn
Resort
Darby, MT, USA
DMD

PR#0918
Bitter Root Town
Town Plan
Darby, MT, USA
PJT

PR#0902
City National Bank and Hotel
Bank/Hotel
W State/S Federal
Mason City, IA 50401, USA
EXE

PR#0903
Clark, Robert Remodelling
Residence
1505 W Moss Avenue
Peoria, IL 61606, USA
EXE

(Francis Little House)

PR#0925
Coonley, Avery
Residence
Riverside, IL, USA
PJT

PR#0922
Copeland, Dr W H
Garage
408 Forest Avenue
Oak Park, IL 60302, USA
EXE

PR#0904
Copeland, Dr W H #2
Residence
400 Forest Avenue
Oak Park, IL 60302, USA
EXE

PR#0905
Gale, Mrs Thomas
Residence
9 Elizabeth Court
Oak Park, IL 60302, USA
EXE

PR#0906
Ingalls, J Kibben
Residence
562 Keystone Avenue
River Forest, IL 60305, USA
EXE

PR#0913
Larwell
Residence
Muskegon, MI, USA
PJT

PR#0914
Lexington Terrace Apartments
Apartments
Chicago, IL, USA
PJT
(For EC Waller)

PR#0927
Martin, D D
Residence/Summer
Lake Erie, NY, USA
PJT

PR#0921
Martin, W E, Pergola
Garden Feature
636 North East Avenue
Oak Park, IL 60302, USA
EXE

PR#0923
Parker, Lawton Remodelling
Residence/Studio
NY, USA
PJT

PR#0924
Puppet Playhouse
Playhouse
Oak Park, IL 60302, USA
EXE

PR#0915
Roberts, Mary
Residence
River Forest, IL, USA
PJT

PR#0912
Screen
Glass
USA
PJT
(Probably much earlier than 1909, closer to 1899)

PR#0909
Steffens, Oscar
Residence

Chicago, IL, USA
DMD

PR#0907
Stewart, George
Residence
196 Hot Springs Road
Montecito, CA 93103, USA
EXE

PR#0910
Stohr Arcade Shops
Shop
Chicago, IL, USA
DMD
(For Peter Stohr)

PR#0919
Study City Dwelling
Residence
USA
PJT
'City Block – Glass Front' FLLW

PR#0920
Study for Concrete
Study
USA
PJT
'Flower Box and Light in Park' FLLW

PR#0911
Thurber Art Gallery
Gallery
Fine Arts Building
Chicago, IL, USA
DMD

PR#0917
Waller E C
Housing/Rental
River Forest, IL, USA
PJT

PR#0916
Waller, E C
Bathing Pavilion
Charlevoix, MI, USA
DMD

1910 **PR#1006**
Blythe-Markley Offices
Office
W State/S Federal
Mason City, IA 50401, USA
EXE
(City National Bank Building)

PR#1005
FLLW Fiesole Studio/Residence
Residence/Studio
Fiesole, Italy
PJT

PR#1003
Irving, E P
Residence
2 Millikin Place
Decatur, IL 62522, USA
EXE

PR#1008
Schoolhouse
Educational
Crosbyton, TX, USA
PJT

PR#1004
Universal Portland Cement Exhibit
Exhibition
Madison Square Garden
New York, NY, USA
DMD

PR#1007
Ziegler, Rev J R
Residence
509 Shelby Street

Frankfort, KY 40601,
USA
EXE

PR#1506
American Homes
Townhouse
Townhouse
USA
PJT
(For Arthur L Richards –
American Homes – American
Ready Cut System)

PR#1101
Angster, Herbert
Residence
Lake Bluff, IL, USA
DMD

PR#1102
Balch, O B
Residence
611 N Kenilworth Avenue
Oak Park, IL 60302, USA
EXE

PR#1210
Balloons and Confetti
Glass Designs
Glass
350 Fairbank Road
Riverside, IL 60546, USA
EXE
(For Coonley Playhouse,
removed from site)

PR#1302
Banff National Park
Recreation Building
Resort
Banff National Park
Alberta, BC, Canada
DMD
(In association with
Francis W Sullivan)

PR#1313
Banff Railway Station
Transport
Banff National park
Alberta, BC, Canada
PJT

PR#1122
Booth Art Gallery
Gallery
Glencoe, IL, USA
PJT
(For Sherman Booth)

PR#1120
Booth Park Features
Park Features
Glencoe, IL, USA
PJT
(For Sherman Booth)

PR#1123
Booth Station #1
Transport
Glencoe, IL, USA
DMD
(Chicago North Shore
and Milwaukee Waiting
Station, for Sherman
Booth)

PR#1124
Booth Station #2
Transport
Glencoe, IL, USA
PJT
(Chicago North Shore
and Milwaukee Waiting
Station, for Sherman
Booth)

PR#1121
Booth Town Hall
Town Hall
Glencoe, IL, USA
PJT
(For Sherman Booth)

PR#1119
Booth, Sherman
Residence/Summer
Glencoe, IL, USA
EXE

PR#1118
Booth, Sherman #1
Residence
Glencoe, IL, USA
PJT

PR#1116
Christian Catholic
Church #1
Religious
Zion City, IL, USA
PJT

PR#1108
Coonley, Avery
Kindergarten
Riverside, IL, USA
PJT
(For Avery Coonley)

PR#1107
Coonley, Avery
Greenhouse
Riverside, IL, USA
PJT
(For Avery Coonley)

PR#1103
Coonley, Avery
Residence/Gardener
281 Bloomingbank
Riverside, IL 60546, USA
EXE
(For Avery Coonley)

PR#1201
Coonley, Avery
Playhouse
350 Fairbank Road
Riverside, IL 60546, USA
EXE
(Playhouse and
Kindergarten
for Avery Coonley)

PR#1115
Cutten, Arthur E
Residence
Downer's Grove, IL, USA
PJT

PR#1109
Esbenshade, E E
Residence
Milwaukee, WI, USA
PJT

PR#1113
FLLW Goethe St
Residence/Studio
Goethe Street
Chicago, IL, USA
PJT

PR#1125
FLLW Oak Park Studio
Remodelling
Residence
951 Chicago Avenue
Oak Park, IL 60302, USA
EXE

PR#1104
FLLW Taliesin I
Residence/Studio
Route 23, Taliesin
Spring Green, WI 53588,
USA
DMD
Taliesin

PR#1114
Gerts, Walter
Remodelling
Residence
River Forest, IL, USA
PJT

PR#1202
Lake Geneva Inn
Hotel
Lake Geneva, WI, USA
DMD
(For Lake Geneva Hotel
Co/Arthur Richards/
John Williams)

PR#1110
Madison Hotel
Hotel
Madison, WI, USA
PJT
(For Arthur L Richards)

PR#1111
Porter, Andrew #2
Residence/Summer
Spring Green, WI, USA
PJT

PR#1112
Schroeder, Edward
Residence
Milwaukee, WI, USA
PJT

PR#1117
Suburban House
Residence
USA
PJT

PR#1126
Taliesin Dam and
Reservoir
Dam
Route 23, Taliesin
Spring Green, WI 53588,
USA
EXE

PR#1104
Wright, Anna Lloyd
Residence
Route 23
Spring Green, WI 53588,
USA
EXE
(Before completion changed
to Residence/Studio for
Frank Lloyd Wright:
Taliesin)

PR#1105
Adams, Harry #1
Residence
Oak Park, IL, USA
PJT

PR#1211
Booth, Sherman Stable
Stables
Glencoe, IL, USA
EXE

PR#1208
FLLW Taliesin
Cottages
Residence
Spring Green, WI, USA
PJT
(Workmen's cottages on the
Taliesin property)

PR#1305
Florida Cottage
Residence
Palm Beach, FL, USA
PJT

PR#1203
Greene, William
Residence
1300 Garfield Avenue
Aurora, IL 60506, USA
EXE

PR#1205
Kehl Dance Academy,
Residence and Shops
Educational/Shops/
Residence

Madison, WI, USA
PJT
(For Frederick W Kehl)

PR#1304
Little, Francis W
Summer House
Residence
Wayzata, MN, USA
DMD
Northome

PR#1204
Park Ridge
Country Club
Country Club
Park Ridge, IL, USA
DMD

PR#1207
Press Building
Office Tower
San Francisco, CA,
USA
PJT
(For Spreckles Estate –
The San Francisco Call)

PR#1206
School House
Educational
La Grange, IL, USA
PJT

PR#1506
Urban House
Townhouse
Milwaukee, WI, USA
PJT
(For Arthur L Richards,
American Ready-Cut
System)

PR#1301
Adams, Harry #2
Residence/Studio
710 Augusta Street
Oak Park, IL 60302,
USA
EXE

PR#1306
Carnegie Library
Library
Pembroke, ON, Canada
PJT
(In association with
Francis W Sullivan)

PR#1507
Chinese Restaurant
Restaurant
Milwaukee, WI,
USA
PJT
(For Arthur L Richards)

PR#1310
Double Residence
Residence
Ottawa, CN, USA
PJT

PR#1303
Hilly, M B
Residence
Brookfield, IL, USA
PJT

PR#1307
Kellog, W J
Residence
Milwaukee, WI, USA
PJT

PR#1308
Mendelson, Jerome
Residence
Albany, NY, USA
PJT

PR#1401
Midway Gardens
Restaurant

Cottage Grove Ave at 60th
Chicago, IL, USA
DMD
(For E C Waller,
Jr, and Oscar Friedman)

PR#1414
Midway Gardens
Dinnerware
Dinnerware
Cottage Grove Ave at 60th
Chicago, IL, USA
DMD
(For E C Waller,
Jr, and Oscar Friedman)

PR#1311
Post Office
Post Office
Ottawa, ON, Canada
PJT

PR#1312
Richards Company
Office Bldg
Office Building
Milwaukee, WI, USA
PJT
(For Arthur L Richards)

PR#1406
Embassy for the USA
Embassy
Tokyo, Japan
PJT

PR#1410
Farmers and
Merchants Bank
Bank
Spring Green, WI, USA
PJT

PR#1403
FLLW Taliesin II
Residence/Studio
Route 23, Taliesin
Spring Green, WI, USA
DMD
Taliesin

PR#1409
Imperial Hotel #1
Hotel
Tokyo, Japan
PJT
(For the Imperial Hotel
Company, Baron Okura
Chairman of the Board)

PR#1404
Jaxon, Honore 3
Residences
Residence
USA
PJT

PR#1515
Kiosk Park Feature
Park Features
Ottawa, ON, Canada
PJT

PR#1402
Mori Oriental Art Shop
Shop
Fine Arts Building
Chicago, IL, USA
DMD
(For S H Mori)

PR#1902
Spaulding Gallery
for Japanese Prints
Gallery
Boston, MA, USA
PJT
(For William and
John T Spaulding)

PR#1413
Spring Green Fairground
Women's Bldg
Fair

Spring Green, WI, USA
DMD

PR#1405
State Bank of S Green
Bank
Spring Green, WI, USA
PJT

PR#1408
Unassigned, V 1407
USA

PR#1407
Vogelsang Dinner
Gardens
Restaurant/Hotel
Chicago, IL, USA
PJT
(Possibly an earlier version
of Midway Gardens, with
hotel)

PR#1506
American Homes
Townhouse
Housing
Milwaukee, WI, USA
PJT
(For Richards Brothers,
American Ready-Cut
System)

PR#1501
Bach, Emil
Residence
7415 Sheridan Road
Chicago, IL 60626, USA
EXE

PR#2005
Barnsdall Olive Hill
Theatre
Theatre
Los Angeles, CA, USA
PJT
(For Aline Barnsdall;
scheme revised through 1920)

PR#1502
Booth, Sherman #2
Residence
265 Sylvan Road
Glencoe, IL 60022, USA
EXE

PR#1503
Brigham, E D
Residence
790 Sheridan Road
Glencoe, IL 60022, USA
EXE

PR#1510
Chinese Hospital
Hospital
USA
PJT
(For The Rockefeller
Foundation)

PR#1512
Christian Catholic
Church #2
Religious
Zion, IL, USA
PJT

PR#0517
Cinema San Diego
Cinema
San Diego, CA, USA
PJT

PR#1504
German, A D Warehouse
Warehouse
316 S Church Street
Richland Center, WI 53581,
USA
EXE

PR#1509
Imperial Hotel #2

Hotel
Tokyo, Japan
DMD
*(For the Imperial Hotel
Company, Baron Okura
Chairman of the Board)*

PR#1517
**Imperial Hotel Oya
Carvings**
Sculpture
Tokyo, Japan
DMD
*(For the Imperial Hotel
Company, Baron Okura
Chairman of the Board)*

PR#1513
Lake Shore Residence
Residence
USA
PJT

PR#1508
Model Quarter Section
Block Plan
Chicago, IL, USA
PJT

PR#1505
Ravine Bluffs Bridge
Bridge
Sylvan Road
Glencoe, IL 60022, USA
EXE
(For Sherman Booth)

PR#1516
Ravine Bluffs Housing
Housing
1023 Meadow Road
Glencoe, IL 60022,
USA
EXE
(For Sherman Booth)

PR#1516
Ravine Bluffs Housing
Housing
1027 Meadow Road
Glencoe, IL 60022, USA
EXE
(For Sherman Booth)

PR#1516
Ravine Bluffs Housing
Housing
1030 Meadow Road
Glencoe, IL 60022, USA
EXE
(For Sherman Booth)

PR#1516
Ravine Bluffs Housing
Housing
1031 Meadow Road
Glencoe, IL 60022, USA
EXE
(For Sherman Booth)

PR#1516
Ravine Bluffs Housing
Housing
*272 Sylvan Road
Glencoe, IL 60022, USA
EXE*
(For Sherman Booth)

PR#1511
Wood, M W
Residence
*Decatur, IL, USA
PJT*

1916 **PR#1701**
Allen, Henry J
Residence
*255 N Roosevelt Blvd
Wichita, KS 67208, USA
EXE*

PR#1601
Bagley, Joseph
Residence

*47017 Lakeview Avenue
Grand Beach, MI 49117,
USA
EXE*

PR#1608
Behn (Voight)
Residence
*Grand Beach, MI, USA
PJT*

PR#1602
Bogk, F C
Residence
*2420 N Terrace Avenue
Milwaukee, WI 53211,
USA
EXE*

PR#1603
Carr, W S
Residence
*46039 Lakeview Avenue
Grand Beach, MI 49117,
USA
EXE*

PR#1609
Converse, Clarence
Residence
Palisades Park, MI, USA
PJT

PR#1514
**Imperial Hotel China
(2 Designs)**
Dinnerware
Tokyo, Japan
EXE
*(Cabaret and main
dining room)*

PR#1611
**Imperial Hotel
Power House**
Hotel
Tokyo, Japan
PJT

PR#1605
**Munkwitz Duplex
Apartments**
Apartments/Duplex
1837 S Layton Blvd
Milwaukee, WI, USA
DMD
*(For Arthur Munkwitz,
American Ready-Cut
System)*

PR#1606
**Richards Company
Duplex Apartments**
Apartments/Duplex
2720–34 W Burnham Blvd
Milwaukee, WI 53215, USA
EXE
*(For Richards Brothers,
American Ready-Cut
System)*

PR#1506
**Richards Company
Small House**
Housing
1835 S Layton Blvd
Milwaukee, WI 53215,
USA
EXE
*(For Richards Brothers,
American Ready-Cut
System)*

PR#1506
**Richards Company
Small House**
Housing
2714 W Burnham Blvd
Milwaukee, WI 53215,
USA
EXE
*(For Richards Brothers
American Ready-Cut
System)*

PR#1607
Vosburgh, Ernest
Residence
46208 Crescent Road
Grand Beach, MI 49117,
USA
EXE

PR#1610
White, William Allen
Residence
Emporia, KS, USA
PJT

1917 **PR#1506**
**American Homes
2 Story**
Housing
10410 S Hoyne Avenue
Chicago, IL 60643, USA
EXE
*(For Richards Brothers
American Ready-Cut
System)*

PR#1506
**American Homes
2 Story**
Housing
10541 S Hoyne Avenue
Chicago, IL 60643, USA
EXE
*(For Richards Brothers
American Ready-Cut
System)*

PR#1506
**American Homes
2 Story**
Housing
2614 Lincolnwood
Evanston, IL 60201, USA
EXE
*(For Richards Brothers
American Ready-Cut
System)*

PR#1506
**American Homes
Bungalow**
Housing
330 Gregory Street
Wilmette, IL 60091, USA
EXE
*(For Richards Brothers
American Ready-Cut
System)*

PR#1506
**American Homes
Bungalow**
Housing
231 Prospect Avenue
Lake Bluff, IL 60044,
USA
EXE
*(For Richards Brothers
American Ready-Cut
System)*

PR#1705
Barnsdall, Aline
Residence
4808 Hollywood Blvd
Los Angeles, CA 90027,
USA
EXE
Hollyhock House

PR#1801
Fukuhara Arinobu
Residence
Hakone, Japan
DMD

PR#1702
Hayashi, Aizaku
Residence
Setagay-U
Tokyo, Japan
EXE

PR#1703
Hunt, Stephen M B

Residence
1165 Algoma Blvd
Oshkosh, WI 54901, USA
EXE

PR#1707
Powell, William
Residence
Wichita, KS, USA
PJT

1918 **PR#1804**
**Inoue, Viscount
Tadashiro**
Residence
Tokyo, Japan
PJT

PR#1807
Mihara
Residence
Tokyo, Japan
PJT

PR#1805
Motion Picture Theatre
Cinema
Tokyo, Japan
PJT

PR#1803
Yamamura, Tazaemon
Residence
Yamate-Cho
Ashiya, Japan
EXE

1919 **PR#1901**
Monolith Homes
Housing
Racine, WI, USA
PJT
(For Thomas P Hardy)

PR#1903
Shampay, G P
Residence
Chicago, IL, USA
PJT

PR#1904
Wenatchee Town Plan
Town Plan
Wenatchee, WA, USA
PJT

1920 **PR#2001**
**Automobile with
Cantilevered Top**
Automobile
USA
PJT

PR#2002
Barnsdall Residence A
Residence
4808 Hollywood Blvd
Los Angeles, CA 90027,
USA
EXE
(For Aline Barnsdall)

PR#2003
Barnsdall Residence B
Residence
4808 Hollywood Blvd
Los Angeles, CA 90027,
USA
DMD
(For Aline Barnsdall)

PR#2012
FLLW Tokyo Studio
Residence/Studio
Tokyo, Japan
EXE
*(For Frank Lloyd Wright,
Tokyo)*

PR#1604
Imperial Hotel Annex
Hotel
Tokyo, Japan
DMD

*(For the Imperial Hotel
Company, Baron Okura
Chairman of the Board)*
(FLLW APT)

PR#2013
Irving, James B House
Residence
1320 Isabella Street
Wilmette, IL, USA
PJT

PR#2007
Motion Picture Theatre
Cinema
Los Angeles, CA, USA
PJT
*(For Aline Barnsdall,
Olive Hill)*

PR#2011
Olive Hill Alphabet
Graphics
Los Angeles, CA, USA
EXE
*(Graphics on folders for
Olive Hill projects for Aline
Barnsdall)*

PR#2010
**Porter, Andrew
Remodelling**
Residence
Chicago, IL, USA
PJT

PR#2008
Staley, C R
Residence
Waukegan, IL, USA
PJT

PR#2006
Taliesin Hydro House
Hydro Plant
Route 23, Taliesin
Spring Green, WI 53588,
USA
DMD
(For Lower Dam at Taliesin)

1921 **PR#2109**
Department Store
Department Store
Tokyo, Japan
PJT
*(In association with Arata
Endo)*

PR#2105
Goto, Baron
Residence
Tokyo, Japan
PJT

PR#2101
Jiyu Gakuen School
Educational
31 Nishi Ikebukuro, Japan
EXE
*(In association with Arata
Endo)*

PR#2133
Poster Design/Japan
Graphics
Takashimaya
Tokyo, TO, Japan
EXE

1922 **PR#2009**
Barnsdall, Aline
Residence
Beverly Hills, CA, USA
PJT

PR#2206
Butterfly Roof House
Residence
CA, USA
PJT

PR#2201
FLLW Harper Ave

**Graphics and
Remodelling**
Graphics/Studio Rem
1284 Harper Avenue
Los Angeles, CA, USA
EXE
*(For Frank Lloyd Wright
Studio, Los Angeles)*

PR#2202
Lowes, G P
Residence
Eagle Rock, CA, USA
PJT

PR#2203
Merchandising Building
Department Store
Los Angeles, CA, USA
PJT

PR#1706
Odawara Hotel
Hotel
Odawara, Japan
PJT
*(For the Imperial Hotel
Company, Baron Okura
Chairman of the Board)*

1923 **PR#2110**
Block House
Residence
Los Angeles, CA, USA
PJT

PR#2108
Block House 2 Story
Residence
Los Angeles, CA, USA
PJT

PR#2106
**Block House,
Los Angeles Ravine**
Residence
Los Angeles, CA, USA
PJT

PR#2307
Commercial Building
Office Tower
Los Angeles, CA, USA
PJT
*(Prototype of National Life
Insurance CompanyBuilding,
Chicago)*

PR#2104
**Doheny Ranch
Development**
Housing
Los Angeles, CA, USA
PJT
*(Possibly for Edward
H Doheny)*

PR#2401
Ennis, Charles
Residence
2655 Glendower Avenue
Los Angeles, CA 90027,
USA
EXE

PR#2305
Foster, Dorothy Martin
Residence
Buffalo, NY, USA
PJT

PR#2402
Freeman, Samuel
Residence
1962 Glencoe Way
Los Angeles, CA 90028,
USA
EXE

PR#2301
**Kindergarten and
Community Theater**
Kindergarten
4808 Hollywood Blvd

Los Angeles, CA 90027,
USA
DMD
The Little Dipper
(for Aline Barnsdall,
partially built then
demolished)

PR#2302
Millard, Alice
Residence
645 Prospect Crescent
Pasadena, CA 91103, USA
EXE
La Miniatura

PR#2303
Moore, Nathan
Rebuilding
Residence
333 Forest Avenue
Oak Park, IL 60302, USA
EXE

PR#2403
Nakoma Country Club
Country Club
Madison, WI, USA
PJT

PR#2405
Nakoma Memorial
Gateway
Sculpture
Madison, WI, USA
PJT
(For the Madison Realty
Company)

PR#2304
Storer, John
Residence
8161 Hollywood Blvd
Hollywood, CA 90069,
USA
EXE

PR#2205
LakeTahoe Summer
Colony,
Resort
Lake Tahoe, CA, USA
PJT
Fallen Leaf, The Fir Tree,
The Wigwam, Emerald Inn,
For Two, Catamaran

1924 **PR#2505**
Automobile Objective
and Planetarium
Planetarium
Sugarloaf Mt, MD, USA
PJT
(For Gordon Strong)

PR#2107
FLLW Desert
Compound
Residence/Studio
Death Valley
Mohave, CA, USA
PJT

PR#2502
Gladney, Mrs Samuel
William #1
Residence
Fort Worth, TX, USA
PJT

PR#2306
Johnson
Compound/Shrine
Residence/Shrine
Grapevine Canyon,
Death Valley, CA, USA
PJT
(Dwelling; Shrine;
Guest House for Albert
M Johnson)

PR#2404
National Life
Insurance Company

Office Tower
Chicago, IL, USA
PJT
(For Albert M Johnson)

PR#2504
Phi Gamma Delta
Fraternity House
Fraternity
Madison, WI, USA
PJT

PR#2204
Sachse, Martin
Residence
Deep Springs
Mohave, CA, USA
PJT

PR#2406
Skyscraper
Office Tower
USA
PJT
(Prototype for St Mark's-
in-the-Bouwerie)

PR#2103
Study for California
Block House
Residence
Los Angeles, CA, USA
PJT

1925 **PR#2501**
FLLW Taliesin III
Residence/Studio
Route 23, Taliesin
Spring Green, WI 53588,
USA
EXE
Taliesin (Rebuilt after fire
destroyed living quarters of
Talesin 1)

PR#2508
Gladney, Mrs Samuel
William #2
Residence
Fort Worth, TX, USA
PJT

PR#2506
Herron, Mary
Remodelling
Residence
Oak Park, IL, USA
PJT

PR#2507
Republic Office
Display Window
Signs
Chicago, IL, USA
PJT
(For Gordon Strong)

1926 **PR#2602**
Broadacre City
Cathedral
Religious
USA
PJT
(Revised design from Steel
Cathedral and Commercial
Arts Festival)

PR#2602
Commercial Arts
Festival
Fair
USA
PJT
(Revised Steel Cathedral
design-V, elevation)

PR#2601
Kindersymphonies/
Oak Park Playground
Association
Playhouse
Oak Park, IL, USA
PJT
Two For A Penny; The

Goblin; Scherzo; The Ann
Baxter; The Iovanna; The
Betty Lloyd

PR#2604
Liberty Magazine
Covers
Graphics
USA
PJT
Frozen Spheres; March
Balloons; Bird in the Cage;
July 4th; Fugue; The Gifts;
Jeweler's Window

PR#2701
Martin, Isabel
Summer House
Residence
6472 Lake Shore Road
Derby, NY 14047, USA
EXE
Graycliff
(For Mrs Darwin
D Martin)

PR#2603
Skyscraper Regulation
Urban Development
USA
PJT

PR#2602
Steel Cathedral
Religious
New York, NY, USA
PJT
(For William Norman
Guthrie, revised as
Commercial Arts Festival;
then Broadacre Cathedral)

1927 **PR#2710**
Arizona Biltmore Hotel
Hotel
2701 E Arizona Biltmore
C, Phoenix, AZ 85013,
USA
EXE
(In association with Albert
Chase McArthur, architect
of record)

PR##4110
Jens Jensen Graphics
Graphics
USA
PJT
(For publication 'Friends of
our Native Landscape')

PR#2709
Jewelry Shop Window
Graphics
USA
EXE
(Related to the Liberty
Cover Graphics)

PR#2711
Ras El Bar
Resort
Damiette, Egypt
PJT

1928 **PR#2801**
Blue Sky Burial Terrace
Mausoleum
Buffalo, NY, USA
PJT
(For Darwin D Martin
family)

PR#2708
Chandler Block House
Residence
Chandler, AZ, USA
PJT
(For Dr Alexander
Chandler)

PR#2802
Colonial Equivalent
Residence

USA
PJT
(Adaptation of Chandler
Block House)

PR#2706
Cudney, Ralph and
Wellington
Residence
Chandler, AZ, USA
PJT
(Detached residence at
San Marcos-in-the-Desert)

PR#3208
Davidson Produce
Markets
Exhibition Pavilion
Exhibition
Buffalo, NY, USA
PJT
Sun, Moon, and Stars
(For Walter V Davidson)

PR#2702
FLLW Desert Camp
Residence/Studio
Chandler, AZ, USA
DMD
Ocotillo

PR#2703
Hillside Home School of
the Allied Arts
Educational
Route 23, Taliesin
Spring Green, WI, USA
PJT
(Expansion of original
Hillside Home School
buildings)

PR#2904
Rosenwald School
Educational
Hampton, VA, USA
PJT
(For Hampton College)

PR#2704
San Marcos-in-the-
Desert
Hotel
Chandler, AZ, USA
PJT
(For Dr Alexander
Chandler)

PR#2803
Wedding Announcement
Graphics
Rancho Santa Fe
La Jolla, CA, USA
PJT
(Wedding of Frank Lloyd
Wright and Olga Ivanovna,
25 August 1928)

PR#2707
Young, Mrs Owen D
Residence
Chandler, AZ, USA
PJT
(Detached residence at
San Marcos-in-the-Desert)

1929 **PR#2804**
Chandler Camp Cabins
Housing
Chandler, AZ, USA
DMD
(For Dr Alexander
Chandler)

PR#2901
Jones, Richard Lloyd #1
Residence
Tulsa, OK, USA
PJT

PR#2902
Jones, Richard Lloyd #2
Residence
3704 S Birmingham
Avenue

Tulsa, OK 74105, USA
EXE
Westhope

PR#3003
Leerdam
Glassware/Dinnerware
Dinnerware/Vases
Leerdam, Holland
PJT
(For P M Cochius, N V
Glasfabriek 'Leerdam', V H
Jeekel, Munssen & Co)

PR#2907
Millard, Alice
Residence
Prospect Crescent
Pasadena, CA, USA
PJT
(Addition to La Miniatura)

PR#2906
Nakoma Sculptures
Sculpture
Bisque Edition, USA
EXE
(Small Bisque Edition
similar to Memorial
Gateway Figures of 1924)

PR#2903
Noble, Elizabeth Apts
Apartments
Los Angeles, CA, USA
PJT
(Per Harold McCormick)

PR#3609
San Marcos
Golf Clubhouse
Clubhouse
Chandler, AZ, USA
PJT
(For Dr A Chandler)

PR#3608
San Marcos
Polo Stables
Stables
Chandler, AZ, USA
PJT
(For Dr Alexander
Chandler)

PR#2705
San Marcos
Water Gardens
Motel
Chandler, AZ, USA
PJT
(For Dr Alexander
Chandler)

PR#2905
St Mark's-in-the-
Bouwerie
Apartment Tower
New York, NY, USA
PJT
(For William Norman
Guthrie)

1930 **PR#3002**
Cabins for YMCA
Resort
Chicago, IL, USA
PJT

PR#3000
Exhibition USA
Exhibition
USA
EXE
(Layout and model stands
for exhibition / New York,
Oregon, Wisconsin, New
Jersey, Illinois)

PR#3001
Grouped Towers
Apartment Tower
Chicago, IL, USA
PJT

PR#2503
Millard, Alice
Gallery
Pasadena, CA, USA
PJT
(Addtion to La Miniatura)

1931 **PR#3101**
Capitol Journal Office
Building/Newspaper
Plant
Office/Newspaper Plant
Salem, OR, USA
PJT
(For George Putnam)

PR#3103
Century of Progress
Fair
Chicago, IL, USA
PJT
(Three designs for the 1933
Chicago World's Fair
'Century of Progress')

PR#3100
Exhibition Europe
Exhibition
Europe
EXE
(Model stands, layouts:
Holland, Germany and
Belgium)

PR#3104
From Generation
to Generation
Graphics
Longmans
Longmans Green, NY,
USA
EXE
(For An Autobiography,
1932 edition)

PR#3102
House on the Mesa
Residence
Denver, CO, USA
PJT
(For George Cranmer and
the Museum of Modern Art)

PR#3106
New Theatre (3 schemes)
Theatre
Woodstock, NY, USA
PJT

PR#3105
Roadside Filling Station
Service Station
USA
PJT

1932 **PR#3203**
Cinema and Shops
Cinema/Shops
Michigan City, IN, USA
PJT
(In association with
John Lloyd Wright)

PR#3201
Conventional House
Residence
USA
PJT
(Adaptation of Chandler
Block House)

PR#3304
Fly Craft Studio
Factory
Madison, WI, USA
PJT
(For Dr Samuel L Chase)

PR#3210
Motor Car/Aeroplane
Filling Station Device
Service Station
USA
PJT

PR#3207
Norm of the Prefab
House
Residence
USA
PJT

PR#3205
Prefabricated Sheet
Steel and Glass Markets
Market
USA
PJT
(For Walter V Davidson)

PR#3202
Prefabricated Sheet
Steel Farm Units
Farm
USA
PJT
(For Walter V Davidson)

PR#3206
Standardized Gas
Station
Service Station
USA
PJT
(Also known as
Standardized Overhead
Service Station)

PR#3211
Taliesin Brochure
Graphics
Route 23, Taliesin
Spring Green, WI 53588,
USA
EXE
(For the Taliesin
Fellowship)

PR#3301
Taliesin Fellowship
Complex
Educational
Route 23, Taliesin
Spring Green, WI 53588,
USA
EXE
(Alterations and additions to
original Hillside Home
School Buildings)

PR#3204
Willey, Malcolm #1
Residence
Minneapolis, MN, USA
PJT

PR#3209
Chicagoan Magazine
Graphics
Chicago, IL, USA
PJT

PR#3305
Hillside Furnishings
Furniture
Route 23, Taliesin
Spring Green, WI 53588,
USA
EXE
(For the Taliesin Fellowship
Complex interiors)

PR#3303
Hillside Playhouse #1
Theatre
Route 23, Taliesin
Spring Green, WI, USA
DMD
(Alteration of Hillside
Home School Gymnasium)

PR#3302
Hillside Theatre
Curtain #1
Textiles
Route 23, Taliesin
Spring Green, WI, USA
DMD

PR#3401
Willey, Malcolm #2
Residence
255 Bedford St SE
Minneapolis, MN 55416,
USA
EXE

PR#3411
Arena
Arena
USA
PJT
(For Broadacre City)

PR#3417
Ball Park
Ball Park
USA
PJT
(For Broadacre City)

PR#3402
Broadacre City
Master Plan
City Plan
USA
PJT
Broadacre City

PR#3406
Broadacre City Model
City Plan
Route 23, Taliesin
Spring Green, WI 53588,
USA
EXE

PR#3418
Cathedral and
Columbarium
Religious/Burial
USA
PJT
(For Broadacre City)

PR#3710
Chapel in
Cast Concrete
Chapel
Cooksville, WI, USA
PJT
(For the Newmann Family)
Memorial Chapel
'To the Soil' FLLW

PR#3415
Community Center
Civic Center
USA
PJT
(For Broadacre City)

PR#3410
County Office Building
Office Tower
USA
PJT
(For Broadacre City)

PR#3414
Education Center
Educational
USA
PJT
(For Broadacre City)

PR#3419
Highway Lighting
Roadway
USA
PJT
(For Broadacre City)

PR#3407
Highway Overpass
Bridge
USA
PJT
(For Broadacre City)

PR#3422
Hillside Hangings
Fabrics/Graphics

Route 23, Taliesin
Spring Green, WI 53588,
USA
EXE
(For the Taliesin
Fellowship Complex)

PR#3403
Hillside Living
Room Rug
Carpets
Route 23, Taliesin
Spring Green, WI 53588,
USA
PJT
Four Seasons (For the
Taliesin Fellowship
Complex)

PR#3404
Hillside Murals
Mural
Route 23, Taliesin
Spring Green, WI 53588,
USA
DMD
(For the Taliesin
Fellowship Complex)

PR#3409
Hospital Group
Hospital
USA
PJT
(For Broadacre City)

PR#3408
Houses
Housing
USA
PJT
(For Broadacre City)

PR#3413
Industrial Park
Factory
USA
PJT
(For Broadacre City)

PR#3412
Little Factory
USA
PJT
(For Broadacre City)

PR#3405
Machine Age Screen
Mural
Machine Age Screen

PR#3416
Stable and Polo Field
Clubhouse
USA
PJT
(For Broadacre City)

PR#3420
Taliesin Farmlands
Landscape
Route 23, Taliesin
Srping Green, WI 53588,
USA
EXE

PR#3504
German Warehouse
Remodelling
Warehouse
Richland Center, WI, USA
PJT
(For A D German)

PR#3701
Hanna, Paul and Jean
Residence
737 Frenchman's Road
Stanford, CA 94305, USA
EXE
Honeycomb House

PR#3602
Kaufmann, Edgar J

Residence
State Highway 381
Mill Run, PA 15464, USA
EXE
Fallingwater

PR#3505
Marcus Housing
Housing
Dallas, TX, USA
PJT
(For Stanley Marcus)

PR#3501
Marcus, Stanley
Residence
Dallas, TX, USA
PJT

PR#3502
Zoned Houses
Housing
USA
PJT
(Designs for Houses for
City, Suburbs, and
Country)

PR#3610
Hillside Gatehouse
Gatehouse
Taliesin
Spring Green, WI, USA
PJT
(For the Taliesin Fellowship
Complex)

PR#3611
Hillside Roadsign
Educational
Taliesin
Spring Green, WI, USA
PJT
(For the Taliesin Fellowship
Complex)

PR#3604
Hoult, C H
Residence
Wichita, KS, USA
PJT

PR#3702
Jacobs, Herbert #1
Residence
441 Toepfer Street
Madison, WI 53711, USA
EXE

PR#3601
Johnson Wax
Administration
Building
Office Building
1525 Howe Street
Racine, WI 53403, USA
EXE
(For the S C Johnson &
Son Company)

PR#3606
Little San Marcos
Resort
Chandler, AZ, USA
PJT
(For Dr A Chandler)

PR#3605
Lusk, Robert
Residence
Huron, SD, USA
PJT

PR#3603
Roberts, Abby Beecher
Residence
County Highway 492
Marquette, MI 49855,
USA
EXE
Deertrack

PR#3607
San Marcos Hotel

Remodelling
Hotel
Chandler, AZ, USA
PJT
(For Dr Alexander
Chandler)

PR#3708
Borglum, Gutzon
Studio
Santa Barbara, CA, USA
PJT

PR#3706
Bramson Dress Shop
Shop/Residence
Oak Park, IL, USA
PJT
(For Leo Bramson)

PR#3715
FLLW Desert Shelter
Residence/Studio
Taliesin West
Scottsdale, AZ 85261
DMD
(Temporary Camp for
Taliesin Fellowship at site
of Taliesin West)

PR#3709
FLLW Sleeping Boxes
Residence
Taliesin West
Scottsdale, AZ, USA
DMD
Sleeping Boxes (Temporary
Residence for Frank Lloyd
Wright and Family;
see Sun Trap)

PR#3709
FLLW Sun Trap
Residence
Taliesin West
Scottsdale, AZ, USA
DMD
The Sun Trap (Temporary
Residence for Frank Lloyd
Wright and Family)

PR#3803
FLLW Taliesin West
Residence/Studio
Taliesin West
Scottsdale, AZ 85261, USA
EXE
Taliesin West

PR#3703
Johnson, Herbert F
Residence
33 E Four Mile
Wind Point, WI 53402,
USA
EXE
Wingspread

PR#3704
Kaufmann, Edgar J
Office Remodelling
Pittsburgh, PA, USA
DMD
(For office in Kaufmann's
Department Store, now at
Victoria & Albert Museum,
London)

PR#3707
Parker, George
Garage
Janesville, WI, USA
PJT

PR#3801
Rebhuhn, Ben
Residence
9A Myrtle Avenue
Great Neck Estates, NY
11021, USA
EXE

PR#3714
Steelcase-Johnson Wax

Furniture
Furniture
1525 Howe Street
Racine, WI, USA
EXE
(Office Furniture for the
Administration Building for
the S C Johnson & Son
Company)

PR#3712
Wright, Frances
Gift Booth
USA
PJT
(Frances Wright was
daughter of Frank Lloyd
Wright)

PR#3705
All Steel Houses
Housing
Los Angeles, CA, USA
PJT
(For Harold Espey)

PR#3906
Ardmore Suntop Houses
Housing
152–8 Sutton Road
Ardmore, PA 19003, USA
EXE
The Ardmore Experiment
(For the Todd Company,
Otto Mallery)

PR#3802
Barns and Farm
Farm
Route 23, Taliesin
Spring Green, WI 53588,
USA
EXE
Midway (for the Taliesin
Fellowship Complex Farm
Buildings)

PR#3908
Bell, L N
Residence
Los Angeles, CA, USA
PJT

PR#3814
FSC Block Details
Educational
111 Lake Hollingsworth Dr
Lakeland, FL 33801, USA
EXE
(Florida Southern College)

PR#3805
FSC Master Plan
Educational
111 Lake Hollingsworth Dr
Lakeland, FL 33801, USA
EXE
(Florida Southern College)

PR#3816
FSC Pfeiffer Chapel
Religious
111 Lake Hollingsworth
Dr, Lakeland, FL 33801,
USA
EXE
(Florida Southern College)

PR#3817
FSC Theatre
Theatre
Lakeland, FL, USA
PJT
(Florida Southern College)

PR#3807
Jester, Ralph
Residence
Palos Verdes, CA, USA
PJT

PR#3808
Johnson, Herbert F
Gatehouse

Wind Point, WI, USA
PJT
*(For entrance to
Wingspread)*

PR#3815
Johnson, Herbert F
Farm
Wind Point, WI, USA
PJT
(For farm at Wingspread)

PR#3809
Jurgenson, Royal
Residence
Evanston, IL, USA
PJT
*(Revision of the norm of
the Prefabricated House)*

PR#3812
**Kaufmann,
Edgar J Guest House**
Residence
Fallingwater
Mill Run, PA 15464, USA
EXE
Fallingwater

PR#3806
Life House for $5000
Residence
Minneapolis, MN, USA
PJT
*(For Life Magazine,
26 September 1938)*

PR#4009
Manson, Charles
Residence
1224 Highland Park Blvd
Wausau, WI 54401, USA
EXE

PR#3810
McCallum, George Bliss
Residence
Northampton, MA, USA
PJT

PR#3909
**Monona Terrace
Civic Center #1**
Civic Center
Madison, WI, USA
PJT

PR#4012
Pew, John C
Residence
3650 Mendota Drive
Shorewood Hills, WI
53705, USA
EXE

PR#3813
**Standard Usonian
Details**
Residence
USA
EXE
*(Instructions and drawings
for Usonian Houses details)*

PR#3901
Armstrong, Andrew F H
Residence
43 Cedar Trail
Ogden Dunes, IN 46368,
USA
EXE

PR#3920
Bantam Remodelling
Automobile
USA
EXE
*Dinky Diner (Travelling
Kitchen Unit for the
Taliesin Fellowship)*

PR#4002
Bazett, Sydney
Residence

101 Reservoir Road
Hillsborough, CA 94010,
USA
EXE

PR#4032
Bazett, Sydney
Residence
Hillsborough, CA,
USA
PJT
('Fir Tree' Type)

PR#3918
Brauner, Erling #1
Residence
Lansing, MI, USA
PJT

PR#3804
Carlson, Edith
Residence
Superior, WI, USA
PJT
Below Zero

PR#4016
Crystal Heights
Hotel/Shops/Theatre
Washington, DC, USA
PJT
*Crystal Heights (For Roy
Thurmond: hotel, shops,
theatre)*

PR#4005
Euchtman, Joseph
Residence
6804 Cross Country Blvd
Baltimore, MD 21215,
USA
EXE

PR#3922
**FSC Dormitory/
Faculty Housing**
Residence
Lakeland, FL, USA
PJT
(Florida Southern College)

PR#3917
Garrison, J J
Residence
Lansing, MI, USA
PJT

PR#3907
Goetsch-Winckler #1
Residence
2410 Hulett Road
Okemos, MI 48864, USA
EXE
*(Alma Goetsch and
Kathrine Winckler)*

PR#3914
Hause, C D
Residence
Lansing, MI, USA
PJT

PR#3919
Kaufmann, Edgar J
Residence
Pittsburgh, PA, USA
PJT
*(Usonian House-: See 'Life'
House, and Schwartz
House)*

PR#4008
Lewis, Lloyd
Residence
153 Little St Mary's Road
Libertyville, IL 60048,
USA
EXE

PR#3923
Lowenstein, Gordon
Residence
Cincinnati, OH, USA
PJT

PR#3910
Mauer, Edgar
Residence
Los Angeles, CA, USA
PJT

PR#3915
Newman, Sydney
Residence
Lansing, MI, USA
PJT

PR#3916
Panshin, Alexis
Residence
Lansing, MI, USA
PJT

PR#4011
Pauson, Rose
Residence
Phoenix, AZ, USA
DMD

PR#4013
Pope, Loren
Residence
9000 Richmond Hwy
Alexandria, VA 22309, USA
*(Located on woodland
plantation)*

PR#4020
Rentz, Frank
Residence
Madison, WI, USA
PJT

PR#3903
Rosenbaum, Stanley
Residence
601 Riverview Drive
Florence, AL 35630, USA
EXE

PR#3904
Schwartz, Bernard
Residence
3425 Adams
Two Rivers, WI 54241,
USA
EXE
*(Based on The Life House,
1938)*

PR#3811
Smith, E A
Residence
Piedmont Pines, CA, USA
PJT

PR#4014
Sondern, Clarence
Residence
3600 Belleview Avenue
Kansas City, MO 64111,
USA
EXE

PR#3911
Spivey, Dr Ludd M
Residence
Fort Lauderdale, FL, USA
PJT

PR#4015
Stevens, Leigh
Plantation
7 River Road
Yemassee, SC 29945, USA
EXE
Auldbrass

PR#4024
Stevens, Leigh
Residence
7 River Road
Yemassee, SC 29945, USA
PJT
Auldbrass (Guest House)

PR#4025
Stevens, Leigh
Residence

7 River Road
Yemassee, SC 29945, USA
EXE
*Auldbrass (Caretaker's
House)*

PR#4026
Stevens, Leigh
Residence
7 River Road
Yemassee, SC 29945, USA
EXE
*Auldbrass (Housekeeper's
House)*

PR#4027
Stevens, Leigh
Stables
7 River Road
Yemassee, SC 29945, USA
EXE
Auldbrass (Stables. kennels)

PR#4028
Stevens, Leigh
Farm
7 River Road
Yemassee, SC 29945, USA
EXE
Auldbrass (Farm building)

PR#4029
Stevens, Leigh
Residence
7 River Road
Yemassee, SC 29945, USA
PJT
Auldbrass (Small cabin)

PR#4030
Stevens, Leigh
Residence
7 River Road
Yemassee, SC 29945, USA
PJT
Auldbrass (Cabin)

PR#3905
Sturges, George
Residence
449 Skyeway Drive,
Brentwood Heights,
CA 90049, USA
EXE

PR#3921
Taliesin Front Gates
Gates
Route 23, Taliesin, Spring
Green, WI 53588, USA
PJT

PR#3912
Usonia I Master Plan
Housing
Lansing, MI, USA
PJT

PR#3902
Van Dusen, C R
Residence
Lansing, MI, USA
PJT

PR#4111
Affleck, Gregor #1
Residence
1925 N Woodward Avenue
Bloomfield Hills,
MI 48013, USA
EXE

PR#4001
Baird, Theodore
Residence
38 Shays Street
Amherst, MA 01002, USA
EXE

PR#4033
Christie, James #1
Residence
Bernardsville, NJ, USA
PJT

PR#4003
Christie, James #2
Residence
190 Jockey Hollow Road
Bernardsville, NJ 07924,
USA
EXE

PR#4004
**Community Christian
Church**
Religious
4601 Main Street
Kansas City, MO 64112,
USA
EXE

PR#4000
**Exhibition Layout for
MoMA 1940**
Exhibition
Museum of Modern Art
NY, NY, USA
EXE
*(Museum of Modern Art,
New York – FLLW
Exhibition)*

PR#4031
FSC Seminar Buildings
Educational
111 Lake Hollingsworth Dr
Lakeland, FL 33801, USA
EXE
(Florida Southern College)

PR#3711
Kaufmann, Edgar J
Farm
Fallingwater
Mill Run, PA, USA
PJT

PR#3713
Kaufmann, Edgar J
Gatehouse
Fallingwater
Mill Run, PA, USA
PJT

PR#4010
Model House for MoMA
Residence
Museum of Modern Art
New York, NY, USA
PJT
*(Museum of Modern Art
FLLW Exhibition)*

PR#4017
Nesbitt, John
Residence
Carmel, CA, USA
PJT
Stoneweb

PR#4018
Oboler, Arch
Residence
32436 W Mulholland Hwy
Malibu, CA, USA
PJT
Eaglefeather

PR#4112
Oboler, Arch
Residence
32436 W Mulholland Hwy
Malibu, CA 90265, USA
EXE
Eleanor's Retreat

PR#4112
Oboler, Arch
Gatehouse
32436 W Mulholland Hwy
Malibu, CA 90265, USA
EXE

PR#4019
Pence, Martin #1
Residence
Hilo, HA, USA
PJT

PR#4007
Pence, Martin #2
Residence
Hilo, HA, USA
PJT

PR#4022
Taliesin Magazine
Graphics
Route 23, Taliesin
Spring Green, WI 53588,
USA
EXE

PR#4210
Terrace Furniture
Furniture
Taliesin West
Scottsdale, AZ, USA
PJT
Slumber Bus

PR#4021
Watkins, Franklin
Residence/Studio
Barnegat City, NJ, USA
PJT
Windswept

PR#4106
Barton, John
Residence
Pine Bluff, WI, USA
PJT

PR#4101
Dayer, Walter
Music Studio
Detroit, MI, USA
PJT

PR#4102
Ellinwood, Alfred
Residence
Deerfield, IL, USA
PJT

PR#4103
Field, Parker B
Residence
Peru, IL, USA
PJT

PR#4118
FSC Roux Library
Library
111 Lake Hollingsworth Dr
Lakeland, FL 33801, USA
EXE
(Florida Southern college)

PR#4115
Guenther, William
Residence
East Caldwell, NJ,
USA
PJT

PR#4117
Horlick-Racine Airport
Airport Lounge
Racine, WI, USA
PJT

PR#4119
**Nesbitt, John
Remodelling**
Residence
2655 Glendower Avenue
Los Angeles, CA, USA
PJT
*Sijistan
(Remodelling of the
Ennis House)*

PR#4116
Peterson, Roy
Residence
Racine, WI, USA
PJT

PR#4104
Richardson, Stuart
Residence

63 Chestnut Hill Place
Glen Ridge, NJ 07028,
USA
EXE

PR#4107
Schevill, Margaret
Residence
Tucson, AZ, USA
PJT

PR#4023
Scott Radio Cabinets
Furniture
USA
PJT
Portable Music Machine

PR#4108
Sigma Chi Fraternity House
Fraternity
Hanover, IN, USA
PJT

PR#4105
Sundt, Vigo
Residence
Madison, WI, USA
PJT

PR#4114
Wall, Carl
Residence
12305 Beck Road
Plymouth, MI 48170, USA
EXE
Snowflake

PR#4109
Waterstreet, Mary
Residence/Studio
Spring Green, WI, USA
PJT

1942 **PR#4202**
Burlingham, Lloyd
Residence
El Paso, TX, USA
PJT
Pottery House

PR#4205
Circle Pines Resort
Resort
Cloverdale, MI, USA
PJT

PR#4201
Co-Operative Homesteads
Housing
Detroit, MI, USA
PJT

PR#4204
Foreman, Clark
Residence
Washington, DC, USA
PJT

PR#4212
FSC Industrial Arts Building
Educational
111 Lake Hollingsworth
Drive
Lakeland, FL 33801, USA
EXE
(Florida Southern College)

PR#4206
Lincoln Continental Remodelling
Auto Remodelling
USA
EXE
(For Frank Lloyd Wright)

PR#4209
Miller, Dr Robert S
Residence
Fremont, OH, USA
PJT

PR#4207
Pittsfield Defense Plant
Factory
Pittsfield, MA, USA
PJT

PR#4203
Quadruple Housing
Housing
Pittsfield, MA, USA
PJT
Cloverleaf
(For the FHA, Clark Foreman)

PR#4213
Schwartz, Bernard
Boathouse
Two Rivers, WI, USA
PJT

PR#4113
Sturges, George
Additions
Residence
Los Angeles, CA, USA
PJT

PR#4208
Wall, Carl
Farm
Plymouth, MI, USA
PJT

PR#4208
Wall, Carl
Gatehouse
Plymouth, MI, USA
PJT

PR#4214
Wall, Carl
Mural
Plymouth, MI, USA
PJT

1943 **PR#4211**
FSC Music Building #1
Educational
Lakeland, FL, USA
PJT
(Florida Southern College)

PR#4305
Guggenheim, Solomon R
Museum
1071 Fifth Avenue
New York, NY 10128,
USA
EXE
(The Solomon R Guggenheim Museum)

PR#4301
Hein, M N
Residence
Chipewa Falls, WI, USA
PJT

PR#4307
Jacobs, Herbert
Residence
Middleton, WI, USA
PJT
(Proposed use of M N Hein Design)

PR#4308
Lewis, Lloyd
Farm
153 Little St Mary's Road
Libertyville, IL 60048,
USA
EXE

PR#4306
Richardson, Glen
Service Station/Restaurant
Spring Green, WI, USA
PJT
(Service Station and Restaurant)

1944 **PR#4405**
FSC Whitney Memorial
Educational
Lakland, FL, USA
PJT
(Florida Southern College)

PR#4510
Glass House
Residence
USA
PJT
Opus 497 – The Glass House
(For Ladies Home Journal)

PR#4403
Harlan, P K
Residence
Omaha, NE, USA
PJT

PR#4406
Hillside Theatre Foyer
Theatre
Route 23, Taliesin, Spring
Green, WI 53588, USA
EXE

PR#4812
Jacobs, Herbert
Residence
3995 Shawn Trail
Middleton, WI 53562,
USA
EXE
The Solar Hemicycle

PR#4401
Johnson Wax Research Tower
Office Tower
1525 Howe Street
Racine, WI 53403, USA
EXE
Helio Laboratory
(S C Johnson & Son Company)

PR#4511
Loeb, Gerald M
Residence
Redding, CT, USA
PJT
Tenaya East

PR#4404
Midway Barns/Farm Cottage
Farm/Farmhouse
Route 23, Taliesin
Spring Green, WI 53588,
USA
EXE

1945 **PR#4507**
Adelman, Benjamin
Laundry
Milwaukee, WI, USA
PJT

PR#4506
Arden, Elizabeth
Spa
Phoenix, AZ, USA
PJT
Sunlight/Moonlight

PR#4501
Berdan, George
Residence
Ludington, MI, USA
PJT

PR#4515
Dana, Malcolm
Residence
Olivet, MI, USA
PJT

PR#4823
Daphne, Nicholas
Mortuary
San Francisco, CA, USA

PJT
(Funeral Chapels)

PR#4512
Friedman, Arnold
Residence
Highway 63
Pecos, NM 87552, USA
EXE
The Fir Tree

PR#4515
FSC Administration Bldg
Office Building
111 Lake Hollingsworth
Dr
Lakeland, FL 33801, USA
EXE
(Florida Southern College)

PR#4710
Grieco, Vito
Residence
Andover, MA, USA
PJT

PR#4502
Haldorn, Stuart
Residence
Carmel, CA, USA
PJT
The Wave

PR#4736
Hillside Garden Contours
Landscape
Route 23, Taliesin
Spring Green, WI 53588,
USA
EXE

PR#4302
McDonald, T L
Residence
Washington, DC, USA
PJT

PR#4303
Morris, V C #1
Residence
San Francisco, CA, USA
PJT
Seacliff

PR#4811
Prout, George
Residence
Columbus, IN, USA
PJT

PR#4513
Stamm, John David
Residence/Boathouse
Lake Delavan, WI, USA
PJT

Taliesin Upper Dam
Dam
Route 23, Taliesin, Spring
Green, WI 53588, USA
EXE

PR#4505
Walter, Lowell
Residence
Cedar Rock Park
Quasqueton, IA 52326,
USA
EXE
Cedar Rock

PR#4402
Wells, Stuart
Residence
Minneapolis, MN, USA
PJT

PR#4718
Wheeler, Frank
Residence
Hinsdale, IL, USA
PJT

1946 **PR#4801**
Adelman, Albert #1
Residence
Fox Point, WI, USA
PJT

PR#4834
Adelman, Albert #2
Residence
7111 N Barnett, Fox
Point, WI 53214, USA
EXE

PR#4703
Alpaugh, Amy
Residence
71 N Pearson Park Road
Northport, MI 49690,
USA
EXE

PR#4508
Calico Mills Store
Department Store
Amedabad, India,
PJT
(For Gautam Sarabhai)

PR#4807
Dayer, Walter
Music Studio
Bloomfield Hills, MI, USA
PJT
Music Pavilion

PR#4809
Feenberg, Ben
Residence
Fox Point, WI, USA
PJT

PR#3814
FSC Esplanades
Educational
111 Lake Hollingsworth
Dr
Lakeland, FL 33801, USA
EXE
(Florida Southern College)

PR#4611
FSC Music Building #2
Educational
Lakeland, FL, USA
PJT
(Florida Southern College)

PR#4835
FSC Water Dome
Landscape
111 Lake Hollingsworth
Dr
Lakeland, FL 33801, USA
(Florida Southern College)

PR#4612
Furniture – Recent
Furniture
USA
EXE

PR#4503
Grant, Douglas
Residence
3400 Adel Drive S E
Cedar Rapids, IA 52403,
USA
EXE

PR#4604
Griggs, Chauncey
Residence
7800 John Dower S W
Tacoma, WA 98467, USA
EXE

PR#4607
Hanna, Paul and Jean Additions
Residence
737 Frenchman's Road
Stanford, CA 94305, USA
EXE
Honeycomb House

PR#4610
Hillside Gate Lodge
Gatehouse
Taliesin
Spring Green, WI, USA
PJT

PR#4605
Home Building Revision
Educational
Route 23, Taliesin, Spring
Green, WI 53588, USA
DMD
(For the Taliesin Fellowship Complex)

PR#4606
Lacy, Rogers
Hotel
Dallas, TX, USA
PJT
(Rogers Lacy Hotel)

PR#5016
Miller, Dr Alvin
Residence
1107 Court Street
Charles City, IA 50616,
USA
EXE

PR#5016
Miller, Drs Alvin & William
Medical Clinic
Charles City, IA, USA
PJT

PR#4914
Mossberg, Herman T
Residence
1404 Ridgedale Road
South Bend, IN 46614,
USA
EXE

PR#4608
Munroe, Joe
Residence
Knox County, OH, USA
PJT

PR#4602
Oboler, Arch
Residence/Studio
Los Angeles, CA, USA
PJT

PR#4603
Pinkerton, W M
Residence
Fairfax County, VA, USA
PJT

PR#4717
Rand, Ayn
Residence
USA
PJT

PR#4815
Rosenbaum, Stanley Additions
Residence
601 Riverview Drive
Florence, AL 35630, USA
EXE

PR#4725
San Antonio Transit
Transport
San Antonio, TX, USA
PJT

PR#4504
Slater, William
Residence
Warwick, RI, USA
PJT

PR#4818
Smith, Melvin Maxwell
Residence
5045 Pon Valley Road

Bloomfield Hills, MI
48013, USA
EXE

1947 PR#4804
Alsop, Carroll
Residence
1907 A Avenue East
Oskaloosa, IA 52577,
USA
EXE

PR#4704
Bell, Dr Charles
Residence
East St Louis, IL, USA
PJT

PR#4706
Black, Dr B Marden
Residence
Rochester, MN, USA
PJT

PR#4709
Bulbulian, Dr A H
Residence
1229 Skyline Drive SW
Rochester, MN 55901,
USA
EXE

PR#4723
Butterfly Wing Bridge
Bridge
Spring Green, WI, USA
PJT

PR#4821
**Community Center
Point Park #1**
Civic Center
Pittsburgh, PA, USA
PJT
(For Edgar J Kaufmann)

PR#4732
**FSC Swimming Pool/
Outdoor Theatre**
Theatre
Lakeland, FL, USA
PJT
(Florida Southern College)

PR#4828
**Galesburg Country
Homes**
Housing
Galesburg, MI 49053,
USA
EXE

PR#4727
**Guggenheim,
Solomon R Annex**
Museum
1071 Fifth Avenue
New York, NY 10128,
USA
PJT

PR#4705
Hamilton, Berta
Residence
Brookline, VT, USA
PJT

PR#4721
**Hartford, H Cottage
Group
Center #1**
Resort
Hollywood, CA, USA
PJT

PR#4731
**Hartford, H Sports
Club/Play Resort**
Clubhouse
Hollywood, CA, USA
PJT

PR#4724
Hartford, Huntington

Residence
Hollywood, CA, USA
PJT

PR#4737
Hartford, Huntington
Stables
Hollywood, CA, USA
PJT

PR#4702
Kaufmann, Edgar J
Additions
Guest House
State Highway 381
Mill Run, PA 15464,
USA
EXE
Fallingwater

PR#4711
Keith, Ruth #1
Residence
Oakland County, PA,
USA
PJT

PR#4735
Keith, Ruth #2
Residence
Oakland County, PA,
USA
PJT

PR#4715
Keys, Thomas #1
Residence
Rochester, MN, USA
PJT

PR#4713
Marting, E L
Residence
Northampton, OH, USA
PJT

PR#4730
**Midway Dairy/Machine
Shed**
Farm
Route 23, Taliesin
Spring Green, WI 53588,
USA
EXE

PR#4820
Muelhberger, C W
Residence
East Lansing, MI,
USA
PJT

PR#4304
Palmer, Dr Paul V
Residence
Phoenix, AZ, USA
PJT

PR#4733
**Parkwyn Village
Community
Center**
Community Center
Kalamazoo, MI, USA
PJT

PR#4806
Parkwyn Village Homes
Housing
Kalamazoo, MI 49008,
USA
EXE

PR#4716
Pike, John J
Residence
Los Angeles, CA, USA
PJT

PR#5031
Unitarian Church
Religious
900 University Bay Drive
Shorewood Hills, WI

53705, USA
EXE
*Country Church for the first
Unitarian Society*

PR#4720
Usonia II New York
Housing
Pleasantville, NY 10570,
USA
EXE

PR#4722
Valley National Bank
Bank
Tucson, AZ, USA
PJT
The Daylight Bank

PR#4726
Wetmore, Roy
Auto Sales/Service
Detroit, MI, USA
PJT

PR#4719
Wilkie, Donald
Residence
Hennepin County, MN,
USA
PJT

1948 PR#4802
Adelman, Benjamin
Residence
Fox Point, WI, USA
PJT
*(Based on the New York
Exhibition House)*

PR#4907
Adler, Arnold
Residence
3600 Belleview Avenue
Kansas City, MO 64111,
USA
EXE
*(Additions to Clarence
Sondern House)*

PR#4803
Barney, Maginel
Residence
Route 23, Taliesin
Spring Green, WI, USA
PJT

PR#4708
Bergman, Dr Alfred
Residence
St Petersburg, FL, USA
PJT

PR#4829
Bimson, Mrs Walter
Penthouse
Phoenix, AZ, USA
PJT

PR#4707
Boomer, Lucius
Residence
Phoenix, AZ, USA
PJT
*(Rebuilding of Pauson
House)*

PR#4601
Brauner, Erling #2
Residence
2527 Arrow Head Road
Okemos, MI 48864, USA
EXE

PR#4805
Buehler, Maynard
Residence
6 Great Oak Circle
Orinda, CA, 94563, USA
EXE

PR#4836
**Community Center/
Twin Bridges**

Bridges/Civic Center
Pittsburgh, PA, USA
PJT
(For Edgar J Kaufmann)

PR#4822
**Crater Resort at
Meteor Crater**
Resort
Meteor Crater, AZ, USA
PJT
(For Burton Tremaine)

PR#4830
Daphne, Nicholas
Residence
San Francisco, CA, USA
PJT

PR#4808
Ellison, Harry
Residence
Bridgewater Twn, NJ,
USA
PJT

PR#4905
Eppstein, Samuel
Residence
11098 Hawthorne Drive
Galesburg, MI 49053,
USA
EXE

PR#4906
Friedman, Sol
Residence
11 Orchard Brook Drive
Pleasantville, NY 10570,
USA
EXE
Toy Hill

PR#5007
Greiner, Ward
Residence
Kalamazoo, MI, USA
PJT

PR#4810
Hageman, Arthur
Residence
Peoria, IL, USA
PJT

PR#4837
**Hartford, H Cottage
Group Center #2**
Resort
Hollywood, CA, USA
PJT

PR#4728
Hawkins, Florence
Apartments
Auburn, CA, USA
PJT

PR#4729
Hawkins, Florence
Residence/Studio
Auburn, CA, USA
PJT

PR#4712
Lamberson, Jack
Residence
511 N Park Avenue
Oskaloosa, IA 52577, USA
EXE

PR#4911
Levin, Robert
Residence
2816 Taliesin Drive
Kalamazoo, MI 49008,
USA
EXE

PR#4833
Lewis, Lloyd
Guest House
Libertyville, IL, USA
PJT

PR#4714
Margolis, Dr Frederick
Residence
Kalamozoo, MI, USA
PJT

PR#4825
Mccord, Glen
Residence
North Arlington, NJ, USA
PJT

PR#5015
Meyer, Curtis
Residence
11108 Hawthorne Drive
Galesburg, MI 49053, USA
EXE

PR#4824
Morris, V C
Gift Shop
140 Maiden Lane
San Francisco, CA 94108,
USA
EXE

PR#4827
Pratt, Eric
Residence
11036 Hawthorne Drive
Galesburg, MI 49053, USA
EXE

PR#4816
Scully, Vincent
Residence
Woodbridge, CT, USA
PJT

PR#4817
Smith, Talbot
Residence
Ann Arbor, MI, USA
PJT

PR#4832
**Sun Cottage at Taliesin
West**
Residence
Taliesin West
Scottsdale, AZ 85261, USA
EXE

PR#4734
Valley National Bank
Bank/Shopping Center
Sunnyslope
Phoenix, AZ, USA
PJT

PR#4831
Walter, Lowell
Boathouse
Cedar Rock Park
Quasqueton, IA 52326,
USA
EXE
River Pavilion

PR#4918
Weisblat, David
Residence
11185 Hawthorne Drive
Galesburg, MI 49053, USA
EXE

PR#4819
Weltzheimer, C R
Residence
127 Woodhaven Drive
Oberlin, OH 44074, USA
EXE

1949 PR#5001
Achuff-Carroll
Residence/Double
Wauwatosa, WI, USA
PJT
*(Harold Achuff and
Thomas Carroll)*

PR#4901
Anthony, Howard

Residence
1150 Miami Road
Benton Harbor, MI 49022,
USA
EXE
Scherzo

PR#5002
Auerback, Irwin
Residence
Pleasantville, NY, USA
PJT

PR#4902
Bloomfield, Louis
Residence
Tucson, AZ, USA
PJT

PR#4928
Bloomfield, Louis
Theatre/Outdoor
Tucson, AZ, USA
PJT

PR#5003
Brown, Eric
Residence
2806 Taliesin Drive
Kalamazoo, MI 49008,
USA
EXE

PR#4926
Cabaret Theatre
Theatre
Taliesin West
Scottsdale, AZ 85261,
USA
EXE
Stone Gallery

PR#4913
Dabney, Charles
Residence
Chicago, IL, USA
PJT

PR#4903
Drummond, Alan
Residence
Santa Fe, NM, USA
PJT

PR#4904
Edwards, James
Residence
2504 Arrow Head Road
Okemos, MI 48864,
USA
EXE

PR#4925
Fresh Air Camp
Resort
Hartland TWP, MI,
USA
PJT

PR#4929
**FSC Crafts and
Childrens Center**
Educational
Lakeland, FL, USA
PJT
(Florida Southern College)

PR#4609
**Gifford Concrete
Block Plant**
Factory
Middleton, WI, USA
PJT

PR#5006
Geotsch-Winckler #2
Residence
Okemos, MI, USA
PJT
*(Alma Goestch and
Kathrine Winckler)*

PR#4915
Griswold,

Senator George
Residence
Greenwich, CT, USA
PJT

PR#4605
Hillside Home
Building Revision
Educational
Route 23, Taliesin
Spring Green, WI 53588,
USA
PJT

PR#4908
Hughes, J Willis
Residence
306 Glenway Drive
Jackson, MS 39216,
USA
EXE

PR#4924
Jacobsen, George #1
Residence
Montreal, Canada
PJT

PR#4909
John, Harry
Residence/Dormitory
Oconomowoc, WI, USA
PJT

PR#4927
Kiva, Lloyd
Shop
Scottsdale, AZ, USA
PJT

PR#4814
Laurent, Kenneth
Residence
4646 Spring Brook Road
Rockford, IL 51114, USA
EXE

PR#4910
Lea, Thomas
Residence
Ashville, NC, USA
PJT

PR#4912
McCartney, Ward
Residence
2662 Taliesin Drive
Kalamazoo,
MI 49008, USA
EXE

PR#4826
Miller, Sydney
Residence
Pleasantville, NY, USA
PJT

PR#5020
Neils, Henry J
Residence
2801 Burnham Blvd
Minneapolis, MN 55416,
USA
EXE

PR#4922
New Theatre, The
Theatre
Hartford, CT, USA
PJT
(For Paton Price)

PR#4921
San Francisco Bridge
Bridge
San Francisco Bay
San Francisco, CA, USA
PJT
*Butterfly-Wing Bridge,
Second Bay Crossing*

PR#4923
Self-Service Garage
Parking Garage

Pittsburgh, PA, USA
PJT
(For Edgar J Kaufmann)

PR#4917
Serlin, Ed
Residence
12 Laurel Hill Drive
Pleasantville, NY 10570,
USA
EXE

PR#5612
Usonian Automatic
Residence
USA,
PJT
(Early Conceptual Studies)

PR#5122
Walker, Mrs Clinton
Residence
Scenic Road at Martin St
Carmel, CA 93921, USA
EXE

PR#4919
Windfohr, Robert
Residence
Fort Worth, TX, USA
PJT
Crownfield

PR#4920
YWCA #1
Clubhouse
Racine, WI, USA
PJT
(For Herbert F Johnson)

1950 PR#5039
Berger, Robert
Residence
259 Redwood Road
San Anselmo, CA 94960,
USA
EXE

PR#5005
Bush, Robert
Residence
Palo Alto, CA, USA
PJT

PR#5004
Carlson, Raymond
Residence
1123 W Palo Verde Doad
Phoenix, AZ 85013, USA
EXE

PR#5014
Carr, John O
Residence
1544 Portage Run
Glenview, IL 60025, USA
EXE

PR#5018
Chahroudi, A K
Residence
Lake Mahopac
Petra Island, NY, USA
PJT

PR#5025
Conklin, Tom
Residence
New Ulm, MN, USA
PJT

PR#5037
Davis, Dr Richard
Residence
1119 Overlook Road
Marion, IN 46952, USA
EXE

PR#5105
Elam, S P
Residence
309 21st Street SW
Austin, MN 55912, USA
EXE

PR#5034
Gillin, John A
Residence
9400 Rockbrook Drive
Dallas, TX 75220, USA
EXE

PR#5009
Grover, Donald
Residence
Syracuse, NY, USA
PJT

PR#5108
Hall, Louis B
Residence
Ann Arbor, MI, USA
PJT

PR#5040
Hanson, Richard
Residence
Corvalis, OR, USA
PJT

PR#5109
Hargrove, Dr Kenneth
Residence
Berkeley, CA, USA
PJT

PR#5010
Harper, Dr Ina
Residence
207 Sunnybank. St Joseph,
MI 49085, USA
EXE

PR#5110
Haynes, John
Residence
3901 N Washington Road
Fort Wayne, IN 46804,
USA
EXE

PR#4701
Houston, Walter
Residence
Schuyler County, IL, USA
PJT

PR#5011
How to Live in the
Southwest
Residence
Phoenix, AZ, USA
EXE
*How to Live in the
Southwest (See David
Wright House)*

PR#5411
Jackson, Dr Arnold
Residence
Madison, WI, USA
PJT

PR#5008
Jacobsen, George #2
Residence
Montreal, Canada
PJT

PR#5012
Keys, Thomas #2
Residence
1243 Skyline Drive SW
Rochester, MN 55901,
USA
EXE

PR#5013
Mathews, Arthur
Residence
83 Wisteria Way
Atherton, CA 94025, USA
EXE

PR#5017
Montooth, George
Residence
Rushville, IL, USA
PJT

PR#5019
Muirhead, Robert
Residence
Rohrscn Road
Plato Center, IL 60170,
USA
EXE

PR#5035
O'Donnell, Dale
Residence
Lansing, MI, USA
PJT

PR#5021
Palmer, William
Residence
227 Orchard Hills Drive
Ann Arbor, MI 48104,
USA
EXE

PR#5114
Pearce, Wilbur
Residence
5 Bradbury Hills Road
Bradbury, CA 91010,
USA
EXE

PR#5036
Sabin, Brainerd
Residence
Battle Creek, MI, USA
PJT

PR#5022
Schaberg, Don
Residence
1155 Wrightwind Drive
Okemos, MI 48864, USA
EXE

PR#5023
Shavin, Seymour
Residence
334 N Crest Road
Chattanooga, TN 37404,
USA
EXE

PR#5042
Sixty Years of Living
Architecture
Exhibition
Palazzo Strozzi
Florence, Italy
DMD

PR#5000
Sixty Years of Living
Architecture
Exhibition
Italy, Switzerland,
Germany, France,
Holland
EXE
*Sixty Years of Living
Architecture*

PR#5000
Sixty Years of Living
Architecture
Exhibition
New York/Los Angeles
USA
EXE
*Sixty Years of Living
Architecture*

PR#5000
Sixty Years of Living
Architecture
Exhibition
Mexico City, DF, Mexico
EXE
*Sixty Years of Living
Architecture*

PR#5024
Small, Dr Leon
Residence/Clinic
West Orange, NJ, USA
PJT

PR#5026
Smith, Richard
Residence
332 E Linden Drive
Jefferson, WI 53549,
USA
EXE

PR#5033
Southwest Christian
Seminary
Religious/Agricultural
Phoenix, AZ, USA
PJT
(For Peyton Canary)

PR#5119
Staley, Karl A
Residence
6363 W Lake Road
N Madison, OH 44057,
USA
EXE

PR#5028
Stevens, Arthur
Residence
Park Ridge, IL, USA
PJT

PR#5120
Strong, Laurence
Residence
Kalamazoo, MI, USA
PJT

PR#5210
Swan, Lawrence
Residence
Detroit, MI, USA
PJT

PR#5027
Sweeton, J A
Residence
375 Kings Highway
Cherry Hill, NJ 08034,
USA
EXE

PR#5029
Wassell, William
Residence
Righters Mill Road
Lower Merion TW, PA,
USA
PJT

PR#4813
Winn, Robert
Residence
2822 Taliesin Drive
Kalamazoo, MI 49008,
USA
EXE

PR#5030
Wright, David
Residence
5212 E Exeter Blvd
Phoenix, AZ 85018, USA
EXE
*(How to Live in the
Southwest)*

PR#5041
YWCA #2
Clubhouse
Racine, WI, USA
PJT
(For Herbert F Johnson)

PR#5214
Zimmerman, Isadore
Residence
223 Heather Street
Manchester, NH 03104,
USA
EXE

1951 PR#5101
Adelman, Benjamin
Residence
5802 N 30th Street

Phoenix, AZ 85016, USA
EXE
(Usonian Automatic)

PR#5102
Austin, Gabrielle &
Charlcey
Residence
9 W Avondale Drive
Greenville, SC 29609,
USA
EXE

PR#5102
Austin, Gabrielle &
Charlcey
Residence
9 W Avondale Drive
Greenville, SC 29609,
USA
EXE

PR#5104
Chahroudi, A K
Residence/Summer
Lake Mahopac
Petra Island, NY 10541,
USA
EXE

PR#5112
Clark, George
Residence
Carmel, CA, USA
PJT
Sun Bonnet

PR#5106
Fuller, Welbie L
Residence
Pass Christian Isl, MS,
USA
DMD

PR#5107
Glore, Charles F
Residence
170 N Mayflower
Lake Forest, IL 60045,
USA
EXE

PR#5103
House for GI Couple
Housing
USA
PJT

PR#5124
Johnson Wax Additions
Office Building
1525 Howe Street
Racine, WI 53403, USA
EXE
*(For the S C Johnson &
Son Company)*

PR#5111
Kaufmann, Liliane and
E J
Residence
Palm Springs, CA, USA
PJT
Boulder House

PR#5038
Kinney, Patrick
Residence
474 N Fillmore Street
Lancaster, WI 53813, USA
EXE

PR#5123
Kraus, Russell
Residence
120 N Ballas Road
Kirkwood, MO 63122,
USA
EXE

PR#4916
Publicker, Robert
Residence
Andover and Tunbridge

Road, Haverford, PA, USA
PJT

PR#5115
Reisley, Roland
Residence
44 Usonia Road
Pleasantville, NY 10570,
USA
EXE

PR#5116
Rubin, Nathan
Residence
518 44th Street NW
Canton, OH 44709, USA
EXE

PR#5125
Stracke, Victor #1
Residence
Appleton, WI, USA
PJT

PR#5113
Vallarino, J J #1
Residence
Panama City, Panama
PJT

PR#5118
Vallarino, J J #2
Residence
Panama City, Panama
PJT

PR#5127
Vallarino, J J #3
Residence
Panama City, Panama
PJT

PR#5117
**Wetmore, Roy
Remodelling**
Auto Sales/Service
Detroit, MI, USA
PJT

PR#5121
Wright, David
Carpets
5212 E Exeter Blvd
Phoenix, AZ 85018, USA
EXE
*(March Balloons Carpet
Design)*

1952 PR#5201
Affleck, Gregor #2
Residence
Bloomfield Hills, MI,
USA
PJT

PR#5032
Anderton Court Shops
Shop
332 N Rodeo Drive
Beverly Hills, CA 90210,
USA
EXE
*(For Nina Anderton and
Eric Bass)*

PR#5202
Bailleres, Raul
Residence
Acapulco, Mexico
PJT

PR#5203
Blair, Quentin
Residence
5588 Greybull Highway
Cody, WY 82414, USA
EXE

PR#5204
Brandes, Ray
Residence
212th Avenue
Issaquah, WA 98027, USA
EXE

PR#5205
Clifton, William
Residence
Oakland, NJ, USA
PJT

PR#5224
Friedman, Arnold
Gatehouse
Highway 63
Pecos, NM 87552, USA
EXE

PR#5206
Goddard, Lewis #1
Residence
Plymouth, MI, USA
PJT

PR#5226
Green, Aaron
Office
319 Grant Street
San Francisco, CA, USA
EXE
*(For Aaron Green
Architectural Office and
West Coast Office of Frank
Lloyd Wright)*

PR#5225
Hillside Kitchen
Educational
Route 23, Taliesin
Spring Green, WI 53588,
USA
EXE
*(For the Taliesin Fellowship
Complex)*

PR#5213
Hillside Playhouse #2
Theater
Route 23, Taliesin
Spring Green, WI 53588,
USA
EXE
*(For the Taliesin Fellowship
Complex)*

PR#5223
**Hillside Theater
Curtain #2**
Textiles
Route 23, Taliesin
Spring Green, WI, 53588,
USA
EXE
*(For the Taliesin Fellowship
Complex)*

PR#5302
Lee, Edgar
Residence
Midland, MI, USA
PJT

PR#5216
**Leesburg Floating
Gardens**
Resort
Leesburg, FL, USA
PJT
*(For the Mess'rs Ottinger,
Byoir, Ferguson, Claiborne
and Company)*

PR#5207
Lewis, George
Residence
3117 Okeeheepkee Rd
Tallahassee, FL 32303,
USA

PR#5208
Lindholm, R W
Residence
Route 33/Stanley
Cloquet, MN 55720, USA
EXE

PR#5227
Morehead, Elizabeth B
Residence

Marin County, CA, USA
PJT

PR#5221
Paradise on Wheels
Housing
Phoenix, AZ, USA
PJT
(For Lee Ackerman)

PR#5303
Penfield, Louis #1
Residence
2203 River Road
Willoughby Hills, OH
44094, USA
EXE

PR#5218
Pieper, Arthur
Residence
6422 E Cheney Road
Paradise Valley, AZ 85253,
USA
EXE
(Usonian Automatic)

PR#5222
**Point View
Residences #1**
Apartment Tower
Pittsburgh, PA, USA
PJT
*(For the Edgar J Kaufmann
Charitable Trust)*

PR#5215
Price Tower
Office Tower/Apartments
NE Sixth Street at
Dewey Bartlesville,
OK 74003, USA
EXE
*(For the H C Price
Company)*

PR#5413
Rebhuhn, Ben
Residence
Fort Meyers, FL, USA
PJT

PR#5308
Rhododendron Chapel
Chapel
Mill Run, PA, USA
PJT
(For Edgar J Kaufmann)

PR#5304
Sander, Frank
Residence
121 Woodchuck Road
Stamford, CT 06903, USA
EXE

PR#5209
Sturtevant, Horace
Residence
Oakland, CA, USA
PJT

PR#5211
Teater, Archie
Residence/Studio
Old Hagerman HWY
Bliss, ID, 83314, USA
EXE

PR#5212
Wainer, Alexis
Residence
Valdosta, GA, USA
PJT

PR#5217
Zeta Beta Tau
Fraternity
Gainesville, FL, USA
PJT

1953 PR#5305
Boomer, Jorgine
Residence

5808 N 30th Street
Phoenix, AZ 85016, USA
EXE

PR#5309
Brewer, Joseph
Residence
East Fiskhill, NY, USA
PJT

PR#5219
Cooke, Andrew B #1
Residence
320 51st Street
Virginia Beach, VA 23455,
USA
EXE

PR#5314
Exhibition House
Residence/Exhibition
1071 Fifth Avenue
New York, NY, USA
DMD
*(For the exhibition Sixty
Years of Living
Architecture)*

PR#5314
**Exhibition Pavilion
New York**
Exhibition
1071 Fifth Avenue
New York, NY, USA
DMD
*(For the exhibition Sixty
Years of Living Architecture)*

PR#5315
FM Radio Station
Radio Station
Jefferson, WI, USA
PJT
(For William Proxmire)

PR#5319
**FSC Science
and Cosmography**
Educational
111 Lake Hollingsworth Dr
Lakeland, FL 33801, USA
EXE
(Florida Southern College)

PR#5317
Goddard, Lewis #2
Residence
12221 Beck Road
Plymouth, MI 48170, USA
EXE

PR#5321
Hillside 'Godown'
Art Storage
Route 23, Taliesin
Spring Green, WI, USA
*(Vault for Frank Lloyd
Wright Drawings)*

PR#5220
Marden, Luis
Residence
600 Chainbridge Road
McLean, VA 22101, USA
EXE

PR#5306
Masieri Memorial
Residence/Pensione
Canal Grande
Venice, Italy
PJT
(For Savina Masieri)

PR#5311
**Pieper-Montooth
Office Building**
Office Building
Scottsdale, AZ, USA
PJT
*(For Arthur Pieper and
Charles Montooth)*

PR#5310
**Point View
Residences #2**
Apartment Tower
Pittsburgh, PA, USA
PJT
*(For the Edgar J Kaufmann
Charitable Trust)*

PR#5421
Price, Harold Jr
Residence
Silver Lake Road
Bartlesville, OK 74003,
USA
EXE
Hillside

PR#5619
**Riverview Terrace
Restaurant**
Restaurant
Route 23, Taliesin
Spring Green, WI 53588,
USA
EXE
*(For the Taliesin Fellowship,
FLLW Foundation, now the
FLLW Visitor Center)*

PR#5316
Taliesin Viaduct
Bridge
Route 23, Taliesin
Spring Green, WI, USA
PJT
*(For the Frank Lloyd
Wright Foundation)*

PR#5301
Taliesin West Sign
Signs
Taliesin West
Scottsdale, AZ 85261, USA
EXE

PR#5414
Thaxton, William
Residence
12024 Tall Oaks
Bunker Hill, TX 77024,
USA

PR#5312
Wright, R Llewellyn #1
Residence
Bethesda, MD, USA
PJT

1954 PR#5501
Adelman, Benjamin
Residence
Whitefish Bay, WI, USA
PJT

PR#5401
Arnold, E Clarke
Residence
954 Dix Street
Columbus, WI 53913, USA
EXE

PR#5402
Bachman-Wilson
Residence
142 S River Road
Millstone, NY 08876, USA
EXE

PR#5313
Beth Sholom Synagogue
Religious
Old York Road at Foxcroft
Elkins Park, PA 19117,
USA
EXE

PR#5403
Boulter, Cedric
Residence
1 Rawson Woods Circle
Cincinnati, OH 45220,
USA
EXE

PR#5416
**Christian Science
Reading Room #1**
Religious
Riverside, IL, USA
PJT

PR#5416
**Christian Science
Reading Room #2**
Religious
Riverside, IL, USA
PJT

PR#5405
Christian, John E
Residence
1301 Woodland Avenue
West Lafayette, IN 47906,
USA
EXE

PR#5423
Cornwell, Gibbons #1
Residence
West Goshen, PA, USA
PJT

PR#5427
**Exhibition Pavilion
Los Angeles**
Exhibition
4808 Hollywood Blvd
Los Angeles, CA, USA
DMD
*(For the exhibition Sixty
Years of Living
Architecture)*

PR#5408
Feiman, Ellis
Residence
452 Santa Clara Drive
NW Canton, OH 44709,
USA
EXE

PR#5532
FLLW Plaza Apartment
Apartment/Studio
Hotel Plaza 59th & 5th
Ave, New York, NY, USA
DMD

PR#5426
Frederick, Louis B
Residence
County Line Road
Barrington Hills, IL 60010,
USA
EXE

PR#5404
FSC Danforth Chapel
Chapel
111 Lake Hollingsworth Dr
Lakeland, FL 33801, USA
EXE
(Florida Southern College)

PR#5409
Greenberg, Dr Maurice
Residence
3902 Highway 67
Dousman, WI 53118, USA
EXE

PR#5429
Hagan Ice Cream Co.
Residence/Offices
Uniontown, PA, USA
PJT

PR#5410
Hagan, IN
Residence
Ohiopyle Road
Chalkhill, PA 15421, USA
EXE

PR#5622
**Hoffman Jaguar
Showroom**
Auto Sales/Service

430 Park Avenue
New York, NY 10022,
USA
EXE
*(Currently the
Mercedes Showroom)*

PR#5430
Hoffman, G M
Residence
Winnetka, IL, USA
PJT

PR#5504
Hoffman, Max #1
Residence
58 Island Drive
Rye, NY, USA
PJT

PR#5534
Hoffman, Max #2
Residence
58 Island Drive
Rye, NY, USA
PJT

PR#5517
Keland, Willard
Residence
1425 Valley View Drive
Racine, WI 54305,
USA
EXE

PR#5509
**Korrick's Department
Store Remodelling**
Department Store/
Residence
Phoenix, AZ, USA
PJT
(For Charles Korrick)

PR#5632
**Monona Terrace
Civic Center #2**
Civic Center
Madison, WI, USA
PJT

PR#5508
Oboler, Arch
Residence/Cinema
Malibu, CA, USA
PJT
Continuation

PR#5419
Price, Harold
Residence
7211 N Tatum Blvd
Paradise Valley, AZ 85253,
USA
EXE
The Grandma House

PR#5420
Price, Harold Jr Rug
Carpets
Silver Lake Road
Bartlesville, OK 74003,
USA
EXE

PR#5415
Schwenn, Roger
Residence
Verona, WI, USA
PJT

PR#5606
Smith, J L
Residence
Kane County, IL, USA
PJT
(Usonian Automatic)

PR#5422
Terne Metal Graphics
Graphics
USA
PJT

PR#5406
Tipshus Medical Clinic
Medical Clinic
Stockton, CA, USA
PJT
(For Dr Alfons Tipshus)

PR#5510
Tonkens, Gerald
Residence
6980 Knoll Road
Amberley Village, OH
45237, USA
EXE
(Usonian Automatic)

PR#5512
Tracy, W B
Residence
18971 Edgecliff Drive SW
Normandy Park, WA
98166, USA
EXE
(Usonian Automatic)

PR#5431
Wright, David
Guest House
5212 E Exeter Blvd
Phoenix, AZ 85018, USA
EXE

PR#5307
**Yosemite National
Park Restaurant**
Restaurant
Yosemite National Park
Yosemite, CA, USA
PJT

1955 **PR#5539**
Air Force Academy
Educational
Boulder, CO, USA
PJT
(Preliminary Sketches)

PR#5517
Barton, A D
Residence
Downer's Grove, IL, USA
PJT

PR#5502
Blumberg, Mel
Residence
Des Moines, IA, USA
PJT

PR#5526
Boswell, William #1
Residence
Cincinnati, OH, USA
PJT

PR#5503
Coats, Robert
Residence
Hillsborough, CA, USA
PJT

PR#5424
Cornwell, Gibbons #2
Residence
West Goshen, PA,
USA
PJT

PR#5519
Dlesk, George #1
Residence
Manistee, MI, USA
PJT

PR#5418
Fawcett, Randall
Residence
21200 Center Avenue
Los Banos, CA 93635,
USA
EXE

PR#5425
Freund Y Cia

Department Store
San Salvador, El Salvador
PJT

PR#5712
Hartman, Stanley
Residence
Lansing, MI, USA
PJT

PR#5714
Herberger, Robert #1
Residence
Maricopa County, AZ,
USA
PJT

PR#5830
Herberger, Robert #2
Residence
Maricopa County, AZ,
USA
PJT
Stonecrest

PR#5529
**Heritage-Henredon
Furniture**
Furniture
USA
EXE
Four Square

PR#5529
**Heritage-Henredon
Furniture**
Furniture
USA
PJT
Burberry

PR#5529
**Heritage-Henredon
Furniture**
Furniture
USA
PJT
Honeycomb

PR#5535
Hoffman, Max #3
Residence
58 Island Drive
Rye, NY 10580, USA
EXE

PR#5505
Jankowski, Leonard #1
Residence
Oakland City, MI, USA
PJT

PR#5538
Jankowski, Leonard #2
Residence
Oakland City, MI, USA
PJT
(Usonian Automatic)

PR#5506
Kalil, Dr Toufic
Residence
117 Heather Street
Manchester, NH 03104,
USA
EXE
(Usonian Automatic)

PR#5514
**Kalita Humphreys
Theater**
Theatre
3636 Turtle Creek Blvd
Dallas, TX 75219,
USA
EXE
*(For Paul Baker and the
Dallas Theater Center)*

PR#5540
Karastan Rug Design
Carpets
USA
PJT

PR#5536
Kinney, Sterling #1
Residence
Amarillo, TX, USA
PJT

PR#5640
**Kundert Medical
Clinic #1**
Medical Clinic
San Luis Obispo, CA
93401, USA
PJT
*(Usonian Automatic for
Dr Kundert and Dr Fogo)*

PR#5614
**Kundert Medical
Clinic #2**
Medical Clinic
1106 Pacific Street
San Luis Obispo, CA
93401, USA
EXE
*(For Dr Kundert and
Dr Fogo)*

PR#5520
**Lenkurt Electric
Company**
Factory
San Carlos, CA, USA
PJT
*(For Lennart Erickson
and Kurt Appert)*

PR#5507
Lovness, Don
Residence
10121 83rd N
Stillwater, MN 55082,
USA
EXE

PR#5541
Martin-Senour Pallette
Paint Color, USA
EXE
*(For William Stuart of the
Martin-Senour Company)*

PR#5640
Medical Building
Medical Clinic
San Luis Obispo, CA,
USA
PJT
*(Usonian Automatic for
Dr Kundert and Dr Fogo)*

PR#5602
Miller, Oscar
Residence
Milford, MN, USA
PJT
(Usonian Automatic)

PR#5530
Morris, V C
Guest House
San Francisco, CA, USA
PJT

PR#5412
Morris, V C #2
Residence
San Francisco, CA,
USA
PJT
Seacliff

PR#5533
**Neurological Treatment
Center**
Hospital
Madison, WI, USA
PJT
*Neuroseum (For the
Wisconsin Neurological
Foundation)*

PR#5516
Pappas, T A
Residence

8654 S Masonridge Road
St Louis, MO 63141, USA
EXE
(Usonian Automatic)

PR#5515
Pieper, C R
Residence
Paradise Valley, AZ, USA
PJT

PR#5523
Rayward, John
Residence
432 Frog Town Road
New Canaan, CT 06840,
USA
EXE

PR#5826
Road Machine
Automobile
USA
PJT
*(Preliminary Study,
V 5826)*

PR#5607
Roberts, Jay
Residence
Seattle, WA, USA
PJT

PR#5511
Schumacher Fabrics
Textiles
New York, NY, USA
EXE
*(For F Schumacher &
Son, NY)*

PR#5608
**Scott, Warren
Remodelling**
Residence
603 Edgewood Place
River Forest, IL 60305,
USA
EXE
*(Remodelling of the Isabel
Roberts House)*

PR#5522
Sunday, Robert #1
Residence
Marshalltown, IA, USA
PJT
(Usonian Automatic)

PR#5636
Sunday, Robert #2
Residence
1701 Woodfield Road
Marshalltown, IA 50158,
USA
EXE

PR#5524
Sussman, Gerald
Residence
Rye, NY, USA
PJT
(Usonian Automatic)

PR#5531
**Townbridge,
Dr Chester**
Residence
Oak Park, IL, USA
PJT

PR#5513
Turkel, Dr Dorothy
Residence
2760 W Seven Mile Road
Detroit, MI 48221, USA
EXE
(Usonian Automatic)

1956 **PR#5701**
Adams, Lee
Residence
St Paul, MN, USA
PJT

PR#5611
**Annunciation Greek
Orthodox Church**
Religious
9400 W Congress Street
Wauwatosa, WI 53225,
USA
EXE
*(For the Milwaukee
Hellenic Community)*

PR#5629
Boebel, Robert
Residence
Boscobel, WI, USA
PJT

PR#5704
Boswell, William #2
Residence
9905 Comargo Club Drive
Indian Hill, OH 45243,
USA
EXE

PR#5627
Bott, Frank
Residence
3640 Briarcliff Road, NW
Kansas City, MO 64116,
USA
EXE

PR#5620
Bramlett Motor Hotel
Motel
Memphis, TN, USA
PJT
(For Percy Bramlett)

PR#5537
**Christian Science
Church #1**
Religious
Bolinas, CA, USA
PJT

PR#5527
**Christian Science
Church #2**
Religious
Bolinas, CA, USA
PJT

PR#5609
City by the Sea (Mural)
Mural
Taliesin West
Scottsdale, AZ 85261,
USA
DMD
*(At Taliesin West Music
Pavilion)*

PR#5525
Cooke, Andrew B #2
Residence
Virginia Beach, VA,
USA
PJT
(Usonian Automatic)

PR#5518
Erdman Prefab #1
Housing
5817 Anchorage Road
Madison, WI 53705,
USA
EXE
(For Marshall Erdman)

PR#5518
Erdman Prefab #1
Housing
2909 W Beltline
Madison, WI 53713, USA
EXE
*Skyview (moved to Beaver
Dam, WI, 1995)*

PR#5518
Erdman Prefab #1
Housing
7655 Indian Hills Road

Beaver Dam, WI 53916, USA
EXE
(Moved February 1985)

PR#5725
Fiberthin Village
Housing
Mishawaka, IN, USA
DMD
The Air House (For the United States Rubber Company)

PR#5624
Friedman, Allen
Residence
200 Thornapple Road
Bannockburn, IL 60015, USA
EXE

PR#5528
Gillin, John
Residence
Hollywood, CA, USA
PJT
Alladin

PR#5615
Golden Beacon
Apartment Tower
Chicago, IL, USA
PJT
(For Charles Glore)

PR#5710
Gordon, C E
Residence
303 SW Gordon Lane
Wilsonville, OR 97070, USA
EXE

PR#5628
Gross, Nelson
Residence
Hackensack, NJ, USA
PJT

PR#5634
Hanna, Paul and Jean Additions
Residence
737 Frenchman's Road
Stanford, CA 94305, USA
EXE
Honeycomb House

PR#5713
Hennessy, Jack #1
Residence
Smoke Rise, NJ, USA
PJT

PR#5639
Hotel Sherman Exhibition Layout
Exhibition
Hotel Sherman
Chicago, IL, USA
DMD

PR#5638
The House Beautiful
Graphics
USA
PJT
(Revisions of 1896 edition)

PR#5715
Kaufmann, Edgar J Jr
Gate Lodge
Mill Run, PA, USA
PJT
(Usonian Automatic)

PR#5520
Lenkurt Electric Company #2
Factory
San Carlos, CA, USA

PJT
(For Lennart Erickson and Kurt Appert)

PR#5633
Levin, Arthur
Residence
Palo Alto, CA, USA
PJT
(Usonian Automatic)

PR#5739
Lindholm Service Station
Service Station
Route#45 At #33
Cloquet, MN 55720, USA
EXE
(For R W Lindholm)

PR#5613
Meyers, Dr Kenneth
Medical Clinic
5441 Far Hills Avenue Dayton, OH 45429, USA
EXE

PR#5617
Mile High
Office Tower
Chicago, IL, USA
PJT
The Illinois

PR#5618
Mills, Bradford #1
Residence
Princeton, NJ, USA
PJT
(Passive Solar Heating)

PR#5720
Moreland, Ralph
Residence
Austin, TX, USA
PJT

PR#5729
Morris, Lillian
Residence
Stinson Beach, CA, USA
PJT
Quietwater

PR#5631
Music Pavilion
Theatre
Taliesin West
Scottsdale, AZ 85261, USA
EXE

PR#5616
New Sports Pavilion
Racetrack
Belmont Park, NY, USA
PJT
The Manhattan Sports Pavilion (For Harry S Guggenheim)

PR#5604
Nooker, Clyde, Remodelling
Residence
951 Chicago Avenue
Oak Park, IL 60302, USA
(Remodelling of Frank Lloyd Wright Oak Park House and Studio)

PR#5603
O'Keeffe, Dr Arthur
Residence
Santa Barbara, CA, USA
PJT

PR#5738
Post Office Spring Green
Post Office
Spring Green, WI, USA
PJT

PR#5630
Schuck, Victoria

Residence
South Hadley, MA, USA
PJT

PR#5722
Sottil, Helen
Residence
Cuernavaca, Mexico
PJT
(Revision of FLLW Residence/Studio, Italy, 1910)

PR#5605
Spencer, Dudley #1
Residence
Brandywine Head, DE, USA
PJT

PR#5635
Spencer, Dudley #2
Residence
619 Shipley Road
Brandywine Head, DE, USA
EXE

PR#5723
Stracke, Victor #2
Residence
Appleton, WI, USA
PJT

PR#5610
Taliesin Parkway Sign
Signs
Taliesin
Spring Green, WI, USA
PJT

PR#5724
Trier, Dr Paul
Residence
6880 NW Beaver Drive
Des Moines, IA 50131
EXE

PR#5612
Usonian Automatic Details
Residence
USA
EXE
(Usonian Automatic)

PR#5521
Weiland, Daniel
Motel
Hagerstown, MD, USA
PJT

PR#5726
Wilson, T Henry
Residence
Morgantown, NC, USA
PJT

PR#5727
Wright, Duey #1
Residence
Wausau, WI, USA
PJT

PR#5318
Wright, R Llewellyn #2
Residence
7927 Deepwell Road
Bethesda, MD 20034, USA
EXE
(Robert Llewellyn Wright was son of Frank Lloyd Wright)

PR#5741
Wyoming Valley School
Educational
Route 23
Wyoming Valley, WI 53588, USA
EXE

PR#5728
Zieger, Dr Allen

Residence
Grosse Pointe, MI, USA
PJT

1957 **PR#5801**
Amery, Nezam
Residence
Teheran, IRAN
PJT

PR#5732
Arizona State Capitol
Government Building
Phoenix, AZ, USA
PJT
Pro Bono Publico/Oasis

PR#5749
Baghdad Art Museum
Museum
Baghdad, IRAQ
PJT

PR#5752
Baghdad Casino
Casino
Baghdad, IRAQ
PJT

PR#5733
Baghdad Crescent Opera
Opera
Baghdad, IRAQ
PJT
Crescent Opera

PR#5733
Baghdad Greater Plan
Civic Centre
Baghdad, IRAQ
PJT

PR#5750
Baghdad Kiosks and Grand Bazaar
Shops/Bazaar
Baghdad, IRAQ
EXE

PR#5751
Baghdad Monument to Haroun-Al-Rashid
Monument
Baghdad, IRAQ
PJT

PR#5734
Baghdad Postal Telegraph
Post Office
Baghdad, IRAQ
PJT

PR#5748
Baghdad Sculpture Museum
Museum
Baghdad, IRAQ
PJT

PR#5759
Baghdad University
Educational
Baghdad, IRAQ
PJT

PR#5428
Barnsdall Park Gallery
Museum
Los Angeles, CA, USA
PJT
(For City of Los Angeles Department of Cultural Affairs, adjacent to Hollyhock House)

PR#5740
Bimson Housing
Housing
Phoenix, AZ, USA
PJT
(Usonian Automatic – for Walter Bimson)

PR#5702
Brooks, Robert
Residence
Middleton, WI, USA
PJT

PR#5703
Dlesk, George #2
Residence
Manistee, MI, USA
PJT

PR#5706
Erdman Prefab #1
Housing
1001 W Jonathan
Bayside, WI 53217, USA
EXE

PR#5706
Erdman Prefab #1
Housing
48 Manor Court
Richmond, NY 10306, USA
EXE

PR#5706
Erdman Prefab #1
Housing
Springville Drive at U.S.5
Stevens Point, WI 54481, USA
EXE

PR#5706
Erdman Prefab #1
Housing
265 Donlea Road
Barrington Hills, IL 60010, USA
EXE

PR#5706
Erdman Prefab #2
Housing
110 Marinette Terrace
Madison, WI 53705, USA
EXE
The One Room House (For Marshall Erdman)

PR#5706
Erdman Prefab #2
Housing
1532 Woodland Drive, SW
Rochester, MN 55901, USA
EXE

PR#5730
Fasbender Clinic
Medical Clinic
MN#55 at Pine
Hastings, MN 55033, USA
EXE
(For Dr Herman Fasbender)

PR#5320
FSC Music Building #3
Theatre
Lakeland, FL, USA
PJT
(Florida Southern College)

PR#5705
Hillside Grounds Plan
Landscape
Route 23, Talicsin
Spring Green, WI 53588, USA
EXE
(For the Taliesin Fellowship Complex, executed in Part)

PR#5707
Hoffman, Max
Carpets
Rye, NY, USA
PJT
(Later executed for the Taliesin living room)

PR#5742
Housing for Negro Families
Housing
Whiteville, NC, USA
PJT
(For Jesse C Fisher)

PR#5716
Hoyer, Carl
Residence
Maricopa County, AZ, USA
PJT

PR#5717
Kinney, Sterling #2
Residence
Tascosa Road
Amarillo, TX 79606, USA
EXE

PR#5755
Marin County Amphitheater
Theater/Aquatic
San Rafael, CA, USA
PJT

PR#5757
Marin County Children's Park
Playground
San Rafael, CA, USA
PJT

PR#5746
Marin County Civic Center
Government Building
N San Pedro Road
San Rafael, CA 94903, USA
EXE

PR#5754
Marin County Fair Pavilion
Fair
San Rafael, CA, USA
PJT

PR#5756
Marin County Health/Services
Office Building
San Rafael, CA, USA
PJT

PR#5753
Marin County Post Office
Post Office
N San Pedro Road
San Rafael, CA 94903, USA
EXE

PR#5718
Mckinney, Darryl
Residence
Cloquet, MN, USA
PJT

PR#5719
Miller, Arthur
Residence
Roxbury, CT, USA
PJT
(Marilyn Monroe)

PR#5711
Mills, Bradford #2
Residence
Princeton, NJ, USA
PJT
(Passive Solar)

PR#5736
Motel for Erdman
Motel
Madison, WI, USA
PJT
(For Marshall Erdman)

PR#5807
Motel for Zeckendorf
Motel
New York, NY, USA
PJT
(For William Zeckendorf)

PR#5747
Rayward, John
Playhouse
432 Frog Town Road
New Canaan, CT 06840,
USA
EXE

PR#5744
Schanbackers Store
Shop
Springfield, IL, USA
PJT

PR#5745
Schultz, Carl
Residence
2704 Highland Court, St
Joseph, MI 49085, USA
EXE

PR#5721
Shelton, Wilson #1
Residence
Oyster Bay
Long Island, NY, USA
PJT

PR#5758
Shelton, Wilson #2
Residence
Oyster Bay
Long Island, NY, USA
PJT

PR#5737
Spring Green
Entrance Sign
Signs
Spring Green, WI, USA
PJT

PR#5625
Stillman, Calvin #1
Residence
Cornwall-on-Hudson, NY,
USA
PJT

PR#5637
Stillman, Calvin #2
Residence
Cornwall-on-Hudson, NY,
USA
PJT

PR#5621
Tonkens Loan Office
Office Building
Cincinnati, OH, USA
PJT
(For Gerald Tonkens)

PR#5735
Valley of the Sun
Signs
Pasadena, CA, USA
PJT
*Valley of the Sun (Rose
Bowl Float for Phoenix,
Arizona)*

PR#5623
Walton, Dr Robert
Residence
417 Hogue Road
Modesto, CA 95350, USA
EXE

PR#5709
Wedding Chapel #1
Chapel
Hotel Claremont
Berkeley, CA, USA
PJT
*The Rococo Chapel
(For Hotel Claremont)*

PR#5731
Wedding Chapel #2
Chapel
Berkeley, CA, USA
PJT
(For Hotel Claremont)

PR#5831
Wright, Duey #2
Residence
904 Grand Avenue
Wausau, WI 54401, USA
EXE

1958 PR#5812
Ablin, Dr George
Residence
4260 Country Club Drive
Bakersfield, CA 93306,
USA
EXE

PR#5822
Colegrove, Ralph
Residence
Hamilton, OH, USA
PJT

PR#5823
Crosby-Lambert, Lillian
Residence
Colbert County, AL, USA
PJT

PR#5803
Franklin, Jesse
Residence
Louisville, KY, USA
PJT

PR#5805
Gutierrez, Dr James
Residence
Albuquerque, NM, USA
PJT

PR#5827
Helicopter
Helicopter
USA
PJT

PR#5817
Hennessy, Jack #2
Residence
Smoke Rise, NJ, USA
PJT
(Erdman Prefab #1)

PR#5708
Juvenile Cultural Center
Building A
Educational
Yale Avenue @21st Street
Wichita, KS 67208, USA
EXE
*(Corbin Educational Center
for the University of
Wichita, Jackson Powell,
Dean)*

PR#5743
Juvenile Cultural Center
Building B
Educational
Brolund at 21st Street
Wichita, KS, USA
PJT
*Cultural Laboratory –
(Corbin Educational Center
for the University of
Wichita)*

PR#5804
Lagomarsino, Frank
Residence
San Jose, CA, USA
PJT

PR#5806
Libbey, Wesley
Residence
Grand Rapids, MI, USA
PJT

PR#5825
The Living City
City Plan
USA
PJT
*The Living City
(Broadacre City Revised)*

PR#5813
Lockridge Medical
Clinic
Medical Clinic
341 Central Avenue
Whitefish, MT 59937,
USA
EXE
*(For Drs Lockridge,
Brown, and Whalen)*

PR#5824
Lovness, Don
Residence
Stillwater, MN, USA
PJT
*(Proposed plans for 3
Cottages)*

PR#5821
Lovness, Don
Residence
10121 83rd North
Stillwater, MN 55082,
USA
EXE
*(Facsimile of Seth Peterson
Cottage, 5821)*

PR#5820
Olfelt, Paul
Residence
2206 Parkland Lane
St Louis Park, MN 55416,
USA
EXE

PR#5821
Petersen, Seth
Residence
Hastings Road
Lake Delton, WI 53940,
USA
EXE

PR#5818
Pilgrim Congregational
Church
Religious
2850 Foothill Blvd
Redding, CA 96001, USA
EXE
(Executed in part)

PR#5802
Rayward, John
Additions
Residence
432 Frog Town Road
New Canaan, CT 06940,
USA
EXE

PR#5826
Road Machine
Automobile, USA
PJT

PR#5815
Spring Green
Community Center
Community Centre
Spring Green, WI, USA
PJT

PR#5808
Spring Green Medical
Center
Medical Clinic
Spring Green, WI, USA
PJT

PR#5626
Stromquist, Don
Residence
1289 Canyon Creek Road

Bountiful, UT 84010,
USA
EXE

PR#5819
Todd A-O Scheme A
Cinema
USA
PJT
(For Mike Todd)

PR#5829
Todd A-O Scheme B
Cinema
USA
PJT
(For Mike Todd)

PR#5828
Train
Train
USA
PJT

PR#5810
Trinity Chapel
Chapel
Norman, OK, USA
PJT
*(For University of
Oklahoma)*

PR#5811
Unity Temple
Taliesin Valley
Chapel/Mortuary
Route 23, Taliesin
Spring Green, WI, USA
PJT

1959 PR#5917
ASU Fine Arts Art
Gallery
Museum/Educational
Tempe, AZ, USA
PJT
*(For Arizona State
University)*

PR#5914
ASU Fine Arts Center
Hexagonal Gallery
Gallery
Tempe, AZ, USA
PJT
*(For Arizona State
University)*

PR#5911
ASU Fine Arts Center,
Master Plan
Fine Arts Centre
Tempe, AZ, USA
PJT
*(Master Plan for Arizona
State University)*

PR#5912
ASU Fine Arts Gallery
Gallery
Tempe, AZ, USA
PJT
*(For Arizona State
University)*

PR#5916
ASU Fine Arts Music
Department
Theatre/Educational
Tempe, AZ, USA
PJT
*(For Arizona State
University)*

PR#5915
ASU Fine Arts
Recital Theater
Theatre/Educational
Tempe, AZ, USA
PJT
*(For Arizona State
University)*

PR#5407
Dobkins, John
Residence
5210 Plain Center Avenue
Canton, OH 44714, USA
EXE

PR#5901
Donahoe, Mrs Helen
Residence
Paradise Valley, AZ, USA
PJT
The Donahoe Triptych

PR#5910
Enclosed Garden
Garden
Route 23, Taliesin
Spring Green, WI 53588,
USA
DMD
*(For Olgivanna Lloyd
Wright)*

PR#5913
Erdman Prefab #3
Housing
Madison, WI, USA
PJT
(For Marshall Erdman)

PR#5907
Furgatch, Harvey
Residence
San Diego, CA, USA
PJT

PR#5904
Grady Gammage
Memorial Auditorium
Auditorium
Apache Blvd at Mill Ave
Tempe, AZ 85281, USA
EXE
*(For Arizona State
University)*

PR#5816
Hanley, Pat
Airplane Hangar
Benton Harbor, MI, USA
PJT

PR#5903
Holy Trinity Greek
Orthodox Church
Religious
San Francisco, CA, USA
PJT

PR#5814
Luechauer Clinic
Medical Clinic
Fresno, CA, USA
PJT
(For Dr Jarvis Luechauer)

PR#5908
Lykes, Norman
Residence
6636 N 36th Street
Phoenix, AZ 85018, USA
EXE

PR#5902
Mann, Dr John D
Residence
Putnam County, NY,
USA
PJT

PR#5909
Penfield, Louis #2
Residence
Willoughby, OH, USA
PJT

PR#5906
Wieland, Daniel
Residence
Hagerstown, MD, USA
PJT

PR#5905
Wieland, Gilbert
Residence
Hagerstown, MD, USA
PJT

BIBLIOGRAPHY
Edited by Robert McCarter

Alofsin, Anthony, *Frank Lloyd Wright: The Lost Years, 1910–1922* (Chicago: University of Chicago, 1993)

Alofsin, Anthony, *Frank Lloyd Wright: The Lessons of Europe, 1910–1922* (Ann Arbor: UMI, 1989)

Alofsin, Anthony, *Frank Lloyd Wright: An Index to the Taliesin Correspondence*, 5 volumes (New York: Garland, 1988)

Auer, Gerhard, 'Licht und Ordnung: uder die Lichtenwurfe Frank Lloyd Wright und Louis Kahn', *Architekt* (September 1990)

Bandes, Susan (ed), *Affordable Dreams, The Goetsch-Winkler House and Frank Lloyd Wright* (East Lansing: Kresge Museum and Michigan State University, 1991)

Badovici, Jean, *Frank Lloyd Wright: architecte americain* (Paris: Editions Albert Morance, 1932)

Banham, Reyner, *The Architecture of the Well-Tempered Environment* (Chicago: University of Chicago Press, 1969, 1984)

Blake, Peter, *Frank Lloyd Wright: Architecture and Space* (Harmondsworth: Penguin, 1964)

Bolon, C, Nelson, R, and Seidel, L (eds), *The Nature of Frank Lloyd Wright* (Chicago: Chicago University Press, 1988)

Brooks, H Allen (ed), *Writings on Wright* (Cambridge, MA: MIT Press, 1981)

Brooks, H Allen, *The Prairie School: Frank Lloyd Wright and His Midwest Contemporaries* (New York: Norten, 1972)

Brooks, H Allen, 'Frank Lloyd Wright and the Wasmuth Drawings', *Art Bulletin* 48, No 2 (June 1966)

Brooks, H Allen, 'Frank Lloyd Wright and the Destruction of the Box', *Journal of the Society of Architectural Historians* 38, No 1 (March 1979)

Brunetti, Fabrizio, *Le Matrici di una Architettura Organica, F. Ll. Wright* (Florence: Alinea, 1974)

Bullock, H D and Morton, T (eds), *The Pope-Leighey House* (Washington: National Trust for Historic Preservation, 1969)

Byrne, Barry, 'On Frank Lloyd Wright and His Atelier', *AIA Journal* 39, No 6 (June 1963)

Ciucci, Giorgio, 'The City in Agrarian Ideology and Frank Lloyd Wright: Origins and Development of Broadacre City', *The American City: From the Civil War to the New Deal* (Cucci, Dal Co, Manieri-Elia, and Tafuri), (Cambridge, MA: MIT Press, 1979)

Condit, Carl, *American Building Art: The Twentieth Century* (New York: Oxford University Press, 1961)

Connors, Joseph, *The Robie House of Frank Lloyd Wright* (Chicago: University of Chicago Press, 1984)

De Long, David (ed), *Frank Lloyd Wright: Designs for an American Landscape* (New York: Abrams, 1996)

Drexler, Arthur, *The Drawings of Frank Lloyd Wright* (New York: Horizon/Museum of Modern Art, 1962)

Dunham, Judith and Scott Zimmerman, *Details of Frank Lloyd Wright: The California Work, 1909–1974* (San Francisco: Chronicle Books, 1994)

Eaton, Leonard, *Two Chicago Architects and their Clients* (Cambridge, MA: MIT Press, 1969)

Emerson, Ralph Waldo, *Emerson: Essays and Lectures* (New York: Library of America, 1983)

Etlin, Richard, *Frank Lloyd Wright and Le Corbusier* (Manchester: Manchester University Press, 1994)

Fallingwater and Edgar Kaufmann, Jr, Proceedings, Temple Hoyne Buell Center for the Study of American Architecture, Columbia University, New York, 1986

Ford, Edward, *The Details of Modern Architecture* (Cambridge, MA: MIT Press, 1990)

Frampton, Kenneth, *Modern Architecture: A Critical History* (London: Thames and Hudson, 1992)

Frampton, Kenneth, *Modern Architecture, 1851–1945* (New York: Rizzoli, 1981)

Frampton, Kenneth, *Studies in Tectonic Culture* (Cambridge, MA: MIT Press, 1994)

Frank, Edward, 'Organic Philosophy, Organic Architecture and Frank Lloyd Wright', manuscript in Avery Architecture and Fine Arts Library, Columbia University

Frank Lloyd Wright, Architecture + Urbanism (September 1989)

'Frank Lloyd Wright's Enchanted Space: Windows for Dimness', *Space Design* (July 1985)

'Frank Lloyd Wright and American Residential Landscaping', *Landscape* (1982)

Froebel, Frederick, *Selected Writings* (ed I M Lilley) (New York, 1898)

Futagawa, Yokio (ed) and Bruce B Pfeiffer *Frank Lloyd Wright Selected Houses*, ADA Edita, Tokyo:
> Volume 1: *Selected Houses* (1991)
> Volume 2: *Selected Houses: Taliesin* (1990)
> Volume 3: *Selected Houses: Taliesin West* (1989)
> Volume 4: *Selected Houses: Fallingwater* (1990)
> Volume 5: *Selected Houses* (1990)
> Volume 6: *Selected Houses* (1991)
> Volume 7: *Selected Houses* (1991)
> Volume 8: *Selected Houses* (1991)

Futagawa, Yokio (ed) and Bruce B Pfeiffer *Frank Lloyd Wright Monograph*, ADA Edita, Tokyo:
> Volume 1: *Monograph, 1887–1901* (1986)
> Volume 2: *Monograph, 1902–1906* (1987)
> Volume 3: *Monograph, 1907–1913* (1987)
> Volume 4: *Monograph, 1914–1923* (1985)
> Volume 5: *Monograph, 1924–1936* (1985)
> Volume 6: *Monograph, 1937–1941* (1986)
> Volume 7: *Monograph, 1942–1950* (1988)
> Volume 8: *Monograph, 1951–1959* (1988)
> Volume 9: *Preliminary Studies, 1889–1916* (1985)
> Volume 10: *Preliminary Studies, 1917–1932* (1986)
> Volume 11: *Preliminary Studies, 1933–1959* (1987)
> Volume 12: *In His Renderings, 1997–1959* (1984)

Futagawa, Yokio (photographer) and Paul Rudolph (text), *Frank Lloyd Wright: Kaufmann House, 'Fallingwater', Bear Run, Pennsylvania, 1936* (Tokyo: ADA Edita, 1970)

Futagawa, Yokio (photographer) and Arata Isozaki (text), *Frank Lloyd Wright: Johnson and Son, Administration Building and Research Tower, Racine, Wisconsin, 1936–9* (Tokyo: ADA Edita, 1970)

Futagawa, Yokio (photographer) and Bruce B Pfeiffer (text), *Frank Lloyd Wright: Solomon R. Guggenheim Museum, New York City, NY, 1943–59; Marin County Civic Center, California, 1957–70* (Tokyo: ADA Edita, 1975)

Futagawa, Yokio (photographer) and Masami Tanigawa (text), *Frank Lloyd Wright: Taliesin East, Spring Green, Wisconsin, 1925–; Taliesin West, Paradise Valley, Arizona, 1938–* (Tokyo: ADA Edita, 1975)

Futagawa, Yokio (ed), *Global Interiors: Houses by Frank Lloyd Wright 1*, Volume 9 (1975), *Global Interiors: Houses by Frank Lloyd Wright 2*, Volume 10 (1976), ADA Edita, Tokyo

Gebhard, David (text) and Scott Zimmerman (photographer), *Romanza: The California Architecture of Frank Lloyd Wright* (San Francisco: Chronicle Books, 1988)

Gebhard, David, 'A Note on the Chicago Fair of 1893 and Frank Lloyd Wright', *Journal of the Society of Architectural Historians* 18, No 2 (May 1959)

Giedion, Sigfried, *Space, Time and Architecture* (Cambridge, MA: Harvard University, 1954)

Gill, Brendan, *Many Masks: A Life of Frank Lloyd Wright* (New York: Putnam's, 1987)

Gossel, Peter (ed), *Frank Lloyd Wright* (Koln: Taschen, 1994)

Graf, Otto, *Die Kunst des Quadrats, Zum Werk von Frank Lloyd Wright*. Volume 1 (Unity Temple), Volume 2 (Imperial Hotel) (Vienna: Verlag Bohlau, 1983)

Gurda, John, *New World Odyssey, Annunciation Greek Orthodox Church and Frank Lloyd Wright* (Milwaukee: Milwaukee Hellenic Community, 1986)

Hamlin, Talbot, 'FLW – An Analysis', *Pencil Points* XIX (March 1938)

Hanks, David, *The Decorative Designs of Frank Lloyd Wright* (New York: Dutton, 1979)

Hanna, Paul and Jean, *Frank Lloyd Wright's Hanna House: The Client's Report* (Carbondale: Southern Illinois University Press, 1981)

Harris, Harwell Hamilton, *Architecture as an Art* (Iowa: Fingernail Moon Press, 1969)

Harrison, Robert P, 'Fallingwater', *Forests: The Shadow of Civilization* (Chicago: Chicago University Press, 1992)

Hearn, M F, 'A Japanese Inspiration for Frank Lloyd Wright's Rigid-Core High-Rise Structures', *Journal of the Society of Architectural Historians*, Vol L, No 1 (March 1991)

Heinz, Thomas, *Dana House* (London: Academy Editions, 1995)

Heinz, Thomas, *Frank Lloyd Wright* (New York: St Martin's Press, 1982)

Heinz, Thomas, *Frank Lloyd Wright* (Architectural Monographs No 18) (New York: St Martin's Press, 1992)

Hertz, David Michael, *Angels of Reality: Emersonian Unfoldings in Wright, Stevens and Ives* (Carbondale: Southern Illinois University Press, 1993)

Hildebrandt, Grant, *The Wright Space: Pattern and Meaning in Frank Lloyd Wright's Houses* (Seattle: University of Washington Press, 1991)

Hitchcock, Henry Russell, 'American Influence Abroad', *The Rise of an American Architecture*, Edgar Kaufmann, Jr (ed) (New York: Praeger, 1970)

Hitchcock, Henry Russell, *In the Nature of Materials; 1887–1941, The Buildings of Frank Lloyd Wright* (New York: Duell, Sloan and Pierce, 1941)

Hitchcock, Henry Russell, 'Frank Lloyd Wright and the "Academic Tradition" of the Early Eighteen-Nineties', *Journal of the Warburg and Courthauld Institutes* VII (January–June 1944)

Hoesli, Bernhard, 'Frank Lloyd Wright: Fallingwater', *Architecture + Urbanism* No 118 (July 1980), pp155–166

Hoffmann, Donald, *Frank Lloyd Wright's Fallingwater: The House and Its History* (New York: Dover, 1978, 1993)

Hoffmann, Donald, *Frank Lloyd Wright's Robie House* (New York: Dover, 1984)

Hoffmann, Donald, *Frank Lloyd Wright's Hollyhock House* (New York: Dover, 1992)

Hoffmann, Donald, *Frank Lloyd Wright: Architecture and Nature* (New York: Dover, 1986)

Hoffmann, Donald, 'Frank Lloyd Wright and Viollet-le-Duc', *Journal of the Society of Architectural Historians* 28, No 3 (October 1969)

Hoffmann, Donald, *Understanding Frank Lloyd Wright's Architecture* (New York: Dover, 1995)

Izzo, Alberto and Camillo Gubitosi (eds), *Frank Lloyd Wright: Drawings, 1887–1959* (Firenze: Centro Di, 1981)

Jacobs, Herbert and Katherine, *Building with Frank Lloyd Wright* (San Francisco: Chronicle Books, 1978)

James, Cary, *The Imperial Hotel* (Vermont: Tuttle, 1968. Reprinted, New York: Dover, 1993)

Johnson, Donald Leslie, *Frank Lloyd Wright versus America: The 1930's* (Cambridge, MA: MIT Press, 1990)

Kakuzo, Okakura, *The Book of Tea* (1906) (Tokyo: Tuttle, 1956)

Kalec, David and Thomas Heinz *Frank Lloyd Wright Home and Studio, Oak Park, Illinois* (Oak Park: Frank Lloyd Wright Home and Studio Foundation, 1975)

Kao, Kenneth Martin, 'Frank Lloyd Wright: Experiments in the Art of Building', *Modulus 22* (University of Virginia, 1993)

Kaufmann, Jr, Edward, *9 Commentaries on Frank Lloyd Wright* (Cambridge, MA: MIT Press, 1989)

Kaufmann, Jr, Edward, *Fallingwater: A Frank Lloyd Wright Country House* (New York: Abbeville Press, 1986)

Kaufmann, Jr, Edward, *Fallingwater* (London: Architectural Press, 1986)

Kief-Niederwohrmeier, Heidi, *Frank Lloyd Wright und Europa* (Stuttgart: Karl Kramer, 1983)

Laseau, Paul and James Tice *Frank Lloyd Wright: Between Principle and Form* (New York: Van Nostrand Reinhold, 1992)

Levine, Neil, 'Frank Lloyd Wright's Diagonal Planning', *In Search of Modern Architecture: A Tribute to Henry Russell Hitchcock* (Cambridge, MA: MIT Press, 1982)

Levine, Neil, 'Abstraction and Representation in Modern Architecture: Frank Lloyd Wright and the International Style', *AA Files* 11, Architectural Association (Spring 1986)

Levine, Neil, *The Architecture of Frank Lloyd Wright* (Princeton: Princeton University Press, 1996)

Lind, Carla, *The Wright Style: Recreating the Spirit of Frank Lloyd*

Wright (New York: Simon and Schuster, 1992)

Lipman, Jonathan, *Frank Lloyd Wright and the Johnson Wax Buildings* (New York: Rizzoli, 1986)

MacCormac, Richard, 'Froebel's Kindergarten Training and the Early Work of Frank Lloyd Wright', *Environment and Planning B* 1 (1974)

MacCormac, Richard, 'The Anatomy of Wright's Aesthetic', *Architectural Review* 143 (February 1968)

Manson, Grant Carpenter, 'Wright in the Nursery: The Influence of Froebel Education on the Work of Frank Lloyd Wright', *The Architectural Review* 113 (February 1953)

Manson, Grant Carpenter, *Frank Lloyd Wright to 1910: The First Golden Age* (New York: Van Nostrand Reinhold, 1958)

March, Lionel and Philip Steadman *The Geometry of the Environment: An Introduction to Spatial Organization in Design* (London: RIBA, 1971)

McArthur, Shirley duFresne, *Frank Lloyd Wright, American System-Built Homes in Milwaukee* (Milwaukee: North Point Historical Society, 1983)

McCarter, Robert, *Fallingwater* (Architecture in Detail) (London: Phaidon, 1994)

McCarter, Robert, 'Folded Space, Boundless Place: Frank Lloyd Wright Houses (1), 1895–1915', *Global Architecture: Houses* (Spring 1994)

McCarter, Robert, 'Squared Space, Constructed Place: Frank Lloyd Wright Houses (2), 1915–1935', *Global Architecture: Houses* (Summer 1994)

McCarter, Robert, 'Woven Space, Anchored Place: Frank Lloyd Wright Houses (3), 1935–1959' *Global Architecture: Houses* (Fall 1994)

McCarter, Robert, (ed), *Frank Lloyd Wright: A Primer on Architectural Principles* (New York: Princeton Architectural Press, 1991)

McCarter, Robert, *Unity Temple* (Architecture in Detail) (London: Phaidon, 1997)

McCarter, Robert, 'Without the Space Within: The Work of Frank Lloyd Wright's Followers in America', *Architektur & Bauforum* No 145 (1991)

Meehan, Patrick, *Frank Lloyd Wright: A Research Guide to Archival Sources* (New York: Garland, 1983)

Meehan, Patrick, *Frank Lloyd Wright Remembered* (Washington: Preservation Press, 1991)

Meehan, Patrick, *Truth Against the World: Frank Lloyd Wright Speaks for an Organic Architecture* (New York: Wiley, 1987)

Menocal, Narciso (ed), *Taliesin 1911–1914* (Wright Studies, Volume 1) (Carbondale: Southern Illinois University Press, 1992)

Muschamp, Herbert, *Man About Town: Frank Lloyd Wright in New York City* (Cambridge, MA: MIT Press, 1983)

Mumford, Lewis (ed), *Roots of Contemporary Architecture* (New York: Dover, 1972)

Museum of Modern Art, *A New House by Frank Lloyd Wright on Bear Run, Pennsylvania* (New York: MOMA, 1938)

Nute, Kevin, *Frank Lloyd Wright and Japan* (New York: Van Nostrand Reinhold, 1993)

O'Gorman, James F, *Three American Architects* (Chicago: University of Chicago, 1991)

Patterson, Terry, *Frank Lloyd Wright and the Nature of Materials* (New York: Van Nostrand Reinhold, 1994)

Peisch, Mark, *The Chicago School of Architecture: Early Followers of Sullivan and Wright* (New York: Random House and Columbia University, 1964)

Pfeiffer, Bruce Brooks (ed), *Frank Lloyd Wright Letters to Apprentices, Frank Lloyd Wright Letters to Architects, Frank Lloyd Wright Letters to Clients* (New York: Rizzoli, 1989)

Pfeiffer, Bruce Brooks (ed), *Frank Lloyd Wright Drawings* (New York: Abrams, 1990)

Plummer, Henry, *The Potential House. Architecture + Urbanism*, Tokyo (September 1989).

Purves, Alexander, 'This goodly frame, the Earth,' *Perspecta* (1989)

Putzel, Max, 'A House that Straddles a Waterfall', *St Louis Post-Dispatch* Sunday Magazine (March 21, 1937)

Quinan, Jack, 'Frank Lloyd Wright, Photography and Architecture', *Frank Lloyd Wright Quarterly*, Vol 2 No 1 (Winter 1991)

Quinan, Jack, *Frank Lloyd Wright's Larkin Building, Myth and Fact* (Cambridge, MA: MIT Press, 1987)

Riley, Terry (ed), *Frank Lloyd Wright, Architect* (New York: Museum of Modern Art/Abrams, 1994)

Rowe, Colin, 'Chicago Frame' (1956), *Mathematics of the Ideal Villa and Other Essays* (Cambridge, MA: MIT Press, 1976)

Rubin, Jeanne, 'The Froebel-Wright Kindergarten Connection: A New Perspective', *Journal of the Society of Architectural Historians* 48, No 1 (March 1989)

Sanderson, Arlene, *Wright Sites: A Guide to Frank Lloyd Wright Public Places* (River Forest: Frank Lloyd Wright Building Conservancy, 1991)

Scully, Vincent, *Frank Lloyd Wright* (New York: George Braziller, 1960)

Scully, Vincent, 'American Houses: Thomas Jefferson to Frank Lloyd Wright', *The Rise of an American Architecture*, Edgar Kaufmann, Jr (ed) (New York: Praeger, 1970)

Scully, Vincent, 'Frank Lloyd Wright and the Stuff of Dreams', *Perspecta* 16 (Cambridge, MA: Yale University/MIT Press, 1980)

Secrest, Meryle, *Frank Lloyd Wright* (New York: Knopf, 1992)

Sergeant, John, *Frank Lloyd Wright's Usonian Houses* (New York: Whitney Library of Design, 1976)

Sergeant, John, 'Warp and Woof: A Spatial Analysis of Frank Lloyd Wright's Usonian Houses', *Environment and Planning B* 3 (1976)

Siry, Joseph, 'Frank Lloyd Wright's Unity Temple and Architecture for Liberal Religion in Chicago, 1885–1909', *Art Bulletin* 73, No 2 (June 1992)

Siry, Joseph, *Unity Temple: Frank Lloyd Wright and Architecture for Liberal Religion* (Cambridge: Cambridge University Press, 1996)

Smith, Kathryn, *Frank Lloyd Wright: Hollyhock House and Olive Hill* (New York: Rizzoli, 1992)

Smith, Kathryn, 'Frank Lloyd Wright and the Imperial Hotel: A Postscript', *Art Bulletin* 67, No 2 (June 1985)

Smith, Norris Kelly, *Frank Lloyd Wright, A Study in Architectural Content* (Englewood Cliffs, NJ: Prentice-Hall, 1979)

Sommer, Robin Langley, *Frank Lloyd Wright: American Architect for the 20th Century* (New York: Smithmark, 1993)

Spenser, Robert, 'The Work of Frank Lloyd Wright', *Architectural Review* Volume 7 (June 1900)

Steele, James, *Barnsdall House* (Architecture in Detail) (London: Phaidon, 1992)

Storrer, William Allin, *The Frank Lloyd Wright Companion* (Chicago: University of Chicago Press, 1993)

Storrer, William Allin, *The Architecture of Frank Lloyd Wright: A Complete Catalog* (Cambridge, MA: MIT Press, 1974, 1978)

Sullivan, Louis, *Kindergarten Chats and Other Writings* (New York: Dover, 1979)

Sullivan, Louis, 'Concerning the Imperial Hotel, Tokyo, Japan', *Architectural Record* 55, No. 2 (February 1924)

Sweeney, Robert, *Frank Lloyd Wright, An Annotated Bibliography* (Los Angeles: Hennessey and Ingalls, 1978)

Sweeney, Robert, *Wright in Hollywood: Visions of a New Architecture* (Cambridge, MA: MIT Press, 1994)

Tafel, Edgar, *Apprentice to Genius: Years with Frank Lloyd Wright* (New York: Dover, 1979, 1985)

Tafel, Edgar, *About Wright* (New York: Wiley, 1993)

Tanigawa, Masami, *Measured Drawing: Frank Lloyd Wright in Japan* (Tokyo: Graphic-sha, 1980)

Twombley, Robert, *Frank Lloyd Wright: An Interpretive Biography* (New York: Harper and Row, 1973)

Twombley, Robert, *Frank Lloyd Wright: His Life and His Architecture* (New York: Wiley, 1979)

The Work of Frank Lloyd Wright, The Art Institute of Chicago, Chicago, 1914

Wright, Frank Lloyd, *Ausgeführte Bauten und Entwürfe von Frank Lloyd Wright*, Wasmuth, Berlin, 1910. Reprinted as *Drawings and Plans of Frank Lloyd Wright* (New York: Dover, 1983). Republished as *Studies and Executed Buildings by Frank Lloyd Wright* (New York: Rizzoli, 1986)

Wright, Frank Lloyd, *Frank Lloyd Wright, Ausgeführte Bauten*, Wasmuth, Berlin, 1911. Reprinted as *The Early Work of Frank Lloyd*

Wright (New York: Bramhall House, 1968)

Wright, Frank Lloyd, 'Frank Lloyd Wright', *Architectural Forum*
LXVIII (January 1938)

Wright, Frank Lloyd, 'Frank Lloyd Wright: His Contribution to the
Beauty of American Life', *House Beautiful* Volume 98, No 11
(November 1955)

Wright, Frank Lloyd, *The Life-Work of Frank Lloyd Wright*,
(Wendigen, 1925. 1965 reprint by Horizon, New York, 1965)

Wright, Frank Lloyd, *In the Cause of Architecture*, F Gutheim
(ed), reprint of *Architectural Record* essays (New York:
McGraw-Hill, 1975)

Wright, Frank Lloyd, *Frank Lloyd Wright: On Architecture*, F Gutheim
(ed) (New York: Grosset and Dunlap, 1941)

Wright, Frank Lloyd, *The Japanese Print – An Interpretation* (1912)
(New York: Horizon, 1967)

Wright, Frank Lloyd, *The Future of Architecture* (New York: Horizon,
1953)

Wright, Frank Lloyd, *Drawings for a Living Architecture* (New York:
Horizon, 1959)

Wright, Frank Lloyd, *Frank Lloyd Wright: Writings and Buildings*.
Kaufmann, Jr, E and B Raeburn (eds), (New York: Horizon, 1960)

Wright, Frank Lloyd, *Frank Lloyd Wright: On Architecture*, F Gutheim
(ed) (New York: Grosset and Dunlap, 1941)

Wright, Frank Lloyd, *An American Architecture* (New York: Horizon,
1955)

Wright, Frank Lloyd, *Sixty Years of Living Architecture* (New York:
Guggenheim Museum, 1953)

Wright, Frank Lloyd, *When Democracy Builds* (Chicago: University of
Chicago, 1945)

Wright, Frank Lloyd, *Genius and the Mobocracy* (New York: Duell,
Sloan and Pearce, 1949)

Wright, Frank Lloyd, *The Natural House* (New York: Horizon, 1954)

Wright, Frank Lloyd, *The Living City* (New York: Horizon, 1958)

Wright, Frank Lloyd, *The Disappearing City* (New York: Payson, 1932)

Wright, Frank Lloyd, *An Autobiography* (New York: Duell, Sloan and
Pierce, 1932, 1943, 1977)

Wright, Frank Lloyd, *A Testament* (New York: Bramhall House, 1957)

Wright, Frank Lloyd, *Frank Lloyd Wright Collected Writings*, Bruce
Brooks Pfieffer (ed), Rizzoli, New York, 1992:
> Volume 1: *Collected Writings, 1894–1930* (1992)
> Volume 2: *Collected Writings, 1930–1932* (1992)
> Volume 3: *Collected Writings, 1932–1939* (1993)
> Volume 4: *Collected Writings, 1939–1949* (1994)
> Volume 5: *Collected Writings, 1949–1959* (1995)

Zevi, Bruno and **Edgar Kaufmann Jr**, *La Casa sulla Cascata di F Ll
Wright: Frank Lloyd Wright's Fallingwater* (Milano: ET/AS Kompass,
1963)

Zevi, Bruno, *Towards an Organic Architecture* (London: Faber and
Faber, 1950)

Zevi, Bruno, *Frank Lloyd Wright* (Bologna: Zanichelli, 1979)

INDEX

AUTHOR'S ACKNOWLEDGEMENTS

After completing an analytical study of Wright in 1990, I had hoped to someday undertake writing a monograph on Wright, to be illustrated with new colour photography, and emphasizing and highlighting the experience of interior space. While in my own mind this project was of necessity always understood to be set a considerable time in the future, I am indeed most grateful to David Jenkins, commissioning editor at Phaidon Press, for encouraging me to undertake it years ahead of schedule, and to James Steele, at whose recommendation I became involved with this publisher.

In my efforts to always go to the source – the building or drawing itself – in my studies of Wright, I am indebted to Kenneth Frampton, whose work continues to be for me an exemplary model of critical insight, and who has never ceased in his insistence that the study of Wright is essential to the future of American architecture. My interest in Wright and his place in American architecture was encouraged early by Henry Kamphoefner and Harwell Hamilton Harris, my teachers in undergraduate school. Earlier still, it is likely that the Wright books given to me in my youth by my artist relatives, Bill and Mickey McCarter, initiated what has become my abiding fascination.

I would like to thank the following people, whose efforts were essential to the completion of this book. Cathy Duncan researched and secured reproduction rights for photographic and drawing material used in this publication, and was in general an outstanding assistant in this endeavour. I would particularly like to thank Oscar Munoz, of the Frank Lloyd Wright Archives, who provided reproductions of Wright's drawings and archival photographs. I must thank my fellow faculty members and my students, who have endured a sometimes distracted professor and chair of department during the period when I was writing this and other texts on Wright, and I am particularly grateful to Dean Wayne Drummond, who has supported my perhaps atypical activity.

The new drawings prepared for this publication were made by fourteen undergraduate and graduate students in the University of Florida's Department of Architecture who participated in a seminar that I taught on Wright's drawings during the summer of 1993: Morris Baptiste, John Beres, Robert Blatter, John Brandies, James Buzbee, Cathy Duncan, Jitendra Jain, Mark Lipchik, Mark Maturo, Karen Sharp, Kricket Snow, Anthony Stefan, Max Strang and Loren Wright. Robert Blatter and James Buzbee had the additional responsibility of preparing these drawings for publication.

Finally, this book is dedicated to my wife Susan, who shares the often difficult life of architecture with me, and to my daughter Katie, who, during her first two years of life, often watched, perplexed, as her father chose to sit at his computer, books strewn around him, typing this manuscript rather than doing the right thing – playing with her.

ACKNOWLEDGEMENTS

AKG London: p24t; Peter Aprahamian: p320, p325; Arcaid/©Richard Bryant 1986: p2, p95, p96/7, p99r, p172br, p269tl,bl,br, p290, p300, p304, p305, p313t, p314, p316/317, p319; Arcaid/Ezra Stoller/Esto: p117, p227b; Arcaid/Farrell Grehan: p124; Avery Library, Columbia University: p207bl, p220; Morris Baptiste: p307t, p312tr, p313b; John Beres: p193r, p198bl,tr; Robert Blatter and James Buzbee: p207tr, p211tl,r; John Brandies: p253r, p258, p260; Buffalo and Erie County Historical Society: p73tl, p75bl; James Buzbee: p228cl; Canadian Centre for Architecture, Montreal: p60, p61cl; Photographs ©1996, The Art Institute of Chicago: p15, p21, p113b, p306tl,cl; Chicago Historical Society/Hedrich Blessing: p203; William Clarkson: p73br, p75tl; Peter Cook: p26, p34, p35, p62, p63, p66tl,tr, p67, p68/9, p76tl,tr, p77, p78, p79bl, p80, p81, p83, p85, p86, p91t, p100, p101tl,tr, p102l, p202, p205, p208/209, p210tl,tr,b, p213cl,t, p214, p215, p216/217, p218/p219, p248, p263tr, p264t, p265tl,tr, p266/267, p272, p279, p280, p282, p283b, p284, p285, p286, p287bl, p326tl,tr, p327; ESTO: p147, p187br, p261; ESTO/©Jeff Goldberg p315, p328cl, p329; ESTO/©Wayne Andrews p330cl,bl; ©Guggenheim Museum/Gwathmey-Siegel & Associates p310bl; John Hewitt: p48, p166b; Jitendra Jain: p283tl; Photograph Jeannette Wilber Scofield, courtesy Donald Hoffmann: p102b; Photographs courtesy of Johnson Wax: p287tr, p288c,tr; Balthazar Korab: p10, p22, p32, p36, p38b, p42, p47, p49tl,cr,cl, p50, p51, p56tr, p58, p65, p98t, p102, p106, p107, p111, p113t, p118, p119tl, p125, p155, p172bl, p199, p227t, p228tr, p259, p268, p270t, p271cl, p275, p276t, p293, p294, p298t,c, p299, p301tl,c, p309, p331; ©Al Krescanko: p6; SC Johnson Wax photo, courtesy of Jonathan Lipman: p287; Mark Maturo: p98b, p99l, p102br, p115b, p116; Mark Lipchik: p328r, Photos courtesy of The Museum of Modern Art, New York: p289, p318; Netherlands Architecture Institute, Rotterdam: p158; Paul Rocheleau Photographer: p52, p53t, p54b, p55, p150tl,tr, p151, p253tl, p254,

p255l,r; Karen Sharp: p79r, 82r; Julius Shulman: p174, p181t,b, p307cl,tr; Anthony Stefan: p72br, p73bl; Max Strang: p53c,b, p59; Tim Street-Porter: p110, p127, p128bl, p130/131, p132, p133, p134, p135t,b, p160, p163, p164, p166t, p169, p170/171, p172t, p173, p175br, p177, p178, p179tl,cl, p181tl,c; Frank Lloyd Wright drawings are Copyright © 1997 The Frank Lloyd Wright Foundation: p18; p23; p28; p38t; p40; p41 tl,tr; p43; p44c; p45tl,tr,cr,cl; p46t,c,b; p54t; p56b; p57t,c,b,r; p60t; p64; p70t,c,b; p71t,c,ml,bl; p72cr; p82bl; p87; p88tl,tr; p89; p90t,c,b; p91b; p92; p93tl,cl; p94t,c,b; p104tl,tr; p105; p107c,r; p108l,c,r; p109tl; p112; p115t; p119b; p121t; p123tl; p126; p128br; p136; p137; p138; p139t,cl,cr,b; p140; p144t,c; p146b; p152l,r; p154tr; p156tl,cl; p159c,tr,cr; p162l,r; p165; p167; p168;p175t; p176; p180; p182tl,cl,b; p183tl; p184; p186; p187bl; p188; p189; p190; p192; p193tl; p194; p195; p196; p197t,b; p198tl; p200; p201; p204; p206; p207t; p211cl; p212; p221bl,br; p222t,b; p224bl,cr; p225; p226tl,tr; p228tl; p230; p231; p232tl,tr,bl; p233tr; p234/5; p236l,tr,cr,br; p237; p238; p239; p240; p241; p242t,bl,br; p244; p245; p247t,b; p249; p250; p251tl,tr; p252t,bl,br; p256; p257; p262; p263tl; p264c,b; p269cr; p270bl,cr,br; p271b; p274; p276b; p277; p278; p288bl; p291; p292; p295br; p296 p297t,cl; p298b; p302cl,c,bl,cr; p303; p306bl; p308; p310t,c; p311 p322tl,tr; p323t,c; p324cl,bl,cr,br; p328tl; p330tl,tr,cr; Photogra Courtesy The Frank Lloyd Wright Archives: p17 tl, tr; p44 t p61t; p72bl; p114tl,tr; p120; p121b; p122; p123tr; p141; p142; p144bl; p145 t,b; p146cl; p148, p149; p153l,r; p154bl; p156tr; p182tr; p183tr; p223; p224t; p228cl,cb; p229; p233 tl; p246; p306 p306 br; Irma Strauss Collection. Courtesy The Frank Lloyd V Archives, Scottsdale, AZ: p20, p29tl; p30t. Courtesy Frank Llc Wright Home & Studio Foundation: p13; p74, p93tr; p109 bl Wright: p295l, p301r. Frank Lloyd Wright Complete List of The Frank Lloyd Wright Foundation 1997.